THE SCIENCE OF

Self-Realization

BOOKS by His Divine Grace
A. C. Bhaktivedanta Swami Prabhupāda

Bhagavad-gītā As It Is
Śrīmad-Bhāgavatam (completed by disciples)
Śrī Caitanya-caritāmṛta
Kṛṣṇa, the Supreme Personality of Godhead
Teachings of Lord Caitanya
The Nectar of Devotion
The Nectar of Instruction
Śrī Īśopaniṣad
Light of the Bhāgavata
Easy Journey to Other Planets
Teachings of Lord Kapila, the Son of Devahūti
Teachings of Queen Kuntī
Message of Godhead
The Science of Self-Realization
The Perfection of Yoga
Beyond Birth and Death
On the Way to Kṛṣṇa
Rāja-vidyā: The King of Knowledge
Elevation to Kṛṣṇa Consciousness
Kṛṣṇa Consciousness: The Matchless Gift
Kṛṣṇa Consciousness: The Topmost Yoga System
Perfect Questions, Perfect Answers
Life Comes from Life
The Nārada-bhakti-sūtra (completed by disciples)
The Mukunda-mālā-stotra (completed by disciples)
Geetār-gān (Bengali)
Vairāgya-vidyā (Bengali)
Buddhi-yoga (Bengali)
Bhakti-ratna-boli (Bengali)
Back to Godhead magazine (founder)

BOOKS compiled from the teachings of His Divine Grace
A. C. Bhaktivedanta Swami Prabhupāda after his lifetime

Search for Liberation
A Second Chance
The Journey of Self-Discovery
Civilization and Transcendence
The Laws of Nature
Renunciation Through Wisdom
The Quest for Enlightenment
Dharma, the Way of Transcendence
Beyond Illusion and Doubt
Bhakti-yoga, the Art of Eternal Love
Spiritual Yoga
The Hare Kṛṣṇa Challenge

For more information on these books, please call 1-800-927-4152 or visit the Bhaktivedanta Book Trust website, krishna.com.

THE SCIENCE OF Self-Realization

Articles from *Back to Godhead* magazine

His Divine Grace
A.C. Bhaktivedanta Swami
Prabhupāda

Founder-*Ācārya* of the International
Society for Krishna Consciousness

THE BHAKTIVEDANTA BOOK TRUST
LOS ANGELES • STOCKHOLM • MUMBAI • SYDNEY

THE COVER: Within every atom resides the Supersoul, a four-handed expansion of Lord Kṛṣṇa, the Supreme Personality of Godhead. The Supersoul maintains the whole creation and gives intelligence to all creatures.

Readers interested in the subject matter of this book are invited by the International Society for Krishna Consciousness (ISKCON) to visit one of its centers (see address list in back of book) or to correspond with the publisher at one of the following addresses.

Bhaktivedanta Book Trust
P.O. Box 341445
Los Angeles, California 90034, USA
Phone: 1-800-927-4152 (inside USA); 1-310-837-5283 (outside USA)
Fax: 1-310-837-1056
e-mail: bbt.usa@krishna.com; web: www.krishna.com

Bhaktivedanta Book Trust
P.O. Box 380
Riverstone, NSW 2765, Australia
Phone: +61-2-9627-6306; Fax: +61-2-9627-6052
e-mail: bbt.wp@krishna.com

Layout/Production: Arcita Dāsa
Art: The Supersoul in the Atom. Painting by Parīkṣit Dāsa

Previous Printings: 1,660,000
Current Printing, 2015 (2nd printing): 50,000

The Science of Self-Realization
Library of Congress Catalog Number: 77-95065
ISBN 0-89213-101-2

DEDICATION

According to material vision, our beloved spiritual master, guide, and friend, His Divine Grace A. C. Bhaktivedanta Swami Prabhupāda, passed away from this world on November 14, 1977, but actually he is still present. As Śrīla Prabhupāda often pointed out, there are two ways of associating with the spiritual master: through his physical presence (*vapu*) and through his instructions (*vāṇī*). Sometimes we can associate with the spiritual master through his physical presence and sometimes not, but we can always associate with him through his instructions.

—The Editors

The Science of Self-Realization consists of articles published in *Back to Godhead* magazine from 1958 to 1977. Exceptions: "The Scriptural Basis of Kṛṣṇa Consciousness" was published in 1970 as a separate pamphlet. "Superconsciousness" was adapted from Śrīla Prabhupāda's purport to *Śrīmad-Bhāgavatam* 3.15.45. "The Incarnation of Love of God" was edited from a lecture Śrīla Prabhupāda gave on the *Caitanya-caritāmṛta* (*Madhya-līlā* 20.330–35) in December 1966. "Chanting the Hare Kṛṣṇa *Mahā-mantra*" appeared as a separate pamphlet in 1967. "Śrīla Prabhupāda Arrives in America" is a translation of a Bengali poem Śrīla Prabhupāda wrote in September 1965 entitled *"Mārkine Bhāgavata-dharma."* The articles were variously edited by Rāyarāma Dāsa, Hayagrīva Dāsa, Jayādvaita Swami, and Draviḍa Dāsa. Jayādvaita Swami compiled the articles, and Mukunda Goswami and Drutakarmā Dāsa wrote the introductory material for the book and its chapters.

CONTENTS

FOREWORD

From the very start, I knew that His Divine Grace A.C. Bhaktivedanta Swami Prabhupāda was the most extraordinary person I had ever met. The first meeting occurred in the summer of 1966, in New York City. A friend had invited me to hear a lecture by "an old Indian swami" on lower Manhattan's Bowery. Overwhelmed with curiosity about a swami lecturing on skid row, I went there and felt my way up a pitch-black staircase. A bell-like, rhythmic sound got louder and clearer as I climbed higher. Finally I reached the fourth floor and opened the door, and there he was.

About fifty feet away from where I stood, at the other end of a long, dark room, he sat on a small dais, his face and saffron robes radiant under a small light. He was elderly, perhaps sixty or so, I thought, and he sat cross-legged in an erect, stately posture. His head was shaven, and his powerful face and reddish horn-rimmed glasses gave him the look of a monk who had spent most of his life absorbed in study. His eyes were closed, and he softly chanted a simple Sanskrit prayer while playing a hand drum. The small audience joined in at intervals, in call-and-response fashion. A few played hand cymbals, which accounted for the bell-like sounds I'd heard. Fascinated, I sat down quietly at the back, tried to participate in the chanting, and waited.

After a few moments the swami began lecturing in English, apparently from a huge Sanskrit volume that lay open before him. Occasionally he would quote from the book, but more often from memory. The sound of the language was beautiful, and he followed each passage with meticulously detailed explanations.

He sounded like a scholar, his vocabulary intricately laced with philosophical terms and phrases. Elegant hand gestures and animated facial expressions added considerable impact to his delivery. The subject matter was the most weighty I had ever encountered: "I am not this body. I am not an Indian... You are not

Americans... We are all spirit souls..."

After the lecture someone gave me a pamphlet printed in India. A photo showed the swami handing three of his books to Indian prime minister Lal Bahadur Shastri. The caption quoted Mr. Shastri as saying that all Indian government libraries should order the books. "His Divine Grace A.C. Bhaktivedanta swami Prabhupāda is doing great work," the prime minister said in another small tract, "and his books are significant contributions to the salvation of mankind." I purchased copies of the books, which I learned the swami had brought over from India. After reading the jacket flaps, the small pamphlet, and various other literature, I began to realize that I had just met one of India's most respected spiritual leaders.

But I could not understand why a gentleman of such distinction was residing and lecturing in the Bowery, of all places. He was certainly well educated and, by all appearances, born of an aristocratic Indian family. Why was he living in such poverty? What in the world had brought him here? One afternoon several days later, I stopped in to visit him and find out.

To my surprise, Śrīla Prabhupāda (as I later came to call him) was not too busy to talk with me. In fact, it seemed that he was prepared to talk all day. He was warm and friendly and explained that he had accepted the renounced order of life in India in 1959, and that he was not allowed to carry or earn money for his personal needs. He had completed his studies at the University of Calcutta many years ago and had raised a family, and then he had left his eldest sons in charge of family and business affairs, as the age-old Vedic culture prescribes. After accepting the renounced order, he had arranged a free passage on an Indian freighter (Scindia Steamship Company's *Jaladuta*) through some friends. In September 1965 he had sailed from Bombay to Boston, armed with only seven dollars' worth of rupees, a trunk of books, and a few clothes. His spiritual master, His Divine Grace Bhaktisiddhānta Sarasvatī Ṭhākura, had entrusted him with delivering India's Vedic teachings to the English-speaking world. And this was why, at age sixty-nine, he had come to America. He told me he wanted to teach Americans about Indian music, cooking, languages, and various other arts. I was mildly amazed.

I saw that Śrīla Prabhupāda slept on a small mattress and that his clothes hung on lines at the back of the room, where they were drying in the summer afternoon heat. He washed them himself and cooked his own food on an ingenious utensil he had fashioned with his own hands in India. In this four-layer apparatus he cooked four preparations at once. Stacked all around him and his ancient-looking portable typewriter in another section of the room were seemingly endless manuscripts. He spent almost all of his waking hours about twenty in twenty-four, I learned—typing the sequels to the three volumes I had purchased. It was a projected sixty-volume set called the *Śrīmad-Bhāgavatam,* and virtually it was the encyclopedia of spiritual life. I wished him luck with the publishing, and he invited me back for Sanskrit classes on Saturdays and for his evening lectures on Monday, Wednesday, and Friday. I accepted, thanked him, and left, marveling at his incredible determination.

A few weeks later it was July 1966 I had the privilege of helping Śrīla Prabhupāda relocate in a somewhat more respectable neighborhood, on Second Avenue. Some friends and I pitched in and rented a ground-floor storefront and a second-floor apartment, to the rear of a little courtyard, in the same building. The lectures and chanting continued, and within two weeks a rapidly growing congregation was providing for the storefront (by this time a temple) and the apartment. By now Śrīla Prabhupāda was instructing his followers to print and distribute leaflets, and the owner of a record company had invited him to record an LP of the Hare Kṛṣṇa chant. He did, and it was a huge success. In his new location he was teaching chanting, Vedic philosophy, music, *japa* meditation, fine art, and cooking. At first *he* cooked he always taught by example. The results were the most wonderful vegetarian meals I had ever experienced. (Śrīla Prabhupāda would even serve everything out himself!) The meals usually consisted of a rice preparation, a vegetable dish, *capātīs* (tortilla-like whole-wheat patties), and *dāl* (a zestfully spiced mung-bean or split-pea soup). The spicing, the cooking medium ghee, or clarified butter and the close attention paid to the cooking temperature and other details all combined to produce taste treats totally unknown to me. Others' opinions of the food, called *prasādam* ("the Lord's mercy"), agreed emphatically with mine. A Peace Corps worker who was also a Chinese-language scholar was learning from Śrīla Prabhupāda how to paint in the classical Indian style. I was startled at the high quality of his first canvases.

In philosophical debate and logic Śrīla Prabhupāda was undefeatable and indefatigable. He would interrupt his translating work for discussions that would last up to eight hours. Sometimes seven or eight people jammed into the small, immaculately clean room where he worked, ate, and slept on a two-inch-thick foam cushion. Śrīla Prabhupāda constantly emphasized and exemplified what he called "plain living and high thinking." He stressed that spiritual life was a science provable through reason and logic, not a matter of mere sentiment or blind faith. He began a monthly magazine, and in the autumn of 1966 *The New York Times* published a favorable picture story about him and his followers. Shortly thereafter, television crews came out and did a feature news story.

Śrīla Prabhupāda was an exciting person to know. Whether it was out of my desire for the personal benefits of yoga and chanting or just out of raw fascination, I knew I wanted to follow his progress every step of the way. His plans for expansion were daring and unpredictable except for the fact that they always seemed to succeed gloriously. He was seventyish and a stranger to America, and he had arrived with practically nothing, yet now, within a few months, he had single-handedly started a *movement*! It was mind-boggling.

One August morning at the Second Avenue storefront temple, Śrīla Prabhupāda told us, "Today is Lord Kṛṣṇa's appearance day." We would observe a twenty-four-hour fast and stay inside the temple. That evening some visitors from India happened along. One of them practically in tears described his unbounded rapture at finding this little piece of authentic India on the other side of the world. Never in his wildest dreams could he have imagined such a thing. He offered Śrīla Prabhupāda eloquent praise and deep thanks, left a donation, and bowed at his feet. Everyone was deeply moved. Later, Śrīla Prabhupāda conversed with the gentleman in Hindi, and since what he was saying was unintelligible to me, I was able to observe how his every expression and gesture communicated to the very core of the human soul.

Later that year, while in San Francisco, I sent Śrīla Prabhupāda his first airline ticket, and he flew out from New York. A sizable group of us greeted him at the terminal by chanting the Hare Kṛṣṇa mantra. Then we drove him to the eastern edge of Golden Gate Park, to a newly rented apartment and storefront temple an arrangement very similar to that in New York. We had established a pattern. Śrīla Prabhupāda was ecstatic.

A few weeks later the first *mṛdaṅga* (a long clay drum with a playing head on each end) arrived in San Francisco from India. When I went up to Śrīla Prabhupāda's apartment and informed him, his eyes opened wide, and in an excited voice he told me to go down quickly and open the crate. I took the elevator, got out on the ground floor, and was walking toward the front door when Śrīla Prabhupāda appeared. So eager was he to see the *mṛdaṅga* that he had taken the stairway and had beaten the elevator. He asked us to open the crate, he tore off a piece of the saffron cloth he was wearing, and, leaving only the playing heads exposed, he wrapped the drum with the cloth. Then he said, "This must never come off," and he began giving detailed instructions on how to play and care for the instrument.

Also in San Francisco, in 1967, Śrīla Prabhupāda inaugurated Ratha-yātrā, the Festival of the Chariots, one of several festivals that, thanks to him, people all over the world now observe. Ratha-yātrā has taken place in India's Jagannātha Purī each year for two thousand years, and by 1975 the festival had become so popular with San Franciscans that the mayor issued a formal proclamation "Ratha-yātrā Day in San Francisco."

By late 1966 Śrīla Prabhupāda had begun accepting disciples. He was quick to point out to everyone that they should think of him not as God but as God's servant, and he criticized self-styled gurus who let their disciples worship them as God. "These 'gods' are very cheap," he used to say. One day, after someone had asked, "Are you God?" Śrīla Prabhupāda replied, "No, I am not God I am a servant of God." Then he reflected a moment and went on. "Actually, I am *not* a servant of God. I am *trying* to be a servant of God. A servant of God is no ordinary thing."

In the mid-seventies Śrīla Prabhupāda's translating and publishing intensified dramatically. Scholars all over the world showered favorable reviews on his books, and practically all the universities and colleges in America accepted them as standard texts. Altogether he produced some eighty books, which his disciples have translated into over sixty languages and distributed to the tune of a hundred million copies. He established one hundred eight temples worldwide and initiated some five thousand disciples. His sympathizers numbered in the millions. Śrīla Prabhupāda was writing and translating up to the last days of his eighty-one-year stay on earth.

Śrīla Prabhupāda was not just another oriental scholar, guru, yoga teacher, or meditation instructor. He was the embodiment of a whole culture, and he implanted that culture in the West. To me and many others he was first and foremost someone who truly cared, who completely sacrificed his own comfort to work for the good of others. He had no private life, but lived only for others. He taught spiritual science, philosophy, common sense, the arts, languages, the Vedic way of life hygiene, nutrition, medicine, etiquette, family living, farming, social organization, schooling, economics and many more things to many people. To me he was a master, a father, and my dearmost friend.

I am deeply indebted to Śrīla Prabhupāda, and it is a debt I shall never be able to repay. But I can at least show some gratitude by joining with his other followers in fulfilling his innermost desire publishing and distributing his books.

"I shall never die," Śrīla Prabhupāda once said. "I shall live forever in my books." He passed away from this world on November 14, 1977, but surely he will live forever.

Michael Grant (Mukunda Goswami)

INTRODUCTION

"Who is Śrīla Prabhupāda?" people often ask, and it is always a hard question to answer. For Śrīla Prabhupāda always eclipsed conventional designations. At various times people have called him a scholar, a philosopher, a cultural ambassador, a prolific author, a religious leader, a spiritual teacher, a social critic, and a holy man. In truth, he was all these things and more. Certainly no one could ever have confused him with the modern entrepreneurial "gurus" who come to the West with slickly packaged, watered-down versions of Eastern spirituality (to satisfy our urge for instant well-being and exploit our well-documented spiritual naiveté.) Śrīla Prabhupāda was, rather, a true holy man (sādhu) of deep intellectual and spiritual sensitivity—he had deep concern and compassion for a society that, to such a large degree, lacks real spiritual dimension.

For the enlightenment of human society, Śrīla Prabhupāda produced some eighty volumes of translations and summary studies of India's great spiritual classics, and his work has seen print both in English and in many foreign languages. Also, in 1944 Śrīla Prabhupāda single-handedly launched a magazine called *Back to Godhead,* which today is circulated widely in all the main English-speaking nations of the world. Nearly all the interviews, lectures, essays, and letters chosen for *The Science of Self- Realization* first appeared in *Back to Godhead.*

In these pages Śrīla Prabhupāda presents the same message that the great sage Vyāsadeva recorded thousands of years ago, the message of ancient India's Vedic literatures. As we shall see, he quotes freely and often from the *Bhagavad-gītā, Śrīmad-Bhāgavatam,* and other classic Vedic texts. He transmits in modern English the same timeless knowledge that other great self-realized teachers have spoken for millennia—knowledge that opens up the secrets of the self within us, of nature and the universe, and of the Supreme Self within and without. Śrīla Prabhupāda speaks with startling clarity and a kind of convincing, simple eloquence and proves just how relevant the science of self-realization is to our modern world and our own lives.

Among the thirty-six selections chosen for this special book, we hear Śrīla Prabhupāda's moving poem upon his arrival in America, his exchange with a noted cardiologist on "soul research," his revelations to London Broadcasting Company on reincarnation, his telling remarks to the *Times of London* on real and false gurus, his dialogue with a German Benedictine monk on Kṛṣṇa and Christ, his insights on superconsciousness and the law of karma, his conversation with a leading Russian scholar on spiritual communism, and his intimate talk with his disciples on the sham of modern science.

Read the selections in order, if you like, or start with the ones that first catch your interest. (The glossary at the back will explain unfamiliar words and names.) *The Science of Self-Realization* will challenge you and bring you inspiration and enlightenment.

—The Publishers

APPRECIATIONS OF ŚRĪLA PRABHUPĀDA'S WORK

Over the years, many people have expressed their appreciation for Śrīla Prabhupāda's work—bringing India's timeless science of self-realization to the West.

* * *

"His Divine Grace A. C. Bhaktivedanta Swami Prabhupāda is doing valuable work, and his books are significant contributions to the salvation of mankind."

Sri Lal Bahadur Shastri
former prime minister of India

"Swami Bhaktivedanta brings to the West a salutary reminder that our highly activistic and one-sided culture is faced with a crisis that may end in self-destruction because it lacks the inner depth of an authentic metaphysical consciousness. Without such depth, our moral and political protestations are just so much verbiage."

Thomas Merton, theologian

"In the diversity of religious approaches offered by the yogis of India, the most significant, of course, is the way of Kṛṣṇa consciousness, shown by Śrīla Prabhupāda Bhaktivedanta Swami, tenth teacher in the tradition of Mahāprabhu Caitanya. It is amazing to see how Śrī Bhaktivedanta Swami has in less than ten years succeeded by his personal devotion and single-minded dedication to the task, untiring energy, and efficient direction, in organizing the International Society for Krishna Consciousness, having thousands of devotees, opening the Rādhā-Kṛṣṇa temples in the major cities of the world, and writing numerous works on *bhakti-yoga* as taught by Śrī Kṛṣṇa and Śrī Caitanya."

Professor Mahesh Mehta
Professor of Religious Studies
University of Windsor, Ontario, Canada

"A. C. Bhaktivedanta Swami Prabhupāda is a prestigious master and heir to a great tradition."

Joseph Jean Lanzo del Vasto
prominent French philosopher and author

"Words fail me to describe the height of scholarship and devotion manifest in Śrīla Prabhupāda's vast writings. Our future generations will definitely find a better world to live in through the efforts of Śrīla Prabhupāda. He stands for international brotherhood and the spiritual integration of all mankind. The literary world outside India, particularly of the West, is indebted to Śrīla Prabhupāda, who has so scientifically acquainted them with what is best in Kṛṣṇa conscious India."

Sri Viswanath Shukla, Ph.D.
Professor of Hindi, M.U. Aligarh, U.P., India

"As a native of India now living in the West, it has given me much grief to see so many of my fellow countrymen coming to the West in the role of gurus and spiritual leaders. Just as any ordinary man in the West becomes conscious of Christian culture from his very birth, any ordinary man in India becomes familiar with the principles of meditation and yoga from his very birth. Unfortunately, many unscrupulous persons come from India, exhibit their im-perfect and ordinary knowledge of yoga, cheat the people with their wares consisting of mantras, and present themselves as incarnations of God. So many of these cheaters have come, convincing their foolish followers to accept them as God, that those who are actually well-versed and learned in Indian culture have become very concerned and troubled. For this reason, I am very excited to see the publications of Śrī A. C. Bhaktivedanta Swami Prabhupāda. They will help to stop the terrible cheating of false and unauthorized 'gurus' and 'yogis', and will give an opportunity to all people to understand the actual meaning of Oriental culture."

Dr. Kailash Vajpeye
Director of Indian Studies

Center for Oriental Studies, University of Mexico

"The books of A. C. Bhaktivedanta Swami Prabhupāda are not only beautiful, but also relevant to our times, as we as a nation search for new cultural patterns for our way of life."

Dr. C. L. Spreadbury
Professor of Sociology
Stephen F. Austin State University, Nacogdoches, Texas

"It is a great honor for me to have the pleasure of examining the publications of the Bhaktivedanta Book Trust, which I find to be of exceptional value for use in educational institutions and libraries. I particularly recommend the ancient classic *Śrīmad-Bhāgavatam* to all students and professors of Indian philosophy and culture. The learned author, His Divine Grace A. C. Bhaktivedanta Swami, is a world-renowned saint and savant in the field of Vedic philosophy and its practical application in the modern world. He has established over one hundred spiritual ashrams, for the study and cultivation of Vedic knowledge, throughout the world. Factually, he is unequaled in his efforts to establish the Vedic way of life, *sanātana-dharma,* in all countries of the world. Certainly I am most grateful that this message of the *Bhāgavata* is being spread for the benefit of the world by such a qualified personality as Swami Bhaktivedanta."

Dr. R. Kalia
President, Indian Library Association

"Swami Bhaktivedanta has offered to devotees of God a blessed service with his English translations and commentaries. The universal application of these truths is shown to be a promised blessing in these times of challenge when light is illumining darkness. Truly this is a holy, inspired writing for all aspiring souls seeking the why, whence, and whither of life!"

Dr. Judith M. Tyberg
Founder and Director
East-West Cultural Center, Los Angeles, California

"As a successor in direct line from Caitanya, the author is entitled, according to Indian custom, to the majestic title of His Divine Grace

A. C. Bhaktivedanta Swami Prabhupāda. Swami Prabhupāda possesses total mastery of the Sanskrit language. The great interest that his reading of the *Bhagavad-gītā* holds for us is that it offers us an authorized interpretation according to the principles of the Caitanya tradition. . . . This appreciation, coming from a Christian philosopher and Indologist, is a gesture of sincere friendship."

Oliver Lacombe
Professeur Honoraire
Université de Paris, Sorbonne
former director, Institute of Indian Civilization, Paris

"I have read Śrī Bhaktivedanta Swami's books with great care, attention, and profound interest and have found them to be of incalculable value to anyone who is curious about India's spiritual and cultural heritage. The author of these books displays on every page an astounding scholarship in the subjects treated, and also an understanding and ease of exposition of abstruse ideas, which are rarest gifts of a man who has been rigorously brought up in the schools of Vaiṣṇava philosophy and has absorbed its teachings so fully that he seems to have reached the highest state of spiritual illumination only few blessed souls achieve."

Dr. H. B. Kulkarni
Professor of English and Philosophy
Utah State University

"Undoubtedly, the work of Swamiji is a great contribution to the troubled human society of today's world."

Dr. Sooda L. Bhatt
Professor of Indian Languages, Boston University

"The appearance of an English translation of Kṛṣṇadāsa Kavirāja Gosvāmī's *Śrī Caitanya-caritāmṛta* by A. C. Bhaktivedanta Swami Prabhupāda is a cause for celebration among both scholars in Indian studies and lay people seeking to enrich their knowledge of Indian spirituality.

". . . Anyone who gives a close reading to the commentary will sense that here, as in his other works, Śrī Bhaktivedanta has combined a healthy mixture of the fervent devotion and aesthetic sensitivity of a devotee and the intellectual rigor of a textual scholar.

". . . These exquisitely wrought volumes will be a welcome addition to the libraries of all persons who are committed to the study of Indian spirituality and religious literature, whether their interests are sparked by the motivations of the scholar, the devotee, or the general reader."

Dr. J. Bruce Long
Department of Asian Studies, Cornell University

I.
LEARNING THE SCIENCE OF THE SOUL

SEEING THE AIM OF HUMAN LIFE

"At present, human society is being misled by leaders who are blind, for they do not know the aim and objective of human life, which is self-realization and the reestablishment of our lost relationship with the Supreme Personality of Godhead. . . . The Kṛṣṇa consciousness movement is trying to enlighten human society in this important matter."

This very important Kṛṣṇa consciousness movement is meant to save human society from spiritual death. At present human society is being misled by leaders who are blind, for they do not know the aim and objective of human life, which is self-realization and the reestablishment of our lost relationship with the Supreme Personality of Godhead. That is the missing point. The Kṛṣṇa consciousness movement is trying to enlighten human society in this important matter.

According to Vedic civilization, the perfection of life is to realize one's relationship with Kṛṣṇa, or God. In the *Bhagavad-gītā,* which is accepted by all authorities in transcendental science as the basis of all Vedic knowledge, we understand that not only human beings but all living entities are parts and parcels of God. The parts are meant for serving the whole, just as the legs, hands, fingers, and ears are meant for serving the total body. We living entities, being parts and parcels of God, are duty-bound to serve Him.

Actually our position is that we are always rendering service to someone, either to our family, country, or society. If we have no one to serve, sometimes we keep a pet cat or dog and render service to it. All these factors prove that we are constitutionally meant to render service, yet in spite of serving to the best of our ability, we are not satisfied. Nor is the person to whom we are rendering that service satisfied. On the material platform, everyone is frustrated. The reason for this is that the service being rendered is not properly directed. For example, if we want to render service to a tree, we must water the root. If we pour water on the leaves, branches, and twigs, there is little benefit. If the Supreme Personality of Godhead is served, all other parts and parcels will be automatically satisfied. Consequently all welfare activities as well as service to society, family, and nation are realized by serving the Supreme Personality of Godhead.

It is the duty of every human being to understand his constitutional position with God and to act accordingly. If this is possible, then our lives become successful. Sometimes, however, we feel challenging and say, "There is no God" or "I am God" or even "I don't care for God." But in actuality this challenging spirit will not save us. God is there, and we can see Him at every moment. If we refuse to see God in our life, then He will be present before us as cruel death. If we do not choose to see Him in one feature, we will see Him in another. There are different features of the Supreme Personality of Godhead because He is the original root of the entire cosmic manifestation. In one sense, it is not possible for us to escape Him.

This Kṛṣṇa consciousness movement is not blind religious fanaticism, nor is it a revolt by some recent upstart; rather, it is an authorized, scientific approach to the matter of our eternal necessity in relation with the Absolute Personality of Godhead, the Supreme Enjoyer. Kṛṣṇa consciousness simply deals with our eternal relationship with Him and the process of discharging our relative duties to Him. Thus, Kṛṣṇa consciousness enables us to achieve the highest perfection of life attainable in the present human form of existence.

We must always remember that human life is attained only after an evolution of many millions of years in the cycle of transmigration of the spirit soul. In this particular form of life, the economic question is more easily solved than in the lower, animal forms. There are swine, dogs, camels, asses, and so on, whose economic necessities are just as important to them as ours are to us, but the economic questions of these animals and others are solved under primitive conditions, whereas the human being is given all the facilities for leading a comfortable life by the laws of nature.

Why is a man given a better chance to live than swine or other animals? Why is a highly posted government officer given better facilities for a comfortable life than an ordinary clerk? The answer is very simple: the important officer has to discharge duties of a more responsible nature than those of an ordinary clerk. Similarly, the human being has to discharge higher duties than the animals, who are always busy with filling their hungry stomachs. But by the laws of nature, the modern animalistic standard of civilization has only increased the problems of filling the stomach. When we approach some of these polished animals for spiritual life, they say that they only want to work for the satisfaction of their stomachs and that there is no necessity of inquiring about the Godhead. Yet despite their eagerness to work hard, there is always the question of unemployment and so many other impediments incurred by the laws of nature. Despite this, they still denounce the necessity of acknowledging the Godhead.

We are given this human form of life not just to work hard like the swine or dog, but to attain the highest perfection of life. If we do not want that perfection, then we will have to work very hard, for we will be forced to by the laws of nature. In the closing days of Kali-yuga (this present age) men will have to work hard like asses for only a scrap of bread. This process has already begun, and every year the necessity for harder work for lesser wages will increase. Yet human beings are not meant to work hard like animals, and if a man fails to discharge his duties as a human being, he is forced to transmigrate to the lower species of life by the laws of nature. The *Bhagavad-gītā* very vividly describes how a spirit soul, by the laws of nature, takes his birth and gets a suitable body and sense organs for enjoying matter in the material world.

In the *Bhagavad-gītā* it is also stated that those who attempt but do not complete the path of approaching God—in other words, those who have failed to achieve complete success in Kṛṣṇa consciousness—are given the chance to appear in the families of the spiritually advanced or in financially well-to-do mercantile families. If the unsuccessful spiritual aspirants are offered such chances of noble parentage, what of those who have actually attained the required success? Therefore an attempt to go back to Godhead, even if half finished, guarantees a good birth in the next life. Both the spiritual and the financially well-to-do families are beneficial for spiritual progress because in both families one can get a good chance to make further progress from the point where he stopped in his previous birth. In spiritual realization the atmosphere generated by a good family is favorable for the cultivation of spiritual knowledge. The *Bhagavad-gītā* reminds such fortunate well-born persons that their good fortune is due to their past devotional activities. Unfortunately, the children of these families do not consult the *Bhagavad-gītā,* being misguided by *māyā* (illusion).

Birth in a well-to-do family solves the problem of having to find sufficient food from the beginning of life, and later a comparatively easier and more comfortable way of life can be led. Being so situated, one has a good chance to make progress in spiritual realization, but as ill luck would have it, due to the influence of the present iron age (which is full of machines and mechanical people) the sons of the wealthy are misguided for sense enjoyment, and they forget the good chance they have for spiritual enlightenment. Therefore nature, by her laws, is setting fires in these golden homes. It was the golden city of Laṅkā, under the regime of the demoniac Rāvaṇa, that was burned to ashes. That is the law of nature.

The *Bhagavad-gītā* is the preliminary study of the transcendental science of Kṛṣṇa consciousness, and it is the duty of all responsible heads of state to chalk out their economic and other programs by referring to the *Bhagavad-gītā*. We are not meant to solve economic questions of life by balancing on a tottering platform; rather, we are meant to solve the ultimate problems of life which arise due to the laws of nature. Civilization is static unless there is spiritual movement. The soul moves the body, and the living body moves the world. We are concerned about the body, but we have no knowledge of the spirit that is moving that body. Without the spirit, the body is motionless, or dead.

The human body is an excellent vehicle by which we can reach eternal life. It is a rare and very important boat for crossing over the ocean of nescience which is material existence. On this boat there is the service of an expert boatman, the spiritual master. By divine grace, the boat plies the water in a favorable wind. With all these auspicious factors, who would not take the opportunity to cross over the ocean of nescience? If one neglects this good chance, it should be known that he is simply committing suicide.

There is certainly a great deal of comfort in the first-class coach of a train, but if the train does not move toward its destination, what is the benefit of an air-conditioned compartment? Contemporary civilization is much too concerned with making the material body comfortable. No one has information of the real destination of life, which is to go back to Godhead. We must not just remain seated in a comfortable compartment; we should see whether or not our vehicle is moving toward its real destination. There is no ultimate benefit in making the material body comfortable at the expense of forgetting the prime necessity of life, which is to regain our lost spiritual identity. The boat of human life is constructed in such a way that it must move toward a spiritual destination. Unfortunately, this body is anchored to mundane consciousness by five strong chains, which are: (1) attachment to the material body due to ignorance of spiritual facts, (2) attachment to kinsmen due to bodily relations, (3) attachment to the land of birth and to material possessions such as house, furniture, estates, property, business papers, etc., (4) attachment to material science, which always remains mysterious for want of spiritual light, and (5) attachment to religious forms and holy rituals without knowing the Personality of Godhead or His devotees, who make them holy. These attachments, which anchor the boat of the human body, are explained in detail in the Fifteenth Chapter of the *Bhagavad-gītā*. There they are compared to a deeply rooted banyan tree which is ever increasing its hold on the earth. It is very difficult to uproot such a strong banyan tree, but the Lord recommends the following process: "The real form of this tree cannot be perceived in this world. No one can understand where it ends, where it begins, or where its foundation is. But with determination one must cut down this strongly rooted tree with the weapon of detachment. Thereafter, one must seek that place from which, having gone, one never returns, and there surrender to that Supreme Personality of Godhead from whom everything began and from whom everything has extended since time immemorial." [*Bhagavad-gītā* 15.3-4]

Neither the scientists nor speculative philosophers have yet arrived at any conclusion concerning the cosmic situation. All they have done is posit different theories about it. Some of them say that the material world is real, others say that it is a dream, and yet others say that it is ever existing. In this way different views are held by mundane scholars, but the fact is that no mundane scientist or speculative philosopher has ever discovered the beginning of the cosmos or its limitations. No one can say when it began or how it floats in space. They theoretically propose some laws, like the law of gravitation, but actually they cannot put this law to practical use. For want of actual knowledge of the truth, everyone is anxious to promote his own theory to gain certain fame, but the actual fact is that this material world is full of miseries and that no one can overcome them simply by promoting some theories about the subject. The Personality of Godhead, who is fully cognizant of everything in His creation, informs us that it is in our best interest that we desire to get out of this miserable existence. We must detach ourselves from everything material. To make the best use of a bad bargain, our material existence must be one-hundred-percent spiritualized. Iron is not fire, but it can be turned into fire by constant association with fire. Similarly, detachment from material activities can be effected by spiritual activities, not by material inertia. Material inertia is the negative side of material action, but spiritual activity is not only the negation of material action but the activation of our real life. We must be anxious to search out eternal life, or spiritual existence in Brahman, the Absolute. The eternal kingdom of Brahman is described in the *Bhagavad-gītā* as that eternal country from which no one returns. That is the kingdom of God.

The beginning of our present material life cannot be traced, nor is it necessary for us to know how we became conditioned in material existence. We have to be satisfied with the understanding that somehow or other this material life has been going on since time immemorial and now our duty is to surrender unto the Supreme Lord, who is the original cause of all causes. The preliminary qualification for going back to Godhead is given in the *Bhagavad-gītā* [15.5]: "One who is free from illusion, false prestige, and false association, who understands the eternal, who is done with material lust and is free from the duality of happiness and distress, and who knows how to surrender unto the Supreme Person attains that eternal kingdom."

One who is convinced of his spiritual identity and is freed from the material conception of existence, who is free from illusion and is transcendental to the modes of material nature, who constantly engages in understanding spiritual knowledge and who has completely severed himself from sense enjoyment can go back to Godhead. Such a person is called *amūḍha,* as distinguished from *mūḍha,* or the foolish and ignorant, for he is freed from the duality of happiness and distress.

And what is the nature of the kingdom of God? It is described in the *Bhagavad-gītā* [15.6] as follows: "That abode of Mine is not illumined by the sun or moon, nor by electricity. One who reaches it never returns to this material world."

Although every place in the creation is within the kingdom of God because the Lord is the supreme proprietor of all planets, there is still the Lord's personal abode, which is completely different from the universe in which we are now living. And this abode is called *paramam,* or the supreme abode. Even on this earth there are countries where the standard of living is high and countries where the standard of living is low. Besides this earth, there are innumerable other planets distributed all over the universe, and some are considered superior places and some inferior places. In any case, all planets within the jurisdiction of the external energy, material nature, require the rays of a sun or the light of fire for their existence, because the material universe is a region of darkness. Beyond this region, however, is the spiritual realm, which is described as func-tioning under the superior nature of God. That realm is described in the *Upaniṣads* thus: "There is no need of sun, moon, or stars, nor is that abode illumined by electricity or any form of fire. All these material universes are illumined by a reflection of that spiritual light, and because that superior nature is always self-luminous, we can experience a glow of light even in the densest darkness of night." In the *Hari-vaṁśa* the spiritual nature is explained by the Supreme Lord Himself as follows: "The glaring effulgence of the impersonal Brahman [the impersonal Absolute] illuminates all existences, both material and spiritual. But, O Bhārata, you must understand that this Brahman illumination is the effulgence of My body." In the *Brahma-saṁhitā* this conclusion is confirmed. We should not think that we can attain that abode by any material means such as spaceships, but we should know for certain that one who can attain that spiritual abode of Kṛṣṇa can enjoy eternal, spiritual bliss without interruption. As fallible living entities, we have two phases of existence. One is called material existence, which is full of the miseries of birth, death, old age, and disease, and the other is called spiritual existence, in which there is an incessant spiritual life of eternity, bliss, and knowledge. In material existence we are ruled by the material conception of the body and the mind, but in spiritual existence we can always relish the happy, transcendental contact of the Personality of Godhead. In spiritual existence, the Lord is never lost to us.

The Kṛṣṇa consciousness movement is trying to bring that spiritual existence to humanity at large. In our present material consciousness, we are attached to the sensual material conception of life, but this conception can be removed at once by devotional service to Kṛṣṇa, or Kṛṣṇa consciousness. If we adopt the principles of devotional service, we can become transcendental to the ma-terial conceptions of life and be liberated from the modes of goodness, passion, and ignorance, even in the midst of various material engagements. Everyone who is engaged in material affairs can derive the highest benefit from the pages of *Back to Godhead* and the other literatures of this Kṛṣṇa consciousness movement. These literatures help all people sever the roots of the indefatigable banyan tree of material existence. These literatures are authorized to train us to renounce everything related to the material conception of life and to relish spiritual nectar in every object. This stage is obtainable only by devotional service and nothing else. By rendering such service, one can at once get liberation (*mukti*) even during this present life. Most spiritual endeavors are tinged with the colors of materialism, but pure devotional service is transcendental to all material pollution. Those who desire to go back to Godhead need only adopt the principles of this Kṛṣṇa consciousness movement and simply aim their consciousness at the lotus feet of the Supreme Lord, the Personality of Godhead, Kṛṣṇa.

"YOUR ORIGINAL CONSCIOUSNESS IS KṚṢṆA CONSCIOUSNESS"

"Your original consciousness is Kṛṣṇa consciousness," Śrīla Prabhupāda tells freelance reporter Sandy Nixon. "Now your consciousness is covered with so much rubbish. You have to cleanse it, and then—Kṛṣṇa consciousness. Our consciousness is like water. Water is by nature clear and transparent, but sometimes it becomes muddy. If you filter all the mud out of the water, it again comes to its original clear, transparent state."

Ms. Nixon: My first question is very basic. What is Kṛṣṇa consciousness?

Śrīla Prabhupāda: *Kṛṣṇa* means God. We are all intimately connected with Him because He is our original father. But we have forgotten this connection. When we become interested in knowing "What is my connection with God? What is the aim of life?" then we are called Kṛṣṇa conscious.

Ms. Nixon: How does Kṛṣṇa consciousness develop in the practitioner?

Śrīla Prabhupāda: Kṛṣṇa consciousness is already there in the core of everyone's heart. But because of our materially conditioned life, we have forgotten it. The process of chanting the Hare Kṛṣṇa *mahā-mantra*—Hare Kṛṣṇa, Hare Kṛṣṇa, Kṛṣṇa Kṛṣṇa, Hare Hare/ Hare Rāma, Hare Rāma, Rāma Rāma, Hare Hare—revives the Kṛṣṇa consciousness we already have. For example, a few months ago these American and European boys and girls did not know about Kṛṣṇa, but just yesterday we saw how they were chanting Hare Kṛṣṇa and dancing in ecstasy throughout the whole Ratha-yātrā procession [an annual festival sponsored by the Kṛṣṇa consciousness movement in cities around the world]. Do you think that was artificial? No. Artificially, nobody can chant and dance for hours together. They have actually awakened their Kṛṣṇa consciousness by following a bona fide process. This is explained in the

Caitanya-caritāmṛta [*Madhya* 22.107]:

> *nitya-siddha kṛṣṇa-prema 'sādhya' kabhu naya*
> *śravaṇādi-śuddha-citte karaye udaya*

Kṛṣṇa consciousness is dormant in everyone's heart, and when one comes in contact with devotees, it is awakened. Kṛṣṇa consciousness is not artificial. Just as a young boy awakens his natural attraction for a young girl in her association, similarly, if one hears about Kṛṣṇa in the association of devotees, he awakens his dormant Kṛṣṇa consciousness.

Ms. Nixon: What is the difference between Kṛṣṇa consciousness and Christ consciousness?

Śrīla Prabhupāda: Christ consciousness is also Kṛṣṇa consciousness, but because at present people do not follow the rules and regulations of Christianity—the commandments of Jesus Christ—they do not come to the standard of God consciousness.

Ms. Nixon: What is unique about Kṛṣṇa consciousness among all religions?

Śrīla Prabhupāda: Primarily, religion means to know God and to love Him. That is religion. Nowadays, because of a lack of training, nobody knows God, what to speak of loving Him. People are satisfied simply going to church and praying, "O God, give us our daily bread." In the *Śrīmad-Bhāgavatam* this is called a cheating religion, because the aim is not to know and love God but to gain some personal profit. In other words, if I profess to follow some religion but I do not know who God is or how to love Him, I am practicing a cheating religion. As far as the Christian religion is concerned, ample opportunity is given to understand God, but no one is taking it. For example, the Bible contains the commandment "Thou shall not kill," but Christians have built the world's best slaughterhouses. How can they become God conscious if they disobey the commandments of Lord Jesus Christ? And this is going on not just in the Christian religion but in every religion. The title "Hindu," "Muslim," or "Christian" is simply a rubber stamp. None of them knows who God is and how to love Him.

Ms. Nixon: How can one tell a bona fide spiritual master from a fake?

Śrīla Prabhupāda: Whoever teaches how to know God and how to love Him—he is a spiritual master. Sometimes bogus rascals mislead people. "I am God," they claim, and people who do not know what God is believe them. You must be a serious student to understand who God is and how to love Him. Otherwise, you will simply waste your time. So the difference between others and us is that we are the only movement that can actually teach one how to know God and how to love Him. We are presenting the science of how one can know Kṛṣṇa, the Supreme Personality of Godhead, by practicing the teachings of the *Bhagavad-gītā* and the *Śrīmad-Bhāgavatam.* They teach us that our only business is to love God. Our business is not to ask God for our necessities. God gives necessities to everyone—even to one who has no religion. For example, cats and dogs have no religion, yet Kṛṣṇa supplies them with the necessities of life. So why should we bother Kṛṣṇa for our daily bread? He is already supplying it. Real religion means to learn how to love Him. The *Śrīmad-Bhāgavatam* [1.2.6] says,

sa vai puṁsāṁ paro dharmo yato bhaktir adhokṣaje
ahaituky apratihatā yayātmā suprasīdati

First-class religion teaches one how to love God without any motive. If I serve God for some profit, that is business—not love. Real love of God is *ahaituky apratihatā:* it cannot be checked by any material cause. It is unconditional. If one actually wants to love God, there is no impediment. One can love Him whether one is poor or rich, young or old, black or white.

Ms. Nixon: Do all paths lead to the same end?

Śrīla Prabhupāda: No. There are four classes of men—the *karmīs,* the *jñānīs,* the *yogīs,* and the *bhaktas*—and each achieves a different goal. The *karmīs* work for some material profit. For example, in the city, many people work hard day and night, and their purpose is to get some money. Thus, they are fruitive workers, or *karmīs.* A *jñānī* is a person who thinks, "Why am I working so hard? The birds, bees, elephants, and other creatures have no profession, yet they are also eating. So why should I unnecessarily work so hard? Rather, let me try to solve the problems of life—birth, death, old age, and disease." *Jñānīs* try to become immortal. They think that if they merge into God's existence then they will become immune to birth, death, old age, and disease. And *yogīs* try to acquire some mystic power to exhibit a wonderful show. For instance, a *yogī* can become very small: if you put him into a locked room, he can come out through any little space. By showing this kind of magic, the *yogī* is immediately accepted as a very wonderful man. Of course, modern *yogīs* simply show some gymnastics—they have no real power. But a real *yogī* has some power, which is not spiritual but material.

So the *yogī* wants mystic power, the *jñānī* wants salvation from the miseries of life, and the *karmī* wants material profit. But the *bhakta*—the devotee—doesn't want anything for himself. He simply wants to serve God out of love, just as a mother serves her child. There is no question of profit in a mother's service to her child. Out of pure affection and love, she cares for him.

When you come to this stage of loving God, that is perfection. Neither the *karmī,* the *jñānī,* nor the *yogī* can know God—only the *bhakta.* As Kṛṣṇa says in the *Bhagavad-gītā* [18.55], *bhaktyā mām abhijānāti:* "Only through the process of *bhakti* can one understand God." Kṛṣṇa never says one can understand Him by other processes. No. Only through *bhakti.* If you are interested in knowing God and loving Him, then you must accept the devotional process. No other process will help you.

Ms. Nixon: What transformation does one undergo on the path—

Śrīla Prabhupāda: No transformation—your original consciousness is Kṛṣṇa consciousness. Now your consciousness is covered with so much rubbish. You have to cleanse it, and then—Kṛṣṇa consciousness. Our consciousness is like water. Water is by nature clear and transparent, but sometimes it becomes muddy. If you filter all the mud out of the water, it again comes to its original clear, transparent state.

Ms. Nixon: Can one function better in society by becoming Kṛṣṇa conscious?

Śrīla Prabhupāda: Yes, you can see that my disciples are not drunkards or meat-eaters, and from a physiological point of view they are very clean—they'll never be attacked by serious diseases. Actually, giving up meat-eating is not a question of Kṛṣṇa consciousness but of civilized human life. God has given human society so many things to eat—nice fruits, vegetables, grain, and first-class milk. From milk one can prepare hundreds of nutritious foods, but no one knows the art. Instead, people maintain big slaughterhouses and eat meat. They are not even civilized. When man is uncivilized, he kills poor animals and eats them.

Civilized men know the art of preparing nutritious foods from milk. For instance, on our New Vṛndāvana farm in West Virginia, we make hundreds of first-class preparations from milk. Whenever visitors come, they are astonished that from milk such nice foods can be prepared. The blood of the cow is very nutritious, but civilized men utilize it in the form of milk. Milk is nothing but cow's blood transformed. You can make milk into so many things—yogurt, curd, ghee (clarified butter), and so on—and by combining these milk products with grains, fruits, and vegetables, you can make hundreds of preparations. This is civilized life—not directly killing an animal and eating its flesh. The innocent cow is simply eating grass given by God and supplying milk, which you can live on. Do you think cutting the cow's throat and eating its flesh is civilized?

Ms. Nixon: No, I agree with you one hundred percent. One thing I'm very curious about: can the *Vedas* be taken symbolically as well as literally?

Śrīla Prabhupāda: No. They must be taken as they are, not symbolically. That is why we are presenting the *Bhagavad-gītā As It Is.*

Ms. Nixon: Are you attempting to revive the ancient Indian caste system in the West? The *Gītā* mentions the caste system—

Śrīla Prabhupāda: Where does the *Bhagavad-gītā* mention the caste system? Kṛṣṇa says, *cātur-varṇyaṁ mayā sṛṣṭaṁ guṇa-karma-vibhāgaśaḥ:* "I created four divisions of men according to their quality and work." [Bg. 4.13] For instance, you can understand that there are engineers as well as medical practitioners in society. Do you say they belong to different castes—that one is in the engineer caste and the other is in the medical caste? No. If a man has qualified himself in medical school, you accept him as a doctor, and if another man has a degree in engineering, you accept him as an engineer. Similarly, the *Bhagavad-gītā* defines four classes of men in society: a class of highly intelligent men, a class of administrators, a class of productive men, and ordinary workers. These divisions are natural. For example, one class of men is very intelligent. But to actually meet the qualifications of first-class men as described in the *Bhagavad-gītā*, they need to be trained, just as an intelligent boy requires training in a college to become a qualified doctor. So in the Kṛṣṇa consciousness movement we are training the intelligent men how to control their minds, how to control their senses, how to become truthful, how to become clean internally and externally, how to become wise, how to apply their knowledge in practical life, and how to become God conscious. All these boys [*gestures toward seated disciples*] have first-class intelligence, and now we are training them to use it properly.

We are not introducing the caste system, in which any rascal born in a *brāhmaṇa* family is automatically a *brāhmaṇa*. He may have the habits of a fifth-class man, but he is accepted as first class because of his birth in a *brāhmaṇa* family. We don't accept that. We recognize a man as first class who is trained as a *brāhmaṇa*. It doesn't matter whether he is Indian, European, or American, lowborn or highborn—it doesn't matter. Any intelligent man can be trained to adopt first-class habits. We want to stop the nonsensical idea that we are imposing the Indian caste system on our disciples. We are simply picking out men with first-class intelligence and training them how to become first class in every respect.

Ms. Nixon: How do you feel about women's liberation?

Śrīla Prabhupāda: So-called equal rights for women means that the men cheat the women. Suppose a woman and a man meet, they become lovers, they have sex, the woman becomes pregnant, and the man goes away. The woman has to take charge of the child and beg alms from the government, or else she kills the child by having an abortion. This is the woman's independence. In India, although a woman may be poverty-stricken, she stays under the care of her husband, and he takes responsibility for her. When she becomes pregnant, she is not forced to kill the child or maintain him by begging. So, which is real independence—to remain under the care of the husband or to be enjoyed by everyone?

Ms. Nixon: How about in spiritual life—can women also succeed in Kṛṣṇa consciousness?

Śrīla Prabhupāda: We make no distinction on the basis of sex. We give Kṛṣṇa consciousness to both men and women equally. We welcome women, men, the poor, the rich—everyone. Kṛṣṇa says in the *Bhagavad-gītā* [5.18]:

vidyā-vinaya-sampanne brāhmaṇe gavi hastini
śuni caiva śva-pāke ca paṇḍitāḥ sama-darśinaḥ

"The humble sages, by virtue of true knowledge, see with equal vision a learned and gentle *brāhmaṇa,* a cow, an elephant, a dog, and a dog-eater."

Ms. Nixon: Could you explain the meaning of the Hare Kṛṣṇa mantra?

Śrīla Prabhupāda: It is very simple. *Hare* means "O energy of the Lord," and *Kṛṣṇa* means "O Lord Kṛṣṇa." Just as there are males and females in the material world, similarly, God is the original male (*puruṣa*), and His energy (*prakṛti*) is the original female. So, when we chant Hare Kṛṣṇa, we are saying, "O Lord Kṛṣṇa, O energy of Kṛṣṇa, kindly engage me in Your service."

Ms. Nixon: Could you please tell me a little bit about your life and how you knew that you were the spiritual master of the Kṛṣṇa consciousness movement?

Śrīla Prabhupāda: My life is simple. I was a householder with a wife and children—now I have grandsons—when my spiritual master ordered me to go to the Western countries and preach the cult of Kṛṣṇa consciousness. So I left everything on the order of my spiritual master, and now I am trying to execute his order and the orders of Kṛṣṇa.

Ms. Nixon: How old were you when he told you to go to the West?

Śrīla Prabhupāda: At our first meeting, he ordered me to preach Kṛṣṇa consciousness in the West. I was then twenty-five years old, a married man with two children. I tried my best to carry out his orders and started managing *Back to Godhead* magazine in 1944, when I was still in household life. I started writing books in 1959 after retiring from family life, and in 1965 I came to the United States.

Ms. Nixon: You have said that you are not God, and yet it appears to me, as an outsider, that your devotees treat you as if you were God.

Śrīla Prabhupāda: Yes, that is their duty. Because the spiritual master is executing God's order, he should be respected as much as God, just as a government officer should be respected as much as the government because he executes the government's order. Even if an ordinary policeman comes, you have to respect him because he is a government man. But that does not mean he *is* the government. *Sākṣād-dharitvena samasta-śāstrair/ uktas tathā bhāvyata eva sadbhiḥ:* "The spiritual master is to be honored as much as the

Supreme Lord because he is the most confidential servitor of the Lord. This is acknowledged in all revealed scriptures and followed by all authorities."

Ms. Nixon: I also wonder about the many beautiful material things that the devotees bring you. For instance, you left the airport in a beautiful, fancy car. I wonder about this because—

Śrīla Prabhupāda: That teaches the disciples how to regard the spiritual master as good as God. If you respect the government representative as much as you respect the government, then you must treat him opulently. If you respect the spiritual master as much as God, then you must offer him the same facilities you would offer to God. God travels in a golden car. If the disciples offer the spiritual master an ordinary motorcar, it would not be sufficient, because the spiritual master has to be treated like God. If God comes to your home, will you bring Him an ordinary motorcar—or will you arrange for a golden car?

Ms. Nixon: One of the most difficult aspects of Kṛṣṇa consciousness for an outsider to accept is the Deity in the temple—how it represents Kṛṣṇa. Could you talk a little bit about that?

Śrīla Prabhupāda: Yes. At the present moment, because you have not been trained to see Kṛṣṇa, He kindly appears before you so you can see Him. You can see wood and stone, but you cannot see what is spiritual. Suppose your father is in the hospital, and he dies. You are crying by his bedside, "Now my father is gone!" But why do you say he is gone? What is that thing which is gone?

Ms. Nixon: Well, his spirit is gone.

Śrīla Prabhupāda: And have you seen that spirit?

Ms. Nixon: No.

Śrīla Prabhupāda: So you cannot see spirit, and God is the Supreme Spirit. Actually, He is everything—spirit and matter—but you cannot see Him in His spiritual identity. Therefore, to show kindness toward you, He appears out of His unbounded mercy in the form of a wooden or stone Deity so that you can see Him.

Ms. Nixon: Thank you very much.

Śrīla Prabhupāda: Hare Kṛṣṇa!

"REAL ADVANCEMENT MEANS KNOWING GOD"

"The purpose of this Kṛṣṇa consciousness movement is to propagate God's name, God's glories, God's activities, God's beauty, and God's love. . . . This Kṛṣṇa consciousness movement is meant to give perfect knowledge to human society."

Ladies and gentlemen, I thank you very much for kindly participating in this Kṛṣṇa consciousness movement. When this society was registered in 1966 in New York, a friend suggested that it be named the Society for God Consciousness. He thought that the name Kṛṣṇa was sectarian. The dictionary also says that Kṛṣṇa is a Hindu god's name. But in actuality, if any name can be attributed to God, it is "Kṛṣṇa."

Actually God has no particular name. By saying He has no name, we mean that no one knows how many names He has. Since God is un-limited, His names also must be unlimited. Therefore we cannot settle on one name. For instance, Kṛṣṇa is sometimes called Yaśodā-nandana, the son of mother Yaśodā; or Devakī-nandana, the son of Devakī; or Vasudeva-nandana, the son of Vasudeva; or Nanda-nandana, the son of Nanda. Sometimes He is called Pārtha-sārathi, indicating that He acted as the charioteer of Arjuna, who is sometimes called Pārtha, the son of Pṛthā.

God has many dealings with His many devotees, and according to those dealings, He is called certain names. Since He has innumerable devotees and innumerable relations with them, He also has innumerable names. We cannot hit on any one name. But the name Kṛṣṇa means "all-attractive." God attracts everyone; that is the definition of *God*. We have seen many pictures of Kṛṣṇa, and we see that He attracts the cows, calves, birds, beasts, trees, plants, and even the water in Vṛndāvana. He is attractive to the cowherd boys, to the *gopīs*, to Nanda Mahārāja, to the Pāṇḍavas, and to all human society. Therefore if any particular name can be given to God, that name is "Kṛṣṇa."

Parāśara Muni, a great sage and the father of Vyāsadeva, who compiled all the Vedic literatures, gave the following definition of God:

aiśvaryasya samagrasya vīryasya yaśasaḥ śriyaḥ
jñāna-vairāgyayoś caiva ṣaṇṇāṁ bhaga itīṅganā
[*Viṣṇu Purāṇa* 6.5.47]

Bhagavān, the Supreme Personality of Godhead, is thus defined by Parāśara Muni as one who is full in six opulences—who has full strength, fame, wealth, knowledge, beauty, and renunciation.

Bhagavān, the Supreme Personality of Godhead, is the proprietor of all riches. There are many rich men in the world, but no one can claim that he possesses all the wealth. Nor can anyone claim that no one is richer than he. We understand from the *Śrīmad-Bhāgavatam,* however, that when Kṛṣṇa was present on this earth He had 16,108 wives, and each wife lived in a palace made of marble and bedecked with jewels. The rooms were filled with furniture made of ivory and gold, and there was great opulence everywhere. These descriptions are all given vividly in the *Śrīmad-Bhāgavatam.* In the history of human society we cannot find anyone who had sixteen thousand wives or sixteen thousand palaces. Nor did Kṛṣṇa go to one wife one day and another wife another day. No, He was personally present in every palace at the same time. This means that He expanded Himself in 16,108 forms. This is impossible for an ordinary man, but it is not very difficult for God. If God is unlimited, He can expand Himself in unlimited forms; otherwise there is no meaning to the word *unlimited.* God is omnipotent: He can maintain not only sixteen thousand wives but sixteen million and still encounter no difficulty; otherwise there is no meaning to the word *omnipotent.*

These are all attractive features. We experience in this material world that if a man is very rich, he is attractive. In America, for instance, Rockefeller and Ford are very attractive because of their riches. They are attractive even though they do not possess all the wealth of the world. How much more attractive, then, is God, who is the possessor of all riches.

Similarly, Kṛṣṇa has unlimited strength. His strength was present from the moment of His birth. When Kṛṣṇa was only three months old, the Pūtanā demon attempted to kill Him, but instead she was killed by Kṛṣṇa. That is God. God is God from the beginning. He does not become God by some meditation or mystic power. Kṛṣṇa is not that type of God. Kṛṣṇa was God from the very beginning of His appearance.

Kṛṣṇa also has unlimited fame. Of course, we are devotees of Kṛṣṇa and know of Him and glorify Him, but apart from us, many millions in the world are aware of the fame of the *Bhagavad-gītā*. In all countries all over the world the *Bhagavad-gītā* is read by philosophers, psychologists, and religionists. We are also finding very good sales with our *Bhagavad-gītā As It Is*. This is because the commodity is pure gold. There are many editions of the *Bhagavad-gītā*, but they are not pure. Ours is selling more because we are presenting the *Bhagavad-gītā* as it is. The fame of the *Bhagavad-gītā* is Kṛṣṇa's fame.

Beauty, another opulence, is possessed unlimitedly by Kṛṣṇa. Kṛṣṇa Himself is very beautiful, as are all His associates. Those who were pious in a previous life receive an opportunity in this material world to take birth in good families and good nations. The American people are very rich and beautiful, and these opulences are a result of pious activities. All over the world people are attracted to the Americans because they are advanced in scientific knowledge, riches, beauty, and so on. This planet is an insignificant planet within the universe, yet within this planet, one country—America—has so many attractive features. We can just imagine, then, how many attractive features must be possessed by God, who is the creator of the entire cosmic manifestation. How beautiful He must be—He who has created all beauty.

A person is attractive not only because of his beauty but also because of his knowledge. A scientist or philosopher may be attractive because of his knowledge, but what knowledge is more sublime than that given by Kṛṣṇa in the *Bhagavad-gītā*? There is no comparison in the world to such knowledge. At the same time, Kṛṣṇa possesses full renunciation (*vairāgya*). So many things are working under Kṛṣṇa's direction in this material world, but actually Kṛṣṇa is not present here. A big factory may continue to work although the owner may not be present. Similarly, Kṛṣṇa's potencies are working under the direction of His assistants, the demigods. Thus Kṛṣṇa Himself is aloof from the material world. This is all described in the revealed scriptures.

God, therefore, has many names according to His activities, but because He possesses so many opulences, and because with these opulences He attracts everyone, He is called Kṛṣṇa. The Vedic literature asserts that God has many names, but "Kṛṣṇa" is the principal name.

The purpose of this Kṛṣṇa consciousness movement is to propagate God's name, God's glories, God's activities, God's beauty, and God's love. There are many things within this material world, and all of them are within Kṛṣṇa. The most prominent feature of this material world is sex, and that also is present in Kṛṣṇa. We are worshiping Rādhā and Kṛṣṇa, and attraction exists between Them, but material attraction and spiritual attraction are not the same. In Kṛṣṇa, sex is real, but here in the material world it is unreal. Everything we deal with here is present in the spiritual world, but here it has no real value. It is only a reflection. In store windows we see many mannequins, but no one cares about them, because everyone knows they are false. A mannequin may be very beautiful, but still it is false. When people see a beautiful woman, however, they are attracted because they think she is real. In actuality, the so-called living are also dead, because this body is simply a lump of matter; as soon as the soul leaves the body, no one would care to see the so-called beautiful body of the woman. The real factor, the real attracting force, is the spiritual soul.

In the material world everything is made of dead matter; therefore it is simply an imitation. The reality of things exists in the spiritual world. Those who have read the *Bhagavad-gītā* can understand what the spiritual world is like, for there it is described:

paras tasmāt tu bhāvo 'nyo 'vyakto 'vyaktāt sanātanaḥ
yaḥ sa sarveṣu bhūteṣu naśyatsu na vinaśyati

"Yet there is another unmanifest nature, which is eternal and is transcendental to this manifested and unmanifested matter. It is supreme and is never annihilated. When all in this world is annihilated, that part remains as it is." [*Bhagavad-gītā* 8.20]

Scientists are attempting to calculate the length and breadth of this material world, but they cannot begin. It will take them thousands of years simply to travel to the nearest star. And what to speak of the spiritual world? Since we cannot know the material world, how can we know what is beyond it? The point is that we must know from authoritative sources.

The most authoritative source is Kṛṣṇa, for He is the reservoir of all knowledge. No one is wiser or more knowledgeable than Kṛṣṇa. Kṛṣṇa informs us that beyond this material world is a spiritual sky, which is filled with innumerable planets. That sky is far, far greater than material space, which constitutes only one fourth of the entire creation. Similarly, the living entities within the material world are but a small portion of the living entities throughout the creation. This material world is compared to a prison, and just as prisoners represent only a small percentage of the total population, so the living entities within the material world constitute but a fragmental portion of all living entities.

Those who have revolted against God—who are criminal—are placed in this material world. Sometimes criminals say that they don't care for the government, but nonetheless they are arrested and punished. Similarly, living entities who declare their defiance of God are placed in the material world.

Originally the living entities are all part and parcel of God and are related to Him just as sons are related to their father. Christians also consider God the supreme father. Christians go to church and pray, "Our Father, who art in heaven . . ." The conception of God as father is also in the *Bhagavad-gītā* [14.4]:

sarva-yoniṣu kaunteya mūrtayaḥ sambhavanti yāḥ
tāsāṁ brahma mahad yonir ahaṁ bīja-pradaḥ pitā

"It should be understood that all species of life, O son of Kuntī, are made possible by birth in this material nature, and that I am the seed-giving father."

There are 8,400,000 species of life—including aquatics, plants, birds, beasts, insects, and human beings. Of the human species, most are uncivilized, and out of the few civilized species only a small number of human beings take to religious life. Out of many so-called religionists, most identify themselves by designations, claiming "I am Hindu," "I am Muslim," "I am Christian," and so on. Some engage in philanthropic work—giving to the poor or opening schools and hospitals. This altruistic process is called *karma-kāṇḍa*. Out of millions of these *karma-kāṇḍīs,* there may be one *jñānī* ("one who knows"). Out of millions of *jñānīs,* one may be liberated, and out of billions of liberated souls, one may be able to understand Kṛṣṇa. This, then, is the position of Kṛṣṇa. As Kṛṣṇa Himself says in the *Bhagavad-gītā* [7.3]:

manuṣyāṇāṁ sahasreṣu kaścid yatati siddhaye
yatatām api siddhānāṁ kaścin māṁ vetti tattvataḥ

"Out of many thousands among men, one may endeavor for perfection, and of those who have achieved perfection, hardly one knows Me in truth."

Understanding Kṛṣṇa, then, is very difficult. But although the understanding of God is a difficult subject, God explains Himself in the *Bhagavad-gītā*. He says, "I am like this, and I am like this. The material nature is like this, and the spiritual nature is like that. The living entities are like this, and the Supreme Soul is like that." Thus everything is completely described in the *Bhagavad-gītā.* Although understanding God is very difficult, it is not difficult when God Himself gives us His own knowledge. Actually that is the only process by which we can understand God. To understand God by our own speculation is not possible, for God is unlimited and we are limited. Our knowledge and perception are both very limited, so how can we understand the unlimited? If we simply accept the version of the unlimited that God Himself gives, we can come to understand Him. That understanding is our perfection.

Speculative knowledge of God will lead us nowhere. If a boy wants to know who his father is, the simple process is to ask his mother. The mother will then say, "This is your father." This is the way of perfect knowledge. Of course, one may speculate about one's father, wondering if this is the man or if that is the man, and one may wander over the whole city, asking, "Are you my father? Are you my father?" The knowledge derived from such a process, however, will always remain imperfect. One will never find his father in this way. The simple process is to take the knowledge from an authority—in this case, the mother. She simply says, "My dear boy, here is your father." In this way our knowledge is perfect.

Transcendental knowledge is similar. I was just previously speaking of a spiritual world. This spiritual world is not subject to our speculation. God says, "There is a spiritual world, and that is My headquarters." In this way we receive knowledge from Kṛṣṇa, the best authority. We may not be perfect, but our knowledge is perfect because it is received from the perfect source.

The Kṛṣṇa consciousness movement is meant to give perfect knowledge to human society. By such knowledge one can understand who he is, who God is, what the material world is, why we have come here, why we must undergo so much tribulation and misery, and why we have to die. Of course, no one wants to die, but death will come. No one wants to become an old man, but still old age comes. No one wants to suffer from disease, but surely enough, disease comes. These are the real problems of human life, and they are yet to be solved. Civilization attempts to improve eating, sleeping, mating, and defense, but these are not the real problems. A man sleeps, and a dog sleeps. A man is not more advanced simply because he has a nice apartment. In both cases, the business is the same—sleeping. Man has discovered atomic weapons for defense, but the dog also has teeth and claws and can also defend himself. In both cases, defense is there. Man cannot say that because he has the atomic bomb he can conquer the entire world or the entire universe. That is not possible. Man may possess an elaborate method for defense, or a gorgeous method for eating, sleeping, or mating, but that does not make him advanced. We may call his advancement polished animalism, and that is all.

Real advancement means knowing God. If we are lacking knowledge of God, we are not actually advanced. Many rascals deny the existence of God because if there is no God they can continue their sinful activities. It may be very nice for them to think that there is no God, but God will not die simply because we deny Him. God is there, and His administration is there. By His orders the sun is rising, the moon is rising, the water flows, and the ocean abides by the tide. Thus everything functions under His order. Since everything is going on very nicely, how can one realistically think that God is dead? If there is mismanagement, we may say that there is no government, but if there is good management, how can we say that there is no government? Just because people do not know God, they say that God is dead, that there is no God, or that

God has no form. But we are firmly convinced that there is God and that Kṛṣṇa is God. Therefore we are worshiping Him. That is the process of Kṛṣṇa consciousness. Try to understand it. Thank you very much.

REINCARNATION AND BEYOND

Mike Robinson, an interviewer for the London Broadcasting Company, inquires about the science of the soul: Have we been here before? Will we be back again, or. . . ? Śrīla Prabhupāda calls upon the age-old Vedic literatures for some striking answers.

Mike Robinson: Can you tell me what you believe—what the philosophy of the Hare Kṛṣṇa movement is?
Śrīla Prabhupāda: Yes. Kṛṣṇa consciousness is not a question of belief; it is a science. The first step is to know the difference between a living body and a dead body. What is the difference? The difference is that when someone dies, the spirit soul, or the living force, leaves the body. And therefore the body is called "dead." So, there are two things: one, this body; and the other, the living force within the body. We speak of the living force within the body. That is the difference between the science of Kṛṣṇa consciousness, which is spiritual, and ordinary material science. As such, in the beginning it is very, very difficult for an ordinary man to appreciate our movement. One must first understand that he is a soul, or something other than his body.
Mike Robinson: And when will we understand that?
Śrīla Prabhupāda: You can understand at any moment, but it requires a little intelligence. For example, as a child grows, he becomes a boy, the boy becomes a young man, the young man becomes an adult, and the adult becomes an old man. Throughout all this time, although his body is changing from a child to an old man, he still feels himself to be the same person, with the same identity. Just see: the body is changing, but the occupier of the body, the soul, is remaining the same. So we should logically conclude that when our present body dies, we get another body. This is called transmigration of the soul.
Mike Robinson: So when people die it is just the physical body that dies?

Śrīla Prabhupāda: Yes. That is explained very elaborately in the *Bhagavad-gītā* [2.20]: *na jāyate mriyate vā kadācin . . . na hanyate hanyamāne śarīre.*
Mike Robinson: Do you often quote references?
Śrīla Prabhupāda: Yes, we quote many references. Kṛṣṇa consciousness is a serious education, not an ordinary religion. [*To a devotee:*] Find that verse in the *Bhagavad-gītā*.
Disciple:

na jāyate mriyate vā kadācin
nāyaṁ bhūtvā bhavitā vā na bhūyaḥ
ajo nityaḥ śāśvato 'yaṁ purāṇo
na hanyate hanyamāne śarīre

"For the soul there is neither birth nor death at any time. He has not come into being, does not come into being, and will not come into being. He is unborn, eternal, ever-existing and primeval. He is not slain when the body is slain."
Mike Robinson: Thank you very much for reading that. So can you explain to me just a bit more? If the soul is undying, does everybody's soul go to be with God when they die?
Śrīla Prabhupāda: Not necessarily. If one is qualified—if he qualifies himself in this life to go back home, back to Godhead—then he can go. If he does not qualify himself, then he gets another material body. And there are 8,400,000 different bodily forms. According to his desires and karma, the laws of nature give him a suitable body. It is just like when a man contracts some disease and then develops that disease. Is that difficult to understand?
Mike Robinson: It's very difficult to understand all of it.
Śrīla Prabhupāda: Suppose somebody has contracted smallpox. So, after seven days he develops the symptoms. What is that period called?
Mike Robinson: Incubation?
Śrīla Prabhupāda: Incubation. So you cannot avoid it. If you have contracted some disease it will develop, by nature's law. Similarly, during this life you associate with various modes of material nature, and that association will decide what kind of body you are going to get in the next life. That is strictly under the laws of nature. Everyone is controlled by the laws of nature—they're completely

dependent—but out of ignorance people think that they are free. They're not free; they're *imagining* that they're free, but they are completely under the laws of nature. So, your next birth will be decided according to your activities—sinful or pious, as the case may be.
Mike Robinson: Your Grace, could you go back over that just for a minute? You said that nobody is free. Are you saying that if we live a good life, we in some way determine a good future for ourselves?
Śrīla Prabhupāda: Yes.
Mike Robinson: So we are free to choose what we believe to be important? Religion is important, because if we believe in God and lead a good life—
Śrīla Prabhupāda: It is not a question of belief. Do not bring in this question of belief. It is law. For instance, there is a government. You may believe or not believe, but if you break the law you'll be punished by the government. Similarly, whether you believe or don't believe, there is a God. If you don't believe in God and you independently do whatever you like, then you'll be punished by the laws of nature.
Mike Robinson: I see. Does it matter what religion you believe? Would it matter if one was a devotee of Kṛṣṇa?
Śrīla Prabhupāda: It is not a question of religion. It is a question of science. You are a spiritual being, but because you are materially conditioned, you are under the laws of material nature. So you may believe in the Christian religion and I may believe in the Hindu religion, but that does not mean that you are going to become an old man and I am not. We're talking of the science of growing old. This is natural law. It is not that because you are Christian you are becoming old or because I am Hindu I am not becoming old. Everyone is becoming old. So, similarly, all the laws of nature are applicable to everyone. Whether you believe this religion or that religion, it doesn't matter.
Mike Robinson: So, you're saying that there's only one God controlling all of us?
Śrīla Prabhupāda: There's one God, and one nature's law, and we are all under that nature's law. We are controlled by the Supreme. So if we think that we are free or that we can do anything we like, that is our foolishness.
Mike Robinson: I see. Can you explain to me what difference it makes, being a member of the Hare Kṛṣṇa movement?

Śrīla Prabhupāda: The Hare Kṛṣṇa movement is meant for those who are serious about understanding this science. There's no question of our being some sectarian group. No. Anyone can join. Students in college can be admitted. You may be a Christian, you may be a Hindu, you may be a Muhammadan—it doesn't matter. The Kṛṣṇa consciousness movement admits anyone who wants to understand the science of God.

Mike Robinson: And what difference would it make to someone—being taught how to be a Hare Kṛṣṇa person?

Śrīla Prabhupāda: His real education would begin. The first thing is to understand that you are a spirit soul. And because you are a spirit soul, you are changing your body. This is the *ABC* of spiritual understanding. So, when your body is finished, annihilated, you are not finished. You get another body, just as you may change your coat and shirt. If you come to see me tomorrow wearing a different shirt and a different coat, does that mean you are a different person? No. Similarly, each time you die you change bodies, but *you*, the spirit soul within the body, remain the same. This point has to be understood; then one can make further progress in the science of Kṛṣṇa consciousness.

Mike Robinson: I am beginning to understand, but what I'm finding difficult is how this ties in with the large numbers of your people we see handing out Hare Kṛṣṇa literature on Oxford Street.

Śrīla Prabhupāda: This literature is meant to convince people about the need for spiritual life.

Mike Robinson: And you're really not concerned whether or not they join the Hare Kṛṣṇa movement?

Śrīla Prabhupāda: It doesn't matter. Our mission is to educate them. People are in ignorance; they are living in a fool's paradise, thinking that when their body is finished, everything is finished. That is foolishness.

Mike Robinson: And you are basically just concerned to tell them that there is a spiritual dimension to life?

Śrīla Prabhupāda: Our first concern is to tell you that you are not this body, that the body is your covering (your shirt and coat) and that within the body you are living.

Mike Robinson: Yes, I think I've got that now. If we could go on from there—you said that how you lived made a difference in your life after death, that there are natural laws that determine your next

life. How does the process of transmigration work?
Śrīla Prabhupāda: The process is very subtle. The spirit soul is invisible to our material eyes. It is atomic in size. After the destruction of the gross body, which is made up of the senses, blood, bone, fat, and so forth, the subtle body of mind, intelligence, and ego goes on working. So at the time of death this subtle body carries the small spirit soul to another gross body. The process is just like air carrying a fragrance. Nobody can see where this rose fragrance is coming from, but we know that it is being carried by the air. You cannot see how, but it is being done. Similarly, the process of transmigration of the soul is very subtle. According to the condition of the mind at the time of death, the minute spirit soul enters into the womb of a particular mother through the semen of a father, and then the soul develops a particular type of body given by the mother. It may be a human being, it may be a cat, a dog, or anything.
Mike Robinson: Are you saying we were something else before this life?
Śrīla Prabhupāda: Yes.
Mike Robinson: And we keep coming back as something else the next time?
Śrīla Prabhupāda: Yes, because you are eternal. According to your work, you are simply changing bodies. Therefore, you should want to know how to stop this business, how you can remain in your original, spiritual body. That is Kṛṣṇa consciousness.
Mike Robinson: I see. So if I become Kṛṣṇa conscious, I wouldn't risk coming back as a dog?
Śrīla Prabhupāda: No. [*To a devotee:*] Find this verse: *janma karma ca me divyam . . .*
Disciple:

janma karma ca me divyam evaṁ yo vetti tattvataḥ
tyaktvā dehaṁ punar janma naiti mām eti so 'rjuna

"One who knows the transcendental nature of My appearance and activities does not, upon leaving the body, take his birth again in this material world, but attains My eternal abode, O Arjuna." [*Bhagavad-gītā* 4.9]
Śrīla Prabhupāda: God is saying, "Anyone who understands Me is

free from birth and death." But one cannot understand God by materialistic speculation. That is not possible. One must first come to the spiritual platform. Then he gets the intelligence required to understand God. And when he understands God, he does not get any more material bodies. He goes back home, back to Godhead. He lives eternally; no more change of body.

Mike Robinson: I see. Now, you've read twice from your scriptures. Where do these scriptures come from? Can you briefly explain that?

Śrīla Prabhupāda: Our scriptures are coming from Vedic literature, which has existed from the beginning of creation. Whenever there is some new material creation—like this microphone, for instance—there is also some literature explaining how to deal with it. Isn't that so?

Mike Robinson: Yes, that's right, there is.

Śrīla Prabhupāda: And that literature comes along with the creation of the microphone.

Mike Robinson: That's right, yes.

Śrīla Prabhupāda: So, similarly, the Vedic literature comes along with the cosmic creation, to explain how to deal with it.

Mike Robinson: I see. So, these scriptures have been in existence since the beginning of creation. Now, if we could move on to something I believe you feel very strongly about. What is the main difference between Kṛṣṇa consciousness and the other Eastern disciplines being taught in the West?

Śrīla Prabhupāda: The difference is that we are following the original literature, and they are manufacturing their own literature. That is the difference. When there is some question on spiritual matters, you must consult the original literature, not some literature issued by a bogus man.

Mike Robinson: What about the chanting of Hare Kṛṣṇa, Hare Kṛṣṇa—

Śrīla Prabhupāda: Chanting Hare Kṛṣṇa is the easiest process by which to become purified, especially in this age, when people are so dull that they cannot very easily understand spiritual knowledge. If one chants Hare Kṛṣṇa, then his intelligence becomes purified, and he can understand spiritual things.

Mike Robinson: Can you tell me how you are guided in what you do?

Śrīla Prabhupāda: We take guidance from the Vedic literature.

Mike Robinson: From the scriptures you quoted?
Śrīla Prabhupāda: Yes, it's all in the literatures. We're explaining them in English. But we're not manufacturing anything. If we were to manufacture knowledge, then everything would be spoiled. The Vedic literature is something like the literature that explains how to set up this microphone. It says, "Do it like this: some of the screws should be on this side, around the metal." You cannot make any change; then everything would be spoiled. Similarly, because we are not manufacturing anything, one simply has to read one of our books, and he receives real spiritual knowledge.
Mike Robinson: How can the philosophy of Kṛṣṇa consciousness affect the way people live?
Śrīla Prabhupāda: It can relieve people's suffering. People are suffering because they are misunderstanding themselves to be the body. If you think that you are your coat and shirt, and you very carefully wash the coat and shirt but you forget to eat, will you be happy?
Mike Robinson: No, I wouldn't.
Śrīla Prabhupāda: Similarly, everyone is simply washing the "coat and shirt" of the body, but forgetting about the soul within the body. They have no information about what is within the "coat and shirt" of the body. Ask anybody what he is, and he will say, "Yes, I am an Englishman," or "I am an Indian." And if we say, "I can see you have an English or an Indian body, but what are *you*?"—that he cannot say.
Mike Robinson: I see.
Śrīla Prabhupāda: The whole modern civilization is operating on the misunderstanding that the body is the self (*dehātma-buddhi*). This is the mentality of the cats and dogs. Suppose I try to enter England, and you stop me at the border: "I am an Englishman," you say, "but you are Indian. Why have you come here?" And the dog barks, "*Rau, rau,* why are you coming?" So what is the difference in mentality? The dog is thinking he's a dog and I'm a stranger, and you are thinking you are an Englishman and I am an Indian. There's no difference in mentality. So if you keep people in the darkness of a dog's mentality and declare that you are advancing in civilization, you are most misguided.
Mike Robinson: Now, moving on to another point, I gather the Hare Kṛṣṇa movement has some concern for areas of the world where there is suffering.
Śrīla Prabhupāda: Yes, we have the only concern. Others are sim-

ply avoiding the main problems: birth, old age, disease, and death. Others have no solutions to these problems; they are simply talking all kinds of nonsense. People are being misguided. They are being kept in darkness. Let us start to give them some light.

Mike Robinson: Yes, but apart from giving spiritual enlightenment, are you also concerned for people's physical well-being?

Śrīla Prabhupāda: Physical well-being automatically follows spiritual well-being.

Mike Robinson: And how does that work?

Śrīla Prabhupāda: Suppose you have a car. So, naturally, you take care of the car as well as yourself. But you don't *identify* yourself as the car. You don't say, "I am this car." That is nonsense. But this is what people are doing. They are taking too much care of the bodily "car," thinking that the car is the self. They forget that they are different from the car, that they are a spirit soul and have a different business. Just as no one can drink petrol and be satisfied, no one can be satisfied with bodily activities. One must find out the proper food for the soul. If a man thinks, "I am a car, and I must drink this petrol," he is considered insane. Similarly, one who thinks that he is this body, and who tries to become happy with bodily pleasures, is also insane.

Mike Robinson: There's a quote here that I'd like you to comment on. I was given this literature by your people before I came, and one of the things you say here is that "Religion without a rational basis is just sentiment." Can you explain that?

Śrīla Prabhupāda: Most religious people say, "We believe . . ." But what is the value of this belief? You may believe something which is not actually correct. For instance, some of the Christian people say, "We believe that animals have no soul." That is not correct. They believe animals have no soul because they want to eat the animals, but actually animals do have a soul.

Mike Robinson: How do you know that the animal has a soul?

Śrīla Prabhupāda: You can know also. Here is the scientific proof: the animal eats, you eat; the animal sleeps, you sleep; the animal has sex, you have sex; the animal also defends, you also defend. Then what is the difference between you and the animal? How can you say that you have a soul but the animal doesn't?

Mike Robinson: I can see that completely. But the Christian scriptures say—

Śrīla Prabhupāda: Don't bring in any scriptures; this is a commonsense topic. Try to understand. The animal is eating, you are eating; the animal is sleeping, you are sleeping; the animal is defending, you are defending; the animal is having sex, you are having sex; the animals have children, you have children; they have a living place, you have a living place. If the animal's body is cut, there is blood; if your body is cut, there is blood. So, all these similarities are there. Now, why do you deny this one similarity, the presence of the soul? This is not logical. You have studied logic? In logic there is something called analogy. Analogy means drawing a conclusion by finding many points of similarity. If there are so many points of similarity between human beings and animals, why deny one similarity? That is not logic. That is not science.
Mike Robinson: But if you take that argument and use it the other way—
Śrīla Prabhupāda: There is no other way. If you are not arguing on the basis of logic, then you are not rational.
Mike Robinson: Yes, OK, but let's start from another hypothesis. Suppose we assume that a human being has no soul—
Śrīla Prabhupāda: Then you must explain the difference between a living body and a dead body. I have already explained this at the beginning. As soon as the living force, the soul, is gone from the body, even the most beautiful body has no value. No one cares for it; it's thrown away. But now, if I touch your hair, there will be a fight. That is the distinction between a living body and a dead body. In a living body the soul is there, and in a dead body the soul is not there. As soon as the soul leaves the body, the body has no value. It is useless. This is very simple to understand, but even the biggest so-called scientists and philosophers are too dull-headed to understand it. Modern society is in a very abominable condition. There is no man with a real brain.
Mike Robinson: Are you referring to all the scientists who fail to understand the spiritual dimension in life?
Śrīla Prabhupāda: Yes. Real science means full knowledge of everything, material and spiritual.
Mike Robinson: But you were a chemist in secular life, were you not?
Śrīla Prabhupāda: Yes, I was a chemist in my earlier life. But it doesn't require any great intelligence to become a chemist. Any commonsense man can do it.

Mike Robinson: But presumably you think that material science is also important, even if today's scientists are dull-headed.
Śrīla Prabhupāda: Material science is important just so far. It is not all-important.
Mike Robinson: I see. Can I come back to a question I had from before? When we were differing a few minutes ago you were saying, "Don't bring the scriptures in; just use common sense." But what part do the scriptures play in your religion? How important are they?
Śrīla Prabhupāda: Our religion is a science. When we say that a child grows into a boy, it is science. It is not religion. Every child grows into a boy. What is the question of religion? Every man dies. What is the question of religion? And when a man dies, the body becomes useless. What is the question of religion? It is science. Whether you're Christian or Hindu or Muslim, when you die your body becomes useless. This is science. When your relative dies, you cannot say, "We are Christian; we believe he has not died." No, he has died. Whether you are Christian or Hindu or Muslim, he has died. So when we speak, we speak on this basis: that the body is important only as long as the soul is in the body. When the soul is not there, it is useless. This science is applicable to everyone, and we are trying to educate people on this basis.
Mike Robinson: But if I understand you correctly, you seem to be educating people on a purely scientific basis. Where does religion come into it at all?
Śrīla Prabhupāda: Religion also means science. People have wrongly taken religion to mean faith—"I believe." [*To a devotee:*] Look up the word *religion* in the dictionary.
Disciple: Under *religion* the dictionary says, "recognition of superhuman control or power, and especially of a personal God entitled to obedience, and effecting such recognition with the proper mental attitude."
Śrīla Prabhupāda: Yes. Religion means learning how to obey the supreme controller. So, you may be Christian and I may be Hindu; it doesn't matter. We must both accept that there is a supreme controller. Everyone has to accept that; that is real religion. Not this "We believe animals have no soul." That is not religion. That is most unscientific. Religion means scientific understanding of the supreme controller: to understand the supreme controller and obey

Him—that's all. In the state, the good citizen is he who understands the government and obeys the laws of the government, and the bad citizen is the one who doesn't care for the government. So, if you become a bad citizen by ignoring God's government, then you are irreligious. And if you are a good citizen, then you are religious.

Mike Robinson: I see. Can you tell me what you believe to be the meaning of life? Why do we exist in the first place?

Śrīla Prabhupāda: The meaning of life is to enjoy. But now you are on a false platform of life, and therefore you are suffering instead of enjoying. Everywhere we see the struggle for existence. Everyone is struggling, but what is their enjoyment in the end? They are simply suffering and dying. Therefore, although life means enjoyment, at the present moment your life is not enjoyment. But if you come to the real, spiritual platform of life, then you'll enjoy.

Mike Robinson: Can you explain to me, finally, some of the stages you go through in spiritual life? What are the spiritual stages a new devotee of Kṛṣṇa goes through?

Śrīla Prabhupāda: The first stage is that you are inquisitive. "So," you say, "what is this Kṛṣṇa consciousness movement? Let me study it." This is called *śraddhā,* or faith. This is the beginning. Then, if you are serious, you mix with those who are cultivating this knowledge. You try to understand how they are feeling. Then you'll feel, "Why not become one of them?" And when you become one of them, then all your misgivings soon go away. You become more faithful, and then you get a real taste for Kṛṣṇa consciousness. Why aren't these boys going to see the cinema? Why don't they eat meat or go to the nightclub? Because their taste has changed. They hate all these things now. In this way, you make progress. First faith, then association with devotees, then removal of all misgivings, then firm faith, then taste, then God realization, and then love of God, the perfection. That is first-class religion. Not some ritualistic ceremony of "I believe, you believe." That is not religion. That is cheating. Real religion means to develop your love for God. That is the perfection of religion.

Mike Robinson: Thank you very much for talking with me. It's been a pleasure talking to you.

Śrīla Prabhupāda: Hare Kṛṣṇa.

TRUTH AND BEAUTY

"Beauty is truth, truth is beauty," said Keats. "That is all ye know on earth, and all ye need to know." Or is it? In this charming yet cutting essay, which first appeared in the old tabloid version of Back to Godhead *(November 20, 1958), Śrīla Prabhupāda tells the unforgettable story of "liquid beauty."*

There may sometimes be arguments about whether "truth" and "beauty" are compatible terms. One would willingly agree to express the truth, one might say, but since truth is not always beautiful—indeed, it is frequently rather startling and unpleasant—how is one to express truth and beauty at the same time?

In reply, we may inform all concerned that "truth" and "beauty" *are* compatible terms. Indeed, we may emphatically assert that the actual truth, which is absolute, is always beautiful. The truth is so beautiful that it attracts everyone, including the truth itself. Truth is so beautiful that many sages, saints, and devotees have left everything for the sake of truth. Mahatma Gandhi, an idol of the modern world, dedicated his life to experimenting with truth, and all his activities were aimed toward truth only.

Why only Mahatma Gandhi? Every one of us has the urge to search for truth alone, for the truth is not only beautiful but also all-powerful, all-resourceful, all-famous, all-renounced, and all-knowledgeable.

Unfortunately, people have no information of the actual truth. Indeed, 99.9 percent of men in all walks of life are pursuing untruth only, in the name of truth. We are actually attracted by the beauty of truth, but since time immemorial we have been habituated to love of untruth appearing like truth. Therefore, to the mundaner "truth" and "beauty" are incompatible terms. The mundane truth and beauty may be explained as follows.

Once a man who was very powerful and strongly built but

whose character was very doubtful fell in love with a beautiful girl. The girl was not only beautiful in appearance but also saintly in character, and as such she did not like the man's advances. The man, however, was insistent because of his lustful desires, and therefore the girl requested him to wait only seven days, and she set a time after that when he could meet her. The man agreed, and with high expectations he began waiting for the appointed time.

The saintly girl, however, in order to manifest the real beauty of absolute truth, adopted a method very instructive. She took very strong doses of laxatives and purgatives, and for seven days she continually passed loose stool and vomited all that she ate. Moreover, she stored all the loose stool and vomit in suitable pots. As a result of the purgatives, the so-called beautiful girl became lean and thin like a skeleton, her complexion turned blackish, and her beautiful eyes sank into the sockets of her skull. Thus at the appointed hour she waited anxiously to receive the eager man.

The man appeared on the scene well dressed and well behaved and asked the ugly girl he found waiting there about the beautiful girl he was to meet. The man could not recognize the girl he saw as the same beautiful girl for whom he was asking; indeed, although she repeatedly asserted her identity, because of her pitiable condition he was unable to recognize her.

At last the girl told the powerful man that she had separated the ingredients of her beauty and stored them in pots. She also told him that he could enjoy those juices of beauty. When the mundane poetic man asked to see these juices of beauty, he was directed to the store of loose stool and liquid vomit, which were emanating an unbearably bad smell. Thus the whole story of the beauty-liquid was disclosed to him. Finally, by the grace of the saintly girl, this man of low character was able to distinguish between the shadow and the substance, and thus he came to his senses.

This man's position was similar to the position of every one of us who is attracted by false, material beauty. The girl mentioned above had a beautifully developed material body in accordance with the desires of her mind, but in fact she was apart from that temporary material body and mind. She was in fact a spiritual spark, and so also was the lover who was attracted by her false skin.

Mundane intellectuals and aesthetics, however, are deluded by the outward beauty and attraction of the relative truth and are unaware of the spiritual spark, which is both truth and beauty at the same time. The spiritual spark is so beautiful that when it leaves the so-called beautiful body, which in fact is full of stool and vomit, no one wants to touch that body, even if it is decorated with a costly costume.

We are all pursuing a false, relative truth, which is incompatible with real beauty. The actual truth, however, is permanently beautiful, retaining the same standard of beauty for innumerable years. That spiritual spark is indestructible. The beauty of the outer skin can be destroyed in only a few hours merely by a dose of a strong purgative, but the beauty of truth is indestructible and always the same. Unfortunately, mundane artists and intellectuals are ignorant of this beautiful spark of spirit. They are also ignorant of the whole fire which is the source of these spiritual sparks, and they are ignorant of the relationships between the sparks and the fire, which take the form of transcendental pastimes. When those pastimes are displayed here by the grace of the Almighty, foolish people who cannot see beyond their senses confuse those pastimes of truth and beauty with the manifestations of loose stool and vomit described above. Thus in despair they ask how truth and beauty can be accommodated at the same time.

Mundaners do not know that the whole spiritual entity is the beautiful person who attracts everything. They are unaware that He is the prime substance, the prime source and fountainhead of everything that be. The infinitesimal spiritual sparks, being parts and parcels of that whole spirit, are qualitatively the same in beauty and eternity. The only difference is that the whole is eternally the whole and the parts are eternally the parts. Both of them, however, are the ultimate truth, ultimate beauty, ultimate knowledge, ultimate energy, ultimate renunciation, and ultimate opulence.

Although written by the greatest mundane poet or intellectual, any literature which does not describe the ultimate truth and beauty is but a store of loose stool and vomit of the relative truth. Real literature is that which describes the ultimate truth and beauty of the Absolute.

RELEVANT INQUIRIES

Again in the old tabloid Back to Godhead, *this time dated April 20, 1960, Śrīla Prabhupāda talks about the science of the soul: "[S]ince a human being is a rational animal, he is born to make inquiries. The greater the number of questions, the greater the advancement of knowledge and science. . . . The most intelligent man, however, inquires about what happens after death."*

A small child walking with his father goes on inquiring constantly. He asks his father so many odd things, and the father has to satisfy him with proper answers. When I was a young father in my householder life, I was overflooded with hundreds of questions from my second son, who was my constant companion. One day it so happened that a bridegroom's party was passing our tramcar, and the four-year-old boy, as usual, inquired what the big procession was. He was given all possible answers to his thousand and one questions regarding the marriage party, and finally he asked whether his own father was married! This question gave rise to loud laughter from all the elderly gentlemen present, although the boy was perplexed as to why we were laughing. Anyway, the boy was somehow satisfied by his married father.

The lesson from this incident is that since a human being is a rational animal, he is born to make inquiries. The greater the number of questions, the greater the advancement of knowledge and science. The whole of material civilization is based on this originally large volume of questions put by young men to their elders. When elderly persons give the proper answers to the questions of the youngsters, civilization makes progress, one step after another. The most intelligent man, however, inquires about what happens after death. The less intelligent make lesser inquiries, but the questions of those who are more intelligent go higher and still higher.

Among the most intelligent of men was Mahārāja Parīkṣit, the great king of the entire world, who was accidentally cursed by a *brāhmaṇa* to meet death from the bite of a serpent within seven days. The *brāhmaṇa* who cursed him was only a boy, yet he was very powerful, and because he did not know the importance of the great king, the boy foolishly cursed him to meet death within seven days. This was later lamented by the boy's father, whom the king had offended. When the king was informed of the unfortunate curse, he at once left his palatial home and went to the bank of the Ganges, which was near his capital, to prepare for his impending death. Because he was a great king, almost all the great sages and learned scholars assembled at the place where the king was fasting prior to leaving his mortal body. At last, Śukadeva Gosvāmī, the youngest contemporary saint, also arrived there, and he was unanimously accepted to preside at that meeting, although his great father was also present. The king respectfully offered Śukadeva Gosvāmī the principal seat of esteem and asked him relevant questions regarding the king's passing from the mortal world, which was to take place on the seventh day thenceforward. The great king, as a worthy descendant of the Pāṇḍavas, who were all great devotees, placed the following relevant inquiries before the great sage Śukadeva. "My dear sir, you are the greatest of the great transcendentalists, and therefore I submissively beg to ask you about my duties at this moment. I am just on the verge of my death. Therefore, what should I do at this critical hour? Please tell me, my lord—what should I hear, what should I worship, or whom should I remember now? A great sage like you does not stay at the home of a householder more than necessary, and therefore it is my good fortune that you have kindly come here at the time of my death. Please, therefore, give me your directions at this critical hour."

The great sage, having thus been pleasingly requested by the king, answered his questions authoritatively, for the sage was a great transcendental scholar and was also well equipped with godly qualities, since he was the worthy son of Bādarāyaṇa, or Vyāsadeva, the original compiler of the Vedic literature.

Śukadeva Gosvāmī said, "My dear king, your inquiry is very much relevant, and it is also beneficial for all people of all times. Such inquiries, which are the highest of all, are relevant because they are confirmed by the teachings of the *vedānta-darśana*, the conclusion of the Vedic knowledge, and are *ātmavit-sammataḥ;* in other words, liberated souls, who have full knowledge of their spiritual identity, put forward such relevant inquiries in order to elucidate further information about the Transcendence."

The *Śrīmad-Bhāgavatam* is the natural commentary upon the great *Vedānta* (or *Śārīraka*) *sūtras,* which were compiled by Śrīla Vyāsadeva. The *Vedānta-sūtras* are the topmost Vedic literature, and they contain the nucleus of basic inquiries about the transcendental subject of spiritual knowledge. Yet although Śrīla Vyāsadeva compiled this great treatise, his mind was not satisfied. Then he happened to meet Śrī Nārada, his spiritual master, who advised him to describe the identity of the Personality of Godhead. Upon receiving this advice, Vyāsadeva meditated on the principle of *bhakti-yoga,* which showed him distinctly what is the Absolute and what is the relativity, or *māyā.* Having achieved perfect realization of these facts, he compiled the great narration of the *Śrīmad-Bhāgavatam,* or beautiful *Bhāgavatam,* which begins with actual historical facts concerning the life of Mahārāja Parīkṣit.

The *Vedānta-sūtra* begins with the key inquiry about the Transcendence, *athāto brahma jijñāsā:* "One should now inquire about Brahman, or the Transcendence."

As long as a man is in the full vigor of life, he forgets the naked truth of death, which he has to meet. Thus a foolish man makes no relevant inquiry about the real problems of life. Everyone thinks that he will never die, although he sees evidence of death before his eyes at every second. Here is the distinction between animalism and humanity. An animal like a goat has no sense of its impending death. Although its brother goat is being slaughtered, the goat, being allured by the green grass offered to it, will stand peacefully waiting to be slaughtered next. On the other hand, if a human being sees his fellow man being killed by an enemy, he either fights to save his brother or leaves, if possible, to save his own life. That is the difference between a man and a goat.

An intelligent man knows that death is born along with his own birth. He knows that he is dying at every second and that the final touch will be given as soon as his term of life is finished. He therefore prepares himself for the next life or for liberation from the disease of repeated birth and death.

A foolish man, however, does not know that this human form of life is obtained after a series of births and deaths imposed in the past by the laws of nature. He does not know that a living entity is an eternal being, who has no birth and death. Birth, death, old age, and disease are external impositions on a living entity and are due to his contact with material nature and to his forgetfulness of his eternal, godly nature and qualitative oneness with the Absolute Whole.

Human life provides the opportunity to know this eternal fact, or truth. Thus the very beginning of the *Vedānta-sūtra* advises that because we have this valuable form of human life, it is our duty—now—to inquire, What is Brahman, the Absolute Truth?

A man who is not intelligent enough does not inquire about this transcendental life; instead, he inquires about many irrelevant matters which do not concern his eternal existence. From the very beginning of his life, he inquires from his mother, father, teachers, professors, books, and so many other sources, but he does not have the right type of information about his real life.

As mentioned before, Parīkṣit Mahārāja was given a warning notice that he would meet death within seven days, and he at once left his palace to prepare himself for the next stage. The king had at least seven days at his disposal in which to prepare for death, but as far as we are concerned, although at least we know that our death is sure, we have no information of the date fixed for the occurrence. I do not know whether I am going to meet death at the next moment. Even such a great man as Mahatma Gandhi could not calculate that he was going to meet with death in the next five minutes, nor could his great associates guess his impending death. Nonetheless, all such gentlemen present themselves as great leaders of the people.

It is ignorance of death and life that distinguishes an animal from a man. A man, in the real sense of the term, inquires about himself and what he is. Wherefrom has he come into this life, and where is he going after death? Why is he put under the troubles of threefold miseries although he does not want them? Beginning from one's childhood, one goes on inquiring about so many things in his life, but he never inquires about the real essence of life. This is animalism. There is no difference between a man and an animal as far as the four principles of animal life are concerned, for every living being exists by eating, sleeping, fearing, and mating. But only the human life is meant for relevant inquiries into the facts about eternal life and the Transcendence. Human life is therefore meant for research into eternal life, and the *Vedānta-sūtra* advises one to conduct this research now or never. If one fails to inquire now into these relevant matters about life, one is sure to go back again to the animal kingdom by the laws of nature. Therefore, even if a foolish man appears advanced in material science—that is, in eating, sleeping, fearing, mating, and so on—he cannot get free from the cruel hands of death by the law of nature. The law of nature works under three modes—goodness, passion, and ignorance. Those who live under conditions of goodness are promoted to the higher, spiritual status of life, and those who live under conditions of passion remain stationed in the same place in the material world where they are now, but those who live under conditions of ignorance are sure to be degraded to the lower species.

The modern setup of human civilization is a risky one because it offers no education about relevant inquiries into the essential principles of life. Like animals, people do not know that they are going to be slaughtered by the laws of nature. They are satisfied with a bunch of green grass, or a so-called jolly life, like the waiting goat in a slaughterhouse. Considering such a condition of human life, we are just trying to make a humble attempt to save the human being by the message of *Back to Godhead*. This method is not fictitious. If there is at all to be an era of reality, this message of *Back to Godhead* is the beginning of that era.

According to Śrī Śukadeva Gosvāmī, the real fact is that a *gṛhamedhī*, or a person who has tied himself, like the goat meant for slaughter, in the business of family, society, community, nation, or humanity at large in regard to the problems and necessities of animal life—namely eating, sleeping, fearing, and mating—and who has no knowledge of the Transcendence is no better than an animal. He may have inquired about physical, political, economic, cultural, educational, or similar other matters of temporary, material concern, but if he has not inquired about the principles of transcendental life, he should be regarded as a blind man driven ahead by uncontrolled senses and about to fall into a ditch. That is the description of the *gṛhamedhī*.

The opposite of the *gṛhamedhī*, however, is the *gṛhastha*. The *gṛhastha-āśrama*, or the shelter of spiritual family life, is as good as the life of a *sannyāsī*, a member of the renounced order. Regardless of whether one is a householder or a renunciant, the important point is that of relevant inquiries. A *sannyāsī* is bogus if not interested in relevant inquiries, and a *gṛhastha,* or householder, is bona fide if he is inclined to put forward such inquiries. The *gṛhamedhī,* however, is simply interested in the animal necessities of life. By the laws of nature, the *gṛhamedhī's* life is full of calamities, whereas the life of the *gṛhastha* is full of happiness. But in the modern human civilization, the *gṛhamedhīs* are posing as the *gṛhasthas.* We should therefore know who is what. A *gṛhamedhī's* life is full of vices, because he does not know how to live a spiritual family life. He does not know that beyond his control is a power who supervises and controls his activities, and he has no conception of his future life. The *gṛhamedhī* is blind to his future and has no aptitude for making relevant inquiries. His only qualification is that he is bound by the shackles of attachment to the false things he has contacted in his temporary existence.

At night such *gṛhamedhīs* waste their valuable time by sleeping or by satisfying their different varieties of sexual urges by visiting cinema shows and attending clubs and gambling houses, where women and liquor are indulged in lavishly. And during the day, they waste their valuable life in accumulating money or, if they have sufficient money to spend, by adjusting the comforts of their family members. Their standard of living and their personal needs increase with their increase in monetary income. Thus there is no limit to their expenses, and they are never satiated. Consequently there is unlimited competition in the field of economic development, and therefore there is no peace in any society of the human world.

Everyone is perplexed by the same questions about earning and spending, but ultimately one must depend on the mercy of mother nature. When there is a scarcity in production or there are disturbances caused by providence, the poor planmaking politician blames it on cruel nature but carefully avoids studying how and by whom the laws of nature are controlled. The *Bhagavad-gītā,* however, explains that the laws of nature are controlled by the Absolute Personality of Godhead. God alone is the controller of nature and the natural laws. Ambitious materialists sometimes examine a fragment of the law of nature, but they never care to know the maker of these laws. Most of them do not believe in the existence of an absolute person or God who controls the laws of nature. Rather, they simply concern themselves with the principles by which different elements interact, but they make no reference to the ultimate direction which makes such interactions possible. They have no relevant questions or answers in this regard. The second of the *Vedānta-sūtras,* however, answers the essential question about Brahman by asserting that the Supreme Brahman, the Supreme Transcendence, is He from whom everything is generated. Ultimately, He is the Supreme Person.

Not only is the foolish *gṛhamedhī* ignorant of the temporary nature of the particular type of body he has obtained, but he is also blind to the actual nature of what is happening before him in the daily affairs of his life. He may see his father die, his mother die, or a relative or neighbor die, yet he does not make the relevant inquiries about whether or not the other existing members of his family will die. Sometimes he thinks and knows that all the members of his family will die today or tomorrow and that he also will die. He may know that the whole family show—or, for that matter, the whole show of community, society, nation, and all such things—is but a temporary bubble in the air, having no permanent value. Yet he is mad after such temporary arrangements and does not concern himself with any relevant inquiries. He has no knowledge as to where he has to go after his death. He works very hard for the temporary arrangements of his family, society, or nation, but he never makes any future arrangement either for himself or for others who will pass away from this present phase of life.

In a public vehicle like a railway carriage, we meet and sit down together with some unknown friends and become members of the same vehicle for a short time, but in due course we separate, never to meet again. Similarly, in a long sojourn of life, we get a temporary sitting accommodation in a so-called family, country, or society, but when the time is up, we are unwillingly separated from one another, never to meet again. There are so many questions relevant to our temporary arrangements in life and our friends in these temporary arrangements, but a man who is a *gṛhamedhī* never inquires about things of a permanent nature. We are all busy making permanent plans in various degrees of leadership, without knowing the permanent nature of things as they are. Śrīpāda Śaṅkarācārya, who especially strove to remove this ignorance in society and who advocated the cult of spiritual knowledge in regard to the all-pervading impersonal Brahman, said in despair, "Children are engaged in playing, young boys are engaged in so-called love affairs with young girls, and the old are seriously thoughtful about adjusting a baffled life of struggle. But, alas, no one is prepared to *inquire* relevantly into the science of Brahman, the Absolute Truth."

Śrī Śukadeva Gosvāmī, who was asked for direction by Mahārāja Parīkṣit, responded to the king's relevant inquiries by advising him as follows:

tasmād bhārata sarvātmā bhagavān īśvaro hariḥ
śrotavyaḥ kīrtitavyaś ca smartavyaś cecchatābhayam

"O descendant of Bharata, it is the duty of mortal men to inquire about, hear about, glorify, and meditate upon the Personality of Godhead, who is the most attractive person because of His fullness in opulence. He is called Hari because He alone can undo the conditioned existence of a living being. If we at all want to be freed from conditioned existence, we must make relevant inquiries about the Absolute Truth so that He may be pleased to bestow upon us perfect freedom in life." (*Śrīmad-Bhāgavatam* 2.1.5)

Śrī Śukadeva Gosvāmī has particularly used four words in regard to the Absolute Personality of Godhead. These words distinguish the Absolute Person, or Parabrahman, from other persons, who are qualitatively one with Him. The Absolute Personality of Godhead is addressed as *sarvātmā,* or all-pervading, because no one is aloof from Him, although not everyone has this realization. The Personality of Godhead, by His plenary representation, resides in everyone's heart as Paramātmā, the Supersoul, along with each individual soul. Therefore every individual soul has an intimate relationship with Him. Forgetfulness of this eternally existing intimate relationship with Him is the cause of conditioned life since time immemorial. But because He is Bhagavān, or the supreme personality, He can at once reciprocate the responsive call of a devotee. Moreover, because He is the perfect person, His beauty, opulence, fame, strength, knowledge, and renunciation are all unlimited sources of transcendental bliss for the individual soul. The individual soul becomes attracted by all these different opulences when they are imperfectly represented by other conditioned souls, but the individual soul is not satisfied by such imperfect representations, and therefore he perpetually seeks the perfect one. The Personality of Godhead's beauty has no comparison, nor do His knowledge and renunciation. But above all, He is *īśvara,* or the supreme controller. We are at present being controlled by the police action of this great king. This police control is imposed upon us because of our disobedience of law. But because the Lord is Hari, He is able to cause the disappearance of our conditioned life by giving us full freedom in spiritual existence. It is therefore the duty of every man to make relevant inquiries about Him and thus go back to Godhead.

SOUL RESEARCH

Śrīla Prabhupāda writes a letter to a noted cardiologist, Dr. Wilfred G. Bigelow: "The central question, you say, is 'Where is the soul, and where does it come from?' That is not difficult to understand."

In 1968, speaking before a gathering of students at Massachusetts Institute of Technology, Śrīla Prabhupāda points out an important lag in technological research. "Although you have so many departments of knowledge," he says, "there is no department aiming to find the difference between a living body and a dead body."

Although advanced in understanding the mechanical workings of the physical body, modern science gives but little attention to studying the spiritual spark that animates the body. In the *Montreal Gazette* article reproduced below, we find world-famous cardiologist Wilfred G. Bigelow urging systematic research to determine what the soul is and where it comes from. Reproduced next is Śrīla Prabhupāda's letter in response to Dr. Bigelow's plea. Śrīla Prabhupāda offers substantial Vedic knowledge on the science of the soul and suggests a practical method for scientifically understanding the spiritual spark.

Gazette Headline:
Heart Surgeon Wants to Know What a Soul Is

WINDSOR—A world-famous Canadian heart surgeon says he believes the body has a soul which departs at death and theologians ought to try to find out more about it.

Dr. Wilfred G. Bigelow, head of the cardiovascular surgery unit at Toronto General Hospital, said that "as a person who believes there is a soul," he thought the time had come "to take the mystery out of this and find out what it is."

Bigelow was a member of a panel which appeared before the Essex County Medical-Legal Society to discuss problems associated with attempts to define the exact moment of death.

The question has become vital in the age of transplants of hearts and other organs in cases when the donors are inevitably dying.

The Canadian Medical Association has produced a widely accepted definition of death as the moment when the patient is in coma, responds to no stimulus of any kind, and brain waves recorded on a machine are flat.

The other members of the panel were Mr. Justice Edson L. Haines of the Ontario Supreme Court and J. Francis Leddy, president of the University of Windsor.

Bigelow, elaborating on points he had raised during the discussion, said in an interview later that his thirty-two years as a surgeon had left him no doubts that there is a soul.

"There are certain cases where you happen to be present at the moment when people pass from a living state to death, and some mysterious changes take place.

"One of the most noticeable is the sudden lack of life or luster to the eyes. They become opaque and literally lifeless.

"It's difficult to document what you observe. In fact, I don't think it can be documented very well."

Bigelow, who became world renowned for his pioneering work in the "deep freeze" surgical technique known as hypothermia and for his heart valve surgery, said "soul research" should be undertaken by theology and allied disciplines within the university.

During this discussion Leddy said that "if there is a soul, you are not going to see it. You are not going to find it."

"If there is a principle of vitality or life, what is it?" The problem was that "the soul doesn't exist anywhere specifically, geographically. It's everywhere and yet it's nowhere in the body."

It would "be nice to start experimenting, but I don't know how you are going to get on any of these things," Leddy said. He said the discussion reminded him of the Soviet cosmonaut who returned from space to report there was no God, because he didn't see Him up there.

Maybe so, said Bigelow, but in modern medicine when something was encountered that could not be explained, "the watchword is discover the answer, take it into the laboratory, take it somewhere where you can discover the truth."

The central question, said Bigelow, was "where is the soul and where does it come from?"

Śrīla Prabhupāda Gives the Vedic Evidence

My dear Dr. Bigelow:

Please accept my greetings. Recently I have read an article in the *Gazette* by Rae Corelli entitled "Heart Surgeon Wants to Know What a Soul Is," and it was very interesting. Your comments show great insight, and so I thought to write you on this matter. Perhaps you may know that I am the founder-*ācārya* of the International Society for Krishna Consciousness. I have several temples in Canada—Montreal, Toronto, Vancouver, and Hamilton. This Kṛṣṇa consciousness movement is specifically meant to teach every soul his original, spiritual position.

Undoubtedly the soul is present in the heart of the living entity, and it is the source of all the energies for maintaining the body. The energy of the soul is spread all over the body, and this is known as consciousness. Since this consciousness spreads the energy of the soul all over the body, one can feel pains and pleasures in any part of the body. The soul is individual, and he is transmigrating from one body to another, just as a person transmigrates from babyhood to childhood, from childhood to boyhood, from boyhood to youth, and then to advanced old age. Then the change called death takes place when we change to a new body, just as we change our old dress to a new dress. This is called transmigration of the soul.

When a soul wants to enjoy this material world, forgetting his real home in the spiritual world, he takes this life of hard struggle for existence. This unnatural life of repeated birth, death, disease, and old age can be stopped when his consciousness is dovetailed with the supreme consciousness of God. That is the basic principle of our Kṛṣṇa movement.

As far as heart transplant is concerned, there is no question of success unless the soul is there in the heart. So the presence of the soul has to be accepted. In sexual intercourse, if there is no soul, there is no conception, no pregnancy. Contraception deteriorates the womb so that it no longer is a good place for the soul. That is against the order of God. By the order of God, a soul is sent to a particular womb, but by this contraceptive he is denied that womb and has to be placed in another. That is disobedience to the Supreme. For example, take a man who is supposed to live in a particular apartment. If the situation there is so disturbed that he cannot enter the apartment, then he is put at a great disadvantage. That is illegal interference and is punishable.

The undertaking of "soul research" would certainly mark the advancement of science. But advancement of science will not be able to find the soul. The soul's presence can simply be accepted on circumstantial understanding. You will find in the Vedic literature that the dimension of the soul is one ten-thousandth the size of a point. The material scientist cannot measure the length and breadth of a point. Therefore it is not possible for the material scientist to capture the soul. You can simply accept the soul's existence by taking it from authority. What the greatest scientists are finding, we've explained long ago.

As soon as one understands the existence of the soul, he can immediately understand the existence of God. The difference between God and the soul is that God is a very great soul, and the living entity is a very small soul; but qualitatively they are equal. Therefore God is all-pervading, and the living entity is localized. But the nature and quality are the same.

The central question, you say, is "Where is the soul, and where does it come from?" That is not difficult to understand. We have already discussed that the soul is residing in the heart of the living entity and that it takes shelter in another body after death. Originally the soul comes from God. Just as a spark comes from fire, and when the spark falls down it appears to be extinguished, the spark of soul originally comes from the spiritual world to the material world. In the material world he falls down into three different conditions, which are called the modes of nature. When a spark of fire falls on dry grass, the fiery quality continues; when the spark falls on the ground, it cannot display its fiery manifestation unless the ground is favorably situated; and when the spark falls on water, it becomes extinguished. As such, we find three kinds of living conditions. One living entity is completely forgetful of his spiritual nature; another is almost forgetful but still has an instinct of spiritual nature; and another is completely in search of spiritual perfection. There is a bona fide method for the attainment of spiritual perfection by the spiritual spark of soul, and if he is properly guided then he is very easily sent back home, back to Godhead, wherefrom he originally fell.

It will be a great contribution to human society if this authorized information from the Vedic literature is presented to the modern world on the basis of modern scientific understanding. The fact is already there. It simply has to be presented for modern understanding.

Yours sincerely,
A.C. Bhaktivedanta Swami

II.
CHOOSING A SPIRITUAL MASTER

WHAT IS A GURU?

"In all the śāstras *[scriptures] the guru is described to be as good as God, but the guru never says, 'I am God.' The disciple's duty is to offer respect to the guru just as he offers respect to God, but the guru never thinks, 'My disciples are offering me the same respect they offer to God; therefore I have become God.' As soon as he thinks like this, he becomes a dog."*

oṁ ajñāna-timirāndhasya jñānāñjana-śalākayā
cakṣur unmīlitaṁ yena tasmai śrī-gurave namaḥ

"I was born in the darkest ignorance, and my guru, my spiritual master, opened my eyes with the torch of knowledge. I offer my respectful obeisances unto him."

The word *ajñāna* means "ignorance" or "darkness." If all the lights in this room immediately went out, we would not be able to tell where we or others are sitting. Everything would become confused. Similarly, we are all in darkness in this material world, which is a world of *tamas. Tamas* or *timira* means "darkness." This material world is dark, and therefore it needs sunlight or moonlight for illumination. However, there is another world, a spiritual world, that is beyond this darkness. That world is described by Śrī Kṛṣṇa in the *Bhagavad-gītā* [15.6]:

na tad bhāsayate sūryo na śaśāṅko na pāvakaḥ
yad gatvā na nivartante tad dhāma paramaṁ mama

"That abode of Mine is not illumined by the sun or moon, nor by electricity. One who reaches it never returns to this material world."

The guru's business is to bring his disciples from darkness to light. At present everyone is suffering due to ignorance, just as one contracts a disease out of ignorance. If one does not know hygienic principles, he will not know what will contaminate him. Therefore due to ignorance there is infection, and we suffer from disease. A criminal may say, "I did not know the law," but he will not be excused if he commits a crime. Ignorance is no excuse. Similarly, a child, not knowing that fire will burn, will touch the fire. The fire does not think, "This is a child, and he does not know I will burn." No, there is no excuse. Just as there are state laws, there are also stringent laws of nature, and these laws will act despite our ignorance of them. If we do something wrong out of ignorance, we must suffer. This is the law. Whether the law is a state law or a law of nature, we risk suffering if we break it.

The guru's business is to see that no human being suffers in this material world. No one can claim that he is not suffering. That is not possible. In this material world, there are three kinds of suffering: *adhyātmika, adhibhautika,* and *adhidaivika*. These are miseries arising from the material body and mind, from other living entities, and from the forces of nature. We may suffer mental anguish, or we may suffer from other living entities—from ants or mosquitoes or flies—or we may suffer due to some superior power. There may be no rain, or there may be flood. There may be excessive heat or excessive cold. So many types of suffering are imposed by nature. Thus there are three types of miseries within the material world, and everyone is suffering from one, two, or three of them. No one can say that he is completely free from suffering.

We may then ask *why* the living entity is suffering. The answer is: out of ignorance. He does not think, "I am committing mistakes and am leading a sinful life; that is why I am suffering." Therefore the guru's first business is to rescue his disciple from this ignorance. We send our children to school to save them from suffering. If our children do not receive an education, we fear that they will suffer in the future. The guru sees that suffering is due to ignorance, which is compared to darkness. How can one in darkness be saved? By light. The guru takes the torchlight of knowledge and presents it before the living entity enveloped in darkness. That knowledge relieves him from the sufferings of the darkness of ignorance.

One may ask whether the guru is absolutely necessary. The *Vedas* inform us that he is:

tad-vijñānārthaṁ sa gurum evābhigacchet
samit-pāṇiḥ śrotriyaṁ brahma-niṣṭham
[*Muṇḍaka Upaniṣad* 1.2.12]

The *Vedas* enjoin us to seek out a guru; actually, they say to seek out *the* guru, not just *a* guru. The guru is one because he comes in disciplic succession. What Vyāsadeva and Kṛṣṇa taught five thousand years ago is also being taught now. There is no difference between the two instructions. Although hundreds and thousands of *ācāryas* have come and gone, the message is one. The real guru cannot be two, for the real guru does not speak differently from his predecessors. Some spiritual teachers say, "In my opinion you should do this," but this is not a guru. Such so-called gurus are simply rascals. The genuine guru has only one opinion, and that is the opinion expressed by Kṛṣṇa, Vyāsadeva, Nārada, Arjuna, Śrī Caitanya Mahāprabhu, and the Six Gosvāmīs. Five thousand years ago Lord Śrī Kṛṣṇa spoke the *Bhagavad-gītā,* and Vyāsadeva recorded it. Śrīla Vyāsadeva did not say, "This is my opinion." Rather, he wrote, *śrī-bhagavān uvāca,* that is, "The Supreme Personality of Godhead says." Whatever Vyāsadeva wrote was originally spoken by the Supreme Personality of Godhead. Śrīla Vyāsadeva did not give his own opinion.

Consequently, Śrīla Vyāsadeva is a guru. He does not misinterpret the words of Kṛṣṇa, but transmits them exactly as they were spoken. If we send a telegram, the person who delivers the telegram does not have to correct it, edit it, or add to it. He simply presents it. That is the guru's business. The guru may be this person or that, but the message is the same; therefore it is said that guru is one.

In the disciplic succession we simply find repetition of the same subject. In the *Bhagavad-gītā* [9.34] Śrī Kṛṣṇa says:

man-manā bhava mad-bhakto mad-yājī māṁ namaskuru
mām evaiṣyasi yuktvaivam ātmānaṁ mat-parāyaṇaḥ

"Engage your mind always in thinking of Me, become My devotee, offer obeisances to Me, and worship Me. Being completely absorbed in Me, surely you will come to Me." These very instructions were reiterated by all the *ācāryas,* such as Rāmānujācārya, Madhvācārya, and Caitanya Mahāprabhu. The Six Gosvāmīs also transmitted the same message, and we are simply following in their footsteps. There is no difference. We do not interpret the words of Kṛṣṇa by saying, "In my opinion, the Battlefield of Kurukṣetra represents the human body." Such interpretations are set forth by rascals. In the world there are many rascal gurus who give their own opinion, but we can challenge any rascal. A rascal guru may say, "I am God," or, "We are all God." That is all right, but we should find out from the dictionary what the meaning of *God* is. Generally, a dictionary will tell us that the word *God* indicates the Supreme Being. Thus we may ask such a guru, "Are you the Supreme Being?" If he cannot understand this, then we should give the meaning of *supreme*. Any dictionary will inform us that *supreme* means "the greatest authority." We may then ask, "Are you the greatest authority?" Such a rascal guru, even though proclaiming himself to be God, cannot answer such a question. God is the Supreme Being and the highest authority. No one is equal to Him or greater than Him. Yet there are many guru-gods, many rascals who claim to be the Supreme. Such rascals cannot help us escape the darkness of material existence. They cannot illumine our darkness with the torchlight of spiritual knowledge.

The bona fide guru will simply present what the supreme guru, God, says in bona fide scripture. A guru cannot change the message of the disciplic succession.

We must understand that we cannot carry out research to find the Absolute Truth. Caitanya Mahāprabhu Himself said, "My Guru Mahārāja, My spiritual master, considered Me a great fool." He who remains a great fool before his guru is a guru himself. However, if one says, "I am so advanced that I can speak better than my guru," he is simply a rascal. In the *Bhagavad-gītā* [4.2] Śrī Kṛṣṇa says:

evaṁ paramparā-prāptam imaṁ rājarṣayo viduḥ
sa kāleneha mahatā yogo naṣṭaḥ parantapa

"This supreme science was thus received through the chain of disciplic succession, and the saintly kings understood it in that way. But in course of time the succession was broken, and therefore the science as it is appears to be lost."

Taking on a guru is not simply a fashion. One who is serious about understanding spiritual life requires a guru. A guru is a question of necessity, for one must be very serious to understand spiritual life, God, proper action, and one's relationship with God. When we are very serious about understanding these subjects, we need a guru. We shouldn't go to a guru simply because a guru may be fashionable at the moment. Surrender must be there, for without surrender we cannot learn anything. If we go to a guru simply to challenge him, we will learn nothing. We must accept the guru just as Arjuna accepted his guru, Śrī Kṛṣṇa Himself:

kārpaṇya-doṣopahata-svabhāvaḥ
pṛcchāmi tvāṁ dharma-sammūḍha-cetāḥ
yac chreyaḥ syān niścitaṁ brūhi tan me
śiṣyas te 'haṁ śādhi māṁ tvāṁ prapannam

"Now I am confused about my duty and have lost all composure because of miserly weakness. In this condition I am asking You to tell me clearly what is best for me. Now I am Your disciple and a soul surrendered unto You. Please instruct me." [*Bhagavad-gītā* 2.7]

This is the process for accepting a guru. The guru is Kṛṣṇa's representative, the former *ācāryas'* representative. Kṛṣṇa says that all *ācāryas* are His representatives; therefore the guru should be offered the same respect one would offer to God. As Viśvanātha Cakravartī Ṭhākura says in his prayers to the spiritual master, *yasya prasādād bhagavat-prasādaḥ:* "By the mercy of the spiritual master, one receives the benediction of Kṛṣṇa." Thus, if we surrender to the bona fide guru, we surrender to God. God accepts our surrender to the guru.

In the *Bhagavad-gītā* [18.66] Kṛṣṇa instructs:

sarva-dharmān parityajya   mām ekaṁ śaraṇaṁ vraja
ahaṁ tvāṁ sarva-pāpebhyo   mokṣayiṣyāmi mā śucaḥ

"Abandon all varieties of religion and just surrender unto Me. I shall deliver you from all sinful reactions. Do not fear." Someone may argue, "Where is Kṛṣṇa? I shall surrender to Him." But no, the process is that we first surrender to Kṛṣṇa's representative; then we surrender to Kṛṣṇa. Therefore it is said, *sākṣād-dharitvena samasta-śāstraiḥ:* the guru is as good as God. When we offer respects to the guru, we are offering respects to God. Because we are trying to be God conscious, it is required that we learn how to offer respects to God through God's representative. In all the *śāstras* the guru is described to be as good as God, but the guru never says, "I am God." The disciple's duty is to offer respect to the guru just as he offers respect to God, but the guru never thinks, "My disciples are offering me the same respect they offer to God; therefore I have become God." As soon as he thinks like this, he becomes a dog instead of God. Therefore Viśvanātha Cakravartī says, *kintu prabhor yaḥ priya eva tasya*. Because he is the most confidential servitor of God, the guru is offered the same respect that we offer God. God is always God, guru is always guru. As a matter of etiquette, God is the worshipable God, and guru is the worshiper God (*sevaka-bhagavān*). Therefore the guru is addressed as *prabhupāda*. The word *prabhu* means "lord," and *pāda* means "position." Thus *prabhupāda* means "he who has taken the position of the Lord." This is the same as *sākṣād-dharitvena samasta-śāstraiḥ*.

Only if we are very serious about understanding the science of God is a guru required. We should not try to keep a guru as a matter of fashion. One who has accepted a guru speaks intelligently. He never speaks nonsense. That is the sign of having accepted a bona fide guru. We should certainly offer all respect to the spiritual master, but we should also remember how to carry out his orders. In the *Bhagavad-gītā* [4.34] Śrī Kṛṣṇa Himself tells us the method of seeking out and approaching the guru:

tad viddhi praṇipātena paripraśnena sevayā
upadekṣyanti te jñānaṁ jñāninas tattva-darśinaḥ

"Just try to learn the truth by approaching a spiritual master. Inquire from him submissively and render service unto him. The self-realized soul can impart knowledge unto you because he has seen the truth." The first process is that of surrender. We have to find an exalted person and willingly surrender before him. The *śāstras* enjoin that before we take a guru we study him carefully to find out whether we can surrender to him. We should not accept a guru suddenly, out of fanaticism. That is very dangerous. The guru should also study the person who wants to become a disciple to see if he is fit. That is the way a relationship is established between the guru and disciple. Everything is provided, but we must take up the process seriously. Then we can be trained to become a bona fide disciple. First we must find a bona fide guru, establish our relationship with him, and act accordingly. Then our life will be successful, for the guru can enlighten the sincere disciple who is in darkness.

Everyone is born a rascal and a fool. If we are born learned, why do we need to go to school? If we do not cultivate knowledge, we are no better than animals. An animal may say that there is no need of books and that he has become a guru, but how can anyone obtain knowledge without the study of authoritative books on science and philosophy? Rascal gurus try to avoid these things. We must understand that we are all born rascals and fools and that we have to be enlightened. We have to receive knowledge to make our lives perfect. If we do not perfect our lives, we are defeated. What is this defeat? The struggle for existence. We are trying to obtain a better life, to attain a superior position, and for this we are struggling very hard. But we do not know what a superior position actually is.

Whatever position we have in this material world must be given up. We may have a good position or a bad position; in any case, we cannot remain here. We may earn millions of dollars and think, "Now I am in a good position," but a little dysentery or cholera will finish our position. If the bank fails, our position is gone. So actually there is no good position in this material world. It is a farce. Those who try to attain a better position in the material world are ultimately defeated, because there is no better position. The *Bhagavad-gītā* [14.26] says what the better position is:

māṁ ca yo 'vyabhicāreṇa bhakti-yogena sevate
sa guṇān samatītyaitān brahma-bhūyāya kalpate

"One who engages in the spiritual activities of unalloyed devotional service at once transcends the modes of material nature and is elevated to the spiritual platform."

Is there any science that gives us the knowledge by which we may become immortal? Yes, we may become immortal, but not in the material sense. We cannot receive this knowledge in so-called universities. However, there is knowledge contained in the Vedic scriptures by which we may become immortal. That immortality is our better position. No more birth, no more death, no more old age, no more disease. Thus the guru takes on a very great responsibility. He must guide his disciple and enable him to become an eligible candidate for the perfect position—immortality. The guru must be competent to lead his disciple back home, back to Godhead.

SEPARATING THE SAINTS FROM THE SWINDLERS

Śrīla Prabhupāda speaks out in an interview with the London Times: *"If you want to be cheated, you will find many cheating gurus. But if you are sincere, you will find a sincere guru. . . . The genuine guru is God's representative, and he speaks about God and nothing else. . . . A genuine guru is not a businessman. He is a representative of God. Whatever God says, the guru repeats. He does not speak otherwise."*

Reporter: Your Grace, it seems that more people than ever are seeking some kind of spiritual life. I wonder if you could tell me why this is so.

Śrīla Prabhupāda: The desire for spiritual life is an absolutely natural hankering. Because we are spirit souls, we cannot be happy in the material atmosphere. If you take a fish out of the water, it cannot be happy on land. Similarly, if we are without spiritual consciousness, we can never be happy. Today, so many people are after scientific advancement and economic development, but they are not happy because these are not the actual goals of life. Many young people are realizing this, and they are rejecting materialistic life and are trying to search for spiritual life. Actually, this is the proper search. Kṛṣṇa consciousness is the proper goal of life. Unless you take to Kṛṣṇa consciousness, you cannot be happy. That is a fact. Therefore, we invite everyone to study and understand this great movement.

Reporter: What frankly worries me is that since the arrival in Britain some time ago of an Indian yogī, who was the first "guru" that most people had ever heard of, a lot of "gurus" have suddenly appeared out of nowhere. Sometimes I get the feeling that not all of them are as genuine as they ought to be. Would it be right to warn people who are thinking of taking up spiritual life that they should make sure that they have a genuine guru to teach them?

Śrīla Prabhupāda: Yes. Of course, to search out a guru is very nice, but if you want a cheap guru, or if you want to be cheated, then you will find many cheating gurus. But if you are sincere, you will find a sincere guru. Because people want everything very cheaply, they are cheated. We ask our students to refrain from illicit sex, meat-eating, gambling, and intoxication. People think that this is all very difficult—a botheration. But if someone else says, "You may do whatever nonsense you like, simply take my mantra," then people will like him. The point is that people want to be cheated, and therefore cheaters come. No one wants to undergo any austerity. Human life is meant for austerity, but no one is prepared to undergo austerity. Consequently, cheaters come and say, "No austerity. Whatever you like, you do. Simply pay me, and I'll give you some mantra, and you'll become God in six months." All this is going on. If you want to be cheated like this, the cheaters will come.
Reporter: What about the person who seriously wants to find spiritual life but who happens to finish up with the wrong guru?
Śrīla Prabhupāda: If you simply want an ordinary education, you have to devote so much time, labor, and understanding to it. Similarly, if you are going to take to spiritual life, you must become serious. How is it that simply by some wonderful mantras, someone can become God in six months? Why do people want something like that? This means that they want to be cheated.
Reporter: How can a person tell he has a genuine guru?
Śrīla Prabhupāda: Can any of my students answer this question?
Disciple: Once I remember John Lennon asked you, "How will I know who is the genuine guru?" And you answered, "Just find out the one who is most addicted to Kṛṣṇa. He is genuine."
Śrīla Prabhupāda: Yes. The genuine guru is God's representative, and he speaks about God and nothing else. The genuine guru is he who has no interest in materialistic life. He is after God, and God only. That is one of the tests of a genuine guru: *brahma-niṣṭham.* He is absorbed in the Absolute Truth. In the *Muṇḍaka Upaniṣad* it is stated, *śrotriyaṁ brahma-niṣṭham:* "The genuine guru is well versed in the scriptures and Vedic knowledge, and he is completely dependent on Brahman." He should know what Brahman [spirit] is and how to become situated in Brahman. These signs are given in the Vedic literature. As I said before, the real guru is God's representative. He represents the Supreme Lord, just as a viceroy represents

a king. The real guru will not manufacture anything. Everything he says is in accordance with the scriptures and the previous *ācāryas*. He will not give you a mantra and tell you that you will become God in six months. This is not a guru's business. A guru's business is to canvass everyone to become a devotee of God. That is the sum and substance of a real guru's business. Indeed, he has no other business. He tells whomever he sees, "Please become God conscious." If he canvasses somehow or other on behalf of God and tries to get everyone to become a devotee of God, he is a genuine guru.

Reporter: What about a Christian priest?

Śrīla Prabhupāda: Christian, Muhammadan, Hindu—it doesn't matter. If he is simply speaking on behalf of God, he is a guru. Lord Jesus Christ, for instance. He canvassed people, saying, "Just try to love God." Anyone—it doesn't matter who—be he Hindu, Muslim, or Christian, is a guru if he convinces people to love God. That is the test. The guru never says, "I am God," or "I will make you God." The real guru says, "I am a servant of God, and I will make you a servant of God also." It doesn't matter how the guru is dressed. As Caitanya Mahāprabhu said, "Whoever can impart knowledge about Kṛṣṇa is a spiritual master." A genuine spiritual master simply tries to get people to become devotees of Kṛṣṇa, or God. He has no other business.

Reporter: But the bad gurus—

Śrīla Prabhupāda: And what is a "bad" guru?

Reporter: A bad guru just wants some money or some fame.

Śrīla Prabhupāda: Well, if he is bad, how can he become a guru? [*Laughter*] How can iron become gold? Actually, a guru cannot be bad, for if someone is bad, he cannot be a guru. You cannot say "bad guru." That is a contradiction. What you have to do is simply try to understand what a genuine guru is. The definition of a genuine guru is that he is simply talking about God—that's all. If he's talking about some other nonsense, then he is not a guru. A guru cannot be bad. There is no question of a bad guru, any more than a red guru or a white guru. Guru means "genuine guru." All we have to know is that the genuine guru is simply talking about God and trying to get people to become God's devotees. If he does this, he is genuine.

Reporter: To be initiated into your society, what would I have to do?

Śrīla Prabhupāda: First of all, you'd have to give up illicit sex life.

Reporter: Does that include all sex life? What is illicit sex life?
Śrīla Prabhupāda: Illicit sex is sex outside of marriage. Animals have sex with no restrictions, but in human society there are restrictions. In every country and in every religion, there is some system of restricting sex life. You would also have to give up all intoxicants, including tea, cigarettes, alcohol, marijuana—anything that intoxicates.
Reporter: Anything else?
Śrīla Prabhupāda: You'd also have to give up eating meat, eggs, and fish. And you'd have to give up gambling as well. Unless you gave up these four sinful activities, you could not be initiated.
Reporter: How many followers do you have throughout the world?
Śrīla Prabhupāda: For anything genuine, the followers may be very few. For something rubbish, the followers may be many. Still, we have about five thousand initiated disciples.
Reporter: Is the Kṛṣṇa consciousness movement growing all the time?
Śrīla Prabhupāda: Yes, it is growing—but slowly. This is because we have so many restrictions. People do not like restrictions.
Reporter: Where is your following the greatest?
Śrīla Prabhupāda: In the United States, Europe, South America, and Australia. And, of course, in India there are millions who practice Kṛṣṇa consciousness.
Reporter: Could you tell me what the goal of your movement is?
Śrīla Prabhupāda: The purpose of this Kṛṣṇa consciousness movement is to awaken man's original consciousness. At the present moment our consciousness is designated. Someone is thinking, "I am an Englishman," and another is thinking, "I am an American." Actually, we do not belong to any of these designations. We are all part and parcel of God; that is our real identity. If everyone simply comes to that consciousness, all the problems of the world will be solved. Then we shall come to know that we are one—the same quality of spirit soul. The same quality of spirit soul is within everyone, although it may be in a different dress. This is the explanation given in the *Bhagavad-gītā*.

Kṛṣṇa consciousness is actually a purificatory process (*sarvopādhi-vinirmuktam*). Its purpose is to make people free from all designations (*tat-paratvena nirmalam*). When our consciousness becomes purified of all designations, the activities we carry out with our purified senses make us perfect. Eventually, we reach the ideal perfection of human life. Kṛṣṇa consciousness is also a very simple process. It is not necessary to become a great philosopher, scientist, or whatever. We need only chant the holy name of the Lord, understanding that His personality, His name, and His qualities are all absolute.

Kṛṣṇa consciousness is a great science. Unfortunately, in the universities there is no department for this science. Therefore we invite all serious men who are interested in the welfare of human society to understand this great movement and, if possible, take part in it and cooperate with us. The problems of the world will be solved. This is also the verdict of the *Bhagavad-gītā,* the most important and authoritative book of spiritual knowledge. Many of you have heard of the *Bhagavad-gītā.* Our movement is based on it. Our movement is approved by all great *ācāryas* in India—Rāmānujācārya, Madhvācārya, Lord Caitanya, and so many others. You are all representatives of newspapers, so I ask you to try to understand this movement as far as possible for the good of all human society.

Reporter: Do you think your movement is the only way to know God?

Śrīla Prabhupāda: Yes.

Reporter: How are you assured of that?

Śrīla Prabhupāda: From the authorities and from God, Kṛṣṇa. Kṛṣṇa says:

sarva-dharmān parityajya mām ekaṁ śaraṇaṁ vraja
ahaṁ tvāṁ sarva-pāpebhyo mokṣayiṣyāmi mā śucaḥ

"Abandon all varieties of religion and just surrender unto Me. I shall deliver you from all sinful reactions. Do not fear." [Bg. 18.66]

Reporter: Does "surrender" mean that one has to leave his family?

Śrīla Prabhupāda: No.

Reporter: But suppose I were to become an initiate. Wouldn't I have to come and live in the temple?

Śrīla Prabhupāda: Not necessarily.

Reporter: I can stay at home?

Śrīla Prabhupāda: Oh, yes.

Reporter: What about work? Would I have to give up my job?

Śrīla Prabhupāda: No, you would simply have to give up your bad

habits and chant the Hare Kṛṣṇa mantra on these beads—that's all.
Reporter: Would I have to give any financial support?
Śrīla Prabhupāda: No, that is your voluntary wish. If you give, that's all right. And if you don't, we don't mind. We do not depend on anyone's financial contribution. We depend on Kṛṣṇa.
Reporter: I wouldn't have to give any money at all?
Śrīla Prabhupāda: No.
Reporter: Is this one of the main things that distinguishes the genuine guru from the fake guru?
Śrīla Prabhupāda: Yes, a genuine guru is not a businessman. He is a representative of God. Whatever God says, the guru repeats. He does not speak otherwise.
Reporter: But would you expect to find a real guru, say, traveling in a Rolls Royce and staying in a penthouse suite in a classy hotel?
Śrīla Prabhupāda: Sometimes people provide us with a room in a first-class hotel, but we generally stay in our own temples. We have some one hundred temples around the world, so we don't require to go to any hotels.
Reporter: I wasn't trying to make any accusations. I was merely trying to illustrate that I think your warning is a valid one. There are so many people interested in finding a spiritual life, and at the same time there are a lot of people interested in cashing in on the "guru business."
Śrīla Prabhupāda: Are you under the impression that spiritual life means voluntarily accepting poverty?
Reporter: Well, I don't know.
Śrīla Prabhupāda: A poverty-stricken man may be materialistic, and a wealthy man may be very spiritual. Spiritual life does not depend on either poverty or wealth. Spiritual life is transcendental. Consider Arjuna, for instance. Arjuna was a member of a royal family, yet he was a pure devotee of God. And in the *Bhagavad-gītā* [4.2] Śrī Kṛṣṇa says, *evaṁ paramparā-prāptam imaṁ rājarṣayo viduḥ:* "This supreme science was received through the chain of disciplic succession, and the saintly kings understood it in that way." In the past, all kings who were saintly understood spiritual science. Therefore, spiritual life does not depend on one's material condition. Whatever a person's material condition may be—he may be a king or a pauper—he can still understand spiritual life. Generally people do not know what spiritual life is, and therefore, they unnecessarily criticize us. If

I asked you what spiritual life is, how would you answer?
Reporter: Well, I'm not sure.
Śrīla Prabhupāda: Although you do not know what spiritual life is, you still say, "It is this," or "It is that." But first you should know what spiritual life is. Spiritual life begins when you understand that you are not your body. This is the real beginning of spiritual life. By seeing the difference between your self and your body, you come to understand that you are a spirit soul (*ahaṁ brahmāsmi*).
Reporter: Do you think this knowledge should be a part of everyone's education?
Śrīla Prabhupāda: Yes. People should first be taught what they are. Are they their bodies, or something else? That is the beginning of education. Now everyone is educated to think he is his body. Because someone accidentally gets an American body, he thinks, "I am an American." This is just like thinking "I am a red shirt" just because you are wearing a red shirt. You are not a red shirt; you are a human being. Similarly, this body is like a shirt or coat over the real person—the spirit soul. If we recognize ourselves simply by our bodily "shirt" or "coat," then we have no spiritual education.
Reporter: Do you think that such education should be given in schools?
Śrīla Prabhupāda: Yes—in schools, colleges, and universities. There is an immense literature on this subject—an immense fund of knowledge. What is actually required is that the leaders of society come forward to understand this movement.
Reporter: Have you ever had people come to you who had previously been involved with a fake guru?
Śrīla Prabhupāda: Yes, there are many.
Reporter: Were their spiritual lives in any way spoiled by the fake gurus?
Śrīla Prabhupāda: No, they were genuinely seeking something spiritual, and that was their qualification. God is within everyone's heart, and as soon as someone genuinely seeks Him, He helps that person find a genuine guru.
Reporter: Have the real gurus like yourself ever tried to put a stop to the false gurus—that is, put pressure on them to put them out of business, so to speak?
Śrīla Prabhupāda: No, that is not my purpose. I started my movement simply by chanting Hare Kṛṣṇa. I chanted in New York in a

place called Tompkins Square Park, and soon people began to come to me. In this way, the Kṛṣṇa consciousness movement gradually developed. Many accepted, and many did not accept. Those who are fortunate have accepted.

Reporter: Don't you feel that people are suspicious because of their experience with fake gurus? If you went to a quack dentist and he broke your tooth, you might be suspicious about going to another dentist.

Śrīla Prabhupāda: Yes. Naturally, if you are cheated, you become suspicious. But this does not mean that if you are cheated once, you will always be cheated. You should find someone genuine. But to come to Kṛṣṇa consciousness, you must be either very fortunate or well aware of this science. From the *Bhagavad-gītā* we understand that the genuine seekers are very few: *manuṣyāṇāṁ sahasreṣu kaścid yatati siddhaye.* Out of many millions of people, there may be only one who is interested in spiritual life. Generally, people are interested in eating, sleeping, mating, and defending. So how can we expect to find many followers? It is not difficult to notice that people have lost their spiritual interest. And almost all those who are actually interested are being cheated by so-called spiritualists. You cannot judge a movement simply by the number of its followers. If one man is genuine, then the movement is successful. It is not a question of quantity, but quality.

Reporter: I wonder how many people you think might have been taken in by fake gurus.

Śrīla Prabhupāda: Practically everyone. [*Laughter*] There is no question of counting. Everyone.

Reporter: This would mean thousands of people, wouldn't it?

Śrīla Prabhupāda: Millions. Millions have been cheated, because they want to be cheated. God is omniscient. He can understand your desires. He is within your heart, and if you want to be cheated, God sends you a cheater.

Reporter: Is it possible for everyone to attain the perfectional stage you spoke of previously?

Śrīla Prabhupāda: Within a second. Anyone can attain perfection within a second—providing he is willing. The difficulty is that no one is willing. In the *Bhagavad-gītā* [18.66] Kṛṣṇa says, *sarva-dharmān parityajya mām ekaṁ śaraṇaṁ vraja:* "Simply surrender unto Me." But who is going to surrender to God? Everyone says,

"Oh, why should I surrender to God? I will be independent." If you simply surrender, it is a second's business. That's all. But no one is willing, and that is the difficulty.

Reporter: When you say that lots of people want to be cheated, do you mean that lots of people want to carry on with their worldly pleasures and at the same time, by chanting a mantra or by holding a flower, achieve spiritual life as well? Is this what you mean by wanting to be cheated?

Śrīla Prabhupāda: Yes, this is like a patient thinking, "I shall continue with my disease, and at the same time I shall become healthy." It is contradictory. The first requirement is that one become educated in spiritual life. Spiritual life is not something one can understand by a few minutes' talk. There are many philosophy and theology books, but people are not interested in them. That is the difficulty. For instance, the *Śrīmad-Bhāgavatam* is a very long work, and if you try to read this book, it may take many days just to understand one line of it. The *Bhāgavatam* describes God, the Absolute Truth, but people are not interested. And if, by chance, someone becomes a little interested in spiritual life, he wants something immediate and cheap. Therefore, he is cheated. Actually, human life is meant for austerity and penance. That is the way of Vedic civilization. In Vedic times they would train boys as *brahmacārīs;* no sex life was allowed at all up to the age of twenty-five. Where is that education now? A *brahmacārī* is a student who lives a life of complete celibacy and obeys the commands of his guru at the *gurukula* [school of the spiritual master]. Now schools and colleges are teaching sex from the very beginning, and twelve- or thirteen-year-old boys and girls are having sex. How can they have a spiritual life? Spiritual life means voluntarily accepting some austerities for the sake of God realization. That is why we insist on no illicit sex, meat-eating, gambling, or intoxication for our initiated students. Without these restrictions, any "yoga meditation" or so-called spiritual discipline cannot be genuine. It is simply a business deal between the cheaters and the cheated.

Reporter: Thank you very much.

Śrīla Prabhupāda: Hare Kṛṣṇa.

"WITH ALL THE HUMILITY AT MY COMMAND"

It is February 1936, in Bombay. The pure devotee who three decades later will become the world-renowned spiritual master of the Kṛṣṇa consciousness movement glorifies his own spiritual master. Here we learn the time-honored meaning of the spiritual master, the disciple, and their relationship.

sākṣād-dharitvena samasta-śāstrair
uktas tathā bhāvyata eva sadbhiḥ
kintu prabhor yaḥ priya eva tasya
vande guroḥ śrī-caraṇāravindam

"In the revealed scriptures it is declared that the spiritual master should be worshiped like the Supreme Personality of Godhead, and this injunction is obeyed by pure devotees of the Lord. The spiritual master is the most confidential servant of the Lord. Thus let us offer our respectful obeisances unto the lotus feet of our spiritual master."

Gentlemen, on behalf of the members of the Bombay branch of the Gauḍīya Maṭha, let me welcome you all because you have so kindly joined us tonight in our congregational offerings of homage to the lotus feet of the world teacher, Ācāryadeva, who is the founder of this Gauḍīya Mission and is the president-*ācārya* of Śrī Śrī Viśva-vaiṣṇava Rāja-sabhā—I mean my eternal divine master, Paramahaṁsa Parivrājakācārya Śrī Śrīmad Bhaktisiddhānta Sarasvatī Gosvāmī Mahārāja.

Sixty-two years ago, on this auspicious day, the Ācāryadeva made his appearance by the call of Ṭhākura Bhaktivinoda at Śrī-kṣetra Jagannātha-dhāma at Purī.

Gentlemen, the offering of such an homage as has been arranged this evening to the Ācāryadeva is not a sectarian concern, for when we speak of the fundamental principle of *gurudeva*, or *ācāryadeva*, we speak of something that is of universal application. There does not arise any question of discriminating my guru from yours or anyone else's. There is only one guru, who appears in an infinity of forms to teach you, me, and all others.

The guru, or *ācāryadeva,* as we learn from the bona fide scriptures, delivers the message of the absolute world, the transcendental abode of the Absolute Personality, where everything nondifferentially serves the Absolute Truth. We have heard so many times: *mahājano yena gataḥ sa panthāḥ* ("Traverse the trail which your previous *ācārya* has passed"), but we have hardly tried to understand the real purport of this *śloka.* If we scrutinizingly study this proposition, we understand that the *mahājana* is one and the royal road to the transcendental world is also one. In the *Muṇḍaka Upaniṣad* [1.2.12] it is said:

tad-vijñānārthaṁ sa gurum evābhigacchet
samit-pāṇiḥ śrotriyaṁ brahma-niṣṭham

"In order to learn the transcendental science, one must approach the bona fide spiritual master in disciplic succession, who is fixed in the Absolute Truth."

Thus it has been enjoined herewith that in order to receive that transcendental knowledge, one must approach the guru. Therefore, if the Absolute Truth is one, about which we think there is no difference of opinion, the guru also cannot be two. The Ācāryadeva for whom we have assembled tonight to offer our humble homage is not the guru of a sectarian institution or one out of many differing exponents of the truth. On the contrary, he is the Jagad-guru, or the guru of all of us; the only difference is that some obey him wholeheartedly, while others do not obey him directly.

In the *Śrīmad-Bhāgavatam* [11.17.27] it is said:

ācāryaṁ māṁ vijānīyān nāvamanyeta karhicit
na martya-buddhyāsūyeta sarva-devamayo guruḥ

"One should understand the spiritual master to be as good as I am," said the Blessed Lord. "Nobody should be jealous of the spiritual master or think of him as an ordinary man, because the spiritual master is the sum total of all demigods." That is, the *ācārya* has been identified with God Himself. He has nothing to do with the affairs of this mundane world. He does not descend here to meddle with the affairs of temporary necessities, but to deliver the fallen, conditioned souls—the souls, or entities, who have come here to the material world with a motive of enjoyment by the mind and the five organs of sense perception. He appears before us to reveal the light of the *Vedas* and to bestow upon us the blessings of full-fledged freedom, after which we should hanker at every step of our life's journey.

The transcendental knowledge of the *Vedas* was first uttered by God to Brahmā, the creator of this particular universe. From Brahmā the knowledge descended to Nārada, from Nārada to Vyāsadeva, from Vyāsadeva to Madhva, and in this process of disciplic succession the transcendental knowledge was transmitted by one disciple to another till it reached Lord Gaurāṅga, Śrī Kṛṣṇa Caitanya, who posed as the disciple and successor of Śrī Īśvara Purī. The present Ācāryadeva is the tenth disciplic representative from Śrī Rūpa Gosvāmī, the original representative of Lord Caitanya who preached this transcendental tradition in its fullness. The knowledge that we receive from our Gurudeva is not different from that imparted by God Himself and the succession of the *ācāryas* in the preceptorial line of Brahmā. We adore this auspicious day as Śrī Vyāsa-pūjā-tithi, because the Ācārya is the living representative of Vyāsadeva, the divine compiler of the *Vedas,* the *Purāṇas,* the *Bhagavad-gītā,* the *Mahābhārata,* and the *Śrīmad-Bhāgavatam.*

One who interprets the divine sound, or *śabda-brahma,* by his imperfect sense perception cannot be a real spiritual guru, because, in the absence of proper disciplinary training under the bona fide *ācārya,* the interpreter is sure to differ from Vyāsadeva (as the Māyāvādīs do). Śrīla Vyāsadeva is the prime authority of Vedic revelation, and therefore such an irrelevant interpreter cannot be accepted as the guru, or *ācārya,* howsoever equipped he may be with all the acquirements of material knowledge. As it is said in the *Padma Purāṇa:*

sampradāya-vihīnā ye mantrās te niṣphalā matāḥ

"Unless you are initiated by a bona fide spiritual master in the disciplic succession, the mantra that you might have received is without any effect."

On the other hand, one who has received the transcendental knowledge by aural reception from the bona fide preceptor in the disciplic chain, and who has sincere regard for the real *ācārya,* must needs be enlightened with the revealed knowledge of the *Vedas*. But this knowledge is permanently sealed to the cognitive approach of the empiricists. As it is said in the *Śvetāśvatara Upaniṣad* [6.23]:

yasya deve parā bhaktir yathā deve tathā gurau
tasyaite kathitā hy arthāḥ prakāśante mahātmanaḥ

"Only unto those great souls who simultaneously have implicit faith in both the Lord and the spiritual master are all the imports of Vedic knowledge automatically revealed."

Gentlemen, our knowledge is so poor, our senses are so imperfect, and our sources are so limited that it is not possible for us to have even the slightest knowledge of the absolute region without surrendering ourselves at the lotus feet of Śrī Vyāsadeva or his bona fide representative. Every moment we are being deceived by the knowledge of our direct perception. It is all the creation or concoction of the mind, which is always deceiving, changing, and flickering. We cannot know anything of the transcendental region by our limited, perverted method of observation and experiment. But all of us can lend our eager ears for the aural reception of the transcendental sound transmitted from that region to this through the unadulterated medium of Śrī Gurudeva or Śrī Vyāsadeva. Therefore, gentlemen, we should surrender ourselves today at the feet of the representative of Śrī Vyāsadeva for the elimination of all our differences bred by our unsubmissive attitude. It is accordingly said in *Śrī Gītā* [4.34]:

tad viddhi praṇipātena paripraśnena sevayā
upadekṣyanti te jñānaṁ jñāninas tattva-darśinaḥ

"Just approach the wise and bona fide spiritual master. Surrender unto him first and try to understand him by inquiries and service. Such a wise spiritual master will enlighten you with transcendental knowledge, for he has already known the Absolute Truth."

To receive the transcendental knowledge we must completely surrender ourselves to the real *ācārya* in a spirit of ardent inquiry and service. Actual performance of service to the Absolute under the guidance of the *ācārya* is the only vehicle by which we can assimilate the transcendental knowledge. Today's meeting for offering our humble services and homage to the feet of the Ācāryadeva will enable us to be favored with the capacity for assimilating the transcendental knowledge so kindly transmitted by him to all persons, without distinction.

Gentlemen, we are all more or less proud of our past Indian civilization, but we actually do not know the real nature of that civilization. We cannot be proud of our past material civilization, which is now a thousand times greater than in days gone by. It is said that we are passing through the age of darkness, the Kali-yuga. What is this darkness? The darkness cannot be due to backwardness in material knowledge, because we now have more of it than formerly. If not we ourselves, our neighbors, at any rate, have plenty of it. Therefore, we must conclude that the darkness of the present age is not due to a lack of material advancement, but that we have lost the clue to our spiritual advancement, which is the prime necessity of human life and the criterion of the highest type of human civilization. Throwing of bombs from airplanes is no advancement of civilization from the primitive, uncivilized practice of dropping big stones on the heads of enemies from the tops of hills. Improvement of the art of killing our neighbors by means of machine guns and poisonous gases is certainly no advancement from primitive barbarism, which prided itself on its art of killing by bows and arrows. Nor does the development of a sense of pampered selfishness prove anything more than intellectual animalism. True human civilization is very different from all these states, and therefore in the *Kaṭha Upaniṣad* [1.3.14] there is the emphatic call:

uttiṣṭhata jāgrata
prāpya varān nibodhata
kṣurasya dhārā niśitā duratyayā
durgaṁ pathas tat kavayo vadanti

"Please wake up and try to understand the boon that you now have in this human form of life. The path of spiritual realization is very difficult; it is sharp like a razor's edge. That is the opinion of learned transcendental scholars."

Thus, while others were yet in the womb of historical oblivion, the sages of India had developed a different kind of civilization, which enabled them to know themselves. They had discovered that we are not at all material entities, but that we are all spiritual, permanent, and indestructible servants of the Absolute. But because we have, against our better judgment, chosen to completely identify ourselves with this present material existence, our sufferings have multiplied according to the inexorable law of birth and death, with its consequent diseases and anxieties. These sufferings cannot be really mitigated by any provision of material happiness, because matter and spirit are completely different elements. It is just as if you took an aquatic animal out of water and put it on the land, supplying all manner of happiness possible on land. The deadly sufferings of the animal are not capable of being relieved at all until it is taken out of its foreign environment. Spirit and matter are completely contradictory things. All of us are spiritual entities. We cannot have perfect happiness, which is our birthright, however much we may meddle with the affairs of mundane things. Perfect happiness can be ours only when we are restored to our natural state of spiritual existence. This is the distinctive message of our ancient Indian civilization, this is the message of the *Gītā,* this is the message of the *Vedas* and the *Purāṇas,* and this is the message of all the real *ācāryas,* including our present Ācāryadeva, in the line of Lord Caitanya.

Gentlemen, although it is imperfectly that we have been enabled by his grace to understand the sublime messages of our Ācāryadeva, Oṁ Viṣṇupāda Paramahaṁsa Parivrājakācārya Śrī Śrīmad Bhaktisiddhānta Sarasvatī Gosvāmī Mahārāja, we must admit that we have realized definitely that the divine message from his holy lips is the congenial thing for suffering humanity. All of us should hear him patiently. If we listen to the transcendental sound without unnecessary opposition, he will surely have mercy upon us. The Ācārya's message is to take us back to our original home, back to God. Let me repeat, therefore, that we should hear him patiently, follow him in the measure of our conviction, and bow down at his lotus feet for releasing us from our present causeless unwillingness for serving the Absolute and all souls.

From the *Gītā* we learn that even after the destruction of the body, the *ātmā,* or the soul, is not destroyed; he is always the same, always new and fresh. Fire cannot burn him, water cannot dissolve him, the air cannot dry him up, and the sword cannot kill him. He is everlasting and eternal, and this is also confirmed in the *Śrīmad-Bhāgavatam* [10.84.13]:

yasyātma-buddhiḥ kuṇape tri-dhātuke
sva-dhīḥ kalatrādiṣu bhauma ijya-dhīḥ
yat-tīrtha-buddhiḥ salile na karhicij
janeṣv abhijñeṣu sa eva go-kharaḥ

"Anyone who accepts this bodily bag of three elements [bile, mucus, and air] as his self, who has an affinity for an intimate relationship with his wife and children, who considers his land worshipable, who takes bath in the waters of the holy places of pilgrimage but never takes advantage of those persons who are in actual knowledge—he is no better than an ass or a cow."

Unfortunately, in these days we have all been turned foolish by neglecting our real comfort and identifying the material cage with ourselves. We have concentrated all our energies for the meaningless upkeep of the material cage for its own sake, completely neglecting the captive soul within. The cage is meant for the undoing of the bird; the bird is not meant for the welfare of the cage. Let us, therefore, deeply ponder this. All our activities are now turned toward the upkeep of the cage, and the most we do is try to give some food to the mind by art and literature. But we do not know that this mind is also material in a more subtle form. This is stated in the *Gītā* [7.4]:

bhūmir āpo 'nalo vāyuḥ khaṁ mano buddhir eva ca
ahaṅkāra itīyaṁ me bhinnā prakṛtir aṣṭadhā

"Earth, fire, water, air, sky, intelligence, mind, and ego are all My separated energies."

We have scarcely tried to give any food to the soul, which is distinct from the body and mind; therefore we are all committing suicide in the proper sense of the term. The message of the Ācāryadeva is to give us a warning to halt such wrong activities. Let us therefore bow down at his lotus feet for the unalloyed mercy and kindness he has bestowed upon us.

Gentlemen, do not for a moment think that my Gurudeva wants to put a complete brake on the modern civilization—an impossible feat. But let us learn from him the art of making the best use of a bad bargain, and let us understand the importance of this human life, which is fit for the highest development of true consciousness. The best use of this rare human life should not be neglected. As it is said in the *Śrīmad-Bhāgavatam* [11.9.29]:

labdhvā su-durlabham idaṁ bahu-sambhavānte
mānuṣyam artha-dam anityam apīha dhīraḥ
tūrṇaṁ yateta na pated anu-mṛtyu yāvan
niḥśreyasāya viṣayaḥ khalu sarvataḥ syāt

"This human form of life is obtained after many, many births, and although it is not permanent, it can offer the highest benefits. Therefore a sober and intelligent man should immediately try to fulfill his mission and attain the highest profit in life before another death occurs. He should avoid sense gratification, which is available in all circumstances."

Let us not misuse this human life in the vain pursuit of material enjoyment, or, in other words, for the sake of only eating, sleeping, fearing, and sensuous activities. The Ācāryadeva's message is conveyed by the words of Śrī Rūpa Gosvāmī [*Bhakti-rasāmṛta-sindhu* 1.2.255–256]:

anāsaktasya viṣayān yathārham upayuñjataḥ
nirbandhaḥ kṛṣṇa-sambandhe yuktaṁ vairāgyam ucyate

prāpañcikatayā buddhyā hari-sambandhi-vastunaḥ
mumukṣubhiḥ parityāgo vairāgyaṁ phalgu kathyate

"One is said to be situated in the fully renounced order of life if he lives in accordance with Kṛṣṇa consciousness. He should be without attachment for sense gratification and should accept only what is necessary for the upkeep of the body. On the other hand, one who renounces things that could be used in the service of Kṛṣṇa, under the pretext that such things are material, does not practice complete renunciation."

The purport of these *ślokas* can only be realized by fully

developing the rational portion of our life, not the animal portion. Sitting at the feet of the Ācāryadeva, let us try to understand from this transcendental source of knowledge what we are, what is this universe, what is God, and what is our relationship with Him. The message of Lord Caitanya is the message for the living entities and the message of the living world. Lord Caitanya did not bother Himself for the upliftment of this dead world, which is suitably named Martyaloka, the world where everything is destined to die. He appeared before us four hundred fifty years ago to tell us something of the transcendental universe, where everything is permanent and everything is for the service of the Absolute. But recently Lord Caitanya has been misrepresented by some unscrupulous persons, and the highest philosophy of the Lord has been misinterpreted to be the cult of the lowest type of society. We are glad to announce tonight that our Ācāryadeva, with his usual kindness, saved us from this horrible type of degradation, and therefore we bow down at his lotus feet with all humility.

Gentlemen, it has been a mania of the cultured (or uncultured) society of the present day to accredit the Personality of Godhead with merely impersonal features and to stultify Him by claiming that He has no senses, no form, no activity, no head, no legs, and no enjoyment. This has also been the pleasure of the modern scholars due to their sheer lack of proper guidance and true introspection in the spiritual realm. All these empiricists think alike: all the enjoyable things should be monopolized by the human society, or by a particular class only, and the impersonal God should be a mere order-supplier for their whimsical feats. We are happy that we have been relieved of this horrible type of malady by the mercy of His Divine Grace Paramahaṁsa Parivrājakācārya Bhaktisiddhānta Sarasvatī Gosvāmī Mahārāja. He is our eye-opener, our eternal father, our eternal preceptor, and our eternal guide. Let us therefore bow down at his lotus feet on this auspicious day.

Gentlemen, although we are like ignorant children in the knowledge of the Transcendence, still His Divine Grace, my Gurudeva, has kindled a small fire within us to dissipate the invincible darkness of empirical knowledge. We are now so much on the safe side that no amount of philosophical argument by the empiric schools of thought can deviate us an inch from the position of our eternal dependence on the lotus feet of His Divine Grace. Furthermore, we

are prepared to challenge the most erudite scholars of the Māyāvāda school and prove that the Personality of Godhead and His transcendental sports in Goloka alone constitute the sublime information of the *Vedas*. There are explicit indications of this in the *Chāndogya Upaniṣad* [8.13.1]:

śyāmāc chavalaṁ prapadye
śavalāc chyāmaṁ prapadye

"For receiving the mercy of Kṛṣṇa, I surrender unto His energy (Rādhā), and for receiving the mercy of His energy, I surrender unto Kṛṣṇa." Also, in the *Ṛg Veda* [1.22.20]:

tad viṣṇoḥ paramaṁ padaṁ sadā paśyanti sūrayaḥ
divīva cakṣur ātatam . . . viṣṇor yat paramaṁ padam

"The lotus feet of Lord Viṣṇu are the supreme objective of all the demigods. These lotus feet are as enlightening as the sun in the sky."

The plain truth so vividly explained in the *Gītā*, which is the central lesson of the *Vedas*, is not understood or even suspected by the most powerful scholars of the empiric schools. Herein lies the secret of Śrī Vyāsa-pūjā. When we meditate on the transcendental pastimes of the Absolute Godhead, we are proud to feel that we are His eternal servitors, and we become jubilant and dance with joy. All glory to my divine master, for it is he who has out of his unceasing flow of mercy stirred up within us such a movement of eternal existence. Let us bow down at his lotus feet.

Gentlemen, had he not appeared before us to deliver us from the thralldom of this gross worldly delusion, surely we should have remained for lives and ages in the darkness of helpless captivity. Had he not appeared before us, we would not have been able to understand the eternal truth of the sublime teaching of Lord Caitanya. Had he not appeared before us, we could not have been able to know the significance of the first *śloka* of the *Brahma-saṁhitā:*

īśvaraḥ paramaḥ kṛṣṇaḥ sac-cid-ānanda-vigrahaḥ
anādir ādir govindaḥ sarva-kāraṇa-kāraṇam

"Kṛṣṇa, who is known as Govinda, is the Supreme Godhead. He

has an eternal, blissful, spiritual body. He is the origin of all. He has no other origin, and He is the prime cause of all causes."

Personally, I have no hope for any direct service for the coming crores of births of the sojourn of my life, but I am confident that some day or other I shall be delivered from this mire of delusion in which I am at present so deeply sunk. Therefore let me with all my earnestness pray at the lotus feet of my divine master to allow me to suffer the lot for which I am destined due to my past misdoings, but to let me have this power of recollection: that I am nothing but a tiny servant of the Almighty Absolute Godhead, realized through the unflinching mercy of my divine master. Let me therefore bow down at his lotus feet with all the humility at my command.

III.
LOOKING AT THE CULTURAL BACKGROUND

INDIA'S GREATEST IMPERSONALIST MEDITATED ON LORD KṚṢṆA AND THE BHAGAVAD-GĪTĀ

Śrīla Prabhupāda rebukes impersonalist yogīs and swamis, the nominal followers of the ninth-century teacher Śaṅkara, in this commentary on the latter's Meditation on the Bhagavad-gītā: *"Fools rush in where angels fear to tread. Whereas Śaṅkara, the greatest of the impersonalists, offers his due respects to Kṛṣṇa and His book* Bhagavad-gītā, *the foolish say that 'we need not surrender to the personal Kṛṣṇa.'"*

— 1 —

O *Bhagavad-gītā,*
Through Thy eighteen chapters
Thou showerest upon man
The immortal nectar
Of the wisdom of the Absolute.
O blessed *Gītā,*
By Thee, Lord Kṛṣṇa Himself
Enlightened Arjuna.
Afterward, the ancient sage Vyāsa
Included Thee in the *Mahābhārata.*
O loving mother,
Destroyer of man's rebirth
Into the darkness of this mortal world,
Upon Thee I meditate.

— 2 —

Salutations to thee, O Vyāsa.
Thou art of mighty intellect,

And thine eyes
Are large as the petals
Of the full-blown lotus.
It was thou
Who brightened this lamp of wisdom,
Filling it with the oil
Of the *Mahābhārata*.

PURPORT

Śrīpāda Śaṅkarācārya was an impersonalist from the materialistic point of view. But he never denied the spiritual form known as *sac-cid-ānanda-vigraha*, or the eternal, all-blissful form of knowledge that existed before the material creation. When he spoke of the Supreme Brahman as impersonal, he meant that the Lord's *sac-cid-ānanda* form was not to be confused with a material conception of personality. In the very beginning of his commentary on the *Gītā*, he maintains that Nārāyaṇa, the Supreme Lord, is transcendental to the material creation. The Lord existed before the creation as the transcendental personality, and He has nothing to do with material personality. Lord Kṛṣṇa is the same Supreme Personality, and He has no connection with a material body. He descends in His spiritual, eternal form, but foolish people mistake His body to be like ours. Śaṅkara's preaching of impersonalism is especially meant for teaching foolish persons who consider Kṛṣṇa to be an ordinary man composed of matter.

No one would care to read the *Gītā* if it had been spoken by a material man, and certainly Vyāsadeva would not have bothered to incorporate it into the history of the *Mahābhārata*. According to the above verses, the *Mahābhārata* is the history of the ancient world, and Vyāsadeva is the writer of this great epic. The *Bhagavad-gītā* is identical with Kṛṣṇa; and because Kṛṣṇa is the Absolute Supreme Personality of Godhead, there is no difference between Kṛṣṇa and His words. Therefore the *Bhagavad-gītā* is as worshipable as Lord Kṛṣṇa Himself, both being absolute. One who hears the *Bhagavad-gītā* "as is" actually hears the words directly from the lotus lips of the Lord. But unfortunate persons say that the *Gītā* is too antiquated for the modern man, who wants to find out God by speculation or meditation.

—3—

I salute Thee, O Kṛṣṇa,
O Thou who art the refuge
Of ocean-born Lakṣmī
And all who take refuge
At Thy lotus feet.
Thou art indeed
The wish-fulfilling tree
For Thy devotee.
Thy one hand holds a staff
For driving cows,
And Thy other hand is raised—
The thumb touching the tip
Of Thy forefinger,
Indicating divine knowledge.
Salutations to Thee, O Supreme Lord,
For Thou art the milker
Of the ambrosia of the *Gītā*.

PURPORT

Śrīpāda Śaṅkarācārya explicitly says, "You fools, just worship Govinda and that *Bhagavad-gītā* spoken by Nārāyaṇa Himself," yet foolish people still conduct their research work to find out Nārāyaṇa; consequently they are wretched, and they waste their time for nothing. Nārāyaṇa is never wretched nor *daridra;* rather, He is worshiped by the goddess of fortune, Lakṣmī, as well as by all living entities. Śaṅkara declared himself to be "Brahman," but he admits Nārāyaṇa, or Kṛṣṇa, to be the Supreme Personality who is beyond the material creation. He offers his respects to Kṛṣṇa as the Supreme Brahman, or Parabrahman, because He (Kṛṣṇa) is worshipable by everyone. Only the fools and enemies of Kṛṣṇa, who cannot understand what the *Bhagavad-gītā* is (though they make commentaries on it), say, *"It is not the personal Kṛṣṇa to whom we have to surrender ourselves utterly, but the unborn, beginningless Eternal who speaks through Kṛṣṇa."* Fools rush in where angels fear to tread. Whereas Śaṅkara, the greatest of the impersonalists, offers his due respects to Kṛṣṇa and His book the *Bhagavad-gītā*, the foolish say that "we need not surrender to the personal Kṛṣṇa." Such unenlightened people do not know that Kṛṣṇa is absolute and that there is no difference between His inside and outside. The difference of inside and outside is experienced in the dual, material world. In the absolute world there is no such difference, because in the absolute everything is spiritual (*sac-cid-ānanda*), and Nārāyaṇa, or Kṛṣṇa, belongs to the absolute world. In the absolute world there is only the factual personality, and there is no distinction between body and soul.

— 4 —

The *Upaniṣads*
Are as a herd of cows,
Lord Kṛṣṇa, son of a cowherd,
Is their milker,
Arjuna is the calf,
The supreme nectar of the *Gītā*
Is the milk,
And the wise man
Of purified intellect
Is the drinker.

PURPORT

Unless one understands spiritual variegatedness, one cannot understand the transcendental pastimes of the Lord. In the *Brahma-saṁhitā* it is said that Kṛṣṇa's name, form, qualities, pastimes, entourage, and paraphernalia are all *ānanda-cinmaya-rasa*—in short, everything of His transcendental association is of the same composition of spiritual bliss, knowledge, and eternity. There is no end to His name, form, etc., unlike in the ma-terial world, where all things have their end. As stated in the *Bhagavad-gītā,* only fools deride Him; whereas it is Śaṅkara, the greatest impersonalist, who worships Him, His cows, and His pastimes as the son of Vasudeva and pleasure of Devakī.

— 5 —

Thou son of Vasudeva,
Destroyer of the demons Kaṁsa and Cāṇūra,

Thou supreme bliss of Mother Devakī,
O Thou, guru of the universe,
Teacher of the worlds,
Thee, O Kṛṣṇa, I salute.

PURPORT

Śaṅkara describes Him as the son of Vasudeva and Devakī. Does he mean thereby that he is worshiping an ordinary, material man? He worships Kṛṣṇa because he knows that Kṛṣṇa's birth and activities are all supernatural. As stated in the *Bhagavad-gītā* [4.9], Kṛṣṇa's birth and activities are mysterious and transcendental, and therefore only the devotees of Kṛṣṇa can know them perfectly. Śaṅkara was not such a fool that he would accept Kṛṣṇa as an ordinary man and at the same time offer Him all devotional obeisances, knowing Him as the son of Devakī and Vasudeva. According to the *Bhagavad-gītā,* only by knowing the transcendental birth and activities of Kṛṣṇa can one attain liberation by acquiring a spiritual form like Kṛṣṇa's. There are five different kinds of liberation. One who merges into the spiritual aura of Kṛṣṇa, known as the impersonal Brahman effulgence, does not fully develop his spiritual body. But one who fully develops his spiritual existence becomes an associate of Nārāyaṇa or Kṛṣṇa in different spiritual abodes. One who enters into the abode of Nārāyaṇa develops a spiritual form exactly like Nārāyaṇa's (four-handed), and one who enters into the highest spiritual abode of Kṛṣṇa, known as Goloka Vṛndāvana, develops a spiritual form of two hands like Kṛṣṇa's. Śaṅkara, as an incarnation of Lord Śiva, knows all these spiritual existences, but he did not disclose them to his then Buddhist followers because it was impossible for them to know about the spiritual world. Lord Buddha preached that the void is the ultimate goal, so how could his followers understand spiritual variegatedness? Therefore Śaṅkara said, *brahma satyaṁ jagan mithyā,* or, material variegatedness is false but spiritual variegatedness is fact. In the *Padma Purāṇa* Lord Śiva has admitted that he had to preach the philosophy of *māyā,* or illusion, in the Kali-yuga as another edition of the "void" philosophy of Buddha. He had to do this by the order of the Lord for specific reasons. He disclosed his real mind, however, by recommending that people worship Kṛṣṇa, for no one can be saved simply by mental speculations composed of word jugglery and grammatical maneuvers. Śaṅkara further instructs:

bhaja govindaṁ bhaja govindaṁ
bhaja govindaṁ mūḍha-mate
samprāpte sannihite kāle
na hi na hi rakṣati ḍukṛñ-karaṇe

"You intellectual fools, just worship Govinda, just worship Govinda, just worship Govinda. Your grammatical knowledge and word jugglery will not save you at the time of death."

— 6 —

Of that terrifying river
Of the Battlefield of Kurukṣetra,
Over which the Pāṇḍavas victoriously crossed,
Bhīṣma and Droṇa were as the high banks,
Jayadratha as the river's water,
The King of Gāndhāra the blue water-lily,
Śalya the shark, Kṛpa the current,
Karṇa the mighty waves,
Aśvatthāmā and Vikarṇa the dread alligators,
And Duryodhana the very whirlpool—
But Thou, O Kṛṣṇa, wast the ferryman!

— 7 —

May the spotless lotus of the *Mahābhārata*,
Which grows on the waters
Of the words of Vyāsa
And of which the *Bhagavad-gītā*
Is the irresistibly sweet fragrance
And its tales of heroes
The full-blown petals
Fully opened by the talk of Lord Hari,
Who destroys the sins
Of Kali-yuga,
And on which daily light
The nectar-seeking souls,

Like so many bees
Swarming joyously—
May this lotus of the *Mahābhārata*
Bestow on us the highest good.

— 8 —

Salutations to Lord Kṛṣṇa,
The embodiment of supreme bliss,
By whose grace and compassion
The dumb become eloquent
And the lame scale mountains—
Him I salute!

PURPORT

Foolish followers of foolish speculators cannot understand the meaning of offering salutations to Lord Kṛṣṇa, the embodiment of bliss. Śaṅkara himself offered his salutations to Lord Kṛṣṇa so that some of his intelligent followers might understand the real fact by the example set by their great master, Śaṅkara, the incarnation of Lord Śiva. But there are many obstinate followers of Śaṅkara who refuse to offer their salutations to Lord Kṛṣṇa and instead mislead innocent persons by injecting materialism into the *Bhagavad-gītā* and confusing innocent readers by their commentaries, and consequently the readers never have the opportunity to become blessed by offering salutations to Lord Kṛṣṇa, the cause of all causes. The greatest disservice to humanity is to keep mankind in darkness about the science of Kṛṣṇa, or Kṛṣṇa consciousness, by distorting the sense of the *Gītā*.

— 9 —

Salutations to that supreme shining one,
Whom the creator Brahmā, Varuṇa,
Indra, Rudra, Marut, and all divine beings
Praise with hymns,
Whose glories are sung
By the verses of the *Vedas*,
Of whom the singers of *Sāma* sing

And of whose glories the *Upaniṣads*
Proclaim in full choir,
Whom the yogīs see
With their minds absorbed
In perfect meditation,
And of whom all the hosts
Of gods and demons
Know not the limitations.
To Him, the Supreme God, Kṛṣṇa, be all salutations—
Him we salute! Him we salute! Him we salute!

PURPORT

By recitation of the ninth verse of his meditation, quoted from the *Śrīmad-Bhāgavatam* [12.13.1], Śaṅkara has indicated that Lord Kṛṣṇa is wor-shipable by one and all, including himself. He gives hints to materialists, impersonalists, mental speculators, "void" philosophers, and all other candidates subjected to the punishment of material miseries—just offer salutations to Lord Kṛṣṇa, who is worshiped by Brahmā, Śiva, Varuṇa, Indra, and all other demigods. He has not mentioned, however, the name of Viṣṇu, because Viṣṇu is identical with Kṛṣṇa. The *Vedas* and the *Upaniṣads* are meant for understanding the process by which one can surrender unto Kṛṣṇa. The yogīs try to see Him (Kṛṣṇa) within themselves by meditation. In other words, it is for all the demigods and demons who do not know where the ultimate end is that Śaṅkara teaches, and he especially instructs the demons and the fools to offer salutations to Kṛṣṇa and His words, the *Bhagavad-gītā*, by following in his footsteps. Only by such acts will the demons be benefited, not by misleading their innocent followers by so-called mental speculations or show-bottle meditations. Śaṅkara directly offers salutations to Kṛṣṇa, as if to show the fools, who are searching after light, that *here is light like the sun*. But the fallen demons are like owls that will not open their eyes on account of their fear of the sunlight itself. These owls will never open their eyes to see the sublime light of Kṛṣṇa and His words, the *Bhagavad-gītā*. They will, however, comment on the *Gītā* with their closed owl-eyes to mislead their unfortunate readers and followers. Śaṅkara, however, discloses the light to his less intelligent followers and shows that the *Bhagavad-gītā* and Kṛṣṇa are the only source of light. This is all to teach the sincere seekers of truth to offer salutation to Lord Kṛṣṇa and thus surrender unto Him without misgivings. That is the highest perfection of life, and that is the highest teaching of Śaṅkara, the great learned scholar whose teachings drove the voidist philosophy of Buddha out of India, the land of knowledge.

Oṁ tat sat.

THE SCRIPTURAL BASIS OF KṚṢṆA CONSCIOUSNESS

After reading an article on the Kṛṣṇa consciousness movement in the Los Angeles Times *(January 11, 1970) Śrīla Prabhupāda begins an unusual correspondence with Dr. J. F. Staal, Professor of Philosophy and of South Asian Languages at the University of California, Berkeley.*

Excerpt from the Los Angeles Times Article

Dr. J. F. Staal, Professor of Philosophy and Near Eastern [sic] Languages at UC Berkeley and an instructor in Indian philosophy, believes that the Krishna sect is an authentic Indian religion and that its adherents are sincere. He attributes the Society's rapid increase in members to the tendency of today's younger generation to reject organized churchgoing while at the same time searching for fulfillment of a belief in mysticism.

He points out, however, that persons who turn away from Christianity, Muhammadanism, and Judaism have usually lost faith with the personal god of those religions and are looking for a mystical religion without absolutes.

"These people in the Krishna movement have turned to Hinduism, but, curiously, it is a cult that is highly personalistic," Staal said. "They accept a personal god, Krishna, and Christianity has that. I feel that they have transferred some of their Christian background to a Hindu sect."

He also feels that they spend too much time chanting to develop a philosophy. On these grounds he and others on the faculty turned down the request to grant credit for an experimental course in Krishna consciousness that will be taught during the winter quarter by Hans Kary, president of the sect's Berkeley temple.

Śrīla Prabhupāda's Letter to the Los Angeles Times

January 14, 1970

Editor
Los Angeles Times

Dear Sir:

With reference to your article in the *Los Angeles Times* dated Sunday, January 11, 1970, under the heading "Kṛṣṇa Chant," I beg to point out that the Hindu religion is perfectly based on the personal conception of God, or Viṣṇu. The impersonal conception of God is a side issue, or one of the three features of God. The Absolute Truth is ultimately the Supreme Personality of Godhead, the Paramātmā conception is the localized aspect of His omnipresence, and the impersonal conception is the aspect of His greatness and eternity. But all these combined together make the Complete Whole.

Dr. J. F. Staal's statement that the Kṛṣṇa cult is a combination of Christian and Hindu religion, as if something manufactured by concoction, is not correct. If Christian, Muhammadan, or Buddhist religions are personal, that is quite welcome. But the Kṛṣṇa religion has been personal from a time long, long ago when Christian, Muhammadan, and Buddhist religions had not yet come into existence. According to the Vedic conception, religion is basically made by the personal God as His laws. Religion cannot be manufactured by man or anyone except God superior to man. Religion is the law of God only.

Unfortunately, all the swamis who came before me in this country stressed the impersonal aspect of God, without sufficient knowledge of God's personal aspect. In the *Bhagavad-gītā*, therefore, it is said that only less intelligent persons consider that God is originally impersonal but assumes a form when He incarnates. The Kṛṣṇa philosophy, however, based on the authority of the *Vedas*, is that originally the Absolute Truth is the Supreme Personality of Godhead. His plenary expansion is present in everyone's heart in His localized aspect, and the impersonal Brahman effulgence is the transcendental light and heat distributed everywhere.

In the *Bhagavad-gītā* it is clearly said that the aim of the Vedic way of searching out the Absolute Truth is to find the personal God. One who is satisfied only with the other aspects of the Absolute Truth, namely the Paramātmā feature or the Brahman feature, is to be considered possessed of a poor fund of knowledge. Recently we have published our *Śrī Īśopaniṣad,* a Vedic literature, and in this small booklet we have thoroughly discussed this point.

As far as the Hindu religion is concerned, there are millions of Kṛṣṇa temples in India, and there is not a single Hindu who does not worship Kṛṣṇa. Therefore, this Kṛṣṇa consciousness movement is not a concocted idea. We invite all scholars, philosophers, religionists, and members of the general public to understand this movement by critical study. And if one does so seriously, one will understand the sublime position of this great movement.

The chanting process is also authorized. Professor Staal's feeling of disgust in the matter of constant chanting of the holy name of Kṛṣṇa is a definite proof of his lack of knowledge in this authorized movement of Kṛṣṇa consciousness. Instead of turning down the request to give Kary's course credit, he and all other learned professors of the University of California at Berkeley should patiently hear about the truth of this authorized movement so much needed at present in godless society. [Credit for the course was later established.] This is the only movement which can save the confused younger generation. I shall invite all responsible guardians of this country to understand this transcendental movement and then give us all honest facilities to spread it for everyone's benefit.

A.C. Bhaktivedanta Swami
Spiritual Master of the Hare Kṛṣṇa Movement

The Exchange Between Śrīla Prabhupāda and Dr. Staal

January 23, 1970

Swami A.C. Bhaktivedanta

Dear Swamiji:

Thank you very much for sending me a copy of your letter to the *Los Angeles Times,* now also published in the *Daily Californian.* I think you will agree with me that apart from publicity, little is gained by discussing religious or philosophic issues through interviews and letters in the press; but allow me to make two brief observations.

First, I know that devotion to Kṛṣṇa is old (though definitely not as old as the *Vedas*) and has never been influenced by Christianity, Islam, or Judaism (I never referred to Buddhism in this connection). The differences between the personal and impersonal are relatively vague, but adopting this distinction for simplicity, I expressed surprise at seeing people who have grown up in a Western culture which stresses the personal take to an Indian cult which does the same. I am less surprised when people who are dissatisfied with Western monotheism take to an Indian philosophy which stresses an impersonal absolute.

Second, I never expressed nor felt disgust at the chanting of the name of Kṛṣṇa. I am not only not irritated at it (like some people), but I rather like it. But it is an indisputable fact that the *Bhagavad-gītā* (not to mention the *Vedas*) does not require such constant chanting. The *Gītā* deals with quite different subjects, which I treat at some length in my courses on the philosophies of India.

Thanking you,

Yours sincerely,
J. F. Staal
Professor of Philosophy
and of South Asian Languages

January 30, 1970

J. F. Staal
Professor of Philosophy and of South Asian Languages
University of California
Berkeley, California

My dear Professor Staal:

I thank you very much for your kind letter dated January 23, 1970. In the last paragraph of your letter you have mentioned that you are not irritated at the chanting of the Hare Kṛṣṇa mantra (like some people), but rather like it. This has given me much satisfaction, and I am sending herewith a copy of our magazine, *Back to Godhead*, issue number 28, in which you will find how the students [at a program at Ohio State University] liked this chanting of the Hare Kṛṣṇa mantra, although all of them were neophytes to this cult of chanting. Actually this chanting is very pleasing to the heart and is the best means of infusing spiritual consciousness, or Kṛṣṇa consciousness, into the hearts of people in general.

This is the easiest process of spiritual realization and is recommended in the *Vedas*. In the *Bṛhan-nāradīya Purāṇa* it is clearly stated that it is only chanting of the holy name of Hari [Kṛṣṇa] that can save people from the problems of materialistic existence, and there is no other alternative, no other alternative, no other alternative in this Age of Kali.

Western culture is monotheistic, but Westerners are being misled by impersonal Indian speculation. The young people of the West are frustrated because they are not diligently taught about monotheism. They are not satisfied with this process of teaching and understanding. The Kṛṣṇa consciousness movement is a boon to them, because they are being really trained to understand Western monotheism under the authoritative Vedic system. We do not simply theoretically discuss; rather, we learn by the prescribed method of Vedic regulations.

But I am surprised to see that in the last paragraph of your letter you say, "It is an indisputable fact that the *Bhagavad-gītā* (not to mention the *Vedas*) does not require such constant chanting." I think that you have missed the following verse in the *Bhagavad-gītā* (9.14), apart from many other similar verses:

satataṁ kīrtayanto māṁ   yatantaś ca dṛḍha-vratāḥ
namasyantaś ca māṁ bhaktyā   nitya-yuktā upāsate

The engagement of the great souls, freed from delusion and perfect in their realization of God, is described here: *satataṁ kīrtayanto māṁ*—they are always (*satataṁ*) chanting (*kīrtayantaḥ*) My glories and—*nitya-yuktā upāsate*—always worshiping Me (Kṛṣṇa).

So I do not know how you can say "indisputable." And, if you want references from the *Vedas*, I can give you many. In the *Vedas*, the chief transcendental vibration *oṁkāra* is also Kṛṣṇa. *Praṇava oṁkāra* is the divine substance of the *Vedas.* Following the *Vedas* means chanting the Vedic mantras, and no Vedic mantra is complete without *oṁkāra.* In the *Māṇḍūkya Upaniṣad, oṁkāra* is stated to be the most auspicious sound representation of the Supreme Lord. This is also confirmed again in the *Atharva Veda. Oṁkāra* is the sound representation of the Supreme Lord and is therefore the principal word in the *Vedas.* In this connection, the Supreme Lord, Kṛṣṇa, says, *praṇavaḥ sarva-vedeṣu:* "I am the syllable *oṁ* in all the Vedic *mantras.*" (Bg. 7.8)

Furthermore, in *Bhagavad-gītā,* Chapter Fifteen, verse 15, Kṛṣṇa says, "I am seated in everyone's heart. By all the *Vedas,* I am to be known; I am the compiler of *Vedānta,* and I know *Veda* as it is." The Supreme Lord, seated in everyone's heart, is described in both the *Muṇḍaka* and *Śvetāśvatara Upaniṣads: dvā suparṇā sayujā sakhāyā* . . . The Supreme Lord and the individual soul are sitting in the body like two friendly birds in a tree. One bird is eating the fruits of the tree, or reactions of material activities, and the other bird, the Supersoul, is witnessing.

The goal of Vedantic study, therefore, is to know the Supreme Lord, Kṛṣṇa. This point is stressed in the *Bhagavad-gītā,* Chapter Eight, verse 13, where it is stated that by the mystic yoga process, ultimately vibrating the sacred syllable *oṁ,* one attains to His supreme spiritual planet. In the *Vedānta-sūtras,* which you have certainly read, the Fourth Chapter, *adhikaraṇa* 4, *sūtra* 22, states positively, *anāvṛttiḥ śabdāt:* "By sound vibration one becomes liberated." By devotional service, by understanding well the Supreme Personality of Godhead, one can go to His abode and never come back again to this material condition. How is it possible? The answer is, simply by chanting His name constantly.

This is accepted by the exemplary disciple, Arjuna, who has perfectly learned the conclusion of spiritual science from the *yogeśvara,* the master of mystic knowledge, Kṛṣṇa. Recognizing Kṛṣṇa to be the Supreme Brahman, Arjuna addresses Him, *sthāne hṛṣīkeśa* . . . : "The world becomes joyful hearing Your name, and thus do all become attached to You." (Bg. 11.36) The process of chanting is herein authorized as the direct means of contacting the Supreme Absolute Truth, the Personality of Godhead. Simply by chanting the holy name Kṛṣṇa, the soul is attracted by the Supreme Person, Kṛṣṇa, to go home, back to Godhead.

In the *Nārada-pañcarātra* it is stated that all the Vedic rituals, mantras, and understanding are compressed into the eight words Hare Kṛṣṇa, Hare Kṛṣṇa, Kṛṣṇa Kṛṣṇa, Hare Hare. Similarly, in the *Kali-santaraṇa Upaniṣad* it is stated that these sixteen words, Hare Kṛṣṇa, Hare Kṛṣṇa, Kṛṣṇa Kṛṣṇa, Hare Hare/ Hare Rāma, Hare Rāma, Rāma Rāma, Hare Hare, are especially meant for counteracting the degrading and contaminating influence of this materialistic Age of Kali.

All these points are elaborately presented in my book *Teachings of Lord Caitanya*.

The process of chanting is, therefore, not only the sublime method for practical perfection of life but the authorized Vedic principle inaugurated by the greatest Vedic scholar and devotee, Lord Caitanya (whom we consider an incarnation of Kṛṣṇa). We are simply following in His authorized footsteps.

The scope of the Kṛṣṇa consciousness movement is universal. The process for regaining one's original spiritual status of eternal life, full with bliss and knowledge, is not abstract, dry theorizing. Spiritual life is not described in the *Vedas* as theoretical, dry, or impersonal. The *Vedas* aim at the inculcation of pure love of God only, and this harmonious conclusion is practically realized by the Kṛṣṇa consciousness movement, or by chanting the Hare Kṛṣṇa mantra.

As the goal of spiritual realization is only one, love of God, so the *Vedas* stand as a single comprehensive whole in the matter of transcendental understanding. Only the incomplete views of various parties apart from the bona fide Vedic lines of teaching give a rapturous appearance to the *Bhagavad-gītā*. The reconciliative factor adjusting all apparently diverse propositions of the *Vedas* is the essence of the *Veda*, or Kṛṣṇa consciousness (love of God).

Thanking you once again,

Yours sincerely,
A.C. Bhaktivedanta Swami

February 8, 1970

Swami A.C. Bhaktivedanta

Dear Swamiji:

Thank you very much for your kindness in sending me your long and interesting letter of January 30, together with the last issue of *Back to Godhead.* So far I have had a few discussions with members of your society here, but they were not entirely satisfactory from my point of view. But now I have your much more authoritative letter, whereby the discussion moves to a higher level.

And yet, I am afraid, you have not convinced me that all the scriptures you quote prescribe only chanting of the name of Kṛṣṇa. Let me refer only to the most important ones.

In the *Bhagavad-gītā* (9.14), *kīrtayantaḥ* need not mean chanting of the name of Kṛṣṇa. It may mean glorifying, chanting, reciting, talking, and refer to songs, hymns, descriptions, or conversations. The commentators take it that way. Śaṅkara in his commentary merely repeats the word, but Ānandagiri in his *vyākhyā* classes *kīrtana* as *vedānta-śravaṇaṁ praṇava-japaś ca,* "listening to the *Vedānta* and muttering *oṁ*" (that the Vedic *oṁ* is Kṛṣṇa is said in the *Bhagavad-gītā,* where Kṛṣṇa is also identified with many other things, and which is *smṛti,* but not in the *Vedas,* which are *śruti*). Another commentator, Hanumān, in his *Paiśāca-bhāṣya,* says that *kīrtayantaḥ* merely means *bhāṣamānaḥ*—"talking [about]."

More important, I think, than the precise meaning of this word, is that the entire verse does not require that everyone always engage in *kīrtana,* but merely states that some great souls do so. This is obvious from the next verse, which states that *anye,* "others," engage in *jñāna: yajñena . . . yajanto mām,* "worshiping me . . . with the worship of knowledge." The *Bhagavad-gītā* is broad-minded and tolerant of a variety of religious approaches, although it also stresses one aspect above all others (i.e., *sarva-phala-tyāga*).*

Finally, in the last *sūtra* of the *Vedānta-sūtra, anāvṛttiḥ śabdāt . . . , śabda* refers to the scripture or to the revelation of the *Vedas,* as is clear from the context and from the commentators. Śaṅkara quotes a number of texts (ending with *ity ādi-śabdebhyaḥ,* "according to these *śabdas*") to support this, i.e., to support the statement that "according to the scripture there is no return." He also refers to *śabda* in this *sūtra* by saying *mantrārtha-vādādi . . . ,* "mantras, descriptions, etc." Vācaspati Miśra in the *Bhāmati* supports this and clarifies it further by adding that a contrary view is *śruti-smṛti-*

**Sarva-phala-tyāga* means "renunciation of all the fruits of one's work."

virodhaḥ, "in conflict with the *smṛti* and the *śruti*."

Thanking you once again for your kind attention.

Yours very sincerely,
J. F. Staal

February 15, 1970

J. F. Staal
Professor of Philosophy
and of South Asian Languages

My dear Dr. Staal:

I am very glad to receive your letter dated Sunday, February 8, 1970. I am very much pleased also to note the contents.

Regarding convincing you that all scriptures prescribe chanting of the name of Kṛṣṇa, I can simply present the authority of Lord Caitanya. Lord Caitanya recommended, *kīrtanīyaḥ sadā hariḥ* ["Hari, Kṛṣṇa, is constantly to be praised" (*Śikṣāṣṭaka* 3)]. Similarly, Madhvācārya quotes, *vede rāmāyaṇe caiva hariḥ sarvatra gīyate* ["Hari is sung about everywhere in the *Vedas* and *Rāmāyaṇa*"]. Similarly, in the *Bhagavad-gītā* (15.15) the Lord says, *vedaiś ca sarvair aham eva vedyaḥ* ["By all the *Vedas,* I am to be known"].

In this way we find all the scriptures aiming at the Supreme Person. In the *Ṛg Veda* (1.22.20) the mantra is *oṁ tad viṣṇoḥ paramaṁ padaṁ sadā paśyanti sūrayaḥ* ["The demigods are always looking to that supreme abode of Viṣṇu"]. The whole Vedic process, therefore, is to understand Lord Viṣṇu, and any scripture is directly or indirectly chanting the glories of the Supreme Lord, Viṣṇu.

Regarding the *Bhagavad-gītā,* verse 9.14, *kīrtayantaḥ* certainly means glorifying, chanting, reciting, and talking, as you have said; but glorifying, chanting, or reciting about whom? It is certainly Kṛṣṇa. The word used in this connection is *mām* ["Me"]. Therefore, we do not disagree when a person glorifies Kṛṣṇa, as Śukadeva did in the *Śrīmad-Bhāgavatam.* This is also *kīrtana.* The highest among all Vedic literatures is the proper place for such glorification of the Supreme Lord, Kṛṣṇa, and this is to be well understood from the verse:

nigama-kalpa-taror galitaṁ phalaṁ
śuka-mukhād amṛta-drava-saṁyutam
pibata bhāgavataṁ rasam ālayaṁ
muhur aho rasikā bhuvi bhāvukāḥ

"O expert and thoughtful men, relish *Śrīmad-Bhāgavatam,* the mature fruit of the desire tree of Vedic literatures. It emanated from the lips of Śrī Śukadeva Gosvāmī. Therefore this fruit has become even more tasteful, although its nectarean juice was already relishable for all, including liberated souls." (*Śrīmad-Bhāgavatam* 1.1.3)

It is said that Mahārāja Parīkṣit attained salvation simply by hearing, and similarly Śukadeva Gosvāmī attained salvation simply by chanting. In our devotional service there are nine different methods for achieving the same goal, love of Godhead, and the first process is hearing. This hearing process is called *śruti.* The next process is chanting. The chanting process is *smṛti.* We accept both *śruti* and *smṛti* simultaneously. We consider *śruti* the mother and *smṛti* the sister, because a child hears from the mother and then again learns from the sister by description.

Śruti and *smṛti* are two parallel lines. Śrīla Rūpa Gosvāmī therefore says:

śruti-smṛti-purāṇādi- pañcarātra-vidhiṁ vinā
aikāntikī harer bhaktir utpātāyaiva kalpate
[*Bhakti-rasāmṛta-sindhu* 1.2.101]

That is, without references to *śruti, smṛti, Purāṇas,* and *Pañcarātras,* un-adulterated devotional service is never achieved. Therefore, anyone who shows a devotional ecstasy without reference to the *śāstras* [Vedic scriptures] simply creates disturbances. On the other hand, if we simply stick to the *śrutis,* then we become *veda-vāda-ratāḥ,** who are not very much appreciated in the *Bhagavad-gītā.*

Therefore *Bhagavad-gītā,* although *smṛti,* is the essence of all Vedic scripture, *sarvopaniṣado gāvaḥ.*† It is just like a cow which is delivering the milk, or the essence of all the *Vedas* and *Upaniṣads,* and all the *ācāryas,* including Śaṅkarācārya, accept the *Bhagavad-*

* (*Bhagavad-gītā* 2.42) Engaged in merely mouthing the words of the scriptures, but not understanding or practicing them.

† See the fourth of Śaṅkarācārya's meditations (p. 79 of this book).

gītā as such. Therefore you cannot deny the authority of the *Bhagavad-gītā* because it is *smṛti;* that view is *śruti-smṛti-virodhaḥ,* "in conflict with the *smṛti* and the *śruti,*" as you have correctly said.

Regarding Ānandagiri's quotation that *kīrtana* means *vedānta-śravaṇaṁ praṇava japaś ca* ["listening to the *Vedānta* and muttering *oṁ*"], the knower of *Vedānta* is Kṛṣṇa, and He is the compiler of *Vedānta.* He is *veda-vit* and *vedānta-kṛt.* So where is there a greater opportunity for *vedānta-śravaṇa* than to hear it from Kṛṣṇa?

Regarding the next verse, in which it is mentioned that *jñāna-yajñena . . . yajanto mām,* the object of worship is Kṛṣṇa, as indicated by *mām* ["Me"]. The process is described in the *Īśopaniṣad,* mantra 11:

vidyāṁ cāvidyāṁ ca yas tad vedobhayaṁ saha
avidyayā mṛtyuṁ tīrtvā vidyayāmṛtam aśnute

"Only one who can learn the process of nescience and that of transcendental knowledge side by side can transcend the influence of repeated birth and death and enjoy the full blessings of immortality."

The culture of *vidyā,* or transcendental knowledge, is essential for the human being; otherwise the culture of *avidyā,* or nescience, binds him to conditional existence on the material platform. Materialistic existence means the pursuit or culture of sense gratification, and this kind of knowledge of sense gratification (*avidyā*) means advancement of repeated birth and death. Those who are absorbed in such knowledge cannot learn any lesson from the laws of nature, and they do the same things over repeatedly, being enamored of the beauty of illusory things. *Vidyā,* or factual knowledge, on the other hand, means to know thoroughly the process of nescient activities while at the same time culturing transcendental science and thereby undeviatingly following the path of liberation.

Liberation is the enjoyment of the full blessings of immortality. This immortality is enjoyed in the eternal kingdom of God (*sambhūty-amṛtam aśnute*), the region of the Supreme Personality of Godhead, and is the result obtained by worshiping the Supreme Lord, the cause of all causes, *sambhavāt.* So in this way real knowledge, *vidyā,* means to worship the Supreme Personality of Godhead, Kṛṣṇa; that is *jñāna-yajñena,* the worship of knowledge.

This *jñāna-yajñena . . . yajanto mām* is the perfection of knowledge, as stated in the *Bhagavad-gītā* (7.19):

bahūnāṁ janmanām ante jñānavān māṁ prapadyate
vāsudevaḥ sarvam iti sa mahātmā sudurlabhaḥ

"After many births and deaths, he who is actually in knowledge surrenders unto Me [Kṛṣṇa], knowing Me to be the cause of all causes, and all that is. Such a great soul is very rare."

If one has not yet come to this conclusion of knowledge and simply indulges in dry speculation without Kṛṣṇa, then his hard speculative labor is something like beating empty husks of grain. The unhulled rice and the empty husks of rice look very much the same. One who knows how to get the grain out of the unhulled rice is wise, but one who beats on the empty husk, thinking to get some result, is simply wasting his labor uselessly. Similarly, if one studies the *Vedas* without finding the goal of the *Vedas*, Kṛṣṇa, he simply wastes his valuable time.

So to cultivate knowledge for worshiping Kṛṣṇa culminates after many, many births and deaths when one actually becomes wise. When one becomes wise in this way, he surrenders to Kṛṣṇa, recognizing Him at last to be the cause of all causes and all that is. That sort of great soul is very rare. So those who have surrendered to Kṛṣṇa life and soul are rare *sudurlabha mahātmās*. They are not ordinary *mahātmās*.

By the grace of Lord Caitanya that highest perfectional status of life is being distributed very freely. The effect is also very encouraging; otherwise, how are boys and girls without any background of Vedic culture quickly occupying the posts of rare *mahātmās* simply by vibrating this transcendental sound, Hare Kṛṣṇa? And simply on the basis of this chanting, the majority of them (those who are very sincere) are steady in devotional service and are not falling down to the four principles of material sinful life, namely (1) meat-eating, (2) illicit sexual connection, (3) taking of intoxicants, including coffee, tea, and tobacco, and (4) gambling. And that is the last *sūtra* of the *Vedānta-sūtra*, i.e., *anāvṛttiḥ śabdāt* ["By sound vibration one becomes liberated"].

One has to learn by the result (*phalena parichīyate*). Our students are ordered to act like this, and they are not falling down. That they are remaining on the platform of pure spiritual life without hankering to culture the above principles of *avidyā*, or sense gratification, is the test of their proper understanding of the *Vedas*. They do not come back to the material platform, because they are relishing the nectarean fruit of love of God.

Sarva-phala-tyāga ["renunciation of all the fruits of one's work"] is explained in the *Bhagavad-gītā* by the Lord Himself in the words *sarva-dharmān parityajya mām ekaṁ śaraṇaṁ vraja:* "Give up everything and simply surrender unto Me [Kṛṣṇa]." The Hare Kṛṣṇa mantra means "O Supreme Energy of Kṛṣṇa and O Lord Kṛṣṇa, please engage me in Your eternal service." So we have given up everything and are simply engaged in the service of the Lord. What Kṛṣṇa orders us to do is our only engagement. We have given up all resultant actions of *karma, jñāna,* and *yoga;* and that is the stage of pure devotional service, *bhaktir uttamā.*

Yours sincerely,
A.C. Bhaktivedanta Swami

February 25, 1970

Swami A.C. Bhaktivedanta
Founder-*Ācārya*
International Society for Krishna Consciousness

Dear Swamiji:

Thank you very much for your very interesting letter of February 15, 1970, with enclosure.

I am afraid that whenever you quote a passage purporting to show that only the chanting of the name Kṛṣṇa is required, I can quote another one which requires something else, adding, *yadi śloko 'pi pramāṇam, ayam api ślokaḥ pramāṇaṁ bhavitum arhati:* "If mere verses are authoritative, this verse also ought to be regarded as authoritative." And there may be no end to this in the foreseeable future, as Patañjali also says, *mahān hi śabdasya prayoga-viṣayaḥ:* "For vast is the domain for the use of words."

Yours very sincerely,
J. F. Staal

3764 Watseka Avenue
Los Angeles, California 90034

April 24, 1970

Dear Dr. Staal:

I beg to thank you very much for your kind letter dated February 25, 1970. I am sorry that I could not reply to your letter earlier because I was a little busy in the matter of purchasing a new church estate at the above address. We have secured a very nice place for a separate temple, lecture room, my quarters, and the devotees' residential quarters, all together in a nice place with all the modern amenities.

I beg to request you to visit this place at your convenience, and if you kindly let me know a day before, my students will be very glad to receive you properly.

Regarding our correspondence, actually this quotation and counter-quotation cannot solve the problem. In a court both the learned lawyers quote from law books, but that is not the solution to the case. The determination of the case is the judgment of the presiding judge. So argument cannot bring us to a conclusion.

The scriptural quotations are sometimes contradictory, and every philosopher has a different opinion, because without putting forward a different thesis, no one can become a famous philosopher. It is therefore difficult to arrive at the right conclusion. The conclusion is, as above mentioned, to accept the judgment of authority. We follow the authority of Lord Caitanya Mahāprabhu, who is nondifferent from Kṛṣṇa, and His version according to Vedic scripture is that in this age this chanting is the only solution for all problems of life. And that is actually being shown by practical experience.

Recently there was a big procession of our students in Berkeley on the Advent Day of Lord Caitanya, and the public has remarked as follows: "This crowd of men is not like others, who assemble to break windows and create havoc." This is also confirmed by the police in the following words: "Members of the Kṛṣṇa consciousness movement cooperated fully with the police, and their efforts to maintain peaceful order throughout the parade were so successful that only minimal police involvement was required."

Similarly, in Detroit there was a big peace march, and our men were appreciated as "angels" in the crowd. So this Kṛṣṇa consciousness movement is actually needed at the present moment as the panacea for all kinds of problems in human society.

Other quotations will not act very appreciably at this time. In a drugstore there may be many medicines, and all may be genuine, but what is required is that an experienced physician prescribe medicine for a particular patient. We cannot say in this case, "This is also medicine, and this is also medicine." No. The medicine which is effective for a particular person is the medicine for him—*phalena paricīyate.*

Yours very sincerely,
A.C. Bhaktivedanta Swami

Final Note by Śrīla Prabhupāda

In a court of justice two lawyers put forward their respective relevant arguments taken from the authorized law books to decide a point, but it is up to the judge to decide the case in favor of one of the litigants. When the opposing lawyers put forward their arguments, both of them are legal and bona fide, but the judgment is given as to which argument is applicable to the particular case.

Lord Caitanya gives His judgment on the authority of *śāstras* that the chanting of the holy names of the Lord is the only means to elevate one to the transcendental platform, and actually we can see it is effective. Each and every one of our students who has seriously taken to this process may be examined individually, and any impartial judge will find it easy to see that they have advanced in their transcendental realization further than any philosophers, religionists, *yogīs, karmīs,* etc.

We have to accept everything favorable to the circumstances. Rejection of other methods in a particular circumstance does not mean that the rejected ones are not bona fide. But for the time being, taking into consideration the age, time, and object, methods are sometimes rejected even though bona fide. We have to test everything by its practical result. By such a test, in this age the constant chanting of the Hare Kṛṣṇa *mahā-mantra* undoubtedly proves very effective.

A. C. Bhaktivedanta Swami

KṚṢṆA CONSCIOUSNESS: HINDU CULT OR DIVINE CULTURE?

"Sometimes Indians both inside and outside of India think that we are preaching the Hindu religion, but actually we are not. . . . People should not think that we are preaching a sectarian religion. No. We are simply preaching how to love God. . . . We are giving a spiritual culture that can solve all the problems of life, and therefore it is being accepted all over the world."

There is a misconception that the Kṛṣṇa consciousness movement represents the Hindu religion. In fact, however, Kṛṣṇa consciousness is in no way a faith or religion that seeks to defeat other faiths or religions. Rather, it is an essential cultural movement for the entire human society and does not consider any particular sectarian faith. This cultural movement is especially meant to educate people in how they can love God.

Sometimes Indians both inside and outside of India think that we are preaching the Hindu religion, but actually we are not. One will not find the word *Hindu* in the *Bhagavad-gītā*. Indeed, there is no such word as *Hindu* in the entire Vedic literature. This word has been introduced by the Muslims from provinces next to India, such as Afghanistan, Baluchistan, and Persia. There is a river called Sindhu bordering the northwestern provinces of India, and since the Muslims there could not pronounce Sindhu properly, they instead called the river Hindu, and the inhabitants of this tract of land they called Hindus. In India, according to the Vedic language, the Europeans are called *mlecchas* or *yavanas*. Similarly, Hindu is a name given by the Muslims.

India's actual culture is described in the *Bhagavad-gītā,* where it is stated that according to the different qualities or modes of nature there are different types of men, who are generally classified into four social orders and four spiritual orders. This system of social and spiritual division is known as *varṇāśrama-dharma*. The four *varṇas*, or social orders, are *brāhmaṇa, kṣatriya, vaiśya,* and *śūdra*. The four *āśramas,* or spiritual orders, are *brahmacarya, gṛhastha, vānaprastha,* and *sannyāsa*. The *varṇāśrama* system is described in the Vedic scriptures known as the *Purāṇas*. The goal of this institution of Vedic culture is to educate every man for advancement in knowledge of Kṛṣṇa, or God. That is the entire Vedic program.

When Lord Caitanya talked with the great devotee Rāmānanda Rāya, the Lord asked him, "What is the basic principle of human life?" Rāmānanda Rāya answered that human civilization begins when *varṇāśrama-dharma* is accepted. Before coming to the standard of *varṇāśrama-dharma* there is no question of human civilization. Therefore, the Kṛṣṇa consciousness movement is trying to establish this right system of human civilization, which is known as Kṛṣṇa consciousness, or *daiva-varṇāśrama*—divine culture.

In India, the *varṇāśrama* system has now been taken in a perverted way, and thus a man born in the family of a *brāhmaṇa* (the highest social order) claims that he should be accepted as a *brāhmaṇa*. But this claim is not accepted by the *śāstra* (scripture). One's forefather may have been a *brāhmaṇa* according to *gotra,* or the family hereditary order, but real *varṇāśrama-dharma* is based on the factual *quality* one has attained, regardless of birth or heredity. Therefore, we are not preaching the present-day system of the Hindus, especially those who are under the influence of Śaṅkarācārya, for Śaṅkarācārya taught that the Absolute Truth is impersonal, and thus he indirectly denied the existence of God.

Śaṅkarācārya's mission was special; he appeared in order to reestablish the Vedic influence after the influence of Buddhism. Because Buddhism was patronized by Emperor Aśoka, twenty-six hundred years ago the Buddhist religion practically pervaded all of India. According to the Vedic literature, Buddha was an incarnation of Kṛṣṇa who had a special power and who appeared for a special purpose. His system of thought, or faith, was accepted widely, but Buddha rejected the authority of the *Vedas*. While Buddhism was spreading, the Vedic culture was stopped both in India and in other places. Therefore, since Śaṅkarācārya's only aim was to drive away Buddha's system of philosophy, he introduced a system called Māyāvāda.

Strictly speaking, Māyāvāda philosophy is atheism, for it is a process in which one *imagines* that there is God. This Māyāvāda system of philosophy has been existing since time immemorial. The present Indian system of religion or culture is based on the Māyāvāda philosophy of Śaṅkarācārya, which is a compromise with Buddhist philosophy. According to Māyāvāda philosophy there actually is no God, or if God exists, He is impersonal and all-pervading and can therefore be imagined in any form. This conclusion is not in accord with the Vedic literature. That literature names many demigods, who are worshiped for different purposes, but in every case the Supreme Lord, the Personality of Godhead, Viṣṇu, is accepted as the supreme controller. That is real Vedic culture.

The philosophy of Kṛṣṇa consciousness does not deny the existence of God and the demigods, but Māyāvāda philosophy denies both; it maintains that neither the demigods nor God exist. For the Māyāvādīs, ultimately all is zero. They say that one may imagine any authority—whether Viṣṇu, Durgā, Lord Śiva, or the sun-god—because these are the demigods generally worshiped in society. But the Māyāvāda philosophy does not in fact accept the existence of any of them. The Māyāvādīs say that because one cannot concentrate one's mind on the impersonal Brahman, one may imagine any of these forms. This is a new system, called *pañcopāsanā*. It was introduced by Śaṅkarācārya, but the *Bhagavad-gītā* does not teach any such doctrines, and therefore they are not authoritative.

The *Bhagavad-gītā* accepts the existence of the demigods. The demigods are described in the *Vedas,* and one cannot deny their existence, but they are not to be understood or worshiped according to the way of Śaṅkarācārya. The worship of demigods is rejected in the *Bhagavad-gītā*. The *Gītā* [7.20] clearly states:

kāmais tais tair hṛta jñānāḥ prapadyante 'nya-devatāḥ
taṁ taṁ niyamam āsthāya prakṛtyā niyatāḥ svayā

"Those whose intelligence has been stolen by material desires surrender unto demigods and follow the particular rules and regulations of worship according to their own natures." Furthermore, in *Bhagavad-gītā* 2.44 Lord Kṛṣṇa states:

bhogaiśvarya-prasaktānāṁ tayāpahṛta-cetasām
vyavasāyātmikā buddhiḥ samādhau na vidhīyate

"In the minds of those who are too attached to sense enjoyment and material opulence, and who are bewildered by such things, the resolute determination for devotional service does not take place." Those who are pursuing the various demigods have been described as *hṛta jñānāḥ*, which means "those who have lost their sense." That is further explained in *Bhagavad-gītā* 7.23:

antavat tu phalaṁ teṣāṁ tad bhavaty alpa-medhasām
devān deva-yajo yānti mad-bhaktā yānti mām api

"Men of small intelligence worship the demigods, and their fruits are limited and temporary. Those who worship the demigods go to the planets of the demigods, but My devotees reach My supreme abode." The rewards given by the demigods are temporary, because any material facility must act in connection with the temporary body. Whatever material facilities one gets, whether by modern scientific methods or by deriving benedictions from the demigods, will be finished with the body. But spiritual advancement will never be finished.

People should not think that we are preaching a sectarian religion. No. We are simply preaching how to love God. There are many theories about the existence of God. The atheist, for example, will never believe in God. Atheists like Professor Jacques Monod, who won the Nobel Prize, declare that everything is chance (a theory already put forward long ago by atheistic philosophers of India such as Cārvāka). Then other philosophies, such as the *karma-mīmāṁsā* philosophy, accept that if one goes on doing his work nicely and honestly, automatically the result will come, without need for one to refer to God. For evidence, the proponents of such theories cite the argument that if one is diseased with an infection and takes medicine to counteract it, the disease will be neutralized. But our argument in this connection is that even if one gives a man the best medicine, he still may die. The results are not always predictable. Therefore, there is a higher authority, *daiva-netreṇa,* a supreme director. Otherwise, how is it that the son of a rich and pious man becomes a hippie in the street or that a man who works very hard and becomes rich is told by his doctor, "Now you may not eat any food, but only barley water"?

The *karma-mīmāṁsā* theory holds that the world is going on

without the supreme direction of God. Such philosophies say that everything takes place by lust (*kāma-haitukam*). By lust a man becomes attracted to a woman, and by chance there is sex, and the woman becomes pregnant. There is actually no plan to make the woman pregnant, but by a natural sequence when a man and a woman unite, a result is produced. The atheistic theory, which is described in the Sixteenth Chapter of the *Bhagavad-gītā* as asuric, or demoniac, is that actually everything is going on in this way, because of chance and resulting from natural attraction. This demoniac theory supports the idea that if one wants to avoid children, he may use a contraceptive method.

Actually, however, there is a great plan for everything—the Vedic plan. The Vedic literature gives directions regarding how men and women should unite, how they should beget children, and what the purpose of sex life is. Kṛṣṇa says in the *Bhagavad-gītā* that sex life sanctioned by the Vedic order, or sex life under the direction of the Vedic rules and regulations, is bona fide and is acceptable to Him. But chance sex life is not acceptable. If by chance one is sexually attracted and there are children, they are called *varṇa-saṅkara,* unwanted population. That is the way of the lower animals; it is not acceptable for humans. For humans, there is a plan. We cannot accept the theory that there is no plan for human life or that everything is born of chance and material necessity.

Śaṅkarācārya's theory that there is no God and that one can go on with his work and imagine God in any form just to keep peace and tranquillity in society is also more or less based on this idea of chance and necessity. Our way, however, which is completely different, is based on authority. It is this divine *varṇāśrama-dharma* that Kṛṣṇa recommends, not the caste system as it is understood today. This modern caste system is now condemned in India also, and it should be condemned, for the classification of different types of men according to birth is not the Vedic or divine caste system.

There are many classes of men in society—some men are engineers, some are medical practitioners, some are chemists, tradesmen, businessmen, and so on. These varieties of classes are not to be determined by birth, however, but by quality. No such thing as the caste-by-birth system is sanctioned by the Vedic literature, nor do we accept it. We have nothing to do with the caste system, which is also at present being rejected by the public in India. Rather, we give everyone the chance to become a *brāhmaṇa* and thus attain the highest status of life.

Because at the present moment there is a scarcity of *brāhmaṇas* (spiritual guides) and *kṣatriyas* (administrative men), and because the entire world is being ruled by *śūdras*, or men of the manual laborer class, there are many discrepancies in society. It is to mitigate all these discrepancies that we have taken to this Kṛṣṇa consciousness movement. If the *brāhmaṇa* class is actually re-established, the other orders of social well-being will automatically follow, just as when the brain is perfectly in order, the other parts of the body, such as the arms, the belly, and the legs, all act very nicely.

The ultimate goal of this movement is to educate people in how to love God. Caitanya Mahāprabhu approves the conclusion that the highest per-fection of human life is to learn how to love God. The Kṛṣṇa consciousness movement has nothing to do with the Hindu religion or any system of religion. No Christian gentleman will be interested in changing his faith from Christian to Hindu. Similarly, no Hindu gentleman of culture will be ready to change to the Christian faith. Such changing is for men who have no particular social status. But everyone will be interested in understanding the philosophy and science of God and taking it seriously. One should clearly understand that the Kṛṣṇa consciousness movement is not preaching the so-called Hindu religion. We are giving a spiritual culture that can solve all the problems of life, and therefore it is being accepted all over the world.

IV.
UNDERSTANDING KṚṢṆA AND CHRIST

KṚṢṆA OR CHRIST—THE NAME IS THE SAME

In 1974, near ISKCON's center in Frankfurt am Main, West Germany, Śrīla Prabhupāda and several of his disciples take a morning walk with Father Emmanuel Jungclaussen, a Benedictine monk from Niederalteich Monastery. Noticing that Śrīla Prabhupāda is carrying meditation beads similar to the rosary, Father Emmanuel explains that he also chants a constant prayer: "Lord Jesus Christ, be merciful unto us." The following conversation ensues.

Śrīla Prabhupāda: What is the meaning of the word *Christ*?
Father Emmanuel: *Christ* comes from the Greek word *Christos*, meaning "the anointed one."
Śrīla Prabhupāda: *Christos* is the Greek version of the word *Kṛṣṇa*.
Father Emmanuel: This is very interesting.
Śrīla Prabhupāda: When an Indian person calls on Kṛṣṇa, he often says, "Kṛṣṭa." *Kṛṣṭa* is a Sanskrit word meaning "attraction." So when we address God as "Christ," "Kṛṣṭa," or "Kṛṣṇa," we indicate the same all-attractive Supreme Personality of Godhead. When Jesus said, "Our Father, who art in heaven, sanctified be Thy name," that name of God was "Kṛṣṭa" or "Kṛṣṇa." Do you agree?
Father Emmanuel: I think Jesus, as the son of God, has revealed to us the actual name of God: Christ. We can call God "Father," but if we want to address Him by His actual name, we have to say "Christ."
Śrīla Prabhupāda: Yes. "Christ" is another way of saying *Kṛṣṭa*, and "Kṛṣṭa" is another way of pronouncing *Kṛṣṇa*, the name of God. Jesus said that one should glorify the name of God, but yesterday I heard one theologian say that God has no name—that we can call Him only "Father." A son may call his father "Father," but the father also has a specific name. Similarly, "God" is the general name of the Supreme Personality of Godhead, whose specific name is Kṛṣṇa. Therefore whether you call God "Christ," "Kṛṣṭa," or

"Kṛṣṇa," ultimately you are addressing the same Supreme Personality of Godhead.

Father Emmanuel: Yes, if we speak of God's actual name, then we must say, "Christos." In our religion, we have the Trinity: the Father, Son, and the Holy Spirit. We believe we can know the name of God only by revelation from the Son of God. Jesus Christ revealed the name of the father, and therefore we take the name Christ as the revealed name of God.

Śrīla Prabhupāda: Actually, it doesn't matter—*Kṛṣṇa* or *Christ*—the name is the same. The main point is to follow the injunctions of the Vedic scriptures that recommend chanting the name of God in this age. The easiest way is to chant the *mahā-mantra:* Hare Kṛṣṇa, Hare Kṛṣṇa, Kṛṣṇa Kṛṣṇa, Hare Hare/ Hare Rāma, Hare Rāma, Rāma Rāma, Hare Hare. *Rāma* and *Kṛṣṇa* are names of God, and *Hare* is the energy of God. So when we chant the *mahā-mantra,* we address God together with His energy. This energy is of two kinds, the spiritual and the material. At present we are in the clutches of the material energy. Therefore we pray to Kṛṣṇa that He may kindly deliver us from the service of the material energy and accept us into the service of the spiritual energy. That is our whole philosophy. *Hare Kṛṣṇa* means, "O energy of God, O God [Kṛṣṇa], please engage me in Your service." It is our nature to render service. Somehow or other we have come to the service of material things, but when this service is transformed into the service of the spiritual energy, then our life is perfect. To practice *bhakti-yoga* [loving service to God] means to become free from designations like "Hindu," "Muslim," "Christian," this or that, and simply to serve God. We have created Christian, Hindu, and Muhammadan religions, but when we come to a religion without designations, in which we don't think we are Hindus or Christians or Muhammadans, then we can speak of pure religion, or *bhakti.*

Father Emmanuel: *Mukti*?

Śrīla Prabhupāda: No, *bhakti.* When we speak of *bhakti, mukti* [liberation from material miseries] is included. Without *bhakti* there is no *mukti,* but if we act on the platform of *bhakti,* then *mukti* is included. We learn this from the *Bhagavad-gītā* [14.26]:

māṁ ca yo 'vyabhicāreṇa bhakti-yogena sevate
sa guṇān samatītyaitān brahma-bhūyāya kalpate

"One who engages in full devotional service, who does not fall down under any circumstance, at once transcends the modes of material nature and thus comes to the level of Brahman."

Father Emmanuel: Is Brahman Kṛṣṇa?

Śrīla Prabhupāda: Kṛṣṇa is Parabrahman. Brahman is realized in three aspects: as impersonal Brahman, as localized Paramātmā, and as personal Brahman. Kṛṣṇa is personal, and He is the Supreme Brahman, for God is ultimately a person. In the *Śrīmad-Bhāgavatam* [1.2.11], this is confirmed:

vadanti tat tattva-vidas tattvaṁ yaj jñānam advayam
brahmeti paramātmeti bhagavān iti śabdyate

"Learned transcendentalists who know the Absolute Truth call this nondual substance Brahman, Paramātmā, or Bhagavān." The feature of the Supreme Personality is the ultimate realization of God. He has all six opulences in full: He is the strongest, the richest, the most beautiful, the most famous, the wisest, and the most renounced.

Father Emmanuel: Yes, I agree.

Śrīla Prabhupāda: Because God is absolute, His name, His form, and His qualities are also absolute, and they are nondifferent from Him. Therefore to chant God's holy name means to associate directly with Him. When one associates with God, one acquires godly qualities, and when one is completely purified, one becomes an associate of the Supreme Lord.

Father Emmanuel: But our understanding of the name of God is limited.

Śrīla Prabhupāda: Yes, we are limited, but God is unlimited. And because He is unlimited, or absolute, He has unlimited names, each of which *is* God. We can understand His names as much as our spiritual understanding is developed.

Father Emmanuel: May I ask a question? We Christians also preach love of God, and we try to realize love of God and render service to Him with all our heart and all our soul. Now, what is the difference between your movement and ours? Why do you send your disciples to the Western countries to preach love of God when the gospel of Jesus Christ is propounding the same message?

Śrīla Prabhupāda: The problem is that the Christians do not follow the commandments of God. Do you agree?

Father Emmanuel: Yes, to a large extent you're right.

Śrīla Prabhupāda: Then what is the meaning of the Christians' love for God? If you do not follow the orders of God, then where is your love? Therefore we have come to teach what it means to love God: if you love Him, you cannot be disobedient to His orders. And if you're disobedient, your love is not true.

All over the world, people love not God but their dogs. The Kṛṣṇa consciousness movement is therefore necessary to teach people how to revive their forgotten love for God. Not only the Christians, but also the Hindus, the Muhammadans, and all others are guilty. They have rubber-stamped themselves "Christian," "Hindu," or "Muhammadan," but they do not obey God. That is the problem.

Visitor: Can you say in what way the Christians are disobedient?

Śrīla Prabhupāda: Yes. The first point is that they violate the commandment "Thou shalt not kill" by maintaining slaughterhouses. Do you agree that this commandment is being violated?

Father Emmanuel: Personally, I agree.

Śrīla Prabhupāda: Good. So if the Christians want to love God, they must stop killing animals.

Father Emmanuel: But isn't the most important point—

Śrīla Prabhupāda: If you miss one point, there is a mistake in your calculation. Regardless of what you add or subtract after that, the mistake is already in the calculation, and everything that follows will also be faulty. We cannot simply accept that part of the scripture we like, and reject what we don't like, and still expect to get the result. For example, a hen lays eggs with its back part and eats with its beak. A farmer may consider, "The front part of the hen is very expensive because I have to feed it. Better to cut it off." But if the head is missing there will be no eggs anymore, because the body is dead. Similarly, if we reject the difficult part of the scriptures and obey the part we like, such an interpretation will not help us. We have to accept all the injunctions of the scripture as they are given, not only those that suit us. If you do not follow the first order, "Thou shalt not kill," then where is the question of love of God?

Visitor: Christians take this commandment to be applicable to human beings, not to animals.

Śrīla Prabhupāda: That would mean that Christ was not intelligent enough to use the right word: *murder.* There is *killing,* and there is *murder. Murder* refers to human beings. Do you think Jesus was not intelligent enough to use the right word—*murder*—instead of the word *killing? Killing* means any kind of killing, and especially animal killing. If Jesus had meant simply the killing of humans, he would have used the word *murder.*

Father Emmanuel: But in the Old Testament the commandment "Thou shalt not kill" *does* refer to murder. And when Jesus said, "Thou shalt not kill," he extended this commandment to mean that a human being should not only refrain from killing another human being, but should also treat him with love. He never spoke about man's relationship with other living entities, but only about his relationship with other human beings. When he said, "Thou shalt not kill," he also meant in the mental and emotional sense—that you should not insult anyone or hurt him, treat him badly, and so on.

Śrīla Prabhupāda: We are not concerned with this or that testament but only with the words used in the commandments. If you want to interpret these words, that is something else. We understand the direct meaning. "Thou shalt not kill" means, "The Christians should not kill." You may put forth interpretations in order to continue the present way of action, but we understand very clearly that there is no need for interpretation. Interpretation is necessary if things are not clear. But here the meaning is clear. "Thou shalt not kill" is a clear instruction. Why should we interpret it?

Father Emmanuel: Isn't the eating of plants also killing?

Śrīla Prabhupāda: The Vaiṣṇava philosophy teaches that we should not even kill plants unnecessarily. In the *Bhagavad-gītā* [9.26] Kṛṣṇa says:

patraṁ puṣpaṁ phalaṁ toyaṁ yo me bhaktyā prayacchati
tad ahaṁ bhakty-upahṛtam aśnāmi prayatātmanaḥ

"If someone offers Me with love and devotion a leaf, a flower, a fruit, or a little water, I will accept it." We offer Kṛṣṇa only the kind of food He demands, and then we eat the remnants. If offering vegetarian food to Kṛṣṇa were sinful, then it would be Kṛṣṇa's sin, not ours. But God is *apāpa-viddha*—sinful reactions are not applicable to Him. He is like the sun, which is so powerful that it can purify even urine—something impossible for us to do. Kṛṣṇa is also like a king, who may order a murderer to be hanged but who himself is beyond punishment because he is very powerful. Eating food first offered to the Lord is also something like a soldier's killing during wartime. In a war, when the commander orders a man to attack, the obedient soldier who kills the enemy will get a medal. But if the same soldier kills someone on his own, he will be punished. Similarly, when we eat only *prasāda* [the remnants of food offered to Kṛṣṇa], we do not commit any sin. This is confirmed in the *Bhagavad-gītā* [3.13]:

yajña-śiṣṭāśinaḥ santo mucyante sarva-kilbiṣaiḥ
bhuñjate te tv aghaṁ pāpā ye pacanty ātma-kāraṇāt

"The devotees of the Lord are released from all kinds of sins because they eat food that is first offered for sacrifice. Others, who prepare food for personal sense enjoyment, verily eat only sin."

Father Emmanuel: Kṛṣṇa cannot give permission to eat animals?

Śrīla Prabhupāda: Yes—in the animal kingdom. But the civilized human being, the religious human being, is not meant to kill and eat animals. If you stop killing animals and chant the holy name Christ, everything will be perfect. I have not come to teach you, but only to request you to please chant the name of God. The Bible also demands this of you. So let's kindly cooperate and chant, and if you have a prejudice against chanting the name Kṛṣṇa, then chant "Christos" or "Kṛṣṭa"—there is no difference. Śrī Caitanya said: *nāmnām akāri bahudhā nija-sarva-śaktiḥ*. "God has millions and millions of names, and because there is no difference between God's name and Himself, each one of these names has the same potency as God." Therefore, even if you accept designations like "Hindu," "Christian," or "Muhammadan," if you simply chant the name of God found in your own scriptures, you will attain the spiritual platform. Human life is meant for self-realization—to learn how to love God. That is the actual duty of man. Whether you discharge this duty as a Hindu, a Christian, or a Muhammadan, it doesn't matter—but discharge it!

Father Emmanuel: I agree.

Śrīla Prabhupāda [*pointing to a string of 108 meditation beads*]: We always have these beads, just as you have your rosary. You are chanting, but why don't the other Christians also chant? Why should they miss this opportunity as human beings? Cats and dogs cannot chant, but we can, because we have a human tongue. If we chant the holy names of God, we cannot lose anything; on the contrary, we gain greatly. My disciples practice chanting Hare Kṛṣṇa constantly. They could also go to the cinema or do so many other things, but they have given everything up. They eat neither fish nor meat nor eggs, they don't take intoxicants, they don't drink, they don't smoke, they don't partake in gambling, they don't speculate, and they don't maintain illicit sexual connections. But they do chant the holy name of God. If you would like to cooperate with us, then go to the churches and chant, "Christ," "Kṛṣṭa," or "Kṛṣṇa." What could be the objection?

Father Emmanuel: There is none. For my part, I would be glad to join you.

Śrīla Prabhupāda: No, we are speaking with you as a representative of the Christian church. Instead of keeping the churches closed, why not give them to us? We would chant the holy name of God there twenty-four hours a day. In many places we have bought churches that were practically closed because no one was going there. In London I saw hundreds of churches that were closed or used for mundane purposes. We bought one such church in Los Angeles. It was sold because no one came there, but if you visit this same church today, you will see thousands of people. Any intelligent person can understand what God is in five minutes; it doesn't require five hours.

Father Emmanuel: I understand.

Śrīla Prabhupāda: But the people do not. Their disease is that they don't want to understand.

Visitor: I think understanding God is not a question of intelligence, but a question of humility.

Śrīla Prabhupāda: Humility means intelligence. The humble and meek own the kingdom of God. This is stated in the Bible, is it not? But the philosophy of the rascals is that everyone is God, and today this idea has become popular. Therefore no one is humble and meek. If everyone thinks that he is God, why should he be humble and meek? Therefore I teach my disciples how to become humble and meek. They always offer their respectful obeisances in the temple and to the spiritual master, and in this way they make advancement. The qualities of humbleness and meekness lead very quickly to spiritual realization. In the Vedic scriptures it is said, "To those who have firm faith in God and the spiritual master, who is His representative, the meaning of the Vedic scriptures is revealed."

Father Emmanuel: But shouldn't this humility be offered to everyone else, also?

Śrīla Prabhupāda: Yes, but there are two kinds of respect: special and ordinary. Śrī Kṛṣṇa Caitanya taught that we shouldn't expect honor for ourselves, but should always respect everyone else, even if he is disrespectful to us. But special respect should be given to God and His pure devotee.

Father Emmanuel: Yes, I agree.

Śrīla Prabhupāda: I think the Christian priests should cooperate with the Kṛṣṇa consciousness movement. They should chant the name Christ or Christos and should stop condoning the slaughter of animals. This program follows the teachings of the Bible; it is not my philosophy. Please act accordingly and you will see how the world situation will change.

Father Emmanuel: I thank you very much.

Śrīla Prabhupāda: Hare Kṛṣṇa.

CHRIST, CHRISTIANS, AND KṚṢṆA

"A Vaiṣṇava [a pure devotee of the Lord] is unhappy to see the suffering of others. Therefore, Lord Jesus Christ agreed to be crucified—to free others from their suffering. But his followers are so unfaithful that they have decided, 'Let Christ suffer for us, and we'll go on committing sin.' They love Christ so much that they think, 'My dear Christ, we are very weak. We cannot give up our sinful activities. So you please suffer for us.'"

The *Śrīmad-Bhāgavatam* states that any bona fide preacher of God consciousness must have the qualities of *titikṣā* (tolerance) and *karuṇā* (compassion). In the character of Lord Jesus Christ we find both these qualities. He was so tolerant that even while he was being crucified, he didn't condemn anyone. And he was so compassionate that he prayed to God to forgive the very persons who were trying to kill him. (Of course, they could not actually kill him. But they were thinking that he could be killed, so they were committing a great offense.) As Christ was being crucified he prayed, "Father, forgive them. They know not what they are doing."

A preacher of God consciousness is a friend to all living beings. Lord Jesus Christ exemplified this by teaching, "Thou shalt not kill." But the Christians like to misinterpret this instruction. They think the animals have no soul, and therefore they think they can freely kill billions of innocent animals in the slaughterhouses. So although there are many persons who profess to be Christians, it would be very difficult to find one who strictly follows the instructions of Lord Jesus Christ.

A Vaiṣṇava is unhappy to see the suffering of others. Therefore, Lord Jesus Christ agreed to be crucified—to free others from their suffering. But his followers are so unfaithful that they have decided, "Let Christ suffer for us, and we'll go on committing sin." They love Christ so much that they think, "My dear Christ, we are very weak. We cannot give up our sinful activities. So you please suffer for us."

Jesus Christ taught, "Thou shalt not kill." But his followers have now decided, "Let us kill anyway," and they open big, modern, scientific slaughterhouses. "If there is any sin, Christ will suffer for us." This is a most abominable conclusion.

Christ can take the sufferings for the previous sins of his devotees. But first they have to be sane: "Why should I put Jesus Christ into suffering for my sins? Let me stop my sinful activities."

Suppose a man—the favorite son of his father—commits a murder. And suppose he thinks, "If there is any punishment coming, my father can suffer for me." Will the law allow it? When the murderer is arrested and says, "No, no. You can release me and arrest my father; I am his pet son," will the police officials comply with that fool's request? *He* committed the murder, but he thinks *his father* should suffer the punishment! Is that a sane proposal? "No. *You* have committed the murder; *you* must be hanged." Similarly, when you commit sinful activities, you must suffer—not Jesus Christ. This is God's law.

Jesus Christ was such a great personality—the son of God, the representative of God. He had no fault. Still, he was crucified. He wanted to deliver God consciousness, but in return they crucified him—they were so thankless. They could not appreciate his preaching. But we appreciate him and give him all honor as the representative of God.

Of course, the message that Christ preached was just according to his particular time, place, and country, and just suited for a particular group of people. But certainly he is the representative of God. Therefore we adore Lord Jesus Christ and offer our obeisances to him.

Once, in Melbourne, a group of Christian ministers came to visit me. They asked, "What is your idea of Jesus Christ?" I told them, "He is our guru. He is preaching God consciousness, so he is our spiritual master." The ministers very much appreciated that.

Actually, anyone who is preaching God's glories must be accepted as a guru. Jesus Christ is one such great personality. We should not think of him as an ordinary human being. The scriptures say that anyone who considers the spiritual master to be an ordinary man has a hellish mentality. If Jesus Christ were an ordinary man, then he could not have delivered God consciousness.

"THOU SHALT NOT KILL"

In July of 1973, at ISKCON'S Paris center, Śrīla Prabhupāda talks with Cardinal Jean Daniélou: "The Bible does not simply say, 'Do not kill the human being.' It says broadly, 'Thou shalt not kill.' . . . Why do you interpret this to suit your own convenience? . . . When there is no food, someone may eat meat in order to keep from starving. That is another thing. But it is most sinful to regularly maintain slaughterhouses just to satisfy your tongue."

Śrīla Prabhupāda: Jesus Christ said, "Thou shalt not kill." So why is it that the Christian people are engaged in animal killing?
Cardinal Daniélou: Certainly in Christianity it is forbidden to kill, but we believe that there is a difference between the life of a human being and the life of the beasts. The life of a human being is sacred because man is made in the image of God; therefore, to kill a human being is forbidden.
Śrīla Prabhupāda: But the Bible does not simply say, "Do not kill the human being." It says broadly, "Thou shalt not kill."
Cardinal Daniélou: We believe that only human life is sacred.
Śrīla Prabhupāda: That is your interpretation. The commandment is "Thou shalt not kill."
Cardinal Daniélou: It is necessary for man to kill animals in order to have food to eat.
Śrīla Prabhupāda: No. Man can eat grains, vegetables, fruits, and milk.
Cardinal Daniélou: No flesh?
Śrīla Prabhupāda: No. Human beings are meant to eat vegetarian food. The tiger does not come to eat your fruits. His prescribed food is animal flesh. But man's food is vegetables, fruits, grains, and milk products. So how can you say that animal killing is not a sin?
Cardinal Daniélou: We believe it is a question of motivation. If the killing of an animal is for giving food to the hungry, then it is justified.

Śrīla Prabhupāda: But consider the cow: we drink her milk; therefore, she is our mother. Do you agree?
Cardinal Daniélou: Yes, surely.
Śrīla Prabhupāda: So if the cow is your mother, how can you support killing her? You take the milk from her, and when she's old and cannot give you milk, you cut her throat. Is that a very humane proposal? In India those who are meat-eaters are advised to kill some lower animals like goats, pigs, or even buffalo. But cow killing is the greatest sin. In preaching Kṛṣṇa consciousness we ask people not to eat any kind of meat, and my disciples strictly follow this principle. But if, under certain circumstances, others are obliged to eat meat, then they should eat the flesh of some lower animal. Don't kill cows. It is the greatest sin. And as long as a man is sinful, he cannot understand God. The human being's main business is to understand God and to love Him. But if you remain sinful, you will never be able to understand God—what to speak of loving Him.
Cardinal Daniélou: I think that perhaps this is not an essential point. The important thing is to love God. The practical commandments can vary from one religion to the next.
Śrīla Prabhupāda: So, in the Bible God's practical commandment is that you cannot kill; therefore killing cows is a sin for you.
Cardinal Daniélou: God says to the Indians that killing is not good, and he says to the Jews that—
Śrīla Prabhupāda: No, no. Jesus Christ taught, "Thou shalt not kill." Why do you interpret this to suit your own convenience?
Cardinal Daniélou: But Jesus allowed the sacrifice of the Paschal Lamb.
Śrīla Prabhupāda: But he never maintained a slaughterhouse.
Cardinal Daniélou: [*Laughs*] No, but he did eat meat.
Śrīla Prabhupāda: When there is no other food, someone may eat meat in order to keep from starving. That is another thing. But it is most sinful to regularly maintain slaughterhouses just to satisfy your tongue. Actually, you will not even have a human society until this cruel practice of maintaining slaughterhouses is stopped. And although animal killing may sometimes be necessary for survival, at least the mother animal, the cow, should not be killed. That is simply human decency. In the Kṛṣṇa consciousness movement our practice is that we don't allow the killing of any animals. Kṛṣṇa

says, *patraṁ puṣpaṁ phalaṁ toyaṁ yo me bhaktyā prayacchati:* "Vegetables, fruits, milk, and grains should be offered to Me in devotion." [*Bhagavad-gītā* 9.26] We take only the remnants of Kṛṣṇa's food (*prasāda*). The trees offer us many varieties of fruits, but the trees are not killed. Of course, one living entity is food for another living entity, but that does not mean you can kill your mother for food. Cows are innocent; they give us milk. You take their milk—and then kill them in the slaughterhouse. This is sinful.

Student: Śrīla Prabhupāda, Christianity's sanction of meat-eating is based on the view that lower species of life do not have a soul like the human being's.

Śrīla Prabhupāda: That is foolishness. First of all, we have to understand the evidence of the soul's presence within the body. Then we can see whether the human being has a soul and the cow does not. What are the different characteristics of the cow and the man? If we find a difference in characteristics, then we can say that in the animal there is no soul. But if we see that the animal and the human being have the same characteristics, then how can you say that the animal has no soul? The general symptoms are that the animal eats, you eat; the animal sleeps, you sleep; the animal mates, you mate; the animal defends, and you defend. Where is the difference?

Cardinal Daniélou: We admit that in the animal there may be the same type of biological existence as in men, but there is no soul. We believe that the soul is a human soul.

Śrīla Prabhupāda: Our *Bhagavad-gītā* says *sarva-yoniṣu,* "In all species of life the soul exists." The body is like a suit of clothes. You have black clothes; I am dressed in saffron clothes. But within the dress you are a human being, and I am also a human being. Similarly, the bodies of the different species are just like different types of dress. There are 8,400,000 species, or dresses, but within each one is a soul, a part and parcel of God. Suppose a man has two sons, not equally meritorious. One may be a Supreme Court judge and the other may be a common laborer, but the father claims both as his sons. He does not make the distinction that the son who is a judge is very important and the worker-son is not important. And if the judge-son says, "My dear father, your other son is useless; let me cut him up and eat him," will the father allow this?

Cardinal Daniélou: Certainly not, but the idea that all life is part of the life of God is difficult for us to admit. There is a great differ-

ence between human life and animal life.
Śrīla Prabhupāda: That difference is due to the development of consciousness. In the human body there is developed consciousness. Even a tree has a soul, but a tree's consciousness is not very developed. If you cut a tree it does not resist. Actually, it does resist, but only to a very small degree. There is a scientist named Jagadish Chandra Bose who has made a machine which shows that trees and plants are able to feel pain when they are cut. And we can see directly that when someone comes to kill an animal, it resists, it cries, it makes a horrible sound. So it is a matter of the development of consciousness. But the soul is there within all living beings.
Cardinal Daniélou: But metaphysically, the life of man is sacred. Human beings think on a higher platform than the animals do.
Śrīla Prabhupāda: What is that higher platform? The animal eats to maintain his body, and you also eat in order to maintain your body. The cow eats grass in the field, and the human being eats meat from a huge slaughterhouse full of modern machines. But just because you have big machines and a ghastly scene, while the animal simply eats grass, this does not mean that you are so advanced that only within your body is there a soul and that there is not a soul within the body of the animal. That is illogical. We can see that the basic characteristics are the same in the animal and the human being.
Cardinal Daniélou: But only in human beings do we find a metaphysical search for the meaning of life.
Śrīla Prabhupāda: Yes. So metaphysically search out why you believe that there is no soul within the animal—that is metaphysics. If you are thinking metaphysically, that's all right. But if you are thinking like an animal, then what is the use of your metaphysical study? *Metaphysical* means "above the physical" or, in other words, "spiritual." In the *Bhagavad-gītā* [14.4] Kṛṣṇa says, *sarva-yoniṣu kaunteya:* "In every living being there is a spirit soul." That is metaphysical understanding. Now either you accept Kṛṣṇa's teachings as metaphysical, or you'll have to take a third-class fool's opinion as metaphysical. Which do you accept?
Cardinal Daniélou: But why does God create some animals who eat other animals? There is a fault in the creation, it seems.
Śrīla Prabhupāda: It is not a fault. God is very kind. If you want to eat animals, then He'll give you full facility. God will give you the

body of a tiger in your next life so that you can eat flesh very freely. "Why are you maintaining slaughterhouses? I'll give you fangs and claws. Now eat." So the meat-eaters are awaiting such punishment. The animal-eaters become tigers, wolves, cats, and dogs in their next life—to get more facility.

V.
PRACTICING YOGA IN THE AGE OF QUARREL

SUPERCONSCIOUSNESS

"The Supersoul, being present within everyone, situated everywhere, is conscious of every existence. The theory that the soul and the Supersoul are one is not acceptable, because the individual soul's consciousness cannot act in superconsciousness. This superconsciousness can only be achieved by dovetailing individual consciousness with the superconsciousness; and this dovetailing process is called surrender, or Kṛṣṇa consciousness."

Kṛṣṇa consciousness is the highest yoga performance by trained devotional yogīs. The yoga system, as is stated in the standard yoga practice formula given by Lord Kṛṣṇa in the *Bhagavad-gītā*, and as recommended in the Patañjali yoga discipline, is different from the nowadays practiced *haṭha-yoga* as is generally understood in the Western countries.

Real yoga practice means to control the senses and, after such control is established, to concentrate the mind on the Nārāyaṇa form of the Supreme Personality of Godhead, Śrī Kṛṣṇa. Lord Kṛṣṇa is the original Absolute Personality, the Godhead, and all the other Viṣṇu forms—with four hands, decorated with conch, lotus, club, and wheel—are plenary expansions of Kṛṣṇa.

In the *Bhagavad-gītā* it is recommended that we should meditate upon the form of the Lord. For practicing concentration of the mind, one has to sit down in a secluded place sanctified by a sacred atmosphere, and the yogī should observe the rules and regulations of *brahmacarya*—to live a life of strict self-restraint and celibacy. No one can practice yoga in a congested city, living a life of extravagance, including unrestricted sex indulgence and adultery of the tongue.

We have already stated that yoga practice means controlling the senses, and the beginning of controlling the senses is to control the tongue. You cannot allow the tongue to take all kinds of forbidden food and drink, and at the same time improve in the practice of yoga. It is a very regrettable fact that many stray, unauthorized so-called yogīs now come to the West and exploit the leaning of the people toward yoga. Such unauthorized yogīs even dare to say publicly that one can indulge in drinking and at the same time practice meditation.

Five thousand years ago, in the *Bhagavad-gītā* dialogue, Lord Kṛṣṇa recommended the yoga practice to His disciple Arjuna, but Arjuna flatly expressed his inability to follow the stringent rules and regulations of yoga. One should be practical in every field of activity. One should not waste his valuable time simply in practicing some gymnastic feats in the name of yoga. Real yoga is to search out the four-handed Supersoul within one's heart and to see Him perpetually in meditation. Such continued meditation is called *samādhi.* If, however, one wants to meditate upon something void or impersonal, it will require a very long time to achieve anything by yoga practice. We cannot concentrate our mind on something void or impersonal. Real yoga practice is to fix the mind on the person of the four-handed Nārāyaṇa who dwells in everyone's heart.

Sometimes it is said that by meditation one will understand that God is seated within one's heart always, even when one does not know it. God is seated within the heart of everyone. Not only is He seated in the heart of the human being, but He is also within the hearts of the cats and dogs. The *Bhagavad-gītā* certifies this with the declaration that Īśvara, the supreme controller of the world, is seated in the heart of everyone. He is present not only in everyone's heart, but also within the atoms. No place is vacant; no place is without the presence of the Lord.

The feature of the Lord by which He is present everywhere is called the Paramātmā. *Ātmā* means the individual soul, and Paramātmā means the individual Supersoul. Both *ātmā* and Paramātmā are individual persons. The difference between them, however, is that the *ātmā,* or soul, is present only in one particular place, whereas the Paramātmā is present everywhere.

In this connection, the example of the sun is very nice. An individual person may be situated in one place, but the sun, even though a specific individual entity, is present over the head of every individual person. In the *Bhagavad-gītā* this is very nicely explained. Therefore, even though the qualities of all entities, including the Lord, are equal, the Supersoul is different from the individual soul by quantity of expansion. The Lord, or Supersoul, can expand Himself into millions of different forms, while the individual soul cannot do so.

The Supersoul, being seated in everyone's heart, can witness every-one's activities, past, present, and future. In the *Upaniṣads* the Supersoul is said to be sitting with the individual soul as a friend and witness. As a friend He is always anxious to get the individual soul back home, back to Godhead. As a witness, He is the endower of all benedictions that result from the individual's actions. The Supersoul gives the individual soul all facility for achieving whatever he may desire. But He instructs His friend, so that he may ultimately give up all other engagements and simply surrender unto God for perpetual bliss and eternal life, full of knowledge. This is the last instruction of the *Bhagavad-gītā*, the most authorized and widely read book on all forms of yoga.

The last word of the *Bhagavad-gītā*, as stated above, is the last word in the matter of perfecting the yoga system. It is further stated in the *Bhagavad-gītā* that a person who is always absorbed in Kṛṣṇa consciousness is the topmost yogī. What is this Kṛṣṇa consciousness?

Just as the individual soul is present by his consciousness throughout the whole body, so the Supersoul, or Paramātmā, is present throughout the whole creation by His superconsciousness. This superconsciousness cannot be imitated by the individual soul, who has limited awareness: I can understand what is going on within my limited body, but I cannot feel what is going on in another's body. I am present all over my body by my consciousness, but I am not present in any other's body by my consciousness. However, the Supersoul, or Paramātmā, being present within everyone, situated everywhere, is conscious of every existence. The theory that the soul and the Supersoul are one is not acceptable, because the in-dividual soul's consciousness cannot act in superconsciousness. This superconsciousness can only be achieved by dovetailing individual consciousness with the superconsciousness; and this dovetailing process is called surrender, or Kṛṣṇa consciousness.

From the teachings of the *Bhagavad-gītā* we learn very clearly that Arjuna in the beginning did not want to fight with his relatives, but after understanding the *Bhagavad-gītā,* when he dovetailed his consciousness with the superconsciousness of Kṛṣṇa, his consciousness was Kṛṣṇa consciousness. A person in full Kṛṣṇa consciousness acts by the dictation of Kṛṣṇa, and so Arjuna agreed to fight the Battle of Kurukṣetra.

In the beginning of Kṛṣṇa consciousness this dictation of the Lord is received through the transparent medium of the spiritual master. When one is sufficiently trained and acts with submissive faith and love for Kṛṣṇa, under the direction of the bona fide spiritual master, the dovetailing process becomes more firm and accurate. At this stage Kṛṣṇa dictates from within. From without, the devotee is helped by the spiritual master, the bona fide representative of Kṛṣṇa, and from within the Lord helps the devotee as *caitya-guru,* being seated within the heart of everyone.

Simply to understand that God is seated in everyone's heart is not perfection. One has to be acquainted with God from within and without and thus act in Kṛṣṇa consciousness. This is the highest perfectional stage for the human form of life, and the topmost stage in all yoga systems.

For a perfect yogī there are eight kinds of superachievements:

1. One can become smaller than an atom.
2. One can become bigger than a mountain.
3. One can become lighter than the air.
4. One can become heavier than any metal.
5. One can achieve any material effect he likes (create a planet, for example).
6. One can control others like the Lord can.
7. One can freely travel anywhere within (or beyond) the universe.
8. One can choose his own time and place of death, and take rebirth wherever he may desire.

But when one rises to the perfectional stage of receiving dictation from the Lord, one is above the stage of the material achievements above mentioned.

The breathing exercise of the yoga system that is generally practiced is just the beginning of the system. Meditation on the Supersoul is just a step forward. Achievement of wonderful material success is also only a step forward. But to attain direct contact with the Supersoul and to take dictation from Him is the highest perfectional stage.

The breathing exercises and meditational practices of yoga are very difficult in this age. They were difficult even five thousand years ago, or else Arjuna would not have rejected the proposal of Kṛṣṇa. This Age of Kali is called a fallen age. At the present moment, people in general are short-living and very slow in understanding self-realization, or spiritual life. They are mostly unfortunate, and as such, if someone is a little bit interested in self-realization, he is misguided by so many frauds. The only actual way to realization of the perfect stage of yoga is to follow the principles of the *Bhagavad-gītā* as they were practiced by Lord Caitanya Mahāprabhu. This is the simplest and highest perfection of yoga practice.

Lord Caitanya practically demonstrated Kṛṣṇa consciousness yoga simply by chanting the holy names of Kṛṣṇa, as they are mentioned in the *Vedānta,* the *Śrīmad-Bhāgavatam,* and many important *Purāṇas.* The largest number of Indians follow this yoga practice, and in the United States and other countries also it is gradually growing in many cities. It is very easy and practical for this age, especially for those who are serious about success in yoga. No other process can be successful in this age.

The meditational process in right earnest was possible in the Golden Age, Satya-yuga, because the people at that time lived for a hundred thousand years on the average.

In the present age, however, if you want success in practical yoga, take to the chanting of Hare Kṛṣṇa, Hare Kṛṣṇa, Kṛṣṇa Kṛṣṇa, Hare Hare/ Hare Rāma, Hare Rāma, Rāma Rāma, Hare Hare, and feel for yourself how you are making progress. One should know for himself how much he is progressing in yoga practice.

In the *Bhagavad-gītā* this practice of Kṛṣṇa consciousness is described as *rāja-vidyā,* the king of all erudition; *rāja-guhyam,* the most confidential system of spiritual realization; *pavitram,* the purest of all that is pure; *su-sukham,* very happily performed; and *avyayam,* inexhaustible.

Those who have taken to this most sublime *bhakti-yoga* system, this practice of devotional service in transcendental love of Kṛṣṇa, can testify to how they are nicely enjoying its happy and easy execution. Yoga means controlling the senses, and *bhakti-yoga* means purifying the senses. When the senses are purified, they are also, automatically, controlled. You cannot stop the activities of the senses by artificial means, but if you purify the senses, not only are they kept back from rubbish engagement, but also they become positively engaged in transcendental service to the Lord.

Kṛṣṇa consciousness is not manufactured by us through mental speculation. It is prescribed in the *Bhagavad-gītā*, which says that when we think in Kṛṣṇa, chant in Kṛṣṇa, live in Kṛṣṇa, eat in Kṛṣṇa, talk in Kṛṣṇa, hope in Kṛṣṇa, and sustain in Kṛṣṇa, we return to Kṛṣṇa, without any doubt. And this is the substance of Kṛṣṇa consciousness.

THE INCARNATION OF LOVE OF GOD

"Caitanya Mahāprabhu is Kṛṣṇa Himself, and He is teaching how to develop love of God by a very simple method. . . . People are embarrassed by so many methods of realization. They cannot take to the actual ritualistic processes of meditation or yoga; it is not possible. Therefore Lord Caitanya says that if one takes up this process of chanting, then immediately he can reach the platform of realization."

Śrī Caitanya Mahāprabhu, the golden *avatāra*, appeared in India nearly five hundred years ago. It is the custom in India that when a child is born, an astrologer is called for. When Lord Kṛṣṇa, the Supreme Personality of Godhead, appeared five thousand years ago, Garga Muni was called by His father, and he said, "This child formerly incarnated in three complexions, such as red and golden, and now He has appeared in blackish color." Kṛṣṇa's color is described in the scriptures as blackish, just like the color of a cloud. Lord Caitanya is understood to be Kṛṣṇa appearing in golden complexion.

There is much evidence in Vedic literature that Caitanya Mahāprabhu is an incarnation of Kṛṣṇa, and this is confirmed by scholars and devotees. In the *Śrīmad-Bhāgavatam* it is confirmed that the incarnation of Kṛṣṇa, or God, in this present age, Kali-yuga, will always engage in describing Kṛṣṇa. He is Kṛṣṇa, but as a devotee of Kṛṣṇa He describes Himself. And in this age His bodily complexion will not be blackish. This means that it may be white, it may be red, or it may be yellow, because these four colors—white, red, yellow, and black—are the colors assumed by the incarnations for the different ages. Therefore, since the red, white, and blackish colors were already taken by former incarnations, the remaining color, golden, is assumed by Caitanya Mahāprabhu. His complexion is not blackish, but He is Kṛṣṇa.

Another feature of this *avatāra* is that He is always accompanied by His associates. In the picture of Caitanya Mahāprabhu one will find that He is always followed by many devotees chanting. Whenever God incarnates He has two missions, as stated in the *Bhagavad-gītā*. There Kṛṣṇa says, "Whenever I appear, My mission is to deliver the pious devotees and to annihilate the demons." When Kṛṣṇa appeared, He had to kill many demons. If we see a picture of Viṣṇu we will notice that He has a conch shell, lotus flower, club, and disc. These last two items are meant for killing demons. Within this world there are two classes of men—the demons and the devotees. The devotees are called demigods; they are almost like God because they have godly qualities. Those who are devotees are called godly persons, and those who are nondevotees, atheists, are called demons. So Kṛṣṇa, or God, comes with two missions: to give protection to the devotees and to destroy the demons. In this age Caitanya Mahāprabhu's mission is also like that: to deliver the devotees and to annihilate the nondevotees, the demons. But in this age He has a different weapon. That weapon is not a club or disc or lethal weapon—His weapon is the *saṅkīrtana* movement. He killed the demoniac mentality of the people by introducing the *saṅkīrtana* movement. That is the specific significance of Lord Caitanya. In this age people are already killing themselves. They have discovered atomic weapons with which to kill themselves, so there is no need for God to kill them. But He appeared to kill their demonic mentality. That is possible by this Kṛṣṇa consciousness movement.

Therefore, in the *Śrīmad-Bhāgavatam* it is said that this is the incarnation of God in this age. And who worships Him? The process is very simple. Just keep a picture of Lord Caitanya with His associates. Lord Caitanya is in the middle, accompanied by His principal associates—Nityānanda, Advaita, Gadādhara, and Śrīvāsa. One simply has to keep this picture. One can keep it anywhere. It is not that one has to come to us to see this picture. Anyone can have this picture in his home, chant this Hare Kṛṣṇa mantra, and thus worship Lord Caitanya. That is the simple method. But who will capture this simple method? Those who have good brains. Without much bother, if one simply keeps a picture of Śrī Caitanya Mahāprabhu at home and chants Hare Kṛṣṇa, then one will realize God. Anyone can adopt this simple method. There is no expenditure, there is no tax, nor is there any need to build a very big church or temple. Anyone, anywhere, can sit down on the road or beneath a tree and chant the Hare Kṛṣṇa mantra and worship God. Therefore it is a great opportunity. For example, in business or political life one sometimes finds a great opportunity. Those who are intelligent politicians take a good opportunity and make a success of it the first time it comes. Similarly, in this age, those who have sufficient intelligence take to this *saṅkīrtana* movement, and they advance very quickly.

Lord Caitanya is called "the golden *avatāra*." *Avatāra* means "descending, coming down." Just as one may come down from the fifth story or the one-hundredth story of a building, an *avatāra* comes down from the spiritual planets in the spiritual sky. The sky we see with our naked eyes or with a telescope is only the material sky. But beyond this there is another sky, which is not possible to see with our eyes or instruments. That information is in the *Bhagavad-gītā;* it is not imagination. Kṛṣṇa says that beyond the material sky is another sky, the spiritual sky.

We have to take Kṛṣṇa's word as it is. For example, we teach small children that beyond England there are other places, called Germany, India, etc., and the child has to learn about these places from the version of the teacher because they are beyond his sphere. Similarly, beyond this material sky there is another sky. One cannot experiment to find it, any more than a small child can experiment to find Germany or India. That is not possible. If we want to get knowledge, then we have to accept authority. Similarly, if we want to know what is beyond the material world, then we have to accept the Vedic authority; otherwise there is no possibility of knowing. It is beyond material knowledge. One cannot go to the far planets in this universe, what to speak of going beyond this universe. The estimation is that in order to go to the highest planet of this universe with modern machinery one would have to travel for forty thousand years. So we cannot even travel within this material sky. Our lifetime and means are so limited that we cannot have proper knowledge of even this material world.

In the *Bhagavad-gītā,* when Arjuna asked Kṛṣṇa, "Will you kindly explain the extent to which Your energies are working?" the Supreme Lord gave him so many instances, and at the end He finally said, "My dear Arjuna, what shall I explain about My energies? It is not actually possible for you to understand. But you can just imagine the expansion of My energies: this material world, which consists of millions of universes, is a display of only one fourth of My creation." We cannot estimate the position of even one universe, and there are millions of universes. Then beyond that is the spiritual sky, and there are millions of spiritual planets. All this information is available from the Vedic literature. If one accepts Vedic literature, then he can get this knowledge. If one doesn't accept it, there is no other means. That is our choice. Therefore, according to Vedic civilization, whenever an *ācārya* speaks he immediately gives references from the Vedic literature. Then others will accept it: "Yes, it is correct." In a law court the lawyer gives references from past judgments of the court, and if his case is tight, the judge accepts. Similarly, if one can give evidence from the *Vedas,* then it is understood that his position is factual.

The *avatāra* for this age, Lord Caitanya, is described in Vedic literature. We cannot accept anyone as an *avatāra* unless he has the symptoms described in the scriptures. We do not whimsically accept Lord Caitanya as an *avatāra* on the basis of votes. Nowadays it has become a fashion that any man can come and say that he is God or an incarnation of God, and some fools and rascals will accept it: "Oh, he is God." We do not accept an *avatāra* like that. We take evidence from the *Vedas.* An *avatāra* must conform to descriptions in the *Vedas.* Then we accept him; otherwise no. For each *avatāra* there is a description in the *Vedas:* He will appear at such and such a place, in such and such a form, and He will act like this. That is the nature of Vedic evidence.

In the *Śrīmad-Bhāgavatam* there is a list of the *avatāras,* and there is mention of Lord Buddha's name. This *Śrīmad-Bhāgavatam* was written five thousand years ago, and it mentions different names for future times. It says that in the future the Lord would appear as Lord Buddha, his mother's name would be Añjanā, and he would appear in Gayā. So Buddha appeared twenty-six hundred years ago, and the *Śrīmad-Bhāgavatam,* which was written five thousand years ago, mentioned that in the future he would appear. Similarly, there is mention of Lord Caitanya, and similarly the last *avatāra* of this Kali-yuga is also mentioned in the *Bhāgavatam.* It is mentioned that the last incarnation in this age is Kalki. He will appear as the son of a *brāhmaṇa* whose name is Viṣṇu-yaśā, in a place called Śambhala. There is a place in India with that name, so perhaps it is there that the Lord will appear.

So an *avatāra* must conform to the descriptions in the *Upaniṣads*, *Śrīmad-Bhāgavatam*, *Mahābhārata*, and other Vedic literatures. And on the authority of Vedic literature and the commentary of great, stalwart *gosvāmīs* like Jīva Gosvāmī, who was the greatest scholar and philosopher in the world, we can accept Lord Caitanya as an incarnation of Kṛṣṇa.

Why did Lord Caitanya appear? In the *Bhagavad-gītā* Lord Kṛṣṇa says, "Give up all other engagements and simply engage in My service. I will give you protection from all results of sinful actions." In this material world, in conditional life, we are simply creating sinful reactions. That's all. And because of sinful reactions, we have received this body. If our sinful reactions stopped we would not have to take a material body; we should get a spiritual body.

What is a spiritual body? A spiritual body is a body which is free from death, birth, disease, and old age. It is an eternal body, full of knowledge and bliss. Different bodies are created by different desires. As long as we have desires for different kinds of enjoyment, we have to accept different kinds of material bodies. Kṛṣṇa, God, is so kind that He awards whatever we want. If we want a tiger's body, with tigerlike strength and teeth with which to capture animals and suck fresh blood, then Kṛṣṇa will give us the opportunity. And if we want the body of a saintly person, a devotee engaged only in the service of the Lord, then He will give us that body. This is stated in the *Bhagavad-gītā*.

If a person engaged in yoga, the process of self-realization, somehow or other fails to complete the process, he is given another chance; he is given birth in a family of a pure *brāhmaṇa* or a rich man. If one is fortunate enough to take birth in such a family, he gets all facilities to understand the importance of self-realization. From the very beginning of life our Kṛṣṇa conscious children are getting the opportunity to learn how to chant and dance, so when they are grown up they will not change, but instead will automatically make progress. They are very fortunate. Regardless of whether he is born in America or Europe, a child will advance if his father and mother are devotees. He gets this opportunity. If a child takes birth in a family of devotees, this means that in his last life he had already taken to the yoga process, but somehow or other he could not finish it. Therefore the child is given another opportunity to make progress under the care of a good father and mother so that he will again advance. In this way, as soon as one completes his development of God consciousness, then he no longer has to take birth in this material world, but returns to the spiritual world.

Kṛṣṇa says in the *Bhagavad-gītā:* "My dear Arjuna, if one understands My appearance, disappearance, and activities, simply because of this understanding he is given the opportunity to take birth in the spiritual world after giving up this body." One has to give up this body—today, tomorrow, or maybe the day after that. One has to. But a person who has understood Kṛṣṇa will not have to take another material body. He goes directly to the spiritual world and takes birth in one of the spiritual planets. So Kṛṣṇa says that as soon as one gets this body—it doesn't matter if it is from India or the moon or the sun or Brahmaloka or anywhere within this material world—one should know that it is due to his sinful activities. There are degrees of sinful activities, so according to the degree of sinfulness, one takes a material body. Therefore our real problem is not how to eat, sleep, mate, and defend—our real problem is how to get a body that is not material but spiritual. That is the ultimate solution to all problems. So Kṛṣṇa guarantees that if one surrenders unto Him, if one becomes fully Kṛṣṇa conscious, then He will give one protection from all reactions to sinful life.

This assurance was given by Kṛṣṇa in the *Bhagavad-gītā,* but there were many fools who could not understand Kṛṣṇa. In the *Bhagavad-gītā* they are described as *mūḍhas. Mūḍha* means "rascal," and Kṛṣṇa says in the *Gītā,* "They do not know what I actually am." So many people misunderstood Kṛṣṇa. Although Kṛṣṇa gave us this message of the *Bhagavad-gītā* so that we could understand Him, many people missed the opportunity. Therefore Kṛṣṇa, out of His compassion, came again, as a devotee, and showed us how to surrender unto Kṛṣṇa. Kṛṣṇa Himself came to teach us how to surrender. His last instruction in the *Bhagavad-gītā* is to surrender, but people—*mūḍhas,* rascals—said, "Why should I surrender?" Therefore, although Caitanya Mahāprabhu is Kṛṣṇa Himself, this time He teaches us practically how to execute the mission of the *Bhagavad-gītā.* That's all. Caitanya Mahāprabhu is teaching nothing extraordinary, nothing beyond the process of surrendering to the Supreme Personality of Godhead, which was already taught in the *Bhagavad-gītā.* There is no other teaching, but the same teaching is presented in different ways so that different kinds of people may take it and take the opportunity to approach God.

Caitanya Mahāprabhu gives us the opportunity to reach God directly. When Rūpa Gosvāmī, the principal disciple of Lord Caitanya, first saw Caitanya Mahāprabhu, he was a minister in the government of Bengal but wanted to join Caitanya Mahāprabhu's movement. So he gave up his position as a minister, and after joining, when he surrendered, he offered a nice prayer to Lord Caitanya. This prayer says:

namo mahā-vadānyāya kṛṣṇa-prema-pradāya te
kṛṣṇāya kṛṣṇa-caitanya- nāmne gaura-tviṣe namaḥ

"My dear Lord, You are the most munificent of all the incarnations." Why? *Kṛṣṇa-prema-pradāya te:* "You are directly giving love of God. You have no other purpose. Your process is so nice that one can immediately learn to love God. Therefore You are the most munificent of all incarnations. And it is not possible for any personality other than Kṛṣṇa Himself to deliver this benediction; therefore I say that You are Kṛṣṇa." *Kṛṣṇāya kṛṣṇa-caitanya-nāmne:* "You are Kṛṣṇa, but You have assumed the name Kṛṣṇa Caitanya. I surrender unto You."

So this is the process. Caitanya Mahāprabhu is Kṛṣṇa Himself, and He is teaching how to develop love of God by a very simple method. He says simply to chant Hare Kṛṣṇa.

harer nāma harer nāma harer nāmaiva kevalam
kalau nāsty eva nāsty eva nāsty eva gatir anyathā

"In this age, simply go on chanting the Hare Kṛṣṇa mantra. There is no other alternative." People are embarrassed by so many methods of realization. They cannot take to the actual ritualistic processes of meditation or yoga; it is not possible. Therefore Lord Caitanya says that if one takes up this process of chanting, then immediately he can reach the platform of realization.

The chanting process offered by Lord Caitanya for achieving love of God is called *saṅkīrtana. Saṅkīrtana* is a Sanskrit word. *Sam* means *samyak*—"complete." And *kīrtana* means "glorifying" or "describing." So complete description means complete glorification of the Supreme, or the Supreme Complete Whole. It is not that one can describe anything or glorify anything and that will be *kīrtana.* From the grammatical point of view that may be *kīrtana,* but according to the Vedic system, *kīrtana* means describing the supreme authority, the Absolute Truth, the Supreme Personality of Godhead. That is called *kīrtana.*

This devotional service begins with the method of *śravaṇa. Śravaṇa* means "hearing," and *kīrtana* means "describing." One should describe, and another should hear. Or the same man himself can both describe and hear. He does not need anyone else's help. When we chant Hare Kṛṣṇa, we chant and hear. This is complete. This is a complete method. But what is that chanting and hearing? One must chant and hear about Viṣṇu, Kṛṣṇa. Not of anything else. *Śravaṇaṁ kīrtanaṁ viṣṇoḥ:* one can understand Viṣṇu, the all-pervading Absolute Truth, the Supreme Personality of Godhead, by the method of hearing.

We have to hear; if one simply hears, that is the beginning. One does not need any education or development of material knowledge. Just like a child: as soon as he hears, immediately he can respond and dance. So by nature God has given us these nice instruments—ears—so that we can hear. But we must hear from the right source. That is stated in the *Śrīmad-Bhāgavatam.* One must hear from those who are devoted to the Supreme Personality of Godhead. They are called *satām.* If one hears from the right source, from a realized soul, then it will act. And these words of God, or Kṛṣṇa, are very relishable. If one is intelligent enough, he will listen to what is spoken by the realized soul. Then very soon he will be released from material entanglements.

This human life is meant for advancing on the path of liberation. That is called *apavarga,* freedom from entanglement. We are all entangled. Our acceptance of this material body means that we are already entangled. But we should not progress in the process of entanglement. That process is called karma. As long as the mind is absorbed in karma, we will have to accept a material body. At the time of death, our mind may be thinking, "Oh, I could not complete this work. Oh, I am dying! I have to do this. I have to do that." This means that Kṛṣṇa will give us another chance to do it, and so we will have to accept another body. He will give us the chance: "All right. You could not do it. *Now* do it. Take this body." Therefore the *Śrīmad-Bhāgavatam* says, "These rascals have become madly intoxicated; because of intoxication they are doing something they should not have done." What are they doing? Mahārāja Dhṛtarāṣṭra is a very good example. Mahārāja Dhṛtarāṣṭra was cunningly planning to kill the Pāṇḍavas in order to favor his own sons, so Kṛṣṇa sent His uncle, Akrūra, to advise him not to do that. Dhṛtarāṣṭra understood Akrūra's instructions, but he said, "My dear Akrūra, what you are saying is quite right, but it does not stand in my heart, so I cannot change my policy. I have to follow this policy and let whatever happens take place."

So when men want to satisfy their senses, they become mad, and in this madness they'll do anything and everything. For example, there have been many instances in material life where someone has become mad after something and has committed a criminal act such as murder. The person could not check himself. Similarly, we are accustomed to sense gratification. We are mad, and therefore our minds are fully absorbed in karma. This is very unfortunate, because our body, although temporary, is the reservoir of all misfortunes and miseries; it is always giving us trouble. These matters are to be studied. We should not be mad. Human life is not meant for that. The defect of the present civilization is that people are mad after sense gratification. That is all. They do not know the real value of life, and therefore they are neglecting the most valuable form of life, this human form.

When this body is finished there is no guarantee what kind of body one will take next. Suppose in my next life I by chance get the body of a tree. For thousands of years I will have to stand up. But people are not very serious. They even say, "What is that? Even if I have to stand up, I shall forget." The lower species of life are situated in forgetfulness. If a tree were not forgetful it would be impossible for it to live. Suppose we were told, "You stand up for three days here!" Because we are not forgetful, we would become mad. So, by nature's law, all these lower species of life are forgetful. Their consciousness is not developed. A tree has life, but even if someone cuts it, because its consciousness is not developed, it does not respond. So we should be very careful to utilize this human form of life properly. The Kṛṣṇa consciousness movement is meant for achieving perfection in life. It is not a bluff or exploitation, but unfortunately people are accustomed to being bluffed. There is a verse by an Indian poet: "If one speaks nice things, people will quarrel with him: 'Oh, what nonsense you are speaking.' But if he bluffs them and cheats them, they will be very glad." So if a bluffer says, "Just do this, give me my fee, and within six months you will become God," then they will agree: "Yes, take this fee, and I shall become God within six months." No. These cheating processes will not solve our problem. If one actually wants to solve the problems of life in this age, then he has to take to this process of *kīrtana*. That is the recommended process.

> *harer nāma harer nāma harer nāmaiva kevalam*
> *kalau nāsty eva nāsty eva nāsty eva gatir anyathā*

In this age, Kali-yuga, one cannot execute any process of self-realization or perfection of life other than *kīrtana*. *Kīrtana* is essential in this age.

In all Vedic literatures it is confirmed that one must meditate on the Supreme Absolute Truth, Viṣṇu, not on anything else. But there are different processes of meditation recommended for different ages. The process of mystic yogic meditation was possible in Satya-yuga, when men lived for many thousands of years. Now people will not believe this, but in a previous age there were people who lived for one hundred thousand years. That age was called Satya-yuga, and the meditation of mystic yoga was possible at that time. In that age the great yogī Vālmīki Muni meditated for sixty thousand years. So that is a long-term process, which is not possible to execute in this age. If one wishes to conduct a farce, that is another matter. But if one actually wants to practice such meditation, it takes an extremely long time to perfect. In the next age, Tretā-yuga, the process of realization was to perform the various ritualistic sacrifices recommended in the *Vedas*. In the next age, Dvāpara-yuga, the process was temple worship. In this present age the same result can be achieved by the process of *hari-kīrtana*, glorification of Hari, Kṛṣṇa, the Supreme Personality of Godhead.

No other *kīrtana* is recommended. This *hari-kīrtana* was started five hundred years ago in Bengal by Lord Caitanya. In Bengal there is competition between the Vaiṣṇavas and the *śāktas*. The *śāktas* have introduced a certain type of *kīrtana* called *kālī-kīrtana*. But in the Vedic scriptures there is no recommendation of *kālī-kīrtana*. *Kīrtana* means *hari-kīrtana*. One cannot say, "Oh, you are Vaiṣṇava.

You can perform *hari-kīrtana.* I shall perform *śiva-kīrtana* or *devī-kīrtana* or *gaṇeśa-kīrtana."* No. The Vedic scriptures do not authorize any *kīrtana* other than *hari-kīrtana. Kīrtana* means *hari-kīrtana,* the glorification of Kṛṣṇa.

So this process of *hari-kīrtana* is very simple: Hare Kṛṣṇa, Hare Kṛṣṇa, Kṛṣṇa Kṛṣṇa, Hare Hare/ Hare Rāma, Hare Rāma, Rāma Rāma, Hare Hare. Actually there are only three words: *Hare, Kṛṣṇa,* and *Rāma.* But they are very nicely arranged for chanting so that everyone can take the mantra and chant Hare Kṛṣṇa, Hare Kṛṣṇa, Kṛṣṇa Kṛṣṇa, Hare Hare. Since we have started this movement in the Western countries, Europeans, Americans, Africans, Egyptians, and Japanese are all chanting. There is no difficulty. They are chanting very gladly, and they are getting the results. What is the difficulty? We are distributing this chanting free of charge, and it is very simple. Simply by chanting, one can have self-realization, God realization, and when there is God realization, then nature realization is included also. For example, if one learns one, two, three, four, five, six, seven, eight, nine, and zero, then he has studied the entirety of mathematics, because mathematics means simply changing the places of these ten figures. That's all. Similarly, if one simply studies Kṛṣṇa, then all his knowledge is perfect. And Kṛṣṇa is easily understood simply by chanting this mantra, Hare Kṛṣṇa. So why not take this opportunity?

Take this opportunity that is being offered to human society. It is very ancient and scientific. It is not that it is a concoction that will last for only three or four years. No. In the *Bhagavad-gītā* Kṛṣṇa Himself says, "This philosophy is inexhaustible and indestructible. It is never lost or destroyed." It may be covered for the time being, but it is never destroyed. Therefore it is called *avyayam. Vyaya* means "exhaustion." For example, one may have a hundred dollars, and if they are spent one after another, the next day it will come to zero. That is *vyaya,* exhaustible. But Kṛṣṇa consciousness is not like that. If you cultivate this knowledge of Kṛṣṇa consciousness, then it will increase. That is certified by Lord Caitanya Mahāprabhu. *Ānandāmbudhi-vardhanam. Ānanda* means "pleasure," "transcendental bliss," and *ambudhi* means "ocean." In the material world we see that the ocean does not increase. But if one cultivates Kṛṣṇa consciousness, then his transcendental bliss will simply increase. *Ānandāmbudhi-vardhanam.* And I shall always remind everyone that the process is very simple. Anyone can chant, anywhere, without taxation or loss, but the gain is very great.

Śrī Caitanya Mahāprabhu has explained this *kīrtana* movement in His *Śikṣāṣṭaka*. *Śikṣā* means "instruction," and *aṣṭaka* means "eight." He has given us eight verses to help us understand this Kṛṣṇa consciousness movement, and I shall explain the first of these instructions. The Lord says, *ceto-darpaṇa-mārjanam:* one should cleanse the heart. I have explained this several times, but it does not become monotonous. It is just like the chanting of Hare Kṛṣṇa; it does not become tiresome. Our students can chant the Hare Kṛṣṇa mantra twenty-four hours a day, and they will never get tired. They will continue to dance and chant. And anyone can try it; because it is not material, one will never get tired of chanting Hare Kṛṣṇa. In the material world, if one chants anything, any favorite name, for three, four, or ten times, he will get tired of it. That is a fact. But because Hare Kṛṣṇa is not material, if one chants this mantra, he will never get tired. The more one chants, the more his heart will be cleansed of material dirt and the more the problems of his life within this material world will be solved.

What is the problem of our lives? That we do not know. Modern education never gives enlightenment about the real problem of life. That is indicated in the *Bhagavad-gītā*. Those who are educated and are advancing in knowledge should know what is the problem of life. This problem is stated in the *Bhagavad-gītā:* one should always see the inconveniences of birth, death, old age, and disease. Unfortunately no one pays attention to these problems. When a man is diseased he thinks, "All right. Let me go to the doctor. He will give me some medicine, and I will be cured." But he does not consider the problem very seriously. "I did not want this disease. Why is there disease? Is it not possible to become free from disease?" He never thinks that way. This is because his intelligence is very low-grade, just like that of an animal. An animal suffers, but it has no sense. If an animal is brought to a slaughterhouse and sees that the animal before him is being slaughtered, he will still stand there contentedly eating the grass. This is animal life. He does not know that next time it will be his turn and he will be slaughtered. I have seen it. In a Kālī temple I have seen that a goat was standing there ready to be sacrificed and another goat was very happily eating the grass.

Similarly, Mahārāja Yudhiṣṭhira was asked by Yamarāja, "What is the most wonderful thing in this world? Can you explain?" So Mahārāja Yudhiṣṭhira answered, "Yes. The most wonderful thing is that at every moment one can see that his friends, his fathers, and his relatives have died, but he is thinking, 'I shall live forever.'" He never thinks that he will die, just as an animal never thinks that at the next moment he may be slaughtered. He is satisfied with the grass, that's all. He is satisfied with the sense gratification. He does not know that he is also going to die.

My father has died, my mother has died, he has died, she has died. So I will also have to die. Then what is after death? I do not know. This is the problem. People do not take this problem seriously, but the *Bhagavad-gītā* indicates that that is real education. Real education is to inquire why, although we do not want to die, death comes. That is real inquiry. We do not want to become old men. Why does old age come upon us? We have many problems, but this is the sum and substance of all of them.

In order to solve this problem, Lord Caitanya Mahāprabhu prescribes the chanting of Hare Kṛṣṇa. As soon as our heart is cleansed by chanting this Hare Kṛṣṇa mantra, the blazing fire of our problematic material existence is extinguished. How is it extinguished? When we cleanse our heart we will realize that we do not belong to this material world. Because people are identifying with this material world, they are thinking, "I am an Indian," "I am an Englishman," "I am this, I am that." But if one chants the Hare Kṛṣṇa mantra, he will realize that he is not this material body. "I do not belong to this material body or this material world. I am a spirit soul, part and parcel of the Supreme. I am eternally related with Him, and I have nothing to do with the material world." This is called liberation, knowledge. If I don't have anything to do with this material world, then I am liberated. And that knowledge is called *brahma-bhūta*.

A person with this realization has no duty to perform. Because we are now identifying our existence with this material world, we have so many duties. The *Śrīmad-Bhāgavatam* says that as long as there is no self-realization, we have so many duties and debts. We are indebted to the demigods. The demigods are not merely fictitious. They are real. There are demigods controlling the sun, the moon, and the air. Just as there are directors of government departments, so for the heating department there is the sun-god, for the air department there is Vāyu, and similarly there are other departmental demigods. In the *Vedas* they are described as controlling deities, so we cannot neglect them. Also, there are great sages and philosophers who have given us knowledge, and we are indebted to them. So as soon as we take birth we are indebted to so many living entities, but it is impossible to liquidate all these debts. Therefore the Vedic literature recommends that one take shelter of the lotus feet of Kṛṣṇa. And Kṛṣṇa says, "If one takes shelter of Me, then he doesn't have to take shelter of anyone else."

Therefore those who are Kṛṣṇa conscious devotees have taken shelter of Kṛṣṇa, and the beginning is hearing and chanting. *Śravaṇaṁ kīrtanaṁ viṣṇoḥ*. So our fervent, humble request to everyone is to please accept this chanting. This movement of Kṛṣṇa consciousness was introduced by Lord Caitanya five hundred years ago in Bengal, and now all over India and especially in Bengal there are millions of followers of Caitanya Mahāprabhu. Now this movement is starting in the Western countries, so just be very serious in understanding it. We do not criticize any other religion. Don't take it in that way. We have no business criticizing any other process of religion. Kṛṣṇa consciousness is giving people the most sublime religion—love of God. That's all. We are teaching to love God. Everyone is already loving, but that love is misplaced. We love this boy or this girl or this country or that society or even the cats and dogs, but we are not satisfied. So we must place our love in God. If one places one's love in God, he will be happy.

Don't think that this Kṛṣṇa consciousness movement is a new type of religion. Where is the religion which does not recognize God? One may call God "Allah" or "Kṛṣṇa" or something else, but where is that religion which does not recognize God? We are teaching that one should simply try to love God. We are attracted by so many things, but if our love is reposed in God, then we will be happy. We don't have to learn to love anything else; everything else is automatically included. Just try to love God. Don't try to love just trees or plants or insects. This will never satisfy. Learn to love God. That is Caitanya Mahāprabhu's mission; that is our mission.

CHANTING THE HARE KṚṢṆA MAHĀ-MANTRA

"This simplest method of meditation is recommended for this age. By practical experience also, one can perceive that by chanting this mahā-mantra, *or the Great Chanting for Deliverance, one can feel a transcendental ecstasy coming through from the spiritual stratum."*

The transcendental vibration established by the chanting of Hare Kṛṣṇa, Hare Kṛṣṇa, Kṛṣṇa Kṛṣṇa, Hare Hare/ Hare Rāma, Hare Rāma, Rāma Rāma, Hare Hare is the sublime method for reviving our transcendental consciousness. As living spiritual souls, we are all originally Kṛṣṇa conscious entities, but due to our association with matter from time immemorial, our consciousness is now adulterated by the material atmosphere. The material atmosphere, in which we are now living, is called *māyā*, or illusion. *Māyā* means "that which is not." And what is this illusion? The illusion is that we are all trying to be lords of material nature, while actually we are under the grip of her stringent laws. When a servant artificially tries to imitate the all-powerful master, he is said to be in illusion. We are trying to exploit the resources of material nature, but actually we are becoming more and more entangled in her complexities. Therefore, although we are engaged in a hard struggle to conquer nature, we are ever more dependent on her. This illusory struggle against material nature can be stopped at once by revival of our eternal Kṛṣṇa consciousness.

Hare Kṛṣṇa, Hare Kṛṣṇa, Kṛṣṇa Kṛṣṇa, Hare Hare is the transcendental process for reviving this original, pure consciousness. By chanting this transcendental vibration, we can cleanse away all misgivings within our hearts. The basic principle of all such misgivings is the false consciousness that I am the lord of all I survey.

Kṛṣṇa consciousness is not an artificial imposition on the mind. This consciousness is the original, natural energy of the living entity. When we hear this transcendental vibration, this consciousness is revived. This simplest method of meditation is recommended for this age. By practical experience also, one can perceive that by chanting this *mahā-mantra,* or the Great Chanting for Deliverance, one can at once feel a transcendental ecstasy coming through from the spiritual stratum. In the material concept of life we are busy in the matter of sense gratification, as if we were in the lower, animal stage. A little elevated from this status of sense gratification, one is engaged in mental speculation for the purpose of getting out of the material clutches. A little elevated from this speculative status, when one is intelligent enough, one tries to find out the supreme cause of all causes—within and without. And when one is factually on the plane of spiritual understanding, surpassing the stages of sense, mind, and intelligence, he is then on the transcendental plane. This chanting of the Hare Kṛṣṇa mantra is enacted from the spiritual platform, and thus this sound vibration surpasses all lower strata of consciousness—namely sensual, mental, and intellectual. There is no need, therefore, to understand the language of the mantra, nor is there any need for mental speculation nor any intellectual adjustment for chanting this *mahā-mantra.* It is automatic, from the spiritual platform, and as such, anyone can take part in the chanting without any previous qualification. In a more advanced stage, of course, one is not expected to commit offenses on the grounds of spiritual understanding.

In the beginning, there may not be the presence of all transcendental ecstasies, which are eight in number. These are: (1) being stopped as though dumb, (2) perspiration, (3) standing up of hairs on the body, (4) dislocation of the voice, (5) trembling, (6) fading of the body, (7) crying in ecstasy, and (8) trance. But there is no doubt that chanting for a while takes one immediately to the spiritual platform, and one shows the first symptom of this in the urge to dance along with the chanting of the mantra. We have seen this practically. Even a child can take part in the chanting and dancing. Of course, for one who is too entangled in material life, it takes a little more time to come to the standard point, but even such a materially engrossed man is raised to the spiritual platform very quickly. When the mantra is chanted by a pure devotee of the Lord in love, it has the greatest efficacy on hearers, and as such this chanting should be heard from the lips of a pure devotee of the Lord, so that immediate effects can be achieved. As far as possible, chanting from the lips of nondevotees should be avoided. Milk touched by the lips of a serpent has poisonous effects.

The word *Harā* is the form of addressing the energy of the Lord, and the words *Kṛṣṇa* and *Rāma* are forms of addressing the Lord Himself. Both *Kṛṣṇa* and *Rāma* mean "the supreme pleasure," and *Harā* is the supreme pleasure energy of the Lord, changed to *Hare* in the vocative. The supreme pleasure energy of the Lord helps us to reach the Lord.

The material energy, called *māyā,* is also one of the multienergies of the Lord. And we, the living entities, are also the energy, marginal energy, of the Lord. The living entities are described as superior to material energy. When the superior energy is in contact with the inferior energy, an incompatible situation arises; but when the superior marginal energy is in contact with the superior energy, Harā, it is established in its happy, normal condition.

These three words, namely *Hare, Kṛṣṇa,* and *Rāma,* are the transcen-dental seeds of the *mahā-mantra.* The chanting is a spiritual call for the Lord and His energy to give protection to the conditioned soul. This chanting is exactly like the genuine cry of a child for its mother's presence. Mother Harā helps the devotee achieve the Lord Father's grace, and the Lord reveals Himself to the devotee who chants this mantra sincerely.

No other means of spiritual realization is as effective in this age of quarrel and hypocrisy as the chanting of the *mahā-mantra:* Hare Kṛṣṇa, Hare Kṛṣṇa, Kṛṣṇa Kṛṣṇa, Hare Hare/ Hare Rāma, Hare Rāma, Rāma Rāma, Hare Hare.

KRSNA CONSCIOUSNESS— THE YOGA FOR THE MODERN AGE

"It is not that this movement is simply a sentimental movement. Don't think that these boys are dancing out of some religious sentiment or fanaticism. No. We have the highest philosophical and theosophical background. . . . But it is all simplified. That is the beauty of this movement. Whether one is a great scholar or a child, he can take part without any difficulty."

ceto-darpaṇa-mārjanaṁ bhava-mahā-dāvāgni-nirvāpaṇaṁ
śreyaḥ-kairava-candrikā-vitaraṇaṁ vidyā-vadhū-jīvanam
ānandāmbudhi-vardhanaṁ prati-padaṁ pūrṇāmṛtāsvādanaṁ
sarvātma-snapanaṁ paraṁ vijayate śrī-kṛṣṇa-saṅkīrtanam

All glories to the *saṅkīrtana* movement. *Paraṁ vijayate śrī-kṛṣṇa-saṅkīrtanam.* Lord Caitanya Mahāprabhu, when He was only a sixteen-year-old boy, introduced this *saṅkīrtana* movement five hundred years ago in Navadvīpa, India. It was not that He manufactured some religious system, just as nowadays so many religious systems are being manufactured. Actually, religion cannot be manufactured. *Dharmaṁ tu sākṣād bhagavat-praṇītam.* Religion means the codes of God, the laws of God, that's all. Certainly we cannot live without obeying the state laws, and similarly we cannot live without obeying the laws of God. And in the *Bhagavad-gītā* [4.7] the Lord says that whenever there are discrepancies in the prosecution of religious activities (*yadā yadā hi dharmasya glānir bhavati bhārata*) and there is a predominance of irreligious activities (*abhyutthānam adharmasya*), at that time I [Kṛṣṇa] appear (*tadātmānaṁ sṛjāmy aham*). And in the material world we can see the same principle demonstrated, for whenever there is disobedience of state laws, there is the advent of some particular state officer or policeman to "set things right."

Lord Caitanya Mahāprabhu is worshiped by the Gosvāmīs. There were six Gosvāmīs: Rūpa Gosvāmī, Sanātana Gosvāmī, Raghunātha Bhaṭṭa Gosvāmī, Jīva Gosvāmī, Gopāla Bhaṭṭa Gosvāmī, and Śrī Raghunātha dāsa Gosvāmī. There are three meanings of *go. Go* means "land," *go* means "cow," and *go* means "senses." And *svāmī* means "master." So *gosvāmī* means that they were masters of the senses. When one becomes master of the senses, or *gosvāmī,* he can make progress in spiritual life. That is the real meaning of *svāmī. Svāmī* means that one is not servant of the senses, but master of them.

One of these Six Gosvāmīs, Rūpa Gosvāmī, was the head, and he compiled a nice verse in honor of Lord Caitanya Mahāprabhu. He says:

anarpita-carīṁ cirāt karuṇayāvatīrṇaḥ kalau
samarpayitum unnatojjvala-rasāṁ sva-bhakti-śriyam
hariḥ puraṭa-sundara-dyuti-kadamba-sandīpitaḥ
sadā hṛdaya-kandare sphuratu vaḥ śacī-nandanaḥ
[*Caitanya-caritāmṛta, Ādi* 1.4]

Kalau means this age, this Age of Kali, the Iron Age, which is very much contaminated, an age of quarrel and disagreement. Rūpa Gosvāmī says that in this Age of Kali, when everything is disagreement and quarrel, "You have descended to offer the highest love of God." *Samarpayitum unnatojjvala-rasām:* and not only the topmost, but a very brilliant *rasa,* or transcendental humor. *Puraṭa-sundara-dyuti:* Your complexion is just like gold, like the luster of gold. "You are so kind that I bless everyone [the Gosvāmīs can bless because they are masters of the senses] that this form of the Lord, Lord Caitanya Mahāprabhu, may always remain dancing in everyone's heart."

When Rūpa Gosvāmī first met Lord Caitanya Mahāprabhu at Prayāga, Lord Caitanya was chanting and dancing in the street, "Hare Kṛṣṇa, Hare Kṛṣṇa." At that time also Rūpa Gosvāmī offered one prayer. *Namo mahā-vadānyāya kṛṣṇa-prema-pradāya te:* "Oh, You are the most munificent of all incarnations because You are distributing love of Godhead." *Kṛṣṇa-prema-pradāya te/ kṛṣṇāya kṛṣṇa-caitanya-nāmne gaura-tviṣe namaḥ:* "You are Kṛṣṇa Himself, because if You were not Kṛṣṇa You could not distribute *kṛṣṇa-prema,* or love of God, for love of Kṛṣṇa is not so easily acquired. But You are distributing this love freely to everyone."

In this way the *saṅkīrtana* movement was inaugurated in Bengal, India, in Navadvīpa. In this sense, the Bengalis are very fortunate that in their country this movement was inaugurated by Lord Caitanya, who predicted:

pṛthivīte āche yata nagarādi grāma
sarvatra pracāra haibe mora nāma

"In all the villages and towns all over the world, everywhere, this *saṅkīrtana* movement will be preached." That is His prediction.

So by the grace of Lord Caitanya, this movement is already introduced in the Western countries, beginning from New York. Our *saṅkīrtana* movement was first introduced in New York in 1966. At that time I came and began to chant this Hare Kṛṣṇa mantra in Tompkins Square. I was chanting there for three hours with a small *mṛdaṅga* (drum), and these American boys assembled and gradually joined, and so it is increasing. First of all it was started in a New York storefront, 26 Second Avenue, then we started our branches in San Francisco, Montreal, Boston, Los Angeles, Buffalo, Columbus. We now [1970] have twenty-four branches, including one in London and one in Hamburg. In London they are all American boys and girls, and they are preaching. They are not *sannyāsīs,* nor are they Vedāntists, nor Hindus, nor Indians, but they have taken this movement very seriously. Even in the London *Times* there was an article headlined "Kṛṣṇa Chant Startles London." So we have many in the movement now. All my disciples, at least in this country, are Americans and Europeans. They are chanting, dancing, and distributing a magazine, *Back to Godhead.* Now we have published many books—the *Śrīmad-Bhāgavatam, Bhagavad-gītā As It Is, Teachings of Lord Caitanya,* and *Īśopaniṣad.* It is not that this movement is simply a sentimental movement. Don't think that these boys are dancing out of some religious sentiment or fanaticism. No. We have the highest philosophical and theosophical background.

As an illustration, let us consider Caitanya Mahāprabhu. While He was preaching, He went to Benares, the seat of Māyāvādī *sannyāsīs.* The followers of Śaṅkarācārya are mostly seen in Benares. When Caitanya Mahāprabhu was there, He was chanting and dancing. Some of the people very much appreciated this, and so He quickly became famous. One prominent *sannyāsī,*

Prakāśānanda Sarasvatī, leader of many thousands of Māyāvādī *sannyāsīs*, was informed: "Oh, from Bengal one young *sannyāsī* has come. He is so nicely chanting and dancing." Prakāśānanda Sarasvatī was a great Vedāntist, and he did not like the idea. He said, "Oh, he is a pseudo *sannyāsī*. He is chanting and dancing, and this is not the business of a *sannyāsī*. A *sannyāsī* should always engage himself in the study of philosophy and the *Vedānta*."

Then one of the devotees who did not like the remarks of Prakāśānanda Sarasvatī came back and informed Lord Caitanya that He was being criticized. So the devotee arranged a meeting of all the *sannyāsīs*, and there was a philosophical discussion on the *Vedānta* between Prakāśānanda Sarasvatī and Lord Caitanya Mahāprabhu. These accounts and philosophical discussions are given in our *Teachings of Lord Caitanya*. It is remarkable that Prakāśānanda himself and all his disciples became Vaiṣṇavas. Similarly, Caitanya Mahāprabhu had a great discussion with Sārvabhauma Bhaṭṭācārya, the greatest logician of that time, who was also a Māyāvādī, impersonalist, and he was also converted.

So Caitanya Mahāprabhu's movement is not mere sentimentalism. There is a very rich background if one wants to understand this *saṅkīrtana* movement through philosophy and logic. There is ample opportunity, for this movement is based on science and on the authority of the *Vedas*. But it is all simplified. That is the beauty of this movement. Whether one is a great scholar or philosopher or a child, he can take part without any difficulty. Other systems of self-realization, the *jñāna* process or yoga process, are also recognized, but it is not possible to practice them in this age. That is the verdict of the *Vedas:*

kṛte yad dhyāyato viṣṇuṁ tretāyāṁ yajato makhaiḥ
dvāpare paricaryāyāṁ kalau tad dhari-kīrtanāt
[*Śrīmad-Bhāgavatam* 12.3.52]

In the Satya-yuga, the Golden Age, it was possible to execute the meditation process. For instance, Vālmīki Muni meditated for sixty thousand years to get perfection. But where is our old age? Besides that, for the meditation process, as described in the *Bhagavad-gītā*, one has to select a secluded place, he has to execute it alone, he has to sit down in a rigid posture, he has to lead a life of complete celibacy, and so on. There are many rules and regulations. Thus *aṣṭāṅga-yoga* meditation is not possible. If one is satisfied by imitating, that is a different thing, but if one wants perfection, then he has to execute all the eight stages of *aṣṭāṅga-yoga*. If this is not possible, then it is a waste of time.

What is the ultimate goal of the yoga process or meditation? Contact with the Supreme, the Supersoul, the Supreme Lord, is the aim and object of all yoga processes. Similarly, philosophical research, the *jñāna* process, also aims at understanding the Supreme Brahman. These are recognized processes, undoubtedly, but according to authoritative description, they are not practical in this Iron Age of Kali. Therefore one has to take to this process of *hari-kīrtana*. Anyone can practice without pre-qualification. One doesn't have to study philosophy or Vedānta. This was the purport of Lord Caitanya's meeting with Prakāśānanda Sarasvatī.

When the Vedānta philosophy was thoroughly discussed between Lord Caitanya and Prakāśānanda Sarasvatī, Prakāśānanda Sarasvatī first of all asked Caitanya Mahāprabhu, "I understand that You were a very good scholar in Your early life. [Lord Caitanya was actually a very great scholar. His name was Nimāi Paṇḍita, and at the age of sixteen He defeated a great scholar from Kashmir, Keśava Kāśmīrī.] And I understand that You are a great Sanskrit scholar, and that especially in logic You are a very learned scholar. You were also born in a *brāhmaṇa* family, and now You are a *sannyāsī*. How is it that You are chanting and dancing and not reading the *Vedānta?*" This was the first question asked by Prakāśānanda Sarasvatī, and Lord Caitanya replied, "Yes, the reason is that when I was initiated by My spiritual master, he said that I am fool number one. 'You don't discuss the *Vedānta,*' he told Me. 'You will simply spoil Your time. Just take to this chanting of Hare Kṛṣṇa, and You will be successful.'" That was his reply. Of course, Caitanya Mahāprabhu was not a fool, and certainly the *Vedānta* is not for fools. One needs sufficient education, and one must attain a certain status before he can understand the *Vedānta*. In each and every word there are volumes of meanings, and there are many commentaries by Śaṅkarācārya and Rāmānujācārya, huge volumes in Sanskrit. But how can we understand *Vedānta?* It is not possible. It *may* be possible for one person or two persons to understand, but for the mass of people it is not possible. Nor is it possible to practice yoga. Therefore, if one takes to Caitanya Mahāprabhu's method, chanting Hare Kṛṣṇa, the first installment of gain will be *ceto-darpaṇa-mārjanam:* all the dirty things will be cleansed from the heart simply by chanting. Chant. There is no expenditure and there is no loss. If one simply chants for one week, he will see how much he will progress in spiritual knowledge.

We are attracting many students simply by chanting, and they are understanding the entire philosophy and becoming purified. This Society was started only four years ago, in 1966, and we have so many branches already. The American boys and girls are taking it very seriously, and they are happy. Ask any one of them. *Ceto-darpaṇa-mārjanam.* They are cleansing the dirty things from the heart, simply by chanting Hare Kṛṣṇa, Hare Kṛṣṇa, Kṛṣṇa Kṛṣṇa, Hare Hare/ Hare Rāma, Hare Rāma, Rāma Rāma, Hare Hare.

The next point is *bhava-mahā-dāvāgni-nirvāpaṇam:* as soon as the heart is cleansed of all dirty things, then all the problems of material existence are immediately solved. This world has been compared to *dāvāgni,* which means a blazing fire in the forest. In this material existence no one wants unhappiness, but it comes by force. That is the law of material nature. No one wants fire, but wherever we go in a city the fire brigade is always active. There is always fire. Similarly, there are many things that no one wants. No one wants death—there is death. No one wants disease—there is disease. No one wants old age—there is old age. They are there, against our will, against our desire.

Thus we should consider the state of this material existence. This human form of life is meant for understanding, not for wasting this valuable life like animals by eating, sleeping, mating, and defending. That is not advancement of civilization. The *Bhāgavatam* says that this body is not meant for working hard simply for sense gratification.

nāyaṁ deho deha-bhājāṁ nṛ-loke
kaṣṭān kāmān arhate viḍ-bhujāṁ ye
[*Śrīmad-Bhāgavatam* 5.5.1]

To work very hard and satisfy oneself by sense gratification is the business of hogs, not human beings. The human being should learn *tapasya.* Especially in India, so many great sages, so many great kings, and so many *brahmacārīs* and *sannyāsīs* have passed their lives in great *tapasya* in order not to go further to sleep. Lord Buddha was a prince who gave up everything and engaged himself in *tapasya*. This is life. When King Bhārata, under whose name India was named Bhārata-varṣa, was twenty-four years old, he gave up his kingdom, his young wife, and young children and went away for *tapasya*. When Lord Caitanya Mahāprabhu was only twenty-four, He gave up His young wife, mother, everything. There are many, many examples. India is the land of *tapasya*, but we are forgetting that. Now we are making it the land of technology. It is surprising that India is now no longer propagating this *tapasya*, for India is the land of *dharma: dharma-kṣetre kuru-kṣetre.*

But it is not only in India; everywhere in this age of iron everything is degraded, degraded in this sense: *prāyeṇālpāyuṣaḥ sabhya kalāv asmin yuge janāḥ* [*Śrīmad-Bhāgavatam* 1.1.10]. In this Age of Kali the duration of life is diminished, and men are not moved to understand self-realization, and if they are, they are invariably misled by so many deceitful leaders. The age is very corrupt. Therefore Caitanya Mahāprabhu's process of chanting Hare Kṛṣṇa is the best and the simplest method.

harer nāma harer nāma harer nāmaiva kevalam
kalau nāsty eva nāsty eva nāsty eva gatir anyathā

"In this Age of Kali there is no other religion than glorifying the Lord by utterance of His holy name, and that is the injunction of all the revealed scriptures. There is no other way, there is no other way, there is no other way." This verse appears in the *Bṛhan-nāradīya Purāṇa. Harer nāma harer nāma harer nāmaiva kevalam.* Simply chant Hare Kṛṣṇa. There is no other alternative. *Kalau nāsty eva nāsty eva nāsty eva gatir anyathā.* In this age, Kali, there is no other alternative for self-realization. So we have to accept it.

There is a similar verse in the *Śrīmad-Bhāgavatam*. In the Twelfth Canto, Third Chapter, Parīkṣit Mahārāja was informed by Śukadeva Gosvāmī of the faults of this age, and now all the symptoms of the Age of Kali are apparent. In the conclusive portion, however, Śukadeva Gosvāmī said, *kaler doṣa-nidhe rājann asti hy eko mahān guṇaḥ:* "My dear king, this age, Kali, is full of faulty things, but there is one good opportunity." What is that? *Kīrtanād eva kṛṣṇasya mukta-saṅgaḥ paraṁ vrajet:* "Simply by chanting this Hare Kṛṣṇa mantra one can become liberated and go back to Godhead."

This is practical and authorized, and one can also test himself to see how he is advancing simply by chanting. This Kṛṣṇa consciousness movement is not something new, something that we have introduced or manufactured. It is authorized by the Vedic principles, authorized by *ācāryas* like Caitanya Mahāprabhu and others. And the method is very simple; there is no loss. We are not charging anything—we are not asking for fees and giving the people some secret mantra and promising them that within six months they will become God. No. This is open for everyone—children, women, girls, boys, old people—everyone can chant and see the results.

To further this end we not only are establishing New Vṛndāvana, our farm project in West Virginia, but are establishing other spiritual communities, such as New Navadvīpa and New Jagannātha Purī. We have already started New Jagannātha Purī in San Francisco, and the Ratha-yātrā festival is going on. This year there will be a great ceremony of Ratha-yātrā in London also. There will be three cars, for Jagannātha, Subhadrā, and Balarāma, and they will be taken to the river Thames. And America has imported New England and New York, so why not New Vṛndāvana? We should especially establish this New Vṛndāvana, because Lord Caitanya recommended, *ārādhyo bhagavān vrajeśa-tanayas tad-dhāma vṛndāvanam:* "Kṛṣṇa, the son of Nanda Mahārāja in Vṛndāvana-dhāma, or Vrajabhūmi, is the supreme worshipable Deity, and His place, Vṛndāvana, is also worshipable." The Western boys and girls are taking to Kṛṣṇa consciousness, and they should have a place like Vṛndāvana. Swami Kīrtanānanda, who went to Vṛndāvana with me two years ago, knows what Vṛndāvana is like, so I have instructed him to construct at least seven temples. In Vṛndāvana, there are five thousand temples of Rādhā-Kṛṣṇa, but the most important temples are seven, established by the Gosvāmīs. Our program is to live in New Vṛndāvana, depend on agriculture and cows as an economic solution, and peacefully execute Kṛṣṇa consciousness, chant Hare Kṛṣṇa—that is the Vṛndāvana scheme. *Yuktāhāra-vihārasya. . . yogo bhavati duḥkha-hā* [*Bhagavad-gītā* 6.17]. This human form of life isn't meant for increasing artificial needs. We should be satisfied just to maintain the body and soul together, and the rest of the time we should enhance our Kṛṣṇa consciousness, so that after leaving this body we won't have to take another material body, but will be able to go back home, back to Godhead. That should be the motto of human life.

Material life means eating, sleeping, mating, and defending, and spiritual life means something more than this. This is also the difference between animal life and human life. In animal life, the common formula is eating, sleeping, mating, and defending. A dog eats, a man also eats. A man sleeps, and a dog also sleeps. A man has sex life, and the dog also has sex life. The dog defends in his own way, and man also defends in his own way, maybe by atomic bombs. These four principles are common to human beings and animals, and advancement of these four principles is not human civilization but animal civilization. Human civilization means *athāto brahma jijñāsā.* In the *Vedānta-sūtra* the first aphorism is *athāto brahma jijñāsā:* "Now is the time for inquiry about Brahman." That is human life. As long as one is not spiritually inquisitive, *jijñāsuḥ śreya uttamam,* he is an animal, because he lives according to these four principles, that's all. He must be inquisitive to know what he is and why he is put into these miseries of birth, death, old age, and disease. Is there any remedy? These matters should be questioned. That is human life; that is spiritual life.

Spiritual life means human life, and material life means animal life. That's all. We have to make the adjustments that are recommended in the *Bhagavad-gītā. Yuktāhāra-vihārasya.* For instance, because I am going to be a spiritual man does not mean that I shall give up eating. Rather, my eating should be adjusted. The *Bhagavad-gītā* describes what class of food is first class, in goodness, and what class of food is in passion, and third class, in ignorance. We have to raise ourselves to the sattvic (goodness) platform of human civilization, then revive our transcendental consciousness, or Kṛṣṇa consciousness. Everything is there in the *śāstras.* Unfortunately, we do not consult them.

evaṁ prasanna-manaso bhagavad-bhakti-yogataḥ
bhagavat-tattva-vijñānaṁ mukta-saṅgasya jāyate
[*Śrīmad-Bhāgavatam* 1.2.20]

Unless one is liberated from the clutches of these three modes of material nature, he cannot understand God. *Prasanna-manasaḥ.* One must be a Brahman-realized soul. *Brahma-bhūtaḥ prasannātmā na śocati na kāṅkṣati* [*Bhagavad-gītā* 18.54]. These injunctions are there, so one should take advantage of these *śāstras* and preach. That is the responsibility of intelligent men. The mass of people know that God is great, but they do not know how great God actually is. That we will find in the Vedic literature. That is our duty in this iron age. That is *hari-kīrtana, paraṁ vijayate śrī-kṛṣṇa-saṅkīrtanam:* glorification of the Supreme.

MEDITATION AND THE SELF WITHIN

Can meditation solve our everyday problems? Is there life after death? Can drugs help us achieve self-realization? During a visit to South Africa in 1976, Śrīla Prabhupāda answered these and other questions for interviewer Bill Faill of the Durban Natal Mercury.

Śrīla Prabhupāda: *Kṛṣṇa* is a name for God that means "all-attractive." Unless one is all-attractive he cannot be God. So Kṛṣṇa consciousness means God consciousness. All of us are small particles of God, equal in quality with Him. Our position as living entities is like that of a small particle of gold in relation to a large quantity of gold.

Mr. Faill: Are we something like sparks in a fire?

Śrīla Prabhupāda: Yes. Both the fire and the spark are fire, but one is big, and the other is very small. Unlike the relationship between the spark and the fire, however, our relationship with God is eternal, although at the present moment we have forgotten that relationship due to contact with the material energy. We are facing so many problems only because of this forgetfulness. If we can revive our original God consciousness, then we shall become happy. This is the sum and substance of Kṛṣṇa consciousness. It is the best process by which to revive our original God consciousness. There are different processes of self-realization, but in the present Age of Kali, people are very fallen, and they require the simple process of Kṛṣṇa consciousness. Now they are thinking that so-called material advancement is the solution to their problems, but this is not a fact. The real solution is to get out of the material condition entirely by becoming Kṛṣṇa conscious. Because God is eternal, we are also eternal, but in the material condition we are thinking, "I am this body," and therefore we must repeatedly change from body to body. This is due to ignorance. Actually we are not our bodies but spiritual sparks, parts and parcels of God.

Mr. Faill: Then the body is just like a vehicle for the soul?
Śrīla Prabhupāda: Yes. It is just like a motorcar. Just as you go from one place to another in a car, so due to mental concoction in the material condition of life, we are going from one position to another, trying to become happy. But nothing will make us happy unless we come to our real position, which is that we are all parts and parcels of God and that our real business is to associate with God and help all living entities by cooperating with Him. Civilized human life is attained only after a long evolution through 8,400,000 species of life. So if we don't take advantage of this civilized human life to understand who God is, who we are, and what our relationship is, but instead simply waste our life like cats and dogs, going here and there looking for sense gratification, then we will have missed a great opportunity. The Kṛṣṇa consciousness movement is meant to teach people how to take full advantage of the human form of life by trying to understand God and our relationship with Him.
Mr. Faill: If we don't make the most of this life, do we get a second chance, in another life?
Śrīla Prabhupāda: Yes. According to your desires at the time of death, you get another body. That body is not guaranteed to be a human body, however. As I've already explained, there are 8,400,000 different forms of life. You can enter any of them, according to your mental condition at death. What we think of at the time of death depends on how we act during our life. As long as we are in material consciousness, our actions are under the control of the material nature, which is being conducted in three modes: goodness, passion, and ignorance. These modes are like the three basic colors—yellow, red, and blue. Just as one can mix red, yellow, and blue to produce millions of colors, the modes of nature are being mixed to produce many varieties of life. To stop the repetition of birth and death in different forms of life, we must transcend the covering of material nature and come to the platform of pure consciousness. But if we do not learn the transcendental science of Kṛṣṇa consciousness, then at death we must transfer to another body, either better or worse than our present one. If we cultivate the mode of goodness, then we are promoted to the higher planetary system, where there is a better standard of life. If we cultivate the mode of passion, then we will remain at the present stage. But if out

of ignorance we commit sinful activities and violate nature's laws, then we will be degraded to animal or plant life. Then again we must evolve to the human form, a process that may take millions of years. Therefore a human being must be responsible. He must take advantage of the rare opportunity of human life by understanding his relationship with God and acting accordingly. Then he can get out of the cycle of birth and death in different forms of life and go back home, back to Godhead.

Mr. Faill: Do you think transcendental meditation is helping people?

Śrīla Prabhupāda: They do not know what real meditation is. Their meditation is simply a farce—another cheating process by the so-called swamis and yogīs. You're asking me if meditation is helping people, but do you know what meditation is?

Mr. Faill: A stilling of the mind—trying to sit in the center without swinging either way.

Śrīla Prabhupāda: And what is the center?

Mr. Faill: I don't know.

Śrīla Prabhupāda: So everyone is talking very much about meditation, but no one knows what meditation actually is. These bluffers use the word "meditation," but they do not know the proper subject for meditation. They're simply talking bogus propaganda.

Mr. Faill: Isn't meditation valuable just to get people thinking right?

Śrīla Prabhupāda: No. Real meditation means to achieve a state in which the mind is saturated with God consciousness. But if you do not know what God is, how can you meditate? Besides, in this age people's minds are so agitated that they cannot concentrate. I have seen this so-called meditation; they are simply sleeping and snoring. Unfortunately, in the name of God consciousness or "self-realization," many bluffers are presenting nonstandard methods of meditation without referring to the authorized books of Vedic knowledge. They are simply practicing another type of exploitation.

Mr. Faill: What about some of the other teachers, like Ouspensky and Gurdjieff? In the past they brought to the West a message similar to yours.

Śrīla Prabhupāda: We would have to study the particulars of their teachings to know whether they meet the Vedic standard. God consciousness is a science, just like medical science or any other science. It cannot be different because it is spoken by different men. Two plus two equals four everywhere, never five, or three. That is science.

Mr. Faill: Do you feel that others may have possibly taught the genuine method of God consciousness?

Śrīla Prabhupāda: Unless I study their teachings in detail, it would be very difficult to say. There are so many bluffers.

Mr. Faill: Just doing it for money.

Śrīla Prabhupāda: That's all. They have no standard method. Therefore we are presenting the *Bhagavad-gītā* as it is, without any personal interpretation. This is standard.

Mr. Faill: Yes, if you begin dressing things up, you inevitably change them.

Śrīla Prabhupāda: Kṛṣṇa consciousness is not a new process. It is very, very old—and standard. It cannot be changed. As soon as you try to change it, then the potency is lost. This potency is just like electricity. If you want to generate electricity, you must follow the standard regulations, arranging all the negative and positive poles properly. You cannot construct the generator whimsically and still produce electricity. Similarly, there is a standard method of understanding Kṛṣṇa conscious philosophy from proper authorities. If we follow their instructions, then the process will act. Unfortunately, one of the dangerous diseases of modern man is that everyone wants to do things according to his own whims. No one wants to follow the standard way. Therefore everyone is failing, both spiritually and materially.

Mr. Faill: Is the Kṛṣṇa consciousness movement growing?

Śrīla Prabhupāda: Oh, yes, very much. You may be surprised to know that we are selling books in the tens of thousands. We have about fifty books, and many librarians and college professors are very appreciative of them, because until their publication there was no such literature in existence. It is a new contribution to the world.

Mr. Faill: Kṛṣṇa consciousness seems to involve shaving the head and wearing saffron robes. How can an ordinary man caught up in family life practice Kṛṣṇa consciousness?

Śrīla Prabhupāda: The saffron robes and the shaven head are not essential, although they create a good mental situation, just as when a military man is dressed properly he gets energy—he feels like a military man. Does that mean that unless he is in uniform he cannot fight? No. In the same way, God consciousness cannot be checked—it can be revived in any circumstances—but certain conditions are helpful. Therefore we prescribe that you live in a certain way, dress in a certain way, eat in a certain way, and so on. These things are helpful for practicing Kṛṣṇa consciousness, but they are not essential.

Mr. Faill: Then one can be a student of Kṛṣṇa consciousness while going about normal daily life?

Śrīla Prabhupāda: Yes.

Mr. Faill: How about drugs? Can they help in the process of God realization?

Śrīla Prabhupāda: If drugs could help God realization, then drugs would be more powerful than God. How can we accept that? Drugs are chemical substances, which are material. How can something material help one realize God, who is all-spiritual? It is impossible. What one experiences from taking drugs is simply a kind of intoxication or hallucination; it is not God realization.

Mr. Faill: Do you think the great mystics down through the ages have actually seen the spiritual spark you mentioned earlier?

Śrīla Prabhupāda: What do you mean by "mystic"?

Mr. Faill: It's just a name given to people who have had an experience of another level of reality.

Śrīla Prabhupāda: We don't use the word *mystic.* Our reality is God realization, which occurs when we come to the spiritual platform. As long as we have a bodily concept of life, our understanding is sense gratification, because the body is made of senses. When we progress from the bodily platform and we see the mind as the center of sense activity, we take the mind as the final stage of realization. That is the mental platform. From the mental platform we may come to the intellectual platform, and from the intellectual platform we can rise to the transcendental platform. Finally we can rise above even the transcendental platform and come to the mature, spiritual platform. These are the stages of God realization. However, in this age, because people are so fallen, the *śāstras* [scriptures] give the special recommendation that people come directly to the spiritual platform by chanting the holy names of God: Hare Kṛṣṇa, Hare Kṛṣṇa, Kṛṣṇa Kṛṣṇa, Hare Hare/ Hare Rāma, Hare Rāma, Rāma Rāma, Hare Hare. If we cultivate this practice on the spiritual platform, then immediately we can realize our spiritual identity.

Then the process of God realization becomes successful very quickly.

Mr. Faill: Today a lot of people are saying that we must look inward for the truth rather than outward into the world of the senses.

Śrīla Prabhupāda: Looking inward means knowing that you are a spirit soul. Unless you understand that you are not the body but a soul, there is no question of looking inward.

First we have to study, "Am I this body, or am I something within this body?" Unfortunately, this subject is not taught in any school, college, or university. Everyone is thinking, "I am this body." For example, in this country people everywhere are thinking, "I am South African, they are Indian, they are Greek," and so on. Actually, everyone in the whole world is in the bodily conception of life. Kṛṣṇa consciousness starts when one is above this bodily conception.

Mr. Faill: So the recognition of the spiritual spark comes first?

Śrīla Prabhupāda: Yes. Recognizing the existence of the spirit soul within the body is the first step. Unless one understands this simple fact, there is no question of spiritual advancement.

Mr. Faill: Is it a question of just understanding it intellectually?

Śrīla Prabhupāda: In the beginning, yes. There are two departments of knowledge: theoretical and practical. First one must learn spiritual science theoretically; then, by working on that spiritual platform, one comes to the point of practical realization.

Unfortunately, today almost everyone is in the darkness of the bodily conception of life. Therefore this movement is very important, because it can lift civilized men out of that darkness. As long as they are in the bodily conception of life, they are no better than animals. "I am a dog," "I am a cat," "I am a cow." Animals think like this. As soon as someone passes, a dog will bark, thinking, "I am a dog. I have been appointed here as watchdog." Similarly, if I adopt the dog's mentality and challenge foreigners—"Why have you come to this country? Why have you come to my jurisdiction?"—then what is the difference between the dog and me?

Mr. Faill: There is none. To change the subject a little, is it necessary to follow certain eating habits to practice spiritual life?

Śrīla Prabhupāda: Yes, the whole process is meant to purify us, and eating is part of that purification. I think you have a saying, "You are what you eat," and that's a fact. Our bodily constitution and mental atmosphere are determined according to how and what we eat. Therefore the *śāstras* recommend that to become Kṛṣṇa conscious, you should eat remnants of food left by Kṛṣṇa. If a tuberculosis patient eats something and you eat the remnants, you will be infected with tuberculosis. Similarly, if you eat *kṛṣṇa-prasādam*, then you will be infected with Kṛṣṇa consciousness. Thus our process is that we don't eat anything immediately. First we offer the food to Kṛṣṇa, then we eat it. This helps us advance in Kṛṣṇa consciousness.

Mr. Faill: You are all vegetarians?

Śrīla Prabhupāda: Yes, because Kṛṣṇa is a vegetarian. Kṛṣṇa can eat anything because He is God, but in the *Bhagavad-gītā* [9.26] He says, "If one offers Me with love and devotion a leaf, a flower, a fruit, or water, I will accept it." He never says, "Give Me meat and wine."

Mr. Faill: How about the tobacco question?

Śrīla Prabhupāda: Tobacco is also an intoxicant. We are already intoxicated by being in the bodily conception of life, and if we increase the intoxication, then we are lost.

Mr. Faill: You mean things like meat, alcohol, and tobacco just reinforce bodily consciousness?

Śrīla Prabhupāda: Yes. Suppose you have a disease and you want to be cured. You have to follow the instructions of a physician. If he says, "Don't eat this; eat only this," you have to follow his prescription. Similarly, we also have a prescription for being cured of the bodily conception of life: chanting Hare Kṛṣṇa, hearing about Kṛṣṇa's activities, and eating *kṛṣṇa-prasādam*. This treatment is the process of Kṛṣṇa consciousness.

VI.
FINDING THE CURE FOR TODAY'S SOCIAL ILLS

CRIME: WHY AND WHAT TO DO?

In this July 1975 interview, Chicago Police Department media relations man Lt. David Mozee asks about curbing the upward-spiraling U.S. crime rate. Śrīla Prabhupāda replies, "If human beings are not given the facility to learn about God, then they remain on the level of cats and dogs. You cannot have peace in a society of cats and dogs. . . . The thief and murderer already know the law, yet they still commit violent crimes due to their unclean hearts. So our process is to cleanse the heart."

Lieutenant Mozee: I understand you have some ideas that could help us in our efforts to prevent crime. I'd be very interested to hear them.

Śrīla Prabhupāda: The difference between a pious man and a criminal is that one is pure in heart and the other is dirty. This dirt is like a disease in the form of uncontrollable lust and greed in the heart of the criminal. Today people in general are in this diseased condition, and thus crime is very widespread. When the people become purified of these dirty things, crime will disappear. The simplest process of purification is to assemble in congregation and chant the holy names of God. This is called *saṅkīrtana* and is the basis of our Kṛṣṇa consciousness movement. So, if you want to stop crime, then you must gather as many people as possible for mass *saṅkīrtana.* This congregational chanting of the holy name of God will dissipate all the dirty things in everyone's heart. Then there will be no more crime.

Lieutenant Mozee: Do you have any feelings about crime here in the United States as opposed to the crime in your own country of India?

Śrīla Prabhupāda: What is your definition of crime?

Lieutenant Mozee: Any trampling on the rights of one person by another person.

Śrīla Prabhupāda: Yes. Our definition is the same. In the *Upaniṣads* it is said, *īśāvāsyam idaṁ sarvam:* "Everything belongs to God." So,

His Divine Grace A. C. Bhaktivedanta Swami Prabhupāda
The founder-*ācārya* of the International Society
for Krishna Consciousness and the greatest exponent
of Kṛṣṇa consciousness in the modern world.

As a rational animal, the human being is meant to make inquiries. But the most relevant inquiries—those made by truly intelligent persons—deal with what happens at the time of death. This scene from the great Vedic history *Śrīmad-Bhāgavatam* shows King Parīkṣit placing such inquiries before his spiritual master, Śukadeva Gosvāmī.
(*pp.* 40–48)

The great sage Parāśara Muni has defined God (*bhagavān*) as the person who possesses in full the six attractive opulences—beauty, strength, wealth, knowledge, fame, and renunciation. By carefully analyzing the character of Śrī Kṛṣṇa, spiritual authorities throughout the ages have concluded that He alone possesses these qualities to the fullest extent. (*pp.* 18–24)

Five thousand years ago on the Battlefield of Kurukṣetra: After seeing the opposing army consisting of his relatives, Arjuna has become confused about his duty and surrenders to Lord Kṛṣṇa as His disciple. Then Lord Kṛṣṇa speaks the *Bhagavad-gītā* for Arjuna's enlightenment. (*pp.* 84–92)

As a child grows, he becomes a boy, the boy becomes a young man, the young man becomes an adult, and the adult becomes an old man. After that he changes his body and accepts a new one out of 8,400,000 species of life. According to the law of karma, the kind of body a person gets in his next life depends on his activities and desires in this life. (*pp.* 26–36)

Whether boss or laborer, master or servant, president or prisoner, everyone is under the tight control of the three modes of material nature (goodness, passion, and ignorance). (*pp.* 26–36)

Human beings are not the only organisms with spirit souls. We are all spirit souls—beasts, birds, reptiles, insects, trees, plants, aquatics, and so on. The spirit soul is simply covered by different dresses, just as some persons are dressed in white clothes, some in green, some in red, etc. (*p.* 246)

everyone has the right to utilize whatever is allotted to him by God, but one may not encroach upon others' property. If one does so, he becomes a criminal. Actually the first crime is that you Americans are thinking this land of America is yours. Although two hundred years ago it was not yours, you have come from other parts of the world and claimed it as your land. Actually it is God's land, and therefore it belongs to everyone, since everyone is a child of God. But the vast majority of people have no conception of God. Practically speaking, everyone is godless. Therefore they should be educated to love God. In America, your government has a slogan: "In God we trust." Is that correct?

Lieutenant Mozee: Yes.

Śrīla Prabhupāda: But where is the education about God? To trust is very good, but simple trust will not endure unless it is backed up with scientific knowledge of God. One may know that he has a father, but unless he knows who his father is, his knowledge is imperfect. And that education in the science of God is lacking.

Lieutenant Mozee: Do you feel it's lacking only here in the United States?

Śrīla Prabhupāda: No. Everywhere. The age we live in is called Kali-yuga, the age of forgetting God. It is an age of misunderstanding and quarrel, and the people's hearts are filled with dirty things. But God is so powerful that if we chant His holy name we become purified, just as my disciples have become purified of their bad habits. Our movement is based on this principle of chanting the holy name of God. We give everyone the opportunity, without any distinction. They can come to our temple, chant the Hare Kṛṣṇa mantra, take a little *prasādam* as refreshment, and gradually become purified. So if the governmental authorities give us some facilities, then we can hold mass *saṅkīrtana*. Then, without a doubt, the whole society will change.

Lieutenant Mozee: If I understand you correctly, sir, you are saying that we should emphasize a return to religious principles.

Śrīla Prabhupāda: Certainly. Without religious principles what is the dif-ference between a dog and a man? Man can understand religion, but a dog cannot. That is the difference. So if human society remains on the level of dogs and cats, how can you expect a peaceful society? If you bring a dozen dogs and put them together in a room, will it be possible to keep them peaceful? Similarly, if

human society is filled with men whose mentality is on the level of dogs, how can you expect peace?
Lieutenant Mozee: If some of my questions sound disrespectful, it is only because I do not completely understand your religious beliefs. I mean no disrespect whatsoever.
Śrīla Prabhupāda: No, it is not a question of my religious beliefs. I am simply pointing out the distinction between human life and animal life. Animals cannot possibly learn anything about God, but human beings can. However, if human beings are not given the facility to learn about God, then they remain on the level of cats and dogs. You cannot have peace in a society of cats and dogs. Therefore, it is the duty of the governmental authorities to see that people are taught how to become God conscious. Otherwise, there will be trouble, because without God consciousness there is no difference between a dog and a man: the dog eats, we eat; the dog sleeps, we sleep; a dog has sex, we have sex; a dog tries to defend itself, and we also try to defend ourselves. These are the common factors. The only difference is that a dog cannot be instructed about his relationship with God, but a man can.
Lieutenant Mozee: Wouldn't peace be a precursor to a return to religion? Must we not first have peace?
Śrīla Prabhupāda: No, no, that is the difficulty. At the present moment, no one actually knows the meaning of religion. Religion means to abide by the laws of God, just as good citizenship means to abide by the laws of the government. Because no one has any understanding of God, no one knows the laws of God or the meaning of religion. This is the present status of people in today's society. They are forgetting religion, taking it to be a kind of faith. Faith may be blind faith. Faith is not the real description of religion. Religion means the laws given by God, and anyone who follows those laws is religious, whether a Christian, a Hindu, or a Muslim.
Lieutenant Mozee: With all due respect, isn't it true that in India, where religious customs have been followed for centuries upon centuries, we are seeing not a return to but a drawing away from spiritual life?
Śrīla Prabhupāda: Yes, but it is due only to bad leadership. Otherwise, the vast majority of the Indian people are fully conscious of God, and they try to follow the laws of God. Here in the West, even big college professors do not believe in God or in life after death.

But in India, even the poorest man believes in God and in a next life. He knows that if he commits sins he will suffer and if he acts piously he will enjoy. To this day, if there is a disagreement between two villagers, they will go to the temple to settle it, because everyone knows that the opposite parties will hesitate to speak lies before the Deities. So in most respects, India is still eighty-percent religious. That is the special privilege of taking birth in India, and the special responsibility also. Śrī Caitanya Mahāprabhu has said:

bhārata-bhūmite haila manuṣya-janma yāra
janma sārthaka kari' kara para-upakāra
[*Caitanya-caritāmṛta, Ādi* 9.41]

Anyone who has taken birth in India should make his life perfect by becoming Kṛṣṇa conscious. Then he should distribute Kṛṣṇa consciousness all over the world.

Lieutenant Mozee: Sir, there is a Christian parable that says it is easier for a camel to go through the eye of a needle than for a rich man to come before the throne of God. Do you think the wealth of the United States and other Western countries is a block to spiritual faith?

Śrīla Prabhupāda: Yes. Too much wealth is a block. Kṛṣṇa states in the *Bhagavad-gītā* [2.44]:

bhogaiśvarya-prasaktānāṁ tayāpahṛta-cetasām
vyavasāyātmikā buddhiḥ samādhau na vidhīyate

If one is materially very opulent, he forgets God. Therefore too much material wealth is a disqualification for understanding God. Although there is no absolute law that only the poor man can understand God, generally if one is extraordinarily rich, his only ambition is to acquire money, and it is difficult for him to understand spiritual teachings.

Lieutenant Mozee: In America, those who belong to the Christian faith also believe these things. I don't see any vast differences between the spiritual beliefs of one religious group and another.

Śrīla Prabhupāda: Yes, the essence of all religion is the same. Our proposal is that whatever religious system one follows, he should try to understand God and love Him. If you are a Christian, we do not say,

"That is no good; you must become like us." Our proposition is that whether you are a Christian, Muslim, or Hindu, simply try to understand God and love Him.

Lieutenant Mozee: If I could return to my original purpose for coming, might I ask what advice you could give to assist us in reducing crime? I recognize that the first and foremost way would be a return to God, as you say—there's no doubt about that—but is there something that we could immediately do to diminish this spreading criminal mentality?

Śrīla Prabhupāda: Yes. As I've already outlined in the beginning of our talk, you should give us the facility to chant the holy name of God and distribute *prasādam.* Then there will be a tremendous change in the population. I came alone from India, and now I have many followers. What did I do? I asked them to sit down and chant the Hare Kṛṣṇa mantra, and afterward I distributed a little *prasādam.* If this is done on a mass scale, the entire society will become very pleasing. This is a fact.

Lieutenant Mozee: Would you want to start the program in an area of affluence or an area of poverty?

Śrīla Prabhupāda: We do not draw such distinctions. Any place easily available to all kinds of men would be very suitable to hold *saṅkīrtana.* There is no restriction that only the poor men need the benefit but the rich do not. Everyone needs to be purified. Do you think criminality exists only in the poorer section of society?

Lieutenant Mozee: No. But I meant to ask whether there would be more of a beneficial influence—more of a strengthening of the community—if the program were held in a poorer area rather than an affluent area.

Śrīla Prabhupāda: Our treatment is for the spiritually diseased person. When a person is afflicted with a disease, there are no distinctions between a poor man and a rich man. They are both admitted to the same hospital. Just as the hospital should be in a place where both the poor man and the rich man can easily come, the location of the *saṅkīrtana* facility should be easily accessible to all. Since everyone is materially infected, everyone should be able to take advantage.

The difficulty is that the rich man thinks he's perfectly healthy, although he's the most diseased of all. But as a policeman, you well know that there's criminality among rich men and poor men alike.

So our chanting process is for everyone, because it cleanses the heart, regardless of the man's opulence or poverty. The only way to permanently change the criminal habit is to change the heart of the criminal. As you well know, many thieves are arrested numerous times and put into jail. Although they know that if they commit theft they will go to jail, still they are forced to steal because of their unclean hearts. Therefore without cleansing the heart of the criminal, you cannot stop crime simply by more stringent law enforcement. The thief and the murderer already know the law, yet they still commit violent crimes, due to their unclean hearts. So our process is to cleanse the heart. Then all the troubles of this material world will be solved.

Lieutenant Mozee: That's a very difficult task, sir.

Śrīla Prabhupāda: It is not difficult. Simply invite everyone: "Come, chant Hare Kṛṣṇa, dance, and take sumptuous *prasādam.*" What is the difficulty? We are doing this at our centers, and people are coming. But because we have very little money, we can hold *saṅkīrtana* only on a small scale. We invite everyone, and gradually people are coming to our centers and becoming devotees. If the government would give us a large facility, however, we could expand unlimitedly. And the problem is big; otherwise why are there national news articles asking what to do? No civil state wants this criminality. That's a fact. But the leaders do not know how to stop it. If they listen to us, however, we can give them the answer. Why crime? Because people are godless. And what to do? Chant Hare Kṛṣṇa and take *prasādam.* If you like, you can adopt this process of *saṅkīrtana.* Otherwise, we will continue conducting it on a small scale. We are just like a poor medical man with a small private practice who could open a big hospital if he were given the facility. The government is the executor. If they take our advice and adopt the process of *saṅkīrtana,* then the problem of crime will be solved.

Lieutenant Mozee: There are many Christian organizations in the United States that give the holy communion. Why doesn't this work? Why is this not cleansing the heart?

Śrīla Prabhupāda: To speak frankly, I find it difficult to find even one real Christian. The so-called Christians do not abide by the Bible's order. One of the ten commandments in the Bible is "Thou shalt not kill." But where is that Christian who does not kill by eating the flesh of the cow? The process of chanting the Lord's holy name and distributing *prasādam* will be effective if carried out by persons who are actually practicing religion. My disciples are trained to strictly follow religious principles, and therefore their chanting of the holy name of God is different from others'. Theirs is not simply a rubber-stamped position. They have realized the purifying power of the holy name through practice.

Lieutenant Mozee: Sir, isn't the difficulty that although a small circle of priests and devotees may follow the religious principles, those on the fringe deviate and cause trouble? For example, assume that the Hare Kṛṣṇa movement grows to gigantic proportions, as Christianity has. Wouldn't you then have a problem with people on the fringe of the movement who professed to be followers but were actually not?

Śrīla Prabhupāda: That possibility is always there, but all I am saying is that if you are not a true Christian, then your preaching will not be effective. And because we are strictly following religious principles, our preaching will be effective in spreading God consciousness and alleviating the problem of crime.

Lieutenant Mozee: Sir, let me thank you for your time. I will deliver this tape recording to my superiors. Hopefully, it will be effective, as you are effective.

Śrīla Prabhupāda: Thank you very much.

CAN WE KEEP SOCIETY FROM GOING TO THE DOGS?

Śrīla Prabhupāda speaks out to India's Bhavan's Journal: *"A dog comes when there are some eatables; I say 'Hut!' and he goes away. But again he comes—he has no memory. So when our memory of God is reducing, that means that our human qualities are reducing. . . . There is no religion, simply a dog's race. The dog is running on four legs, and you are running on four wheels—that's all. And you think that the four-wheel race is advancement of civilization!"*

Interviewer: The first question is this: "Is the influence of religion on the wane? And if so, does this factor account for the increase in corruption and the widespread deterioration of moral values?"
Śrīla Prabhupāda: Yes, religion is on the wane. This is predicted in the *Śrīmad-Bhāgavatam* [12.2.1]:

tataś cānudinaṁ dharmaḥ satyaṁ śaucaṁ kṣamā dayā
kālena balinā rājan naṅkṣyaty āyur balaṁ smṛtiḥ

"In the Kali-yuga [the present age of quarrel and hypocrisy] the following things will diminish: religion, truthfulness, cleanliness, mercy, duration of life, bodily strength, and memory."

These are human assets, which make the human being distinct from the animal. But these things will decline. There will be no mercy, there will be no truthfulness, memory will be short, and the duration of life will be cut short. Similarly, religion will vanish. That means that gradually we will come to the platform of animals.
Interviewer: Religion will vanish? We'll become animals?
Śrīla Prabhupāda: Especially when there is no religion, it is simply animal life. Any common man can distinguish that the dog does not understand what religion is. The dog is also a living being, but he is not interested in understanding the *Bhagavad-gītā* or the *Śrīmad-*

Bhāgavatam. He is not interested. That is the distinction between man and dog: the animal is not interested.

So when the human beings become uninterested in religious things, then they are animals. And how can there be happiness or peace in animal society? They want to keep people like animals, and they are making a United Nations. How is it possible? United animals, society for united animals? These things are going on.

Interviewer: Do you see any hopeful signs?

Śrīla Prabhupāda: At least they have detected that religion is declining. That is good. "Declining" means they are going to be animals. In logic it is said that man is a rational animal. When the rationality is missing, then he is simply an animal, not a human being. In human society either you become Christian, Muhammadan, Hindu, or Buddhist; it doesn't matter. There must be some system of religion. Human society without religion is animal society. This is a plain fact. Why are people so unhappy now? Because there is no religion. They are neglecting religion.

One gentleman has written me that Tolstoy once said, "Unless dynamite is put underneath the church, there cannot be any peace." Even now the Russian government is very strictly against God consciousness, because they think that religion has spoiled the whole social atmosphere.

Interviewer: It seems there could be some truth in that.

Śrīla Prabhupāda: The religious system might have been misused, but that does not mean that religion should be avoided. Real religion should be taken. It does not mean that because religion has not been properly executed by the so-called priests, religion should be rejected. If my eye is giving me some trouble on account of a cataract, it does not mean that the eye should be plucked out. The cataract should be removed. That is Kṛṣṇa consciousness.

Interviewer: I think history shows that many people have misused religion. Isn't that a fact?

Śrīla Prabhupāda: These people have no conception of God, and they are preaching religion. What is religion? *Dharmaṁ tu sākṣād bhagavat-praṇītam:* "The path of religion is directly enunciated by the Supreme Lord." They have no conception of God—they do not know what God is—and they are professing some religion. How long can it go on artificially? It will deteriorate.

That has become the present condition. They have no idea of

God, so how will they know what is the order of God? Religion means the order of God. For example, law means the order of the state. If there is no state, then where is the order? We have a clear conception of God—Kṛṣṇa. He is giving His order, and we accept it. It is clear religion. If there is no God, no conception of God, no order of God, then where is religion? If there is no government, then where is the law?

Interviewer: Well, there wouldn't be any law. It would be an outlaw society.

Śrīla Prabhupāda: Outlaw—everyone is an outlaw, manufacturing his own concocted system of religion. That is going on.

Just ask—in any religious system, what is their conception of God? Can anyone tell clearly? No one can tell. But we shall immediately say:

veṇuṁ kvaṇantam aravinda-dalāyatākṣaṁ
barhāvataṁsam asitāmbuda-sundarāṅgam
kandarpa-koṭi-kamanīya-viśeṣa-śobhaṁ
govindam ādi-puruṣaṁ tam ahaṁ bhajāmi

"I worship Govinda, the primeval Lord, who is adept at playing on His flute, whose blooming eyes are like lotus petals, whose head is bedecked with a peacock's feather, whose figure of beauty is tinged with the hue of blue clouds, and whose unique loveliness charms millions of Cupids." [*Brahma-saṁhitā* 5.30] Immediately, we can give a description of God.

If there is no idea of God, then what kind of religion is that?

Interviewer: I don't know.

Śrīla Prabhupāda: It is bogus. People have no conception of God, and therefore they have no understanding of religion. That is the decline, and because religion is declining, the human beings are becoming more and more like animals.

"Animal" means that one has no memory. A dog comes when there are some eatables; I say "Hut!" and he goes away. But again he comes—he has no memory. So when our memory of God is reducing, that means that our human qualities are reducing. In the Kali-yuga these human qualities will be reduced. That means that people are becoming like cats and dogs.

Interviewer: Here's the second question: "The traditional charge against Vedic culture is that it is fatalistic, that it makes people slaves to the belief in predestination, and that it therefore inhibits progress. How far is this charge true?"

Śrīla Prabhupāda: What is that progress? Is a dog's jumping progress? Is that progress? A dog is running here and there on four legs, and you are running here and there on the four wheels of the automobile. Is that progress? That is not the Vedic system. According to the Vedic system, the human being has a certain amount of energy, and since the human being has better consciousness than the animals, the energy of the human beings is more valuable than the energy of the animals.

Interviewer: Probably no one would dispute that the human being has more freedom or, I suppose, responsibility than the animals.

Śrīla Prabhupāda: So human energy should be utilized for spiritual advancement, not to compete with the dog. The saintly person is not busy like the dog. Today people think that "dog-ness" is life, but actual life is spiritual progress. Therefore, the Vedic literature says:

tasyaiva hetoḥ prayateta kovido
na labhyate yad bhramatām upary adhaḥ
tal labhyate duḥkhavad anyataḥ sukhaṁ
kālena sarvatra gabhīra-raṁhasā

"Persons who are actually intelligent and philosophically inclined should endeavor only for that purposeful end which is not obtainable even by wandering from the topmost planet [Brahmaloka] down to the lowest planet [Pātāla]. As far as happiness derived from sense enjoyment is concerned, it can be obtained automatically in the course of time, just as in the course of time we obtain miseries, even though we do not desire them." [*Śrīmad-Bhāgavatam* 1.5.18]

Interviewer: Could you explain that a little further?

Śrīla Prabhupāda: The human being should exert his energy for that thing which he did not get in many, many lives. In many, many lives the soul has been in the forms of dogs, or demigods, or cats, birds, beasts, and many others. There are 8,400,000 different types of bodies. So this transmigration of the soul is going on. The business in every case is sense gratification.

Interviewer: Which means?

Śrīla Prabhupāda: For example, the dog is busy for sense gratification: where is food, where is shelter, where is a female, where is defense? The man is also doing the same business, in different ways. This business is going on, life after life. Even a small insect is trying for the same thing. Birds, beasts, fish—everywhere the same struggle is going on. Where is food, where is sex, where is shelter, and how to defend? The Vedic literature says that these things we have done for many, many lives, and that if we don't get out of this struggle for existence, we will have to do them again for many, many lives.
Interviewer: I'm beginning to see.
Śrīla Prabhupāda: Yes, so these things should be stopped. Therefore, Prahlāda Mahārāja makes this statement:

sukham aindriyakaṁ daityā deha-yogena dehinām
sarvatra labhyate daivād yathā duḥkham ayatnataḥ

"My dear friends born of demoniac families, the happiness perceived with reference to the sense objects by contact with the body can be obtained in any form of life, according to one's past fruitive activities. Such happiness is automatically obtained without endeavor, just as we obtain distress." [*Śrīmad-Bhāgavatam* 7.6.3]

A dog has a body, and I have a body. So, my sex pleasure and the dog's sex pleasure—there is no difference. The pleasure derived out of sex is the same. A dog is not afraid of having sex pleasure on the street before everyone, and we hide it. That's all. People are thinking that to have sex pleasure in a nice apartment is advanced. However, that is not advanced. And they are making a dog's race for this so-called advancement. People do not know that according to whatever kind of body one has acquired, the pleasure is already stored up.
Interviewer: What do you mean, "the pleasure is already stored up"?
Śrīla Prabhupāda: That is called destiny. A pig has got a certain type of body, and his eatable is the stool. You cannot change it. The pig will not like to eat *halavā* [a dessert made of sweetened, buttery toasted grains]. It is not possible. Because he has a particular type of body, he must eat like that. Can any scientist improve the standard of living of the pig?
Interviewer: I doubt it.
Śrīla Prabhupāda: Therefore, Prahlāda Mahārāja says that it is

already stored up. The pleasure is basically the same, but a little different according to the body. The uncivilized man in the jungle is having the same thing.

Now people are thinking that civilization means constructing skyscraper buildings. But Vedic civilization says, No, that is not advance-ment. The real advancement of human life is self-realization, how much you have realized your *self.* Not that you have constructed skyscraper buildings.

Interviewer: But wouldn't what you're saying make sense to most people?

Śrīla Prabhupāda: Sometimes people misunderstand. In a high court, a judge is sitting soberly, apparently doing nothing, and he is getting a high salary. Someone else is thinking, "I am working so hard in the same court, rubber-stamping—and not getting one tenth the salary of the judge." He is thinking, "I am so busy, working so hard, and I am not getting as good a salary as the man who is just sitting on the bench." The situation is like that: the Vedic civilization is meant for self-realization, not for a dog's race.

Interviewer: Still, isn't it usually considered honorable to work hard, to struggle, and eventually "get ahead" in life?

Śrīla Prabhupāda: The *karmīs,* fruitive workers, have been described in the *Bhagavad-gītā* as *mūḍhas,* asses. Why are they compared to the asses? Because the ass works very hard with loads on his back, and in return his master gives him only a little morsel of grass. He stands at the door of the washerman and eats grass while again the washerman loads his back. He doesn't have the sense to think, "If I go out of the cottage of the washer-man, I can get grass anywhere. Why am I carrying so much?"

Interviewer: That brings to mind some people I know.

Śrīla Prabhupāda: The fruitive worker is like that. He is very busy in the office, and if you want to see him he will say, "I am very busy." So what is the result of your being so busy? He takes two pieces of toast and one cup of tea. And for this purpose you are so busy? He does not know why he is busy. In the account books he will find that the balance was one million dollars and now it has become two million. He is satisfied with that, but he will take only two pieces of toast and one cup of tea, and still he will work very hard. That is what is meant by *karmī.* Asses—they work like asses, without any aim in life.

But Vedic civilization is different. The accusation is not correct—people in Vedic civilization are not at all lazy. They are busy for a higher subject matter. Prahlāda Mahārāja stresses that this busyness is so important that it should begin from one's very childhood. *Kaumāra ācaret prājñaḥ:* one should not lose a second's time. That is Vedic civilization. The asses see, "These men are not working like I am"—like dogs and asses—and they consider that we are escaping. Yes, escaping your fruitless endeavor. The Vedic civilization is meant for self-realization.

Interviewer: Could you give us more of an idea what the Vedic civilization is like?

Śrīla Prabhupāda: The Vedic civilization begins from the *varṇāśrama* system. In the *varṇāśrama* system there is this arrangement: *brāhmaṇas* [intellectuals, advisors], *kṣatriyas* [administrators], *vaiśyas* [merchants, farmers], *śūdras* [workers], *brahmacārīs* [celibate students], *gṛhasthas* [householders], *vānaprasthas* [retired married people], and *sannyāsīs* [renounced monks].

The ultimate goal is that Kṛṣṇa, the Supreme Lord, should be worshiped. So if you worship Kṛṣṇa, then you fulfill all your occupational duties, either as a *brāhmaṇa, kṣatriya, vaiśya, śūdra, brahmacārī,* anything. Take to it immediately—take to Kṛṣṇa consciousness. This is so important.

Interviewer: If people really knew about a lifestyle that was more natural, more fulfilling, what would be the problem? They actually would, as you say, take to it.

Śrīla Prabhupāda: But they do *not* know, and therefore there is no religion, simply a dog's race. The dog is running on four legs, and you are running on four wheels—that's all. And you think that the four-wheel race is the advancement of civilization.

Therefore, modern civilization is practically said to do nothing. Whatever is obtainable by destiny you will get, wherever you are. Rather, take to Kṛṣṇa consciousness. The example is given by Prahlāda Mahārāja that you do not want anything distasteful and yet it comes upon you. Similarly, even if you do not want happiness which you are destined, it will come upon you. You should not waste your energy for material happiness. You cannot get more material happiness than you are destined.

Interviewer: How can you be so sure of that?

Śrīla Prabhupāda: How shall I believe it? Because you get some distressful condition, although you do not want it. For instance, President Kennedy died by the hand of his own countryman. Who wanted it, and why did it come? He was a great man, he was protected by so many, and still he was destined to be killed. Who can protect you?

So if the distressful condition comes upon me by destiny, then the opposite position—happiness—will also come. Why shall I waste my time for this rectification? Let me use my energy for Kṛṣṇa consciousness. That is intelligent. You cannot check your destiny. Everyone will experience a certain amount of happiness and a certain amount of distress. No one is enjoying uninterrupted happiness. That is not possible.

Just as you cannot check your distress, so you cannot check your happiness. It will come automatically. So don't waste your time for these things. Rather, you should utilize your time for advancing in Kṛṣṇa consciousness.

Interviewer: Would a Kṛṣṇa conscious person not try for progress?

Śrīla Prabhupāda: The thing is that if you try for progress vainly, then what is the use of that? If it is a fact that you cannot change your destiny, then what is the use of trying? We will be satisfied with the amount of happiness and distress we are destined.

Vedic civilization is meant for realization of God. That is the point. You'll still find in India that during important festivals many millions of people are coming to take bath in the Ganges, because they are interested in how to become liberated. They are not lazy. They are going thousands of miles, two thousand miles away, to take bath in the Ganges. They are not lazy, but they are not busy in the dog's race. Rather, they are busy right from their childhood trying to become self-realized. *Kaumāra ācaret prājño dharmān bhāgavatān iha.* They are so busy that they want to begin the business from their very childhood. So it is the wrong conception to think that they are lazy.

Interviewer: Then the question may be raised that if destiny cannot be checked, then why not let every newborn child simply run around like an animal, and whatever is destined to happen to him will happen?

Śrīla Prabhupāda: No, the advantage is that you can train him spiritually. Therefore it is said, *tasyaiva hetoḥ prayateta kovidaḥ:* you should engage your energy for self-realization. *Ahaituky apratihatā:*

devotional service, Kṛṣṇa consciousness, cannot be checked. Just as material destiny cannot be checked, your advancement in spiritual life cannot be checked if you endeavor for it.

Actually, Kṛṣṇa will change destiny—but only for His devotee. He says, *ahaṁ tvāṁ sarva-pāpebhyo mokṣayiṣyāmi:* "I shall give you all protection from all reactions of sinful activities." [*Bhagavad-gītā* 18.66]

For instance, if one is condemned by the law court to be hanged, no one can check it. Even the same judge who has given this verdict cannot check it. But if the defendant begs for the mercy of the king, who is above all the laws, then the king can check it.

Therefore, our business is to surrender to Kṛṣṇa. If we artificially want to be more happy by economic development, that is not possible. So many men are working so hard, but does it mean that everyone will become a Henry Ford or a Rockefeller? Everyone is trying his best. Mr. Ford's destiny was to become a rich man, but does it mean that every other man who has worked as hard as Ford will become a rich man like Ford? No. This is practical. You cannot change your destiny simply by working hard like an ass or a dog. But you can utilize that energy for improving your Kṛṣṇa consciousness.

Interviewer: Exactly what is Kṛṣṇa consciousness? Could you tell us more?

Śrīla Prabhupāda: Love of God—that is Kṛṣṇa consciousness. If you have not learned to love God, then what is the meaning of your religion? When you are actually on the platform of love of God, you understand your relationship with God—"I am part and parcel of God." Then you extend your love to the animal, also. If you actually love God, then your love for the insect is also there. You understand, "This insect has a different body, but he is also part and parcel of my father; therefore, he is my brother." Then you cannot maintain a slaughterhouse. If you maintain a slaughterhouse and disobey the order of Christ, "Thou shalt not kill," and you proclaim yourself Christian or Hindu, that is not religion. Then it is simply a waste of time—because you do not understand God; you have no love for God, and you are labeling yourself under some sect, but there is no real religion. That is going on all over the world.

Interviewer: How can we cure the situation?

Śrīla Prabhupāda: Kṛṣṇa is the Supreme Personality of Godhead.

If you do not accept that Kṛṣṇa is the supreme entity, then try to understand. That is education: there is someone supreme; Kṛṣṇa is not Indian; He is God. The sun rises first in India, but that does not mean that the sun is Indian; similarly, although Kṛṣṇa appeared in India, now He has come to the Western countries, through this Kṛṣṇa consciousness movement.

THE SUPREME WELFARE WORK

Śrīla Prabhupāda exchanges letters with the Secretary of the Andhra Pradesh Relief Fund Committee of Hyderabad, India. "If you want to perform relief work by collecting funds, I think that will not be successful. You have to please the supreme authority, and that is the way to success. For example, due to the performance of saṅkīrtana *[congregational chanting of Hare Kṛṣṇa] here, the rain has begun to fall after a drought of two years."*

Revered Swamiji,

The residents of the twin cities are happy to have this opportunity to meet you and your esteemed followers. You may be aware that due to inadequate rainfall during the last two years and its complete failure this year, more than half of our state [Andhra Pradesh, a state in southern India] is in the grip of a serious drought. With a view to supplement governmental efforts to combat this evil, a Central Voluntary Organization of citizens drawn from various walks of life has been set up. The members of this organization surveyed the areas affected by drought. The situation is pathetic. There are villages where drinking water is not available for miles. Due to scarcity of fodder, the cattle owners are parting with their cattle for a nominal price. Many of the stray cattle are dying away due to unavailability of fodder and water. The food problem is also very serious. Due to high prices of food grains on the open market, purchase of grains at market prices is beyond the reach of poor villagers, with the result that at least five to six million people are hardly having one meal a day. There are many who are on the verge of starvation. The entire situation is most pathetic and heartrending.

We therefore appeal to your revered self to consider how your Society could best come to the rescue of these millions of souls who are in unimaginable distress. The Committee would like to suggest that members of your Society appeal to the *bhaktas* [devotees] attending your discourses to contribute their mite to the Andhra Pradesh Relief Fund.

The Committee is prepared to send some of its representatives along with members of your Society wherever you wish to distribute *prasāda* to the hungry millions in the state.

As *mānava-sevā* is *mādhava-sevā* ["Service to man is service to God"], the Committee is confident that even a little effort by your gracious Society will go a long way in mitigating the sufferings of hundreds and thousands of people.

Yours ever in the service of the Lord,
T. L. Katidia, Secretary
Andhra Pradesh Relief fund Committee
Hyderabad, India

My dear Mr. Katidia,

Please accept my greetings. With reference to your letter and your personal interview, I beg to inform you that without pleasing the Supreme Personality of Godhead, no one can become happy. Unfortunately people do not know who God is and how to make Him happy. Our Kṛṣṇa consciousness movement is therefore meant to present the Supreme Personality of Godhead directly to the people. As stated in the *Śrīmad-Bhāgavatam*, Seventh Canto, Sixth Chapter: *tuṣṭe ca tatra kim alabhyam ananta ādye/ kiṁ tair guṇa-vyatikarād iha ye sva-siddhāḥ.*

The idea stated in this verse is that by pleasing the Supreme Personality of Godhead we please everyone, and there is no question of scarcity. Because people do not know this secret of success, they are making their own independent plans to be happy. However, it is not possible to achieve happiness in this way. On your letterhead I find many important men in this country who are interested in relieving the sufferings of the people, but they should know for certain that without pleasing the Supreme Personality of Godhead all their attempts will be futile. A diseased man cannot live simply on the strength of the help of an expert physician and medicine. If this were so, then no rich man would ever die. One must be favored by Kṛṣṇa, the Supreme Personality of Godhead.

Therefore if you want to perform relief work simply by collecting funds, I think that it will not be successful. You have to please the supreme authority, and that is the way to success. For example, due to the performance of *saṅkīrtana* here, the rain has begun to fall after a drought of two years. The last time we performed a Hare Kṛṣṇa Festival in Delhi, there was imminent danger of Pakistan's declaring war, and when a newspaper man approached me for my opinion, I said there must be fighting because the other party was aggressive. However, because of our *saṅkīrtana* movement, India emerged victorious. Similarly, when we held a festival in Calcutta, the Naxalite [Communist] movement stopped. These are facts. Through the *saṅkīrtana* movement we can not only get all facilities for living, but also at the end can go back home, back to Godhead. Those who are of a demoniac nature cannot understand this, but it is a fact.

I therefore request you, as leading members of society, to join this movement. There is no loss on anyone's part for chanting the Hare Kṛṣṇa mantra, but the gain is great. According to *Bhagavad-gītā* [3.21], what is accepted by leading men is also accepted by common men:

yad yad ācarati śreṣṭhas tat tad evetaro janaḥ
sa yat pramāṇaṁ kurute lokas tad anuvartate

"Whatever action a great man performs, common men follow in his footsteps. And whatever standards he sets by exemplary acts, all the world pursues."

The *saṅkīrtana* movement of Kṛṣṇa consciousness is very important. Therefore, through you I wish to appeal to all the leading men of India to accept this movement very seriously and give us all facility to spread this movement throughout the world. Then there will be a very happy condition, not only in India but all over the world.

Hoping this will meet you in good health,
Your ever well-wisher,
A.C. Bhaktivedanta Swami

DECLARING OUR DEPENDENCE ON GOD

In a conversation with the Back to Godhead *staff, Śrīla Prabhupāda discusses the American Revolution: "The Americans say they trust in God. But without the science of God, that trust is simply fictitious. First take the science of God very seriously; then put your trust in Him. . . . They're manufacturing their own way of governing. And that is their defect. They will never be successful. . . . There will always be revolutions—one after another. There will be no peace."*

Back to Godhead: Thomas Jefferson put the basic philosophy of the American Revolution into the Declaration of Independence. The important men of the day who signed this document agreed that there are certain very obvious or self-evident truths, the first of which is that all men are created equal. By this they meant that all men are equal before the law and have an equal opportunity to be protected by the law.

Śrīla Prabhupāda: Yes, in that sense men are, as you say, created equal.

BTG: Another point in the Declaration of Independence is that all men are endowed by God with certain natural rights that cannot be taken away from them. These are the rights of life, liberty, and—

Śrīla Prabhupāda: But animals also have the right to life. Why don't animals also have the right to live? The rabbits, for instance, are living in their own way in the forest. Why does the government allow hunters to go and shoot them?

BTG: They were simply talking about human beings.

Śrīla Prabhupāda: Then they have no real philosophy. The narrow idea that my family or my brother is good, and that I can kill all others, is criminal. Suppose that for my family's sake I kill your father. Is that philosophy? Real philosophy is *suhṛdaṁ sarva-bhūtānām:* friendliness to all living entities. Certainly this applies to human beings, but even if you unnecessarily kill one animal, I shall immediately protest, "What nonsense are you doing?"

BTG: The founders of America said that another natural right is the right to liberty, or freedom—freedom in the sense that the government doesn't have the right to tell you what kind of job you have to do.

Śrīla Prabhupāda: If the government is not perfect, it should not be allowed to tell people what to do. But if the government is perfect, then it can.

BTG: The third natural right they mentioned was that every human being has the right to pursue happiness.

Śrīla Prabhupāda: Yes. But your standard of happiness may be different from my standard. You may like to eat meat; I hate it. How can your standard of happiness be equal to mine?

BTG: So should everyone be free to try to achieve whatever standard of happiness he wants?

Śrīla Prabhupāda: No, the standard of happiness should be prescribed according to the qualities of the person. You must divide the whole society into four groups: those with *brāhmaṇa* qualities, those with *kṣatriya* qualities, those with *vaiśya* qualities, and those with *śūdra* qualities.* Everyone should have good facility to work according to his natural qualities.

You cannot engage a bull in the business of a horse, nor can you engage a horse in the business of a bull. Today practically everyone is getting a college education. But what is taught at these colleges? Mostly technical knowledge, which is *śūdra* education. Real higher education means learning Vedic wisdom. This is meant for the *brāhmaṇas*. Alone, *śūdra* education leads to a chaotic condition. Everyone should be tested to find out which education he is suited for. Some *śūdras* may be given technical education, but most *śūdras* should work on the farms. Because everyone is coming to the cities to get an education, thinking, "We can get more money," the agriculture is being neglected. Now there is scarcity because no one is engaged in producing nice foodstuffs. All these anomalies have been caused by bad government. It is the duty of the government to see that everyone is engaged according to his natural qualities. Then people will be happy.

---

* *Brāhmaṇas* are the learned and pious teachers (and spiritual leaders) of society, *kṣatriyas* are the military and administrators, *vaiśyas* are the farmers and merchants, and *śūdras* are the laborers.

BTG: So if the government artificially puts all men into one class, then there can't be happiness.
Śrīla Prabhupāda: No, that is unnatural and will cause chaos.
BTG: America's founding fathers didn't like classes, because they'd had such bad experience with them. Before the revolution, Americans had been ruled by monarchs, but the monarchs would always become tyrannical and unjust.
Śrīla Prabhupāda: Because they weren't trained to be saintly monarchs. In Vedic civilization, boys were trained from the very beginning of life as first-class *brahmacārīs* [celibate students]. They went to the *gurukula,* the school of the spiritual master, and learned self-control, cleanliness, truthfulness, and many other saintly qualities. The best of them were later fit to rule the country.

The American Revolution has no special significance. The point is that when people become unhappy, they revolt. That was done in America, that was done in France, and that was done in Russia.
BTG: The American revolutionaries said that if a government fails to rule the people properly, then the people have the right to dissolve that government.
Śrīla Prabhupāda: Yes. Just as in Nixon's case: they pulled him down. But if they replace Nixon with another Nixon, then what is the value? They must know how to replace Nixon with a saintly leader. Because people do not have that training and that culture, they will go on electing one Nixon after another and never become happy. People can be happy. The formula for happiness is there in the *Bhagavad-gītā.* The first thing they must know is that the land belongs to God. Why do Americans claim that the land belongs to them? When the first settlers went to America, they said, "This land belongs to God; therefore we have a right to live here." So why are they now not allowing others to settle on the land? What is their philosophy? There are so many overpopulated countries. The American gov-ernment should let those people go to America and should give them facility to cultivate the land and produce grains. Why are they not doing that? They have taken others' property by force, and by force they are checking others from going there. What is the philosophy behind this?
BTG: There is no philosophy.
Śrīla Prabhupāda: Roguism is their philosophy. They take the property by force, and then they make a law that no one can take another's

property by force. So they are thieves. They cannot restrict God's property from being occupied by God's sons. America and the other countries in the United Nations should agree that wherever there is enough land, it may be utilized by the human society for producing food. The government can say, "All right, you are overpopulated. Your people can come here. We will give them land, and they can produce food." We would see a wonderful result. But will they do that? No. Then what is their philosophy? Roguism. "I will take the land by force, and then I won't allow others to come here."

BTG: One American motto is "One nation under God."

Śrīla Prabhupāda: Yes, that is Kṛṣṇa consciousness. There should be one nation under God, and one world government under God as well. Everything belongs to God, and we are all His sons. That philosophy is wanted.

BTG: But in America people are very much afraid of a central government because they think that whenever there's a strong government there will always be tyranny.

Śrīla Prabhupāda: If the leaders are properly trained, there cannot be tyranny.

BTG: But one of the premises of the American system of government is that if a leader has too much power, he will inevitably become corrupt.

Śrīla Prabhupāda: You have to train him in such a way that he cannot become corrupt!

BTG: What is that training process?

Śrīla Prabhupāda: That training is the *varṇāśrama-dharma.** Divide the society according to quality and train people in the principle that everything belongs to God and should be used in the service of God. Then there really can be "one nation under God."

BTG: But if society is divided into different groups, won't there be envy?

Śrīla Prabhupāda: No, no. Just as in my body there are different parts that work together, so the society can have different parts working for the same goal. My hand is different from my leg. But when I tell the hand, "Bring a glass of water," the leg will help. The leg is required, and the hand is required.

BTG: But in the Western world we have a working class and a

---

* The system of dividing society into four social and four spiritual orders according to people's natural qualities.

capitalist class, and there is always warfare going on between the two.
Śrīla Prabhupāda: Yes. The capitalist class is required, and the working class is also required.
BTG: But they are fighting.
Śrīla Prabhupāda: Because they are not trained up; they have no common cause. The hand and the leg work differently, but the common cause is to maintain the body. So if you find out the common cause for both the capitalists and the workers, then there will be no fighting. But if you do not know the common cause, then there will always be fighting.
BTG: Revolution?
Śrīla Prabhupāda: Yes.
BTG: Then the most important thing is to find the common cause that people can unite on?
Śrīla Prabhupāda: Yes, just like in our Kṛṣṇa conscious society you come to consult me about every activity, because I can give you the common cause. Otherwise, there will be fighting. The government should be very expert to know the aim of life—the common cause—and they should train the people to work for the common cause. Then they will be happy and peaceful. But if people simply elect rascals like Nixon, they will never find a common cause. Any rascal can secure votes by some arrangement, and then he becomes the head of the government. The candidates are bribing, they are cheating, they are making propaganda to win votes. Somehow or other they get votes and capture the prime post. This system is bad.
BTG: So if we don't choose our leaders by popular election, how will society be governed?
Śrīla Prabhupāda: You require *brāhmaṇas, kṣatriyas, vaiśyas,* and *śūdras.* Just as when you want to construct a building, you require engineers. You don't want sweepers. Isn't that so? What will the sweeper do? No, there must be engineers. So if you follow the division of *varṇāśrama,* only *kṣatriyas* are allowed to govern. And for the legislative assembly—the senators—only qualified *brāhmaṇas.* Now the butcher is in the legislative assembly. What does he know about making laws? He is a butcher, but by winning votes he becomes a senator. At the present moment, by the principle of vox populi, a butcher goes to the legislature. So everything depends on training. In our Kṛṣṇa conscious society, we're actually doing that,

but in the case of politics, they forget it. There cannot be just one class. That is foolishness, because we have to engage different classes of men in different activities. If we do not know the art, then we will fail, because unless there is a division of work, there will be havoc. We have discussed all the responsibilities of the king in the *Śrīmad-Bhāgavatam*. The different classes in society should cooperate exactly as the different parts of the body do. Although each part is meant for a different purpose, they all work for one cause: to maintain the body properly.

BTG: What is the actual duty of the government?

Śrīla Prabhupāda: To understand what God wants and to see that society works toward that aim. Then people will be happy. But if the people work in the wrong direction, how can they be happy? The government's duty is to see that they are working in the right direction. The right direction is to know God and to act according to His instructions. But if the leaders themselves do not believe in the supremacy of God, and if they do not know what God wants to do, or what He wants us to do, then how can there be good government? The leaders are misled, and they are misleading others. That is the chaotic condition in the world today.

BTG: In the United States there has traditionally been the separation of church and state.

Śrīla Prabhupāda: I am not talking about the church. Church or no church—that is not the point. The main thing is that the leaders have to accept that there is a supreme controller. How can they deny it? Everything in nature is going on under the Supreme Lord's control. The leaders cannot control nature, so why don't they accept a supreme controller? That is the defect in society. In every respect, the leaders are feeling that there must be a supreme controller, and yet they are still denying Him.

BTG: But suppose the government is atheistic—

Śrīla Prabhupāda: Then there cannot be good government. The Americans say they trust in God. But without the science of God, that trust is simply fictitious. First take the science of God very seriously, then put your trust in Him. They do not know what God is, but we do. We actually trust in God.

They're manufacturing their own way of governing. And that is their defect. They will never be successful. They are imperfect, and if they go on manufacturing their own ways and means, they will remain imperfect. There will always be revolutions—one after another. There will be no peace.

BTG: Who determines the regulative principles of religion that people should follow?

Śrīla Prabhupāda: God. God is perfect. He does that. According to the Vedic version, God is the leader of all living entities (*nityo nityānāṁ cetanaś cetanānām*). We are different from Him because He is all-perfect and we are not. We are very small. We have the qualities of God, but in very small quantity. Therefore we have only a little knowledge—that's all. With a little knowledge you can manufacture a 747 airplane, but you cannot manufacture a mosquito. God has created the mosquito's body, which is also an "airplane." And that is the difference between God and us: we have knowledge, but it is not as perfect as God's. So the leaders of the government have to consult God; then they will rule perfectly.

BTG: Has God also devised the most perfect government?

Śrīla Prabhupāda: Oh, yes. The *kṣatriyas* ruled the government in Vedic times. When there was a war, the king was the first to fight. Just like your George Washington: he fought when there was a war. But what kind of president is ruling now? When there is a war, he sits very securely and telephones orders. He's not fit to be president. When there is war, the president should be the first to come forward and lead the battle.

BTG: But if man is small and imperfect, how can he execute God's perfect orders for a perfect government?

Śrīla Prabhupāda: Although you may be imperfect, because you are carrying out my order, you're becoming perfect. You have accepted me as your leader, and I accept God as my leader. In this way society can be governed perfectly.

BTG: So good government means first of all to accept the Supreme Being as the real ruler of the government?

Śrīla Prabhupāda: You cannot directly accept the Supreme Being. You must accept the servants of the Supreme Being—the *brāhmaṇas* or Vaiṣṇavas [devotees of the Lord]—as your guides. The government men are *kṣatriyas*—the second class. The *kṣatriyas* should take advice from the *brāhmaṇas* or Vaiṣṇavas and make laws accordingly. The *vaiśyas* should carry out the *kṣatriyas'* orders in practice. And the *śūdras* should work under these three orders. Then society will be perfect.

THE PEACE FORMULA

"The earth is the property of God, but we, the living entities, especially the so-called civilized human beings, are claiming God's property as our own, under both an individual and collective false conception. If you want peace, you have to remove this false conception from your mind and from the world."

The great mistake of modern civilization is to encroach upon others' property as though it were one's own and to thereby create an unnecessary disturbance of the laws of nature. These laws are very strong. No living entity can violate them. Only one who is Kṛṣṇa conscious can easily overcome the stringency of the laws of nature and thus become happy and peaceful in the world.

As a state is protected by the department of law and order, so the state of Universe, of which this earth is only an insignificant fragment, is protected by the laws of nature. This material nature is one of the different potencies of God, who is the ultimate proprietor of everything that be. This earth is, therefore, the property of God, but we, the living entities, especially the so-called civilized human beings, are claiming God's property as our own, under both an individual and collective false conception. If you want peace, you have to remove this false conception from your mind and from the world. This false claim of proprietorship by the human race on earth is partly or wholly the cause of all disturbances of peace on earth.

Foolish and so-called civilized men are claiming proprietary rights on the property of God because they have now become godless. You cannot be happy and peaceful in a godless society. In the *Bhagavad-gītā* Lord Kṛṣṇa says that He is the factual enjoyer of all activities of the living entities, that He is the Supreme Lord of all universes, and that He is the well-wishing friend of all beings. When the people of the world know this as the formula for peace, it is then and there that peace will prevail.

Therefore, if you want peace at all, you will have to change your consciousness into Kṛṣṇa consciousness, both individually and collectively, by the simple process of chanting the holy name of God. This is a standard and recognized process for achieving peace in the world. We therefore recommend that everyone become Kṛṣṇa conscious by chanting Hare Kṛṣṇa, Hare Kṛṣṇa, Kṛṣṇa Kṛṣṇa, Hare Hare/ Hare Rāma, Hare Rāma, Rāma Rāma, Hare Hare.

This is practical, simple, and sublime. Four hundred and eighty years ago this formula was introduced in India by Lord Śrī Caitanya, and now it is available in your country. Take to this simple process of chanting as above mentioned, realize your factual position by reading the *Bhagavad-gītā As It Is*, and reestablish your lost relationship with Kṛṣṇa, God. Peace and prosperity will be the immediate worldwide result.

SPIRITUAL COMMUNISM

During his visit to the Soviet Union, Śrīla Prabhupāda talks with Professor Grigoriy Kotovsky, head of the India Department at the U.S.S.R. Academy of Sciences: "Whether you surrender to monarchy, aristocracy, or dictatorship, you have to surrender; that is a fact. Without surrender there is no life. It is not possible. So we are educating people to surrender to the Supreme, wherefrom you get all protection. . . . Any other surrender you have to change by revolution. But when you come to Kṛṣṇa, then it is sufficient. You are satisfied."

Śrīla Prabhupāda: The other day I was reading the paper, *Moscow News.* There was a Communist congress, and the President declared, "We are ready to take others' experience to improve." So I think the Vedic concept of socialism or communism will much improve the idea of communism. For example, in a socialistic state the idea is that no one should starve; everyone must have his food. Similarly, in the Vedic concept of *gṛhastha* [householder] life it is recommended that a householder see that even a lizard or a snake living in his house should not starve. Even these lower creatures should be given food, and certainly all humans should. It is recommended that the *gṛhastha,* before taking his lunch, stand on the road and declare, "If anyone is still hungry, please come! Food is ready!" If there is no response, then the proprietor of the household takes his lunch. Modern society takes the people as a whole as the proprietor of a certain state, but the Vedic conception is *īśāvāsyam idaṁ sarvam*—everything is owned by *īśa,* the supreme controller. *Tena tyaktena bhuñjīthāḥ*—you may enjoy what is allotted to you by Him. *Mā gṛdhaḥ kasya svid dhanam:* but do not encroach upon others' property. This is the *Īśopaniṣad—Veda.* The same idea is explained in the different *Purāṇas.* There are many good concepts in the Vedic literature about communism. So I thought that these ideas should be distributed to your most thoughtful men. Therefore I was anxious to speak.

Prof. Kotovsky: It is interesting that here in our country there is now great interest in the history of old, old thought. From this point of view, our Institute translated into Russian and published many literary monuments of great Indian culture. You will be interested to discover that we published some of the *Purāṇas* and parts of the *Rāmāyaṇa.* There are volumes in Russian of *Mahābhārata* and also a second edition of *Mahābhārata,* translated in full. We have also published the full translation of *Manu-smṛti* with Sanskrit commentaries. Interest in these publications was so great that they sold out in a week. They are now completely out of stock. It was impossible to get them in the book market after a month. There is great interest among reading people here in Moscow and the U.S.S.R. toward ancient Vedic culture, and from this point of view we published many such books.

Śrīla Prabhupāda: Among these *Purāṇas,* the *Śrīmad-Bhāgavatam* is called the *Mahā-Purāṇa.*

Prof. Kotovsky: *Mahā-Purāṇa.*

Śrīla Prabhupāda: Yes. We have translated the full text—first we present the original Sanskrit text, its transliteration, the English equivalent for each word, then the translation, and then a purport, or explanation of the verse. In this way, there are eighteen thousand verses in *Śrīmad-Bhāgavatam.* We are translating everything literally. You can see. Each and every verse is being done like that for the whole *Bhāgavata Purāṇa.* The opinion of the *ācāryas,* the great saintly sages who are the preachers of the *Bhāgavata* philosophy, is *nigama-kalpa-taror galitaṁ phalam:* this is the ripened fruit of the Vedic desire tree [*Śrīmad-Bhāgavatam* 1.1.3]. It is accepted by all the Indian scholars, and Lord Caitanya especially preached this *Bhāgavatam.* So we have the complete *Bhāgavatam* in its English translation. If you want to see it, I can show you.

Prof. Kotovsky: It seems to me that in the Moscow and Leningrad libraries we have nearly all the major texts of ancient Indian culture, beginning from the *Vedas,* the original texts in Sanskrit. For instance, in the Leningrad branch of our Institute there are six or eight editions of *Manu-smṛti.* This Institute was founded in Imperial Russia in Leningrad, so in Leningrad we now have a branch of our Institute dealing mainly with the history of Asiatic culture. You will find here an account of what is being translated and what studies are being done on the history of Indian religion and also the

state of Indian religion, Hinduism, in Hindu India today.
Śrīla Prabhupāda: Hinduism is a very complex topic.
Prof. Kotovsky: Oh, yes. [*They laugh.*] Really, to my understanding, it is not a religion, from the European point of view; it is a way of life—religion, philosophy, a way of life, whatever you want.
Śrīla Prabhupāda: This word *Hindu* is not a Sanskrit word. It was given by the Muhammadans. You know that there is a river, Indus, which in Sanskrit is called Sindhu. The Muhammadans pronounce *s* as *h*. Instead of *Sindhu*, they made it *Hindu*. So *Hindu* is a term that is not found in the Sanskrit dictionary, but it has come into use. But the real cultural institution is called *varṇāśrama*. There are four *varṇas* [social divisions]—*brāhmaṇa, kṣatriya, vaiśya,* and *śūdra*—and four *āśramas* [spiritual divisions]—*brahmacarya, gṛhastha, vānaprastha,* and *sannyāsa*. According to the Vedic concept of life, unless people take to this system or institution of four *varṇas* and four *āśramas,* actually they do not become civilized human beings. One has to take this process of four divisions of social orders and four divisions of spiritual orders; that is called *varṇāśrama*. India's culture is based on this age-old Vedic system.
Prof. Kotovsky: *Varṇāśrama.*
Śrīla Prabhupāda: *Varṇāśrama*. And in the *Bhagavad-gītā*—perhaps you have read the *Bhagavad-gītā*?
Prof. Kotovsky: Yes.
Śrīla Prabhupāda: There, in the *Bhagavad-gītā* [4.13], is the statement *cātur-varṇyaṁ mayā sṛṣṭam:* this system was created by Viṣṇu [God]. So since *varṇāśrama* is a creation of the Supreme, it cannot be changed. It is prevalent everywhere. It is like the sun. The sun is a creation of the Supreme. The sunshine is there in America, in Russia, and in India—everywhere. Similarly, this *varṇāśrama* system is prevalent everywhere in some form or another. Take, for example, the *brāhmaṇas,* the most intelligent class of men. They are the brains of the society. The *kṣatriyas* are the administrative class; then the *vaiśyas* are the productive class, and the *śūdras* are the worker class. These four classes of men are prevalent everywhere under different names. Because it is created by the original creator, so it is prevalent everywhere, *varṇāśrama-dharma.*
Prof. Kotovsky: It is interesting that in the opinion of some European and old Russian scholars, this *varṇāśrama* system is a later creation, and if you would read the old texts of Vedic literature, you

would find a much more simple and agrarian society. It is the opinion of these scholars that the *varṇāśrama* system was introduced in Indian society in the late age of the Vedic era but not from the beginning. And if you would analyze the old texts, you would find that in the old classical India it was not so prevalent.

Śrīla Prabhupāda: As far as we are concerned, it is mentioned in the *Bhagavad-gītā. Cātur-varṇyaṁ mayā sṛṣṭam.* The *Bhagavad-gītā* was spoken five thousand years ago, and in the *Bhagavad-gītā* it is said, "This system of the *Bhagavad-gītā* was spoken by Me to the sun-god." So if you take an estimation of that period, it comes to forty million years ago. Can the European scholars trace back history five thousand years? Can they go back forty million years? We have evidence that this *varṇāśrama* system has been current at least five thousand years. The *varṇāśrama* system is also mentioned in the *Viṣṇu Purāṇa* [3.8.9]. *Varṇāśramācāravatā puruṣeṇa paraḥ pumān.* That is stated in the *Viṣṇu Purāṇa. Varṇāśrama-dharma* is not a phenomenon of a historical period calculated in the modern age. It is natural. In the *Śrīmad-Bhāgavatam* the comparison is given that just as in the body there are four divisions—the brain division, the arms division, the belly division, and the leg division—so by nature's way these four divisions are existing in the social body. There exist a class of men who are considered the brain, a class of men who are considered the arms of the state, a class of men who are called the productive class, and so on. There is no need of tracing history; it is naturally existing from the day of creation.

Prof. Kotovsky: You have said that in any society there are four divisions, but they are not so easy to distinguish. For instance, one can group together different social classes and professional groups into four divisions in any society; there is no difficulty. The only difficulty is, for instance, in the socialistic society—in our country and other socialist societies—how you can distinguish the productive group from the workers.

Śrīla Prabhupāda: For example, we belong to the intellectual class of men. This is a division.

Prof. Kotovsky: Intelligent class, *brāhmaṇas.* And you can also put together all the intelligentsia in that department.

Śrīla Prabhupāda: Yes.

Prof. Kotovsky: And then the administrative class.

Śrīla Prabhupāda: Yes.

Prof. Kotovsky: But who are the *vaiśyas* and *śūdras*? That is the difficulty. Because all others are workers—factory workers, collective farm workers, and so on. So from this point of view there is a great distinction, in my opinion, between socialist society and all societies preceding socialism, because in modern Western society you can group all social and professional classes in these particular class divisions—*brāhmaṇas, kṣatriyas, vaiśyas,* and *śūdras:* intellectuals, productive class, owners of the productive system (factory owners, for instance), and menial workers. But here you have no *vaiśyas* because you have administrative staffs in factories, and you can call them *kṣatriyas,* and then there are the *śūdras,* the workers themselves, but no intermediate class.

Śrīla Prabhupāda: That is stated. *Kalau śūdra-sambhavaḥ.* In this age practically all men are *śūdras.* But if there are simply *śūdras,* the social order will be disturbed. In spite of your state of *śūdras,* the *brāhmaṇa* is found here, and that is necessary. If you do not divide the social order in such a way, there will be chaos. That is the scientific estimation of the *Vedas.* You may belong to the *śūdra* class, but to maintain social order you have to train some of the *śūdras* to become *brāhmaṇas.* Society cannot depend on *śūdras.* Nor can you depend on the *brāhmaṇas.* To fulfill the necessities of your body, there must be a brain, arms, a stomach, and legs. The legs, the brain, and the arms are all required for cooperation to fulfill the mission of the whole body. So in any society you can see that unless there are these four divisions, there will be chaos. It will not work properly. It will be *māyā,* and there will be disturbances. The brain must be there, but at the present moment there is a scarcity of brains. I am not talking of your state or my state; I am taking the world as a whole. Formerly the Indian administration was a monarchy. For example, Mahārāja Parīkṣit was a *kṣatriya* king. Just before his death, he renounced his royal order. He came to the forest to hear about self-realization. If you want to maintain the peace and prosperity of the whole world society, you must create a very intelligent class of men, a class of men expert in administration, a class of men expert in production, and a class of men to work. That is required; you cannot avoid it. That is the Vedic conception, *mukha-bāhūru-pādajāḥ* [*Śrīmad-Bhāgavatam* 11.17.13]. *Mukha* means "the face," *bāhu* means "the arms," *ūru* means "the waist," and *pāda,* "the legs." Whether you take this state or that state, unless there is a smooth, systematic establishment of these four orders of life, the state or society will not run very smoothly.

Prof. Kotovsky: Generally it seems to me that this whole *varṇāśrama* system to some extent created a natural division of labor in the ancient society. But now division of labor among people in any society is much more complicated and sophisticated. So it is very confusing to group them into four classes.

Śrīla Prabhupāda: Confusion has come to exist because in India, at a later day, the son of a *brāhmaṇa,* without having the brahminical qualifications, claimed to be a *brāhmaṇa;* and others, out of superstition or a traditional way, accepted him as a *brāhmaṇa.* Therefore the Indian social order was disrupted. But in our Kṛṣṇa consciousness movement we are training *brāhmaṇas* everywhere, because the world needs the brain of a *brāhmaṇa.* Although Mahārāja Parīkṣit was a monarch, he had a body of *brāhmaṇas* and learned sages to consult, an advisory body. It is not that the monarchs were independent. In history it is found that if some of the monarchs were not in order, they were dethroned by the brahminical advisory council. Although the *brāhmaṇas* did not take part in politics, they would advise the monarch how to execute the royal function. This is not too far in the past. How long ago was Aśoka?

Prof. Kotovsky: That would be equal to what we call, in our terminology, ancient and medieval India.

Śrīla Prabhupāda: Yes.

Prof. Kotovsky: In old and feudal India—you are right—it was very open, and the major part of the high administrative staff in the legislative department were *brāhmaṇas.* Even in the Mogul era there were *brāhmaṇas* to advise the Muslim emperors and administrators.

Śrīla Prabhupāda: That is a fact—the *brāhmaṇas* were accepted. They formed the advisory committee of the king. For example, Candragupta, the Hindu king, was in the age of Alexander the Great. Just before Candragupta, Alexander the Great went from Greece into India and conquered a portion. When Candragupta became emperor, he had Cāṇakya as his prime minister. Perhaps you have heard this name Cāṇakya?

Prof. Kotovsky: Yes.

Śrīla Prabhupāda: Yes, he was a great *brāhmaṇa* politician, and it is by his name that the quarter of New Delhi where all the foreign embassies are grouped together is called Cāṇakya Purī. Cāṇakya

Paṇḍita was a great politician and *brāhmaṇa*. He was vastly learned. His moral instructions are still valuable. In India, schoolchildren are taught Cāṇakya Paṇḍita's instructions. Although he was the prime minister, Cāṇakya Paṇḍita maintained his *brāhmaṇa* spirit; he did not accept any salary. If a *brāhmaṇa* accepts a salary, it is understood that he has become a dog. That is stated in the *Śrīmad-Bhāgavatam*. He can advise, but he cannot accept employment. So Cāṇakya Paṇḍita was living in a cottage, but he was actually the prime minister. This brahminical culture and the brahminical brain is the standard of Vedic civilization. The *Manu-smṛti* is an example of the standard of brahminical culture. You cannot trace out from history when the *Manu-smṛti* was written, but it is considered so perfect that it is the Hindu law. There is no need for the legislature to pass a new law daily to adjust social order. The law given by Manu is so perfect that it can be applicable for all time. It is stated in Sanskrit to be *tri-kālādau*, which means "good for the past, present, and future."

Prof. Kotovsky: I am sorry to interrupt you, but to my knowledge all of Indian society in the second half of the eighteenth century was, by order of the British administration, under a law divergent from Hindu law. There was a lot of change. The actual Hindu law that was used by the Hindus was quite different from the original *Manu-smṛti*.

Śrīla Prabhupāda: They have now made changes. Even our late Pandit Jawaharlal Nehru introduced his own Hindu code. He introduced the right of divorce in marriage, but this was not in the *Manu-saṁhitā*. There are so many things they have changed, but before this modern age the whole human society was governed by the *Manu-smṛti*. Strictly speaking, modern Hindus are not strictly following the Hindu scriptures.

But our point is not to try to bring back the old type of Hindu society. That is impossible. Our idea is to take the best ideas from the original idea. For example, in the *Śrīmad-Bhāgavatam* there is a description of the communist idea. It is described to Mahārāja Yudhiṣṭhira. If there is something good, a good experience, why shouldn't you adopt it? That is our point of view. Besides that, modern civilization is missing one all-important point—the aim of human life. Scientifically, the aim of human life is self-realization, *ātma-tattva*. It is said that unless the members of human society come to the point of self-realization, they are defeated in whatever they do. Actually it is happening in modern society, despite all economic advancement and other advancement: instead of keeping peace and tranquillity, they are fighting—individually, socially, politically, and nationally. If we think about it in a cool-headed way, we can see that in spite of much improvement in many branches of knowledge, we are keeping the same mentality that is visible in the lower animal society. Our conclusion, according to the *Śrīmad-Bhāgavatam,* is that this human body is not meant for working hard for sense gratification. But people do not know anything beyond that. They do not know about the next life. There is no scientific department of knowledge to study what happens after this body is finished. That is a great department of knowledge.

In the *Bhagavad-gītā* [2.13] it is said, *dehino 'smin yathā-dehe. Deha* means "this body." *Dehinaḥ* means "the one who owns this body." *Dehino 'smin yathā dehe kaumāraṁ yauvanaṁ jarā.* The *dehī,* the owner of the body, is within, and the body is changing from one form to another. The child has a certain type of body that changes to another type when he is older. But the owner of the body still exists throughout. Similarly, when this body is completely changed, we accept another body. People do not understand this. We are accepting different bodies, even in this life, from babyhood to childhood to boyhood to youth. That is a fact—everyone knows it. I was a child, but that childhood body is no more. I have a different body now. What is the difficulty in understanding that when this body will be no more, then I will have to accept another body? It is a great science.

Prof. Kotovsky: As you know, there are two quite opposite approaches to this problem. The approach is slightly different according to different religions, but at the same time, any religion recognizes and searches for the change-of-place experience, or transmigration of spirit. In Christian religion, in Judaism, in—

Śrīla Prabhupāda: I am not talking religions with you. I am talking science and philosophy. One religion may accept one way; that is not our concern. We are concerned with the point that if the owner of the body is permanent in spite of different changes of body, there should be no difficulty in understanding that when this body changes entirely, the owner of the body will have another body.

Prof. Kotovsky: Another approach is that there is no separation.

There are no two phenomena—the body and the owner of the body are the same.
Śrīla Prabhupāda [*emphatically*]: No.
Prof. Kotovsky: When the body dies, the owner also dies.
Śrīla Prabhupāda: No, no. But why is there no department of knowledge in the university to study this fact scientifically? That is my proposition—they are lacking. It may be as you say or it may be as I say, but there must be a department of knowledge to study this. Recently a cardiologist in Toronto, a doctor, has accepted that there is a soul. I had some correspondence with him, and he strongly believes that there is a soul. So there is another point of view, but our process is to accept knowledge from authority. We have Kṛṣṇa's statement on this subject, and He is authoritative. Kṛṣṇa is accepted as the authority by all the *ācāryas*. The *Bhagavad-gītā* is accepted by scholarly and philosophical circles all over the world. Kṛṣṇa says:

dehino 'smin yathā dehe kaumāraṁ yauvanaṁ jarā
tathā dehāntara-prāptir dhīras tatra na muhyati

"Just as the soul gives up the childhood body and comes to the boyhood body and then to youth, the soul also gives up this body and accepts another body." [*Bhagavad-gītā* 2.13] This statement is given by Kṛṣṇa, the greatest authority according to our tradition of knowledge. We accept such a statement without argument. That is the way of Vedic understanding.
Prof. Kotovsky: The difficulty is that our approach is that we do not believe in anything without argument. We can believe only things based on argument.
Śrīla Prabhupāda: Yes, that is allowed. That is stated in the *Bhagavad-gītā* [4.34]. *Tad viddhi praṇipātena paripraśnena sevayā. Paripraśna*, argument, is allowed—but not in the challenging spirit, but rather with the spirit to understand. Argument is not denied. But as far as Vedic statements are concerned, they are infallible, and the scholars of the *Vedas* accept them in that way. For example, cow dung is the stool of an animal. Now, the Vedic statement is that as soon as you touch the stool of any animal—even if you touch your own stool—you are impure and have to purify yourself by taking a bath. According to the Hindu system, after evacuating one has to take a bath.
Prof. Kotovsky: That is quite understandable hygienic knowledge.

Śrīla Prabhupāda: Yes.
Prof. Kotovsky: Yes, that is right.
Śrīla Prabhupāda: But in another place it is stated that cow dung, although the stool of an animal, is pure. Even if you apply it to an impure place, that place becomes purified. This is superficially contradictory. In one place it is said that the stool of an animal is impure and as soon as you touch it you have to be purified, and in another place it says that cow dung is pure. According to our knowledge, it is contradictory—but still it is accepted by those who are followers of the *Vedas.* And the fact is that if you analyze cow dung, you will find that it contains all antiseptic properties.
Prof. Kotovsky: This I don't know.
Śrīla Prabhupāda: Yes, one professor in a medical college analyzed it, and he found it full of antiseptic properties. So Vedic statements, even if found contradictory, if analyzed scrutinizingly will prove correct. There may be an exception. But it is accepted, and when scientifically analyzed and examined, it is found to be correct.
Prof. Kotovsky: Yes, if you analyze from the scientific point of view, that is right.
Śrīla Prabhupāda: There are other instances—for example, the conch shell. The conch shell is the bone of an animal, and according to Vedic instruction if you touch the bone of an animal you become impure and have to take a bath. But this conch shell is kept in the Deity room, because it is accepted as pure by the *Vedas.* My point is that we accept Vedic laws without argument. That is the principle followed by scholars. If you can substantiate your statements by quotations from the *Vedas,* then they are accepted. You are not required to substantiate them in other ways. There are different kinds of *pramāṇas,* or evidences. Proof by Vedic quotation is called *śruti-pramāṇa.* As in the legal court if you can give statements from the law book your statement is accepted, so all statements you give, if supported by *śruti-pramāṇas,* are accepted by scholars. I think you know the *Vedas* are known as *śrutis.*
Prof. Kotovsky: Yes.
Śrīla Prabhupāda:

śruti-smṛti-purāṇādi- pañcarātra-vidhiṁ vinā
aikāntikī harer bhaktir utpātāyaiva kalpate
[*Brahma-yāmala*]

Any system we accept must be supported by evidences of *śruti, smṛti,* the *Purāṇas,* and *Pañcarātra.* That which is not proved by these *pramāṇas* is a disturbance.

Prof. Kotovsky: Could I just say one thing? What is in the *Vedas* could also have been proved in a scientific way. Today, suppose there is a scientific laboratory. What is said by that lab is true. That it is true you accept, without going into the propriety of it. Suppose you have a scientific workshop or institution; if this workshop or scientific institution says, "This is not good," the general body will take it for granted: "Yes. The scientific body has said so, so it is understood."

Śrīla Prabhupāda: Similarly, Vedic authoritative statements are accepted by the *ācāryas* [great teachers]. India is governed by the *ācāryas*—Rāmānujācārya, Madhvācārya, Śaṅkarācārya. They accept the *Vedas,* and their followers accept them. The benefit is that I do not waste my time to research whether cow dung is pure or impure; rather, because it is stated in the *Vedas* to be pure, I accept it. I save my time by accepting the *śruti-pramāṇa.* In that way there are different statements in the *Vedas* for sociology and politics or anything, for *veda* means "knowledge."

sarvasya cāhaṁ hṛdi sanniviṣṭo
mattaḥ smṛtir jñānam apohanaṁ ca
vedaiś ca sarvair aham eva vedyo
vedānta-kṛd veda-vid eva cāham
[*Bhagavad-gītā* 15.15]

Prof. Kotovsky: May I put one question to you? Have you many branches of your society in the world?

Śrīla Prabhupāda: Yes.

Prof. Kotovsky: Where is your main center, and where are the branches of the Kṛṣṇa consciousness society?

Śrīla Prabhupāda: Of course, I have over sixty-five branches.

Prof. Kotovsky: Sixty-five branches.

Śrīla Prabhupāda: Yes, and I have made my main center in Los Angeles. And now we are establishing an important center in Māyāpur, the birthplace of Lord Caitanya. Have you been to India?

Prof. Kotovsky: Six or seven times. Now there is a very difficult situation in Calcutta because of the influx of refugees from Bangladesh.

Śrīla Prabhupāda: Yes, but we had our *saṅkīrtana* for ten days, and it was very wonderful. The gathering was not less than thirty thousand people daily. They were much interested in hearing our lectures, since we lecture from *Śrīmad-Bhāgavatam* and *Bhagavad-gītā*. So people are responding from every part of the world, especially the American boys and girls. They are especially interested, and England and also Germany and France. From here I plan to go to Paris. What is the name of that place?

Disciple: In Paris? Oh, Fontenay-aux-Roses?

Śrīla Prabhupāda: Yes, they have taken a whole house, a nice house. So our process is very simple. We ask our students to observe four prohibitive principles—no illicit sex life, no eating of meat, fish or eggs, no gambling, and no intoxication, including cigarettes, tea, and coffee. One has to obey these four principles and chant the Hare Kṛṣṇa *mahā-mantra,* and you will find how, by this process only, these boys and girls are quickly improving. The process is very simple. Besides that, we have books—volumes of books—the *Śrīmad-Bhāgavatam,* the *Bhagavad-gītā*. Throughout all these years, I have written about one dozen four-hundred-page books—*Kṛṣṇa, the Supreme Personality of Godhead* in two parts, the *Śrīmad-Bhāgavatam* in six parts, *Teachings of Lord Caitanya* in one part, *The Nectar of Devotion* in one part. So we are trying to spread this Kṛṣṇa consciousness. Kṛṣṇa is a historical personality, as much as Lenin is a historical personality. Just as you are trying to understand his philosophy, we are trying to understand Kṛṣṇa's philosophy.

Prof. Kotovsky: Are there many participants in your sixty-five branches?

Śrīla Prabhupāda: Oh yes, more than one thousand initiated, and outside there are many. The one thousand have accepted the principles. Just like these boys. [*Śrīla Prabhupāda points to his two secretaries.*]

Prof. Kotovsky: But does that mean that these students abstain from normal Western, European universities? For instance, can a normal student from one of the various universities who is attending lectures in the normal way also be initiated and admitted to your community?

Śrīla Prabhupāda: If you want to live in our community and be initiated, we welcome you. If not, come try to understand our philosophy, read our books—there are so many books, magazines, questions, and answers. Try to understand the philosophy. It is not that all of a sudden a student comes and becomes our disciple. He first of all comes, associates, and tries to understand. We do not canvass. He voluntarily says that he wants to be a disciple.

Prof. Kotovsky: What happens if, for instance, one is not a student but a young worker or the young son of a farmer? Would he renounce his whole life and join your community in a given center? How would he maintain himself in his day-to-day life, in material life?

Śrīla Prabhupāda: As I told you, this propaganda is meant for creating *brāhmaṇas* all over the world, because the *brāhmaṇa* element is lacking. One who seriously comes to us has to become a *brāhmaṇa,* so he should adopt the occupation of a *brāhmaṇa* and give up the occupation of a *kṣatriya* or *śūdra.* But if one wants to keep his profession and also at the same time understand our movement, that is allowed. We have many professors following our movement. There is Howard Wheeler, a professor at Ohio State University. He is my disciple. He is continuing with his professorship, but almost all the money he is getting he is spending for this Kṛṣṇa consciousness. *Gṛhasthas,* those who are in householder life outside, are expected to contribute fifty percent of their income for our society, keep twenty-five percent for family, and keep twenty-five percent for personal emergencies. But Lord Caitanya Mahāprabhu teaches that it does not matter whether one is a *gṛhastha* [householder], or in the renounced order, or a *brāhmaṇa,* or a *śūdra.* Lord Caitanya says, "Anyone who understands the science of Kṛṣṇa becomes My spiritual master." The actual words in Bengali are *kibā vipra, kibā nyāsī, śūdra kene naya.* Do you understand a little Bengali?

Prof. Kotovsky: A little.

Śrīla Prabhupāda: Yes, as a vibration. *Yei kṛṣṇa-tattva-vettā, sei 'guru' haya.* "Anyone who understands the science of Kṛṣṇa can become a spiritual master." [*Caitanya-caritāmṛta, Madhya* 8.128]

Prof. Kotovsky: But by creating *brāhmaṇas* from different social classes of society, you deny the old prescription of the Hindu scriptures.

Śrīla Prabhupāda: No, I establish it.

Prof. Kotovsky: According to all scriptures—the *Purāṇas,* etc.—every member of one of these four classes of *varṇas* has to be born within it.

Śrīla Prabhupāda: No, no, no, no.
Prof. Kotovsky: That is the foundation of all the *varṇas*—
Śrīla Prabhupāda: No, no. I am sorry.
Prof. Kotovsky: The foundation of all the *varṇas*—
Śrīla Prabhupāda: You have spoken incorrectly. With great respect I beg to submit that you are not speaking correctly. In the *Bhagavad-gītā* [4.13] it is stated, *cātur-varṇyaṁ mayā sṛṣṭaṁ guṇa-karma-vibhāgaśaḥ:* "These four orders of *brāhmaṇas, kṣatriyas, vaiśyas,* and *śūdras* were created by Me according to quality and work." There is no mention of birth.
Prof. Kotovsky: I agree with you that this is the addition of later *brāhmaṇas* who tried to perpetuate these qualities.
Śrīla Prabhupāda: That has killed the Indian culture. Otherwise there would have been no necessity of the division of part of India into Pakistan. Not only that, but from the historical point of view this whole planet was Bhārata-varṣa, and it was controlled by one flag up to the time of Mahārāja Parīkṣit. Then it gradually separated. This is history. Lately they have separated Pakistan. So Bhārata-varṣa is now crippled into a small piece of land. Otherwise, according to Vedic scripture, this whole planet is called Bhārata-varṣa. Formerly it was named Ilāvṛta-varṣa. But since Emperor Bhārata ruled this planet, it is called Bhārata-varṣa. So this culture, Kṛṣṇa consciousness, was always existent. Consider any religion—Christian, Muhammadan, Jewish. They are at most two to three thousand years old. But you cannot trace out the beginning of this Vedic scripture. It is therefore called *sanātana,* eternal. This culture is for this whole human society. It is not a religious faith. Religious faith you can change, but real *dharma* you cannot change. Try to understand Kṛṣṇa. In the *Bhagavad-gītā* [18.66] He says, *sarva-dharmān parityajya mām ekaṁ śaraṇaṁ vraja:* "Give up all other forms of religion and just surrender to Me." That is real knowledge—to surrender to the Supreme. You or I—anyone—is surrendered to someone. That is a fact. Our life is by surrender, is it not? Do you disagree with this point?
Prof. Kotovsky: To some extent you surrender.
Śrīla Prabhupāda: Yes, to the full extent.
Prof. Kotovsky: You have to surrender to the society, for instance. To the whole people.
Śrīla Prabhupāda: Yes, to the whole people, or to the state or to the

king or the government or whatever you say. This surrender must be there.

Prof. Kotovsky: The only difficulty is that we cannot half surrender to a government or a king. The principal difference is of surrender to a king, to a person, or to the society.

Śrīla Prabhupāda: No, that is only a change of color. But the principle of surrender is there. Whether you surrender to monarchy, democracy, aristocracy, or dictatorship, you have to surrender; that is a fact. Without surrender there is no life. It is not possible. So we are educating people to surrender to the Supreme, wherefrom you get all protection, just as Kṛṣṇa says (*sarva-dharmān parityajya mām ekaṁ śaraṇaṁ vraja*). No one can say, "No, I am not surrendered to anyone." Not a single person. The difference is *where* he surrenders. The ultimate surrendering object is Kṛṣṇa. Therefore in the *Bhagavad-gītā* [7.19] Kṛṣṇa says, *bahūnāṁ janmanām ante jñānavān māṁ prapadyate:* "After surrendering to so many things birth after birth, when one is factually wise he surrenders unto Me." *Vāsudevaḥ sarvam iti sa mahātmā sudurlabhaḥ:* "Such a *mahātmā* is very rare."

Prof. Kotovsky: But at the same time it seems to me that surrender is to be accompanied by revolt. The history of mankind has proved that mankind has developed only by revolt against some kind of surrender. In the medieval age there was the French Revolution. It was revolt against surrender. But this revolution itself was surrender to the rank and file of the people. You are agreed?

Śrīla Prabhupāda: Yes.

Prof. Kotovsky: So it is not enough to come to a full stop. Surrender is to be accompanied with revolt against some and surrender to other people.

Śrīla Prabhupāda: But the surrender will be fully stopped when it is surrender to Kṛṣṇa.

Prof. Kotovsky: Ah, ah.

Śrīla Prabhupāda: That is full stop—no more surrender. Any other surrender you have to change by revolution. But when you come to Kṛṣṇa, then it is sufficient. You are satisfied. I'll give you an example: a child is crying, and people move him from one lap to another. Oh, he does not stop. But as soon as the baby comes to the lap of his mother—

Prof. Kotovsky: It stops.

Śrīla Prabhupāda: Yes, full satisfaction. So this surrender, these changes, will go on in different categories. But the sum total of all this surrender is surrender to *māyā*. Therefore, in the *Bhagavad-gītā* it is said that this surrender, neglecting Kṛṣṇa, is all *māyā*. Either you surrender to this or to that, but final surrender is surrender to Kṛṣṇa; then you will be happy. The process of surrender is there, but surrender to Kṛṣṇa keeps one quite satisfied, transcendentally.
Prof. Kotovsky: Haven't you come across hostile attitudes to your teachings from orthodox Hindus or *brāhmaṇas* in India?
Śrīla Prabhupāda: We have subdued them.
Prof. Kotovsky: Ah.
Śrīla Prabhupāda: Any orthodox Hindu may come and challenge, but we have our weapons—the Vedic literatures. So no one has come. Even Christian priests in America love me. They say, "These boys are American, Christian, Jewish, and now they are so much after God. But we could not deliver them." They are admitting it. Their fathers and their parents come to me, offer their obeisances, and say, "Swamiji, it is our great fortune that you have come here to teach God consciousness." So on the contrary, I have been well received. In India also, since you inquired of India, all other sects are admitting that before me many kinds of swamis went to the Western countries, but they could not convert even a single person to Kṛṣṇa consciousness. They are admitting that. As far as I am concerned, I don't take any credit, but I am confident that because I am presenting the Vedic knowledge as it is, without adulteration, it is being effective. That is my confidence. If you have the right medicine and you administer it to a patient, you must be sure that he will be cured.
Prof. Kotovsky: How many out of your one thousand disciples do you have in India itself? How many of your community do you have in India?
Śrīla Prabhupāda: In India?
Prof. Kotovsky: Yes.
Śrīla Prabhupāda: In India there are many Kṛṣṇa conscious persons—hundreds, thousands, millions. In India there is no question. There is not a single Hindu who is not Kṛṣṇa conscious.
Prof. Kotovsky: Yes, I understand.
Śrīla Prabhupāda: Vaiṣṇavas. This is called the Vaiṣṇava cult. You have been in India, so as it is commonly known, there are many

millions of Vaiṣṇavas. For example, this gentleman [an Indian gentleman present] is the commander of Air India airlines. He is not my disciple, but he is a Vaiṣṇava, Kṛṣṇa conscious. Similarly, in India there are millions of Kṛṣṇa conscious persons. There are even Muhammadans who are Kṛṣṇa conscious. At Gorakhpur University there is a Muhammadan professor who is a great devotee of Lord Kṛṣṇa. So this is natural. It is said in the *Caitanya-caritāmṛta* that Kṛṣṇa consciousness is everywhere, in everyone's heart. It simply has to be awakened by this process. That is all. It is there in your heart also. It is not that it is foreign to you. In everyone's heart there is Kṛṣṇa consciousness. By this process we have to awaken it. It is just like the way the sun rises. It is not that all of a sudden the sun comes from nowhere. It is there, but it rises in the morning. Similarly, this Kṛṣṇa consciousness is everywhere, but some way or another it is now covered. By this process it is reawakened and aroused by association.

Prof. Kotovsky: You came yesterday to Moscow. Have you seen something here in Moscow?

Śrīla Prabhupāda: No, I am not very much interested in sightseeing.

Prof. Kotovsky: But in any case, just to stay in an old-style hotel is not interesting—not many people to see. And you are leaving the day after tomorrow?

Śrīla Prabhupāda: That is my program.

Prof. Kotovsky: You are leaving for the United States or for Europe?

Śrīla Prabhupāda: Yes, for Europe. Paris. And we have two very big ceremonies in London and San Francisco. They are making arrangements for the Ratha-yātrā Car Festival. This car festival is observed in Jagannātha Purī. You have been to Jagannātha Purī?

Prof. Kotovsky: Yes, the car festival has been held from immemorial times. A very old tradition. Huge cars.

Śrīla Prabhupāda: Yes, and it has now been introduced in the Western countries in London and San Francisco, and gradually maybe we will introduce it in other countries also.

Prof. Kotovsky: In London there is a large Indian community.

Śrīla Prabhupāda: No, no. This is organized by the Englishmen and Americans. The Indian communities in London and San Francisco are trying to become—you know the word? *Sahib?*

Prof. Kotovsky: [*Laughs.*] Westernized. [*They both laugh.*] A very great social anthropologist at the university has written something very interesting. He says there are two processes—the process of Westernization among *brāhmaṇas,* mainly the upper class, and the process called Sanskritization, which is the process of adopting *brāhmaṇa* rituals, etc., by so-called lower classes, even untouchables. It is a very interesting process in India just now. But India's position, unfortunately, is problematic.

Śrīla Prabhupāda: The difficulty is that India is nowhere. They are trying to imitate Western life, but from a materialistic or technical point of view, they are one hundred years back.

Prof. Kotovsky: Yes, that is right. But what to do for India?

Śrīla Prabhupāda: There is one thing I am experiencing. If India's spiritual asset is distributed, that will increase India's honor. Because everywhere I go, people still adore Indian culture. If this treasure house of India's spiritual knowledge is properly distributed, at least people outside of India will understand that they are getting something from India.

Prof. Kotovsky: Of course, you're right. The Indian cultural heritage is to be made known everywhere. But at the same time, in what way would this benefit the Indian masses themselves? They are sitting in India, and they have nothing to gain from the spreading of the Indian cultural heritage all over the world. Indian villages have to have fertilizers, tractors, etc.

Śrīla Prabhupāda: Yes, we do not object to that.

Prof. Kotovsky: Yes, I don't think you can object, but at the same time, something has to be done in India. One may call it Westernization, but this introduction to an industrial technological revolution is needed in all fields of Indian life—agriculture, industry, etc.

Śrīla Prabhupāda: Arjuna, before understanding the *Bhagavad-gītā,* was a fighter, and after understanding the *Bhagavad-gītā* he remained a fighter. So we don't want to change the position. For example, you are a respectable professor, a teacher. We don't say that you must change your position. We have come to convince you about our philosophy. That is all. Arjuna was refusing to fight. "Kṛṣṇa, I don't want to kill my relatives. I do not want this kingdom." But he was taught the *Bhagavad-gītā,* and at the end when Kṛṣṇa inquired, "What is your decision now?" he said, *kariṣye vacanaṁ tava*—"Yes, I shall act as You say." [*Bhagavad-gītā* 18.73] That means that his consciousness changed. He was a fighter, and he remained a fighter, but he changed his consciousness. We want that. We don't want to disturb the present condition of society. We are not against technology. No, but we try to make one understand this Kṛṣṇa consciousness. That is our program.

Prof. Kotovsky: Of course, at the same time the final goal of any consciousness is to change the society—to make it a better society.

Śrīla Prabhupāda: That is automatic.

Prof. Kotovsky: I am not really so happy that the ultimate goal is not to disturb society, because in modern society there are many things to be changed through consciousness.

Śrīla Prabhupāda: That preliminary change is to follow rules and regulations of austerity. For example, don't take intoxicants.

Prof. Kotovsky: No indulging in intoxicants—simplicity, etc.

Śrīla Prabhupāda: So if one takes to this process—

Prof. Kotovsky: Then the others will come automatically.

Śrīla Prabhupāda: One's whole life will change, because these four things—illicit sex life, intoxicants, meat-eating, and gambling—are very great impediments to social improvement.

Prof. Kotovsky: That will automatically make life simpler, because a person who does not indulge in illicit sex, intoxicants, and such other things has to lead a comparatively simple life.

Śrīla Prabhupāda: The other day I was speaking in Bombay with a respectable gentleman. I was telling him that Kṛṣṇa says:

māṁ hi pārtha vyapāśritya ye 'pi syuḥ pāpa-yonayaḥ
striyo vaiśyās tathā śūdrās te 'pi yānti parāṁ gatim

"Even those who are lowborn [*pāpa-yonayaḥ*]—*strī, vaiśyas,* and *śūdras*—are also included by accepting Me. By accepting My shelter they are also elevated to the transcendental position." [*Bhagavad-gītā* 9.32] Now why have the higher classes of Hindu society neglected this injunction of the *Bhagavad-gītā*? Suppose one is *pāpa-yonayaḥ*, lowborn. Kṛṣṇa says that he can be "elevated to the transcendental position if he accepts Me." Why wasn't this message propagated by the higher class of people so that the so-called lowborn could be elevated? Why did they reject them? The result was that instead of accepting the Muhammadans, the Indians rejected them, and now they are partitioned off. They have become eternal enemies of India. So for the first time we are trying to elevate persons to the higher position of Kṛṣṇa consciousness, even if one is lowborn. Because the soul is pure. In the *Vedas* it is said that the soul is untouched by any material contamination; it is simply temporarily covered. This covering should be removed. Then one becomes pure. That is the mission of human life—to uncover ourselves from this material environment, come to spiritual understanding, and surrender to Kṛṣṇa. Then life is perfect.

THE TINY WORLD OF MODERN SCIENCE

During a morning walk in April 1973, at Venice Beach, Los Angeles, Śrīla Prabhupāda discusses modern science and its high priests: "They claim to have millions of dollars worth of knowledge, but if you ask them a question, they simply give you a postdated check. Why should we accept it? They cannot even produce a spear of grass through their biological or chemical experiments. Nonetheless, they are claiming that the creation is produced by some chemical or biological method. Why does no one question all this nonsense?"

Śrīla Prabhupāda: The whole world of science and technology is running on the false idea that life is born from matter. We cannot allow this nonsensical theory to go unchallenged. Life does not come from matter. Matter is generated from life. This is not theory; it is fact. Science is based on an incorrect theory; therefore all its calculations and conclusions are wrong, and people are suffering because of this. When all these mistaken modern scientific theories are corrected, people will become happy. So we must challenge the scientists and defeat them. Otherwise they will mislead the entire society.

Matter changes in six phases: birth, growth, maintenance, production of by-products, dwindling, and death. But the life within matter, the spirit soul, is eternal; it goes through no such changes. Life *appears* to be developing and decaying, but actually it is simply passing through each of these six phases until the material body can no longer be maintained. Then the old body dies, and the soul enters a new body. When our clothing is old and worn, we change it. Similarly, one day our bodies become old and useless, and we pass on to a new body.

As Kṛṣṇa says in the *Bhagavad-gītā* [2.13], *dehino 'smin yathā dehe kaumāraṁ yauvanaṁ jarā/ tathā dehāntara-prāptiḥ:* "As the embodied soul continuously passes, in this body, from boyhood to youth to old age, the soul similarly passes into another body at death." And a little later [2.18]: *antavanta ime dehā nityasyoktāḥ śarīriṇaḥ.* This means that only the material body of the indestructible and eternal entity is subject to destruction. This material body is perishable, but the life within the body is *nitya,* eternal.

According to the *Vedas,* the measurement of the soul within the body is one ten-thousandth part of the tip of a hair. This is very small; in fact, it is atomic. Yet because of that atomic spiritual energy, my body is working. Is it so difficult to understand? Suppose a man thinks himself very stout and strong. Why is he stout and strong? Only because within his body is a small spiritual spark. But as soon as the spiritual spark is gone, his body dies, and his strength and vigor become void. If scientists say that matter is the cause and origin of life, then let them bring just one dead man back to life by injecting him with chemicals. But this they cannot do.

Dr. Singh: Since scientists cannot see the spirit soul, they say its existence is very doubtful.

Śrīla Prabhupāda: How can they see it? It is too small to see. Where is such seeing power?

Dr. Singh: Still, they want to sense it by some means.

Śrīla Prabhupāda: If you inject just one grain of deadly poison into someone, he immediately dies. No one can see the poison or how it acts. But the poison is acting nevertheless. In the same way, the *Vedas* say that because the minute particle called the soul is within the body, the whole body is working nicely. If I pinch myself, I immediately feel it, because I am conscious all over my skin. But as soon as the soul is absent, which is the case when my body dies, you can take this same skin and cut it and chop it, and no one will protest. Why is this simple thing so hard to understand? Is this not detecting spirit?

Dr. Singh: That is the soul. But what about God?

Śrīla Prabhupāda: First of all let us understand the soul. The soul is a small God. If you understand the sample, then you can understand the whole.

Now here is matter. [*Śrīla Prabhupāda points at a dead tree with his cane.*] Formerly leaves and twigs were growing from this tree. Why are they not growing now? Can the scientists answer this question?

Karandhara Dāsa: They would say the chemical composition has changed.

Śrīla Prabhupāda: All right, then if they are so advanced in knowledge of chemistry, they must supply the proper chemicals to make branches and leaves grow again.
Brahmānanda Swami: Knowledge means that one must be able to demonstrate his theory. They should be able to show in their laboratories that life is caused by a combination of chemicals.
Śrīla Prabhupāda: Yes, the scientific method means first observation, then hypothesis, and then demonstration. But these scientists cannot demonstrate their hypothesis. They simply observe and then speak nonsense.

Scientists say that the chemicals are the cause of life. But all the chemicals that were there when the tree was living are still present. And life energy is also there. There are thousands of microbes in the tree, and they are all living entities. No one can claim that life energy is lacking in the body of this tree.
Dr. Singh: But what about the life energy of the tree itself?
Śrīla Prabhupāda: Yes, that is the difference. The living force is individual, and the particular individual living entity which was the tree has left. This must be the case, since all the chemicals that are necessary to support life are still there yet the tree is dead.

Here is another example: suppose I am living in an apartment, and then I leave it. I am gone, but many other living entities remain there—ants, spiders, and so forth. It is not true that simply because I have left the apartment, it can no longer accommodate life. Other living entities are still living there. It is simply that I—an individual living being—have left. The chemicals in the tree are like the apartment; they are simply the environment for the individual living force—the soul—to act through. Thus the scientists will never be able to produce life in the chemical laboratory.

The so-called scientists say that life begins from chemicals. But the real question is, "Where have the chemicals come from?" The chemicals come from life, and this means that life has mystic power. For example, an orange tree contains many oranges, and each orange contains chemicals—citric acid and others. So where have these chemicals come from? Obviously they have come from the life within the tree. The scientists are missing the origin of the chemicals. They have started their investigation from the chemicals, but they cannot identify the origin of the chemicals. Chemicals come from the supreme life—God. Just as the living body of a man produces many chemicals, the supreme life (the Supreme Lord) is producing all the chemicals found in the atmosphere, in the water, in humans, in animals, and in the earth. And that is called mystic power. Unless the mystic power of the Supreme Lord is accepted, there is no solution to the problem of the origin of life.

Dr. Singh: The scientists will reply that they cannot believe in mystic power.

Śrīla Prabhupāda: But they must explain the origin of the chemicals. Anyone can see that an ordinary tree is producing many chemicals; they cannot deny it. But how does it produce them? Since they cannot answer this, they must accept that the living force has mystic power. I cannot explain how my fingernail is growing out of my finger; it is beyond the power of my brain. In other words, it is growing by inconceivable potency, or *acintya-śakti.* So if *acintya-śakti* exists in an ordinary being, imagine how much *acintya-śakti* God possesses.

The difference between God and me is that although I have the same potencies as God, I can produce only a small quantity of chemicals, whereas He can produce enormous quantities. I can produce a little water in the form of perspiration, but God can produce the seas. Analysis of one drop of seawater gives you the qualitative analysis of the sea, without any mistake. Similarly, the ordinary living being is part and parcel of God, so by analyzing the living beings we can begin to understand God. In God there is great mystic potency. God's mystic potency is working swiftly, exactly like an electric machine. Machines operate by certain energy, and they are so nicely made that all the work is done simply by pushing a button. Similarly, God said, "Let there be creation," and there was creation. Considered in this way, the workings of nature are not very difficult to understand. God has such wonderful potencies that the creation, on His order alone, immediately takes place.

Brahmānanda Swami: Scientists don't accept God or *acintya-śakti.*

Śrīla Prabhupāda: That is their rascaldom. God exists, and His *acintya-śakti* also exists.

Karandhara Dāsa: Scientists say that life was created biochemically.

Śrīla Prabhupāda: And I say to them: "Why don't *you* create life? Your biology and chemistry are very advanced, so why don't you create life?"

Karandhara Dāsa: They say they will create life in the future.

Śrīla Prabhupāda: When in the future? If the scientists know the creative process, why can't they create life now? If life has a biochemical origin, and if biologists and chemists are so advanced, then why can't they create life in their laboratories? When this crucial point is raised, they say, "We shall do it in the future." Why in the future? That is nonsense. Trust no future, however pleasant. What is the meaning of their advancement? They are talking nonsense.

Karandhara Dāsa: They say that they are right on the verge of creating life.

Śrīla Prabhupāda: But that is also the future, in a different way. They must accept that they still do not know the truth about the origin of life. Since they are expecting to be able to create life in the future, presently their knowledge must be imperfect. Their proposal is something like giving someone a postdated check. Suppose I owe you ten thousand dollars and I say, "Yes, I will pay you the entire sum with this postdated check. Is that all right?" If you are intelligent, you will reply, "At present, give me at least five dollars in cash to I can see something tangible." Similarly, the scientists cannot produce even a single blade of grass by biochemistry, yet still they claim that life is produced from matter. What is this nonsense? Is no one questioning this? We can prove that life began from life. Here is the proof: when a father begets a child, the father is living, and the child is living. But where is the scientist's proof that life comes from matter? We can prove that life begins from life, and we can also prove that the original life is Kṛṣṇa. But what evidence exists that a child is ever born out of a dead stone? The scientists cannot prove that life comes from matter. They are leaving that aside for the future.

Karandhara Dāsa: The basis of what the scientists call "scientific integrity" is that they talk only about what they can experience through their senses.

Śrīla Prabhupāda: Then they are suffering from what we call "Doctor Frog's philosophy." There was once a frog who had lived all his life in a well. One day a friend visited him and informed him of the existence of the Atlantic Ocean.

"Oh, what is this Atlantic Ocean?" asked the frog in the well.

"It is a vast body of water," his friend replied.

"How vast? Is it double the size of this well?"

"Oh, no, much larger," his friend replied.

"How much larger? Ten times the size?"

In this way the frog went on calculating. But what was the possibility of his ever understanding the depths and far reaches of the great ocean? Our faculties, experience, and powers of speculation are always limited. The frog was always thinking in terms relative to his well. He had no power to think otherwise. Similarly, the scientists are estimating the Absolute Truth, the cause of all causes, with their imperfect senses and minds, and thus they are bound to be bewildered. The essential fault of the so-called scientists is that they have adopted the inductive process to arrive at their conclusions. For example, if a scientist wants to determine whether or not man is mortal by the inductive process, he must study every man to try to discover if some or one of them may be immortal. The scientist says, "I cannot accept the proposition that all men are mortal. There may be some men who are immortal. I have not yet seen every man. Therefore how can I accept that man is mortal?" This is called the inductive process. And the deductive process means that your father, your teacher, or your guru says that man is mortal, and you accept it.

Dr. Singh: So there is an ascending process of gaining knowledge and a descending process?

Śrīla Prabhupāda: Yes. The ascending process will never be successful, because it relies on information gathered through the senses, and the senses are imperfect. So we accept the descending process.

God cannot be known by the inductive process. Therefore He is called *adhokṣaja,* which means "unknowable by direct perception." The scientists say there is no God, because they are trying to understand by direct perception. But He is *adhokṣaja;* therefore the scientists are ignorant of God because they are missing the method of knowing Him. In order to understand transcendental science, one must approach a bona fide spiritual master, hear from him submissively, and render service to him. Lord Kṛṣṇa explains this in the *Bhagavad-gītā* [4.34]: *tad viddhi praṇipātena paripraśnena sevayā.*

Dr. Singh: There is a scientific journal called *Nature.* It contains articles concerning natural products like plants and animals, but it does not mention God—only nature.

Śrīla Prabhupāda: We may correctly observe that plants are being produced by nature, but we must ask, "What has produced nature?" To ask *this* question is intelligence.

Dr. Singh: The scientists don't think about that.

Śrīla Prabhupāda: So they are fools. As soon as we speak of nature, the next question should be, "*Whose* nature?" For instance, I speak of *my* nature, and you speak of *your* nature. Therefore, as soon as nature is mentioned, the next inquiry should be, "*Whose* nature?"

Nature means energy, and as soon as you speak of energy, you must accept that there is a source of that energy. For example, the source of electric energy is the electric powerhouse. Electricity is not produced automatically. We must install a powerhouse and a generator. Similarly, in the *Vedas* it is said that material nature is working under Kṛṣṇa's direction.

Dr. Singh: So do you mean to say that science has started from an intermediate point—not from the original point?

Śrīla Prabhupāda: Yes, that is it exactly. They are ignorant of the origin. The scientists start from one point—but where does that point come from? That they do not know, in spite of vast research. One has to accept that the original source is God, who is full of all mystic powers and from whom everything emanates. He Himself says in the *Bhagavad-gītā* [10.8], *ahaṁ sarvasya prabhavo mattaḥ sarvaṁ pravartate:* "I am the source of all spiritual and material worlds. Everything emanates from Me." Our conclusions are not based on blind faith; they are most scientific. Matter comes from life. In life—in the origin—there are unlimited material resources; that is the great mystery of creation.

Modern scientific research is just like Sāṅkhya philosophy, which analyzes material elements. *Sāṅkhya* means "to count." We are also Sāṅkhya philosophers to some extent, because we count and analyze the material elements; this is land, this is water, this is air, this is sunshine, this is fire. Furthermore, I can count my mind, my intelligence, and my ego. Beyond my ego, however, I cannot count. But Kṛṣṇa says that there is existence beyond the ego, and that existence is the living force—the spirit soul. This is what the scientists do not know. They think that life is merely a combination of material elements, but Kṛṣṇa denies this in the *Bhagavad-gītā* [7.5]. *Apareyam itas tv anyāṁ prakṛtiṁ viddhi me parām:* "Besides this in-ferior nature there is a superior energy of Mine." The inferior energy is the material elements, and the superior energy is the living entity.

bhūmir āpo 'nalo vāyuḥ khaṁ mano buddhir eva ca
ahaṅkāra itīyaṁ me bhinnā prakṛtir aṣṭadhā

"Earth, water, fire, air, ether, mind, intelligence, and false ego—all together these eight constitute My separated material energies." [*Bhagavad-gītā* 7.4] Kṛṣṇa explains here in the *Bhagavad-gītā* that *vāyu* (gas) comes from Him, and that finer than the gases is *kham* (ether). Finer than ether is the mind, finer than the mind is intelligence, and finer than the intelligence is the soul. But the scientists do not know this. They can perceive only gross things. They mention *vāyu,* but where does the *vāyu* come from? Where does the gas come from?

Dr. Singh: That they cannot answer.

Śrīla Prabhupāda: But *we* can answer. We have the knowledge that gas comes from *kham,* or ether, and ether comes from mind, mind comes from intelligence, and intelligence comes from Kṛṣṇa's superior energy, the spirit soul.

Dr. Singh: Are both inferior and superior energies studied in Sāṅkhya philosophy?

Śrīla Prabhupāda: No. Sāṅkhya philosophers do not know of superior energy. They simply analyze the material elements, just as the scientists do. Neither the scientists nor the Sāṅkhya philosophers know anything of the spirit soul. They are simply analyzing Kṛṣṇa's material energy.

Dr. Singh: They are analyzing the creative material elements?

Śrīla Prabhupāda: Material elements are not creative! The *soul* is creative. No one can create life with only matter, and matter cannot create itself. You, a living entity, can mix hydrogen and oxygen to create water. But matter itself has no creative energy. If you place a bottle of hydrogen near a bottle of oxygen, will they automatically combine, without your help?

Dr. Singh: No. They must be mixed.

Śrīla Prabhupāda: Yes, the superior energy—the living entity—is required. Oxygen and hydrogen are inferior energy, but when the superior energy mixes them, then they can become water.

Inferior energy has no power unless superior energy is involved. This sea [*indicating the Pacific Ocean*] is calm and quiet. But when superior force—air—pushes it, high waves are created. The sea has no power without the superior force. Similarly, there is another force superior to the air, and another, and another, until we arrive at Kṛṣṇa, the most superior force. This is real research. Suppose a railroad train is just starting to move. The engine pushes one car, which pushes another, and so on, until the entire train is moving. And the whole motion originates with the engineer, a living entity. Similarly, in the cosmic creation, Kṛṣṇa gives the first push, and then, by means of many successive pushes, the entire cosmic manifestation comes into being. This is explained in the *Bhagavad-gītā* [9.10]: *mayādhyakṣeṇa prakṛtiḥ sūyate sa-carācaram.* "This material nature is working under My direction, O son of Kuntī, and is producing all moving and unmoving beings." And a little later:

sarva-yoniṣu kaunteya mūrtayaḥ sambhavanti yāḥ
tāsāṁ brahma mahad yonir ahaṁ bīja-pradaḥ pitā

"All species of life are made possible by birth in material nature, and I am the seed-giving father." [*Bhagavad-gītā* 14.4] For example, if we sow a banyan seed, a huge tree eventually grows up and produces millions of new seeds. Each of these seeds, in turn, produces another tree with millions of new seeds, and so on. So Kṛṣṇa is the original seed-giving father.

Unfortunately, the scientists only observe the immediate cause; they do not perceive the remote cause. There are two causes—the immediate cause and the remote cause. Kṛṣṇa is described in the *Vedas* as *sarva-kāraṇa-kāraṇam,* the cause of all causes. If you understand the cause of all causes, then you understand everything. *Yasmin vijñāte sarvam evaṁ vijñātaṁ bhavati:* "If you know the original cause, the later, subordinate causes are automatically known." Although the scientists are searching after the original cause, when the *Vedas,* which contain perfect knowledge, give the original cause, they won't accept. They keep to their partial, imperfect knowledge.

Dr. Singh: Scientists are worried about energy sources, and now they are working to utilize solar energy for cooking, lighting, and various other purposes. They are hoping that when they exhaust all other energy sources, they will be able to use solar energy.

Śrīla Prabhupāda: This is not a very new theory. Everyone knows that because the roots of trees store the sun's energy, it is possible to get fire from a tree. These scientists are tiny creatures, but they are very proud. We don't give them credit, because they are simply stating what everyone knows. As soon as you cut a tree, you cannot get fire from it. It has to be dried in the sun. When the energy is gathered from the sun, the tree can be utilized for fire. Actually everything is being maintained by the sun's energy, but the scientists don't know where the sun's energy comes from. In the *Bhagavad-gītā* [15.12] Kṛṣṇa says:

yad āditya-gataṁ tejo jagad bhāsayate 'khilam
yac candramasi yac cāgnau tat tejo viddhi māmakam

"The splendor of the sun, which dissipates the darkness of this whole world, comes from Me. And the splendor of the moon and the splendor of fire are also from Me."

Again, Kṛṣṇa says, *jyotiṣāṁ ravir aṁśumān:* "Of lights I am the radiant sun." [*Bhagavad-gītā* 10.21] Also, in the Eleventh Chapter of the *Bhagavad-gītā* Arjuna tells Kṛṣṇa, *śaśi-sūrya-netram:* "The sun and moon are among Your great, unlimited eyes." This knowledge is contained in the *Bhagavad-gītā,* but scientists cannot attain this knowledge by their speculation. Can they?

Dr. Singh: It is not possible.

Śrīla Prabhupāda: And what is their knowledge? The scriptures say that even if you counted all the grains of sand on earth, you still would not be able to understand God. All this material counting does not mean that you have the capacity to understand the unlimited. But it is even beyond their capacity to count all the material things. Why are the scientists so proud of their energy and capacities? They do not even know of the material things, and what to speak of the spiritual. As far as scientists and other living entities are concerned, their knowledge is limited. But this is not so for Kṛṣṇa. If we receive knowledge from Kṛṣṇa, that knowledge is perfect. In the scriptures we receive information that there are nine hundred thousand species of life existing within the ocean. The information given in the scriptures is exact, because it comes from Kṛṣṇa, and as Kṛṣṇa Himself says: "As the Supreme Personality of Godhead, I know everything that has happened in the past, all that is happening in the present, and all things that are yet to come." [*Bhagavad-gītā* 7.26]

Dr. Singh: We have to take knowledge from the supreme knower.

Śrīla Prabhupāda: For perfect knowledge we have to approach a superior person, a guru. One may try to learn a subject by reading books at home, but he can learn much better by going to college and approaching a professor. In the same way, we have to approach a guru. Of course, if we encounter a false guru, our knowledge is false. But if our guru is perfect, our knowledge is perfect. We accept Kṛṣṇa as our guru. If He is perfect in knowledge, our knowledge is also perfect. As far as we're concerned, we do not have to be perfect in ourselves, but if we receive knowledge from the perfect, our knowledge is perfect. We cannot say that we understand that there are nine hundred thousand species of life in the ocean because we have studied the entire ocean. Rather, we say that we take this information from scriptures, and therefore it is perfect. This is the Vedic process.

Scientists may carry out much research work, but however great a scientist may be, his senses are imperfect. Therefore he cannot have perfect knowledge. What is the value of our eyes? We cannot see without sunlight, nor can we see small things without a microscope. Our eyes are imperfect, and the instruments our eyes have discovered are also imperfect. How, then, is it possible to get perfect knowledge? Because the living entity is limited, his knowledge is limited. A child may know that two plus two equals four, but when he speaks of higher mathematics, we do not take him seriously. The senses through which a scientist acquires knowledge are limited and imperfect; therefore his knowledge is limited and imperfect. In his ignorance he may claim to know everything, but that is simply nonsense.

A blind man may lead another blind man, but what does it avail them when they both fall into a ditch? The laws of nature bind us hand and foot, yet we think we are free to speculate. This is illusion. Although conditioned by so many of nature's laws, the rascals think they are free. Yet if there is a cloud, they cannot see the sun. What power have we to see? Only when nature's laws give us some facility are we able to see. Indeed, we can only experiment under certain conditions, and if the conditions are not favorable, our experiments fail. Why then are we so proud of experimental knowledge?

Why experiment? Things are already there. The sun's energy is there, given by God for us to use. What else is there to know? So many apples fall from trees. What further need is there to explain the law of gravity? Actually the scientists are lacking in common sense. They are simply concerned with "scientific" explanations.

They say the law of gravity works only under certain conditions, but who has made these conditions? When Kṛṣṇa appeared as Lord Rāmacandra, He threw stones on the water, and the stones floated. The law of gravity did not work in that case. Therefore the law of gravity works only under the direction of the Supreme Lord. The law in itself is not final. A king may give a law, but he can change that law immediately. The ultimate law-giver is Kṛṣṇa, and a law will only work by His will. Scientists try to explain God's will in so many ways, but because they are conditioned by *māyā,* illusion, they can only talk like a person haunted by ghosts. Tell me, what is the scientific explanation that accounts for all the varieties of trees?

Karandhara Dāsa: They say that nature mutates and makes these varieties.

Śrīla Prabhupāda: Then it must be nature's will. And what is that will? Does the land have any will?

Karandhara Dāsa: Well, they are very vague on that point.

Śrīla Prabhupāda: That means that they do not have perfect knowledge. They do not know that behind nature is the will of Kṛṣṇa.

Dr. Singh: They explain that the chemical composition of these different plants is different.

Śrīla Prabhupāda: That's all right, but who made these chemical compositions? As soon as you say "chemical composition," you immediately require a God.

Karandhara Dāsa: They say there is no need for a God, because if you mix two chemicals together—

Śrīla Prabhupāda: God or not, there must be some will. There must be some consciousness. Two chemicals mix and produce such and such. Who mixes them? Consciousness is there. Well, that consciousness is Kṛṣṇa. There is consciousness everywhere, and as soon as you accept that consciousness, you must accept consciousness as a person. Therefore, we speak of Kṛṣṇa consciousness. In the *Bhagavad-gītā* it is stated that consciousness is all-pervading. You may have consciousness, and I may have consciousness, but there is another consciousness, which is all-pervading. My consciousness is limited to my body, and your consciousness is limited to yours, but there is another consciousness, which is within you, me, and everyone. That is Kṛṣṇa consciousness.

Actually everything in the world is relative. That is a scientific fact. Our bodies, lives, intelligence, and everything else are all relative. To us an ant may seem to have a very short life, but for the ant his life is about a hundred years in duration. That hundred years is relative to the body. Similarly, Brahmā, who lives fantastically long from our point of view, only lives a hundred years from his point of view. This is relativity.

Karandhara Dāsa: Then the relativity is based upon our individual situation.

Śrīla Prabhupāda: Yes. Therefore it is said that what is food for one is poison for another. People are thinking that because they cannot survive on the moon, no other living entities can. Everyone thinks of things in a relative way, in his own terms. This is the meaning of "frog philosophy." The frog is always thinking of things in relation to his well. He has no power to conceive of the Atlantic Ocean, because his well is his only experience. God is great, but we are thinking of God's greatness in our own terms, in terms of relative greatness. Some insects are born at night; they grow at night, have their children at night, and die at night. They never see the sun; therefore they conclude that there is no such thing as day. If you asked the insect about the morning, he would say, "There cannot be any morning." Similarly, when people hear of Brahmā's long duration of life from the scriptures, they do not believe it. They say, "How can anyone live for such a long time?" In the *Bhagavad-gītā* [8.17] Kṛṣṇa states:

sahasra-yuga-paryantam ahar yad brahmaṇo viduḥ
rātriṁ yuga-sahasrāntāṁ te 'ho-rātra-vido janāḥ

"By human calculation, a thousand ages taken together is the duration of Brahmā's one day. And such also is the duration of his night."

Thus Brahmā, by these calculations, lives for so many millions and trillions of years. We cannot believe this, although evidence is given in the scriptures. In other words, we conclude that Kṛṣṇa talks nonsensically, while we speak as authorities. Even great scholars say that these scriptural statements are all mental speculations. Although these men are nothing but rascals, they pass for reputable scholars. They place themselves above God's position by attempting to refute or deny the statements of God in the revealed scriptures. In this way so many fools in the guise of scholars, scientists, and philosophers are misguiding the whole world.

Dr. Singh: Of course, so much is being written about Darwin's theory. In any library there are hundreds of books on his theories.

Śrīla Prabhupāda: Do they accept or reject them?

Dr. Singh: Generally they accept him, but some are very critical.

Śrīla Prabhupāda: Darwin speaks about the evolution of the species of life, but he has no real information about spiritual evolution. He knows nothing about the progress of the spirit soul from lower forms of life to higher forms. He claims that man has evolved from monkeys, but we can see that the monkey is not extinct. If the monkey is the immediate forefather of man, why is the monkey still existing?

Dr. Singh: Darwin says that the species are not created independently but are descended from one another.

Śrīla Prabhupāda: If there is no question of independence, how can he abruptly begin with a certain species? He must explain how the original species came into existence.

Karandhara Dāsa: Scientists claim that the earth was created by biological chemistry, and they refuse to teach that God created the earth, because they think everyone will consider them fools.

Śrīla Prabhupāda: If their biology and chemistry are so advanced, why don't they create something? They claim they may be able to create life in the future, but why in the future? Life is already created. Is science based on the future? We should trust no future, however pleasant we may think it will be. Everyone is thinking the future will be very pleasant, but what assurance do we have of this? They have to accept that they do not know what the truth actually is. They cannot even produce a spear of grass through their biological or chemical experiments. Nonetheless they are claiming that the creation is produced by some chemical or biological method. Why does no one question all this nonsense?

Dr. Singh: In the ultimate analysis, when they consider the origin of life, they say that everything started from matter. In other words, living matter comes from nonliving matter.

Śrīla Prabhupāda: From where is this living matter coming now? Did it come from nonliving matter in the past and not at the present? How is the ant coming? Is it materializing from dirt? Even an ant does not come from inert matter. What proof do they have of such a theory? Darwin claims that in the distant past no really intelligent man existed, that man simply evolved from the apes. If there was no intelligent brain in the past, how is it that these Vedic scriptures were written thousands and thousands of years ago? How do they explain a sage like Vyāsadeva?

Dr. Singh: They have no explanation. They simply say these are unknown forest sages.

Śrīla Prabhupāda: Vyāsadeva may be unknown to them, but nonetheless he was there. How is it he got such a brain? He may be unknown to you or to me, but nonetheless his brainwork is there, his philosophy is there, his language, linguistics, poetic arrangements, and verbal strength. You may not know the person, but you can understand the brain.

Dr. Singh: Weren't all the varieties of animals existing from the beginning?

Śrīla Prabhupāda: Yes. Simultaneous creation is verified by the *Bhagavad-gītā*. All the varieties of animals and men as well as demigods were existing from the beginning. A living entity wants a certain type of body, and Kṛṣṇa gives it to him. Because he desires things in a certain way, he associates with certain qualities of nature in matter. According to his association, he receives a particular type of body. The psychological forces of the mind—thinking, feeling, and willing—determine the particular type of situation and body the living entity receives. The evolutionary process is there, but it is not an evolution of species. It is not that one species of life develops from another, for, as Kṛṣṇa states:

bhūta-grāmaḥ sa evāyaṁ bhūtvā bhūtvā pralīyate
rātry-āgame 'vaśaḥ pārtha prabhavaty ahar-āgame

"Again and again, when Brahmā's day arrives, all living entities come into being, and with the arrival of Brahmā's night they are helplessly annihilated." [*Bhagavad-gītā* 8.19]

The evolution is the spiritual evolution of the individual living entity through the various species of life. If one enters into the body of a fish, he has to undergo the evolutionary process step by step. If one is on the top of the stairs and somehow falls down, he again has to go up the evolutionary staircase step by step. Of course, the scientists are busy making so much research that they cannot understand this. If you tell them they are going to be trees in their next life, they think you are speaking nonsense. After all, what can we learn by research? When the cause of all causes is known, then everything knowable becomes known, and nothing remains unknown. As the *Vedas* state: *yasmin vijñāte sarvam evaṁ vijñātaṁ bhavati.* If we know the Absolute Truth, all other truths become known, but if we don't know the Absolute Truth, we are in ignorance. One may not be an official scientist or philosopher, but he may challenge anyone and talk boldly if he only knows one thing—Kṛṣṇa.

This contemporary civilization is so proud of its independence, but actually it is so much dependent on oil. If the oil supply is stopped, then what will these rascal scientists do? They cannot do anything. Let them try to manufacture oil in their test tubes, enough oil to run their civilization on. At present there is a scarcity of water in India. What can the scientists do about this? They may know the chemical composition of water, but they cannot produce it when there is a great scarcity. They require the help of clouds, and all that is God's manipulation. Actually they cannot do anything. They have gone to the moon, but for all their labor they have simply taken away some dust and rocks. The rascal government exacts taxes and spends money unnecessarily. This is their intelligence. It is a state of asses, that's all. The politicians have no sympathy or compassion. They do not consider that the hard-earned money is coming from the public and that they are spending it by shooting big rockets off to other planets. All they do is promise to bring back more dust. First they may get a handful of dust; then they promise to bring back tons of dust. What is the meaning of all this?

Karandhara Dāsa: They believe that there may be life on Mars.

Śrīla Prabhupāda: They may believe or not believe—what is the gain? What we do know is that life is here. They know this, yet they are engaged in fighting and in killing life. Here is life. Here is a human being. Life is here undoubtedly. But they are busy trying to destroy it with their big bombs. This is their scientific advancement.

Dr. Singh: They are very curious to know what is going on on other planets.

Śrīla Prabhupāda: That means that for their childish curiosity they are spending so much money. They can spend so much to satisfy their curiosity, but when so many poverty-stricken countries ask them for help, they say there is no money. They are very proud to go to the moon, but why don't they take information how to go to Kṛṣṇa's Goloka Vṛndāvana? If they go there, all their curiosity will be satisfied. They will learn that beyond this inferior energy there is indeed a superior, spiritual energy. This material energy cannot work independently. The spiritual energy has to join it. Material elements are not created of themselves. It is the soul that is creative. We may try to make something with matter, but matter does not create itself. Hydrogen and oxygen will come in contact only when moved by the superior energy. Only fools can expect the entire cosmic manifestation, which is only matter, to come into being automatically. We may have a nice car, but if there is no driver, what is its use? Unless a man knows how to work a machine, unless a man pushes a button, the machine does not work. Similarly, without the superior energy, the material energy cannot act. Behind this wonderful cosmic manifestation is the direction of a superior energy. All this information is given in the scriptures, but still people will not believe it.

Actually everything is God's property, but people are claiming this property to be theirs or their country's. Now they are talking about the problem of overpopulation, but the fact is that God has supplied enough. Actually there is enough land and enough food if it is properly used. People are artificially creating problems, and the scientists are helping them by giving them so many destructive devices. They simply encourage the rascals and rogues who are trying to use up God's property. If you help a murderer or a thief, you also become a criminal. Is that not so? There is so much trouble in the world because the scientists are helping all the thieves and rogues. Thus they are all criminals. *Stena eva saḥ*. One who does not recognize the proprietorship of the Supreme Lord is a thief.

Our mission is to bring these rascals to their senses. Now one must find out the means to do this. The rascals are suffering, but because they are sons of God they should not suffer. They do not know that there is God or that there is happiness. They know nothing of bliss or of eternal life. They are carrying on so much research and living for fifty, sixty, or seventy years. After that they do not know what is going to happen. They have no knowledge that life is eternal. Actually their position is like that of an animal. An animal does not know what is after death, nor does he actually contemplate death. He does not know why he is here, nor does he know the value of life. Under the influence of *māyā*, the animal simply goes on eating, sleeping, defending, mating, and dying. That's all. People are endeavoring so hard, but for what purpose? They say that they are struggling so hard to make provisions for the next generation, but what are the provisions for? They cannot reply to that. This Kṛṣṇa consciousness movement is meant to give real purpose to life by establishing Kṛṣṇa, God, as the center of everything. It is therefore to the scientists' benefit to understand this important movement.

VII.
RETURNING TO THE ETERNAL RELIGION

ŚRĪLA PRABHUPĀDA ARRIVES IN AMERICA

On September 18, 1965, as the Indian steamship Jaladuta *nears Boston's Commonwealth Pier, Śrīla Prabhupāda prays to Lord Kṛṣṇa in a moving poem. "I am simply praying for Your mercy so that I will be able to convince them about Your message."*

1

My dear Lord Kṛṣṇa, You are so kind upon this useless soul, but I do not know why You have brought me here. Now You can do whatever You like with me.

2

But I guess You have some business here, otherwise why would You bring me to this terrible place?

3

Most of the population here is covered by the material modes of ignorance and passion. Absorbed in material life, they think themselves very happy and satisfied, and therefore they have no taste for the transcendental message of Vāsudeva. I do not know how they will be able to understand it.

4

But I know Your causeless mercy can make everything possible, because You are the most expert mystic.

5

How will they understand the mellows of devotional service? O Lord, I am simply praying for Your mercy so that I will be able to convince them about Your message.

6

All living entities have come under the control of the illusory energy by Your will, and therefore, if You like, by Your will they can also be released from the clutches of illusion.

7

I wish that You may deliver them. Therefore if You so desire their deliverance, then only will they be able to understand Your message.

8

The words of the *Śrīmad-Bhāgavatam* are Your incarnation, and if a sober person repeatedly receives them with submissive aural reception, then he will be able to understand Your message.

9

It is said in the *Śrīmad-Bhāgavatam* [1.2.17–21]: "Śrī Kṛṣṇa, the Personality of Godhead, who is the Paramātmā [Supersoul] in everyone's heart and the benefactor of the truthful devotee, cleanses desire for material enjoyment from the heart of the devotee who has developed the urge to hear His messages, which are in themselves virtuous when properly heard and chanted. By regular attendance in classes on the *Bhāgavatam* and by rendering of service to the pure devotee, all that is troublesome to the heart is almost completely destroyed, and loving service unto the Personality of Godhead, who is praised with transcendental songs, is established as an irrevocable fact. As soon as irrevocable loving service is established in the heart, the effects of nature's modes of passion and ignorance, such as lust, desire, and hankering, disappear from the heart. Then the devotee is established in goodness, and he becomes completely happy. Thus established in the mode of unalloyed goodness, the man whose mind has been enlivened by contact with devotional service to the Lord gains positive scientific knowledge of the Personality of Godhead in the stage of liberation from all material association. Thus the knot in the heart is pierced, and all misgivings are cut to pieces. The chain of fruitive actions is terminated when one sees the self as master."

10

He will become liberated from the influence of the modes of ignorance and passion and thus all inauspicious things accumulated in the core of the heart will disappear.

11

How will I make them understand this message of Kṛṣṇa consciousness? I am very unfortunate, unqualified, and the most fallen. Therefore I am seeking Your benediction so that I can convince them, for I am powerless to do so on my own.

12

Somehow or other, O Lord, You have brought me here to speak about You. Now, my Lord, it is up to You to make me a success or failure as You like.

13

O spiritual master of all the worlds! I can simply repeat Your message, so if You like You can make my power of speaking suitable for their understanding.

14

Only by Your causeless mercy will my words become pure. I am sure that when this transcendental message penetrates their hearts they will certainly feel engladdened and thus become liberated from all unhappy conditions of life.

15

O Lord, I am just like a puppet in Your hands. So if You have brought me here to dance, then make me dance, make me dance. O Lord, make me dance as You like.

16

I have no devotion, nor do I have any knowledge, but I have strong faith in the holy name of Kṛṣṇa. I have been designated as Bhaktivedanta, and now, if You like, You can fulfill the real purport of Bhaktivedanta.

Signed—the most unfortunate, insignificant beggar
A.C. Bhaktivedanta Swami,
on board the ship *Jaladuta,* Commonwealth Pier,
Boston, Massachusetts, U.S.A.
dated 18th of September, 1965

"BUILD YOUR NATIONS ON THE SPIRITUAL PLATFORM"

Śrīla Prabhupāda addresses students, faculty, and government officials at the University of Nairobi in September 1972: "You are trying to develop yourselves, so please develop spiritually, for spiritual development is sound development. Don't imitate the Americans and Europeans, who are living like cats and dogs. . . . The atomic bomb is already there, and as soon as the next war breaks out, all their skyscrapers and everything else will be finished. Try to understand this from the real viewpoint of human life, the spiritual viewpoint."

Ladies and gentlemen, thank you very much for kindly coming here to participate in this meeting for spreading Kṛṣṇa consciousness. The Kṛṣṇa consciousness movement is trying to bring human society to the point where everyone's life can become successful. The subject today is the real meaning of human life. We are trying to instruct the entire world about this meaning.

Human life is attained after many, many millions of years of evolution. We should always remember that there are 8,400,000 species of life according to the *Padma Purāṇa*. Life began with the aquatics, for we can understand from Vedic literature that at the beginning of creation the entire planet was merged in water. This material world is composed of five gross elements—earth, water, fire, air, and ether. Besides these there are three subtle elements—mind, intelligence, and ego. Behind these curtains is the spirit soul, which is covered by these eight elements. This information is given in the *Bhagavad-gītā*.

Human beings are not the only living entities to have a spirit soul. We are all spirit souls—beasts, birds, reptiles, insects, trees, plants, aquatics, and so on. The spirit soul is simply covered by different dresses, just as some of you are dressed in white clothes, some in green, some in red, etc. But we are not concerned with the dress; we are concerned with you as spirit soul. Thus it is said in the *Bhagavad-gītā* [5.18]:

vidyā-vinaya-sampanne brāhmaṇe gavi hastini
śuni caiva śva-pāke ca paṇḍitāḥ sama-darśinaḥ

"The humble sages, by virtue of true knowledge, see with equal vision a learned and gentle *brāhmaṇa*, a cow, an elephant, a dog, and a dog-eater."

The sage does not make any distinction on the basis of color, intelligence, or species. He sees every living entity as a small particle of spirit soul. It is stated:

keśāgra-śata-bhāgasya śatāṁśaḥ sādṛśātmakaḥ
jīvaḥ sūkṣma-svarūpo 'yaṁ saṅkhyātīto hi cit-kaṇaḥ

"There are innumerable particles of spiritual atoms, which are measured as one ten-thousandth of the upper portion of a hair." Because we have no instrument to measure the dimensions of the spirit soul, the small particle of spirit soul is measured in this way. In other words, the soul is so small that it is smaller than an atom. That small particle is within you, within me, within the elephant, within gigantic animals, in all men, in the ant, in the tree, everywhere. However, scientific knowledge cannot estimate the dimensions of the soul, nor can a doctor locate the soul within the body. Consequently material scientists conclude that there is no soul, but that is not a fact. There is a soul. The presence of the soul makes the difference between a living body and a dead body. As soon as the soul departs from the body, the body dies. It has no value. However great a scientist or a philosopher one may be, he must admit that as soon as the soul departs from the body, the body dies. It then has no value and has to be thrown away. We should try to understand this: the soul is valuable, not the body. The fact that the soul is transmigrating is explained in the *Bhagavad-gītā* [2.22]:

vāsāṁsi jīrṇāni yathā vihāya
navāni gṛhṇāti naro 'parāṇi
tathā śarīrāṇi vihāya jīrṇāny
anyāni saṁyāti navāni dehī

"As a person puts on new garments, giving up old ones, the soul similarly accepts new material bodies, giving up the old and useless ones."

When a suit becomes old, we give it up and accept another suit; similarly the soul is changing dresses according to desire. Because the soul is part and parcel of God, it has godly qualities. God is the supreme will, the supreme power, the supreme independent one, and we, being part and parcel of Him, have all these qualities in minute quantity. We have willing, thinking, feeling, and desiring. In the *Vedas* it is stated that God is the supreme living force among all living forces (*cetanaś cetanānām*). He is also supplying the necessities of all living entities.

We living entities are innumerable; there is no limit to our number. God, however, is one. He is also living, as we are, but we are minute particles of that living force. For example, a particle of gold is the same in quality as a gold mine. If we chemically analyze the ingredients in a small drop of water, we will find all of the ingredients that are to be found in the vast ocean. In a similar way, we are one with God, being His part and parcel. This godly particle, the soul, or the living force, is transmigrating from aquatics to trees and plants and then from trees and plants to insect life, then to reptile life, then to the bodies of birds and beasts. Darwin's theory of evolution is but a partial explanation of the transmigration of the soul. Darwin has simply taken information from the Vedic literature, but he has no conception of the soul. The difference is that the soul is transmigrating from aquatic life to plants and trees, then to insect life, then to bird life, then animal life, then human life, and within human life he moves from uncivilized life to civilized life, etc. The civilized life of a human being represents the culmination of evolution. Here is a junction: from this point we can again slide down into the cyclic process of evolution, or we can elevate ourselves to a godly life. The choice is up to us. This is indicated in the *Bhagavad-gītā*.

This human form of life actually means developed consciousness; therefore we should not waste our lives like cats, dogs, and hogs. That is the injunction. Although this body is perishable like a dog's or cat's body, it is different in that one can attain the highest perfection in this life. We are part and parcel of God, but somehow or other we have fallen into this material existence; now we have to evolve in such a way that we can go back home, back to

Godhead. That is the highest perfection.

There is actually another world, a spiritual world. As stated in the *Bhagavad-gītā* [8.20]:

paras tasmāt tu bhāvo 'nyo 'vyakto 'vyaktāt sanātanaḥ
yaḥ sa sarveṣu bhūteṣu naśyatsu na vinaśyati

"Yet there is another unmanifest nature, which is eternal and is transcendental to this manifested and unmanifested matter. It is supreme and is never annihilated. When all in this world is annihilated, that part remains as it is."

In this material nature, everything is created, it stays for some time, produces some by-products, dwindles, and finally vanishes. Our bodies are created at a certain moment by sexual intercourse. The semen of the father emulsifies and takes a pea form, and the living entity, or soul, takes shelter in that form, and because it takes shelter, it develops hands, legs, eyes, etc. This development is complete in the seventh month, and in the ninth month the human being comes out of the womb. It is because the soul is present that the child develops. If the soul is not present, there is no development, and the child is born dead. We can take this dead body and preserve it in chemicals, but it will not develop. Development means change of body. All of us have had baby bodies, but those bodies are no longer existing. The body of a baby develops into the body of a child, and that body develops into the body of a boy, and that body develops into a youth's body, which eventually turns into an old man's body. Finally the body completely vanishes. The whole cosmic manifestation, the gigantic form of this material world, is also working according to this same process. It is created at a certain point, it develops, it is maintained, and at a certain stage it is dissolved. That is the nature of the material world. It is manifest at a certain interval, and again it vanishes (*bhūtvā bhūtvā pralīyate*).

The word *bhāva* means "nature." There is another nature, which never dissolves, which is eternal. As *jīvas,* spirit souls, we are also eternal. This is verified in the *Bhagavad-gītā* [2.20]:

na jāyate mriyate vā kadācin
nāyaṁ bhūtvā bhavitā vā na bhūyaḥ

ajo nityaḥ śāśvato 'yaṁ purāṇo
na hanyate hanyamāne śarīre

"For the soul there is neither birth nor death at any time. He has not come into being, does not come into being, and will not come into being. He is unborn, eternal, ever-existing, and primeval. He is not slain when the body is slain."

Just as God has no birth or death, we spirit souls can have neither birth nor death, but because we think, "I am this body," we consider that we are born and that we die. Such thinking is called *māyā,* or illusion, and as soon as we get out of this illusion of identifying the soul with the body, we attain the stage called *brahma-bhūta*. When one realizes *ahaṁ brahmāsmi,* "I am not this body; I am spirit soul, part and parcel of the Supreme Brahman," he attains what is called Brahman realization. As soon as Brahman realization is attained, one becomes happy.

Is this not a fact? If you understand clearly that you have no birth and death, that you are eternal, will you not become happy? Yes, certainly. Thus when one is Brahman realized, spiritually realized, he has no more to do with hankering or lamentation. The whole world is simply hankering and lamenting. You African people are now hankering to be like Europeans and Americans, but the Europeans have lost their empire, and now they are lamenting. So in this way one party is hankering and another is lamenting. Similarly, this material life is simply a combination of hankering and lamenting. We are hankering for those things which we do not possess, and we are lamenting for those things which we have lost. That is our material business. If we realize, however, that we are part and parcel of the Supreme Personality of Godhead (Parabrahman) and that we are Brahman, then we will transcend this hankering and lamenting.

The so-called universal brotherhood or unity that the United Nations is trying to achieve is possible only when you come to the spiritual platform, or Brahman realization. Brahman realization is the aim of human life. One should not work like cats, dogs, and hogs. The hog is always very busy day and night trying to find stool, and when he finds it, he eats it and becomes sexually agitated and has sex without discrimination. A hog will have sex with its mother or sister or anyone else, and this is a hog's life. However, the scriptures indicate that the human form of life is not meant for working hard for sense gratification like cats, dogs, and hogs. It is meant for realizing, "I do not belong to this material world. I am spirit soul and am eternal, but somehow or other I have fallen into this conditional life of birth, old age, disease, and death." This human form of life is meant for making a solution to these four material miseries—birth, old age, disease, and death. That is the aim of human life. Just try to understand that human life is not meant for working very hard like hogs and then having some sense gratification and then all of a sudden dying.

People who do not believe in the soul are in a most unfortunate condition. They do not know where they came from nor where they are going. Knowledge of the soul is the most important knowledge, but it is not discussed in any university. But what is the constitution of this body? What is the distinction between a dead body and a living body? Why is the body living? What is the condition of the body, and what is its value? No one is presently studying these questions, but by this Kṛṣṇa consciousness movement we are trying to educate people so that they can understand that they are not these bodies but are spirit souls. The business of human life is different from the business of cats and dogs. That is our message.

As far as the soul is concerned, the evolutionary process is going on, and we are struggling for existence, struggling to come to the point of eternal life. That eternal life is possible. If you try your best in this human form of life, in your next life you can get a spiritual body. Your spiritual body is already within you, and it will develop as soon as you become free from the contamination of this material existence. That is the aim of human life. People do not know what actual self-interest is; it is to realize oneself, to realize, "I am part and parcel of God, and I have to return to the kingdom of God to join with God."

Just as we have a social life here, God has a social life in the spiritual kingdom. You can join Him there. It is not that after this body is finished you become void. No. That is a wrong conception. In the *Bhagavad-gītā* [2.12], Kṛṣṇa told Arjuna on the Battlefield of Kurukṣetra:

na tv evāhaṁ jātu nāsaṁ na tvaṁ neme janādhipāḥ
na caiva na bhaviṣyāmaḥ sarve vayam ataḥ param

"Never was there a time when I did not exist, nor you, nor all these kings; nor in the future shall any of us cease to be."

The process for attaining eternal life is very easy, and yet at the same time very difficult. It is difficult because people in the beginning do not believe in the existence of transmigration of the soul. However, if we simply take knowledge from the authorities, the process becomes very simple. Our process of Kṛṣṇa consciousness is to take knowledge from Kṛṣṇa, the most perfect being, and not from an ordinary being conditioned by the laws of material nature. Knowledge taken from a conditioned being is sure to be defective.

What are the defects of the conditioned soul? He is sure to commit mistakes, sure to be illusioned, sure to cheat others, and sure to have imperfect senses. We cannot attain knowledge perfectly, because we want to cheat others and our senses are imperfect. Although our senses are imperfect, we are very proud of our eyes, and we want to see everything. Therefore someone says, "Can you show me God?" Actually the answer is yes. Why can't you see God at every moment? Kṛṣṇa says, *raso 'ham apsu kaunteya:* "I am the taste of water." Everyone drinks water, and the taste is there—so if we think of this taste as God, we begin the process of God realization. Kṛṣṇa also says, *prabhāsmi śaśi-sūryayoḥ:* "I am the sunshine, and I am the moonshine." We all see the sunshine and moonshine every day, and if we think of how it is that the sun and moon are emanating light, we will ultimately reach God. There are so many similar instances. If you want to be God conscious and realize God yourself, it is not very difficult. You have simply to follow the prescribed methods. As stated in the *Bhagavad-gītā* [18.55], *tato māṁ tattvato jñātvā.* We must simply try to understand God in truth and try to understand His appearance, dis-appearance, and functions. When we understand Him in truth, we immediately enter the kingdom of God. After quitting this body, the person who understands God, or Kṛṣṇa, does not come back again to accept another material body. Kṛṣṇa says, *mām eti:* "He comes to Me." That is our aim.

Therefore we should not waste our time living like cats and dogs. We should live comfortably, but at the same time we should be Kṛṣṇa conscious, or God conscious. That will help us become happy. Without understanding God and without becoming God conscious, there is no possibility of peace and happiness. The way of peace and happiness is outlined in the *Bhagavad-gītā.*

If you really want to understand God, He is very easy to understand. God is the proprietor of everything. *Īśāvāsyam idaṁ sarvam.* Unfortunately we are thinking, "I am the proprietor." In your country, for instance, the British have sometimes claimed to be proprietors, and now you are claiming to be the proprietors—so who knows what will happen in the future? Actually no one knows who the real proprietor is. The land is there, and it is the property of God, but we are simply thinking, "I am the proprietor. I own this, and I own that." Actually, America existed before the Europeans came, but now the Americans are thinking, "We are the proprietors." Similarly, before them the Red Indians were thinking, "We are the proprietors." The fact is that no man is an actual proprietor; the proprietor is God.

īśāvāsyam idaṁ sarvaṁ yat kiṁ ca jagatyāṁ jagat
tena tyaktena bhuñjīthā mā gṛdhaḥ kasya svid dhanam

"Everything animate or inanimate that is within the universe is controlled and owned by the Lord. One should therefore accept only those things necessary for himself, which are set aside as his quota, and one should not accept other things, knowing well to whom they belong." [*Īśopaniṣad* 1]

This realization is wanting. Kṛṣṇa claims proprietorship over all forms—including American forms, African forms, cat forms, dog forms, tree forms, etc.—for in actuality He is the proprietor and the supreme father. If we simply realize this, we attain God realization. Actually, if we realize God as prescribed in the authorized books and Vedic literatures, we will find that there will no longer be quarrels between this party and that party. Everything will be peaceful.

Everyone has the right to use God's property, just as a son has the right to live at the cost of his father. It is stated in the scriptures that even a small animal in the home must be given some food. That is spiritual communism. No one should remain hungry, not even a serpent. We are always afraid of serpents, but if we find a serpent to be living in our house, it is our duty to see that the serpent is also fed. This is the conception of God consciousness, or Kṛṣṇa consciousness: *samaḥ sarveṣu bhūteṣu.* One who is transcendentally situated is equally disposed to every living entity. Thus the *Bhagavad-gītā* points out that when one sees everyone equally, as part and parcel of the Supreme Lord, one actually begins his devotional life. This Kṛṣṇa consciousness movement is trying in an authoritative way to make everyone understand what he is and what the aim of life is. This process of purification of the heart is very easily accomplished. One simply has to chant this *mahā-mantra*—Hare Kṛṣṇa, Hare Kṛṣṇa, Kṛṣṇa Kṛṣṇa, Hare Hare/ Hare Rāma, Hare Rāma, Rāma Rāma, Hare Hare. It can actually be seen that in this movement there are boys and girls from different countries and different religions, but no one is concerned with any particular section, country, or religious body. We are simply concerned about knowing ourselves and our relationship with God.

God is the supreme proprietor, and we are all His sons, or servitors. Therefore let us engage ourselves in the service of the Lord, as recommended in the *Bhagavad-gītā*. As soon as we understand that God is the proprietor of everything, then all the troubles of the world will immediately be solved. This may take some time. It is not expected that everyone will understand this high philosophy, but if the intelligent people in every country try to understand it, that will be sufficient. In the *Bhagavad-gītā* [3.21] it is stated:

yad yad ācarati śreṣṭhas tat tad evetaro janaḥ
sa yat pramāṇaṁ kurute lokas tad anuvartate

"Whatever action a great man performs, common men follow in his footsteps. And whatever standards he sets by exemplary acts, all the world pursues."

We therefore invite the most intelligent men in the world to understand this Kṛṣṇa conscious philosophy and try to distribute it all over the world. We have now come to these African countries, and I invite all intelligent Africans to come and understand this philosophy and distribute it. You are trying to develop yourselves, so please develop spiritually, for spiritual development is sound development. Don't imitate the Americans and Europeans, who are living like cats and dogs. Such civilizations built on the consciousness of sense gratification cannot stand. The atomic bomb is already there, and as soon as the next war breaks out, all their skyscrapers and everything else will be finished. Try to understand this from the real viewpoint of human life, the spiritual viewpoint. This is what this Kṛṣṇa consciousness movement is about. We therefore request you to try to understand this philosophy. Thank you very much.

"A DEVOTEE ALWAYS FEELS COMPASSION FOR OTHERS' DISTRESS"

"When Lord Jesus Christ presented himself, for instance, he was greatly afflicted by the miserable conditions of the people. Regardless of which country or sect they belong to, all Vaiṣṇavas, or devotees—any people who are God conscious, or Kṛṣṇa conscious—are thus compassionate."

Today I shall speak to you about the glorification of the holy name of God. This was discussed between Mahārāja Parīkṣit and Śukadeva Gosvāmī in connection with a *brāhmaṇa* who was very fallen and addicted to all kinds of sinful activities but was saved simply by chanting the holy name. This is found in the Sixth Canto of the *Śrīmad-Bhāgavatam*.

The universal planetary systems are very nicely explained in the Fifth Canto of the *Śrīmad-Bhāgavatam*. Within the universe there are some planets which are hellish. Actually, not only the *Bhāgavatam* but all religious scriptures contain descriptions of hell and heaven. In the *Śrīmad-Bhāgavatam* you can find out where those hellish planets are and how distant they are from this planet, just as you can obtain information from modern astronomy. Astronomers have calculated how far the moon is from here and what the distance is between this planet and the sun; similarly, the *Bhāgavatam* contains descriptions of the hellish planets.

We have experience of different atmospheric conditions even on this planet. In the Western countries near the North Pole, the climate is different than in India, which is near the equator. Just as there are differences in atmosphere and living conditions on this planet, similarly there are many planets which have different atmospheres and conditions of life.

After hearing a description of the hellish planets from Śukadeva

Gosvāmī, Parīkṣit Mahārāja said:

adhuneha mahā-bhāga yathaiva narakān naraḥ
nānogra-yātanān neyāt tan me vyākhyātum arhasi

"Sir, I have heard from you about the hellish planets. Men who are very sinful are sent to those planets." [*Śrīmad-Bhāgavatam* 6.1.6] Parīkṣit Mahārāja is a Vaiṣṇava [devotee], and a Vaiṣṇava always feels compassion for others' distress. He is very afflicted by the miseries of others. When Lord Jesus Christ presented himself, for instance, he was greatly afflicted by the miserable conditions of the people. Regardless of which country or sect they belong to, all Vaiṣṇavas, or devotees—any people who are God conscious, or Kṛṣṇa conscious—are thus compassionate. Therefore to blaspheme a Vaiṣṇava, a preacher of God's glories, is a great offense.

Kṛṣṇa, God, is never tolerant of offenses committed at the lotus feet of a Vaiṣṇava. *Kṛpāmbudhi:* a Vaiṣṇava is an ocean of mercy. *Vāñchā-kalpa-taru:* everyone has desires, but a Vaiṣṇava can fulfill all desires. *Kalpa-taru* means "desire tree." There is a tree in the spiritual world which is called a desire tree. In this material world, you get a particular type of fruit from a particular type of tree, but in Kṛṣṇaloka as well as in all the Vaikuṇṭha planets, all the trees are spiritual and will fulfill all your desires. That is described in the *Brahma-saṁhitā: cintāmaṇi-prakara-sadmasu kalpa-vṛkṣa.*

A Vaiṣṇava is addressed as *mahā-bhāga,* which means "fortunate." One who becomes a Vaiṣṇava and is God conscious is understood to be greatly fortunate.

Caitanya Mahāprabhu has explained that the living entities are rotating in different species of life, in different planetary systems all over the universe. A living entity can go anywhere—to hell or heaven—as he likes and as he prepares himself. There are many heavenly planets, many hellish species of life. The living entity is rotating, wandering through these species and creating bodies according to his mentality in the present life. As you sow, so shall you reap.

Caitanya Mahāprabhu says that out of all these numberless living entities who are traveling in the material world, one is fortunate, not everyone. If everyone were fortunate, they would all have taken to Kṛṣṇa consciousness. It is being distributed freely everywhere.

But why are people not taking it? Because they are unfortunate. Therefore Caitanya Mahāprabhu says that only those who are fortunate take to this Kṛṣṇa consciousness, and they get hopeful life, pleasant life, blissful life, a life of knowledge.

It is the duty of a Vaiṣṇava to go door to door to make the unfortunate people fortunate. A Vaiṣṇava thinks, "How can these people be delivered from their hellish life?" That was Parīkṣit Mahārāja's inquiry. "Sir," he said, "you have described that on account of one's sinful activities one is put into a hellish condition of life or in a hellish planetary system. Now, what are the countermethods by which such persons can be saved?" This is the question. When a Vaiṣṇava comes, when God Himself comes, or when God's son or His very confidential devotees come, their only mission is to save the sinful men who are suffering. They have knowledge of how to do this.

When Prahlāda Mahārāja met Nṛsiṁhadeva, he said:

naivodvije para duratyaya-vaitaraṇyās
tvad-vīrya-gāyana-mahāmṛta-magna-cittaḥ
śoce tato vimukha-cetasa indriyārtha-
māyā-sukhāya bharam udvahato vimūḍhān

"My dear Lord," Prahlāda says, "I am not very anxious for my own deliverance." [*Śrīmad-Bhāgavatam* 7.9.43] Māyāvādī philosophers are very careful that their personal salvation is not interrupted. They think, "If I go to preach in association with others, I may fall down, and my realization will be finished." Therefore they do not come. Only the Vaiṣṇavas come, at the risk of falldown—but they do not fall down. They may even go to hell to deliver the conditioned souls. This is Prahlāda Mahārāja's mission. He says, *naivodvije:* "I am not very anxious about living in this material world."

Prahlāda Mahārāja says further, "I have no anxiety for myself, because somehow or other I have been trained to be always Kṛṣṇa conscious." Because he is Kṛṣṇa conscious, he is confident that in his next life he is going to Kṛṣṇa. It is stated in the *Bhagavad-gītā* that if one executes the Kṛṣṇa conscious regulative principles carefully, it is certain that he will reach the supreme destination in his next life.

Prahlāda Mahārāja continues: "There is only one source of anxiety for me." Just see—although he had no anxiety for himself, he still had anxiety. He says, *śoce tato vimukha-cetasaḥ:* "I am anxious for those persons who are not Kṛṣṇa conscious. That is my anxiety. For myself I have no anxiety, but I am thinking of those who are not Kṛṣṇa conscious." Why aren't they Kṛṣṇa conscious? *Māyā-sukhāya bharam udvahato vimūḍhān.* These rascals have created a humbug civilization for temporary happiness.

Māyā-sukhāya. Actually this is a fact. We have a humbug civilization. So many cars are being manufactured every year, and for that purpose so many roads have to be excavated and prepared. This creates problem after problem. Therefore it is *māyā-sukhāya,* illusory happiness, and yet we are trying to be happy in this way. We are trying to manufacture some way to be happy, but this only creates other problems.

In your country you have the greatest number of cars, but that does not solve any problems. You have manufactured cars to help solve the problems of life, but I have experienced that this also creates more problems. When my disciple Dayānanda wanted to take me to a doctor in Los Angeles, I had to take the trouble to travel thirty miles before I could even consult the doctor. Once you create cars, then you must travel thirty or forty miles to meet your friends.

You can fly from New York to Boston in one hour, but it takes even longer than that just to get to the airport. This situation is called *māyā-sukhāya. Māyā* means "false," "illusory." We are trying to create some very comfortable situation, but we have created another uncomfortable situation. This is the way of the material world; if we are not satisfied by the natural comforts offered by God and nature and we want to create artificial comforts, then we have to create some discomfort also. Most people do not know that. They think that they are creating a very comfortable situation, but actually they are traveling fifty miles to go to the office to earn a livelihood and fifty miles to come back. Because of such conditions, Prahlāda Mahārāja says that these *vimūḍhās*—these materialistic persons, these rascals—have created an unnecessary burden on themselves simply for temporary happiness. *Vimūḍhān, māyā-sukhāya bharam udvahato.* Therefore, in Vedic civilization it is recommended that one free himself from material life, take *sannyāsa,* the renounced order of life, and prosecute spiritual life with absolutely no anxiety.

If one can execute Kṛṣṇa consciousness in family life, that is very good. Bhaktivinoda Ṭhākura was a family man, a magistrate, and still he executed devotional service so nicely. Dhruva Mahārāja and Prahlāda Mahārāja were *gṛhasthas,* householders, but they trained themselves in such a way that even as householders they were faced with no interruption in their service. Therefore, Prahlāda Mahārāja says, "I have learned the art of always remaining in Kṛṣṇa consciousness." What is that art? *Tvad-vīrya-gāyana-mahāmṛta-magna-cittaḥ.* Simply glorifying the victorious activities and pastimes of the Lord. *Vīrya* means "very heroic."

Kṛṣṇa's activities are heroic. You can read about them in *Kṛṣṇa, the Supreme Personality of Godhead.* Kṛṣṇa's name, His fame, His activities, His associates, and all other things related to Him are heroic. Prahlāda Mahārāja says in this connection, "I am certain that wherever I go, I can glorify Your heroic activities and be safe. There is no question of my falling down. But I am simply anxious for these persons who have created a type of civilization in which they are always busy working hard. I am thinking of them."

Prahlāda says further:

prāyeṇa deva munayaḥ sva-vimukti-kāmā
maunaṁ caranti vijane na parārtha-niṣṭhāḥ
naitān vihāya kṛpaṇān vimumukṣa eko
nānyaṁ tvad asya śaraṇaṁ bhramato 'nupaśye

"My dear Lord, there are many saintly persons and sages who are very interested in their own liberation." [*Śrīmad-Bhāgavatam* 7.9.44] *Munayaḥ* means "saintly persons" or "philosophers." *Prāyeṇa deva munayaḥ sva-vimukti-kāmāḥ:* they are very interested in their own liberation. They try to live in solitary places like the Himalaya Mountains. They do not talk to anyone, and they are always afraid of mixing with ordinary people in the city and becoming disturbed or maybe even falling down. They think, "Better let me save myself."

Prahlāda Mahārāja regrets that these great saintly persons do not come to the city, where people have manufactured a civilization of very hard work all day and night. Such saints are not very compassionate. He says, "I am anxious for these fallen people who are unnecessarily working so hard simply for sense gratification."

Even if there were some point in working that hard, such people do not know what it is. All they know is sex. Either they go to a naked dance or to a naked club or to this or that. Prahlāda Mahārāja says, *naitān vihāya kṛpaṇān vimumukṣa ekaḥ:* "My Lord, I do not need salvation alone. Unless I take all these fools with me, I shall not go." He refuses to go to the kingdom of God without taking all these fallen souls with him. This is a Vaiṣṇava. *Nānyaṁ tvad asya śaraṇaṁ bhramato 'nupaśye:* "I simply want to teach them how to surrender unto You. That's all. That is my goal."

The Vaiṣṇava knows that as soon as one surrenders, one's path is clear. *Naivodvije para duratyaya-vaitaraṇyās tvad-vīrya-gāyana-mahāmṛta-magna-cittaḥ:* "Somehow or other, let them bow down before Kṛṣṇa." This is a simple method. All you have to do is bow down before Kṛṣṇa with faith and say, "My Lord Kṛṣṇa, I was forgetful of You for so long, for so many lives. Now I have come to consciousness; please accept me." That's all. If one simply learns this technique and sincerely surrenders himself to the Lord, his path is immediately open. These are the philosophical thoughts of a Vaiṣṇava. A Vaiṣṇava is always thinking about how the fallen conditioned souls can be delivered. He is always involved in making plans in that way, just like the Gosvāmīs. What was the business of the Six Gosvāmīs of Vṛndāvana, Lord Caitanya's direct disciples? That is stated by Śrīnivāsa Ācārya:

nānā-śāstra-vicāraṇaika-nipuṇau sad-dharma-saṁsthāpakau
lokānāṁ hita-kāriṇau tribhuvane mānyau śaraṇyākarau
rādhā-kṛṣṇa-padāravinda-bhajanānandena mattālikau
vande rūpa-sanātanau raghu-yugau śrī-jīva-gopālakau

"The Six Gosvāmīs, namely, Śrī Sanātana Gosvāmī, Śrī Rūpa Gosvāmī, Śrī Raghunātha Bhaṭṭa Gosvāmī, Śrī Raghunātha Dāsa Gosvāmī, Śrī Jīva Gosvāmī, and Śrī Gopāla Bhaṭṭa Gosvāmī, are very expert in scrutinizingly studying the revealed scriptures with the aim of establishing eternal religious principles for the benefit of all human beings. They are always absorbed in the mood of the *gopīs* and are engaged in the transcendental loving service of Rādhā and Kṛṣṇa." [*Ṣaḍ-gosvāmy-aṣṭaka* 2]

With similar Vaiṣṇava compassion, Parīkṣit Mahārāja says to Śukadeva Gosvāmī: "You have described the different types of hellish conditions of life. Now, tell me how those who are suffering can be delivered. Kindly explain this to me."

adhuneha mahā-bhāga yathaiva narakān naraḥ
nānogra-yātanān neyāt tan me vyākhyātum arhasi

Nara means human beings, those who are fallen. *Narakān naraḥ/ nānogra-yātanān neyāt tan me:* "How can they be delivered from their fierce miseries and horrible pains?" That is a Vaiṣṇava heart. Mahārāja Parīkṣit says, "Somehow or other they have fallen down to this hellish life. But that does not mean that they should remain in that condition. There must be some means by which they can be delivered, so kindly explain that."

Śukadeva Gosvāmī replied:

na ced ihaivāpacitiṁ yathāṁhasaḥ
kṛtasya kuryān mana-ukta-pāṇibhiḥ
dhruvaṁ sa vai pretya narakān upaiti
ye kīrtitā me bhavatas tigma-yātanāḥ

"Yes, I've already described the different types of hellish conditions and very severe painful life, but one has to counteract it." [*Śrīmad-Bhāgavatam* 6.1.7]

How can this be done? Sinful activities are committed in various ways. We can commit sinful activity or thus make a plan, thinking, "I shall kill that man." Either way, it is sinful. When the mind is thinking, feeling, and willing, then there is action.

The other day I was reading in a book that if someone's dog barks at you when you are passing on the road, then that is an offense on the part of the dog-owner, according to law. No one should have to be scared by dogs barking, so one should take care of his dog. I read this. It is a law in your country. The dog is simply barking, but it is sinful. The dog is not responsible, because it is an animal, but because the owner of the animal has made the dog his best friend, he is responsible by law. If an outside dog enters your house, it may not be killed, but the owners of the dog may be prosecuted.

Just as the barking of the dog is unlawful, so when you speak something offensive to others, that is also sinful. That is just like barking. Therefore sinful activities are committed in so many ways. Whether we think of sinful activities, or we speak something sinful, or we actually commit a sinful activity, they are all considered sinful activities. *Dhruvaṁ sa vai pretya narakān upaiti.* One has to suffer punishment for such sinful activities.

People do not believe in a next life, because they want to avoid this botheration. But we cannot avoid it. We must act according to the law, or we will be punished. Similarly, I cannot avoid God's law. That is not possible. I can cheat others, commit theft, and hide myself, thereby saving myself from the punishment of the state law, but I cannot save myself from the superior law, the law of nature. It is very difficult. There are so many witnesses. The daylight is witness, the moonlight is witness, and Kṛṣṇa is the supreme witness. You cannot say, "I am committing this sin, but no one can see me."

Kṛṣṇa is the supreme witness sitting within your heart. He notes down what you are thinking and what you are doing. He also gives facility. If you want to do something to satisfy your senses, Kṛṣṇa gives the facility for that action. That is stated in the *Bhagavad-gītā. Sarvasya cāhaṁ hṛdi sanniviṣṭaḥ:* "I am sitting in everyone's heart." *Mattaḥ smṛtir jñānam apohanaṁ ca:* "From Me come remembrance, knowledge, and forgetfulness."

In this way Kṛṣṇa gives us a chance. If you want Kṛṣṇa, then He will give you a chance to have Him, and if you don't want Kṛṣṇa, then He will give you a chance to forget Him. If you want to enjoy life forgetting Kṛṣṇa, forgetting God, then Kṛṣṇa will give you all facility so that you can forget, and if you want to enjoy life with Kṛṣṇa consciousness, then Kṛṣṇa will give you the chance to make progress in Kṛṣṇa consciousness. That is up to you.

If you think that you can be happy without Kṛṣṇa consciousness, Kṛṣṇa does not object to that. *Yathecchasi tathā kuru.* After advising Arjuna, He simply said, "Now I have explained everything to you. Whatever you desire you can do." Arjuna replied immediately, *kariṣye vacanaṁ tava:* "Now I shall execute Your order." That is Kṛṣṇa consciousness.

God does not interfere with your little independence. If you want to act according to the order of God, then God will help you. Even if you fall down sometimes, if you become sincere—"From this time on I shall remain Kṛṣṇa conscious and execute His orders"—then Kṛṣṇa will help you. In all respects, even if you fall down, He will excuse you and give you more intelligence. This intelligence will say, "Don't do this. Now go on with your duty." But if you want to forget Kṛṣṇa, if you want to become happy without Kṛṣṇa, He will give you so many chances that you will forget Kṛṣṇa life after life.

Parīkṣit Mahārāja says here, "It is not that if I say there is no God then there will be no God or I will not be responsible for what I do." That is the atheistic theory. Atheists do not want God, because they are always sinful—if they thought that there was a God, then they would be forced to shudder at the thought of punishment. Therefore they deny the existence of God. That is their process. They think that if they do not accept God then there is no punishment and they can do whatever they like.

When rabbits are being attacked by bigger animals, they close their eyes and think, "I am not going to be killed." But they are killed anyway. Similarly, we may deny the existence of God and the law of God, but still God and His law are there. In the high-court you may say, "I don't care for the law of the government," but you will be forced to accept the government law. If you deny the state law, then you will be put into prison and be caused to suffer. Similarly, you may foolishly decry the existence of God—"There is no God" or "I am God"—but nevertheless you are responsible for all your actions, both good and bad.

There are two kinds of activities—good and bad. If you act nicely and perform pious activities, then you get good fortune, and if you act sinfully, then you have to suffer. Therefore Śukadeva Gosvāmī says:

tasmāt puraivāśv iha pāpa-niṣkṛtau
yateta mṛtyor avipadyatātmanā
doṣasya dṛṣṭvā guru-lāghavaṁ yathā
bhiṣak cikitseta rujāṁ nidāna-vit
[*Śrīmad-Bhāgavatam* 6.1.8]

There are different kinds of atonement. If you commit some sin and counteract it by something else, that is atonement. There are examples of this in the Christian Bible. Śukadeva Gosvāmī says, "You should know that you are responsible, and according to the gravity of sinful life, you should accept some type of atonement as described in the *śāstras*, the scriptures."

Actually, just as when one is diseased he must go to a doctor and pay doctor bills as a form of atonement, according to the Vedic way of life there is a class of *brāhmaṇas* to whom one should go for the prescribed atonement according to the sins one commits.

Śukadeva Gosvāmī says that one has to execute the prescribed atonement according to the gravity of one's sinful life. He continues the example: *doṣasya dṛṣṭvā guru-lāghavaṁ yathā bhiṣak cikitseta rujāṁ nidāna-vit.* When you consult a physician, he prescribes an inexpensive medicine or a costly medicine, according to the gravity of the disease. If you simply have a headache, he may prescribe an aspirin, but if you have something very severe, he immediately prescribes a surgical operation that will cost a thousand dollars. Similarly, sinful life is a diseased condition, so one must follow the prescribed cure to become healthy.

Acceptance of the chain of birth and death is a diseased condition of the soul. The soul has no birth and death and no disease, because it is spirit. Kṛṣṇa says in the *Bhagavad-gītā* [2.20]: *na jāyate,* the soul has no birth, and *mriyate,* it has no death. *Nityaḥ śāśvato 'yaṁ purāṇo/ na hanyate hanyamāne śarīre.* The soul is eternal and everlasting. It is not lost with the dissolution of this body. *Na hanyate hanyamāne śarīre. Na hanyate* means that it is not killed or destroyed, even after the destruction of this body.

The missing point of modern civilization is that there is no educational system to instruct people on what happens after death. Thus we have the most defective education, because without this knowledge of what happens after death, one dies like an animal. The animal does not know that he is going to have another body; he has no such knowledge.

Human life is not meant for becoming an animal. One should not simply be interested in eating, sleeping, sex life, and defense. You may have a very nice arrangement for eating, or many nice buildings for sleeping, or a very good arrangement for sex life, or a very good defense force to protect you, but that does not mean that you are a human being. That type of civilization is animal life. Animals are also interested in eating, sleeping, and sex life, and according to their own methods they defend also. Where, then, is the distinction between human life and animal life if you simply engage in these four principles of bodily nature?

The distinction is made when a human being is inquisitive—"Why have I been put into this miserable condition? Is there any remedy for it? Is there any perpetual, eternal life? I do not want to die. I want to live very happily and peacefully. Is there a chance of this? What is that method? What is that science?" When these inquiries are there and steps are taken to answer these questions, that is human civilization; otherwise it is doggish civilization, animal civilization.

Animals are satisfied if they can eat, sleep, have some sex life, and have some defense. Actually there is no defense, because no one can protect himself from the hands of cruel death. Hiraṇyakaśipu, for instance, wanted to live forever, and so he underwent severe austerities. So-called scientists are now saying that we shall stop death by scientific methods. This is also another crazy utterance. That is not possible. You may make great advancement in scientific knowledge, but there is no scientific solution to these four problems—birth, death, old age, and disease.

One who is intelligent will be eager to solve these four prime problems. No one wants to die. But there is no remedy. I have to die. Everyone is very anxious to stop the increase of population by employing so many contraceptive methods, but still, birth is going on. So there is no stoppage of birth. You may invent up-to-date medicines by your scientific methods, but you cannot stop disease. It is not possible just to take a tablet to put an end to disease.

In the *Bhagavad-gītā* it is said, *janma-mṛtyu-jarā-vyādhi-duḥkha-doṣānu-darśanam:* one might think that he has solved all the problems of his life, but where is the solution to these four problems of birth, death, old age, and disease? That solution is Kṛṣṇa consciousness.

Kṛṣṇa also says in the same book,

janma karma ca me divyam evaṁ yo vetti tattvataḥ
tyaktvā dehaṁ punar janma naiti mām eti so 'rjuna
[*Bhagavad-gītā* 4.9]

Every one of us is giving up our body at every moment. The last phase of giving up this body is called death. But Kṛṣṇa says, "If anyone understands My appearance and disappearance and My activities—not superficially, but in truth—after giving up this body he never again accepts a material body."

What happens to such a person? *Mām eti*—he returns to Kṛṣṇa.

If you are to go to Kṛṣṇa, then you have to prepare your spiritual body. That is Kṛṣṇa consciousness. If you keep yourself in Kṛṣṇa consciousness, then gradually you prepare your next body, a spiritual body, which will carry you immediately to Kṛṣṇaloka, the abode of Kṛṣṇa, and you will become happy. You will live there perpetually and blissfully.

"THEY HAVE GIVEN EVERYTHING TO KṚṢṆA—AND THAT IS NEVER A MISTAKE"

In 1973 Śrīla Prabhupāda received an unusual letter from a woman in California who had encountered two of his young disciples. She complained that they had "a very negative outlook toward the people they meet." Moved by her genuine concern, Śrīla Prabhupāda took time out from his busy schedule to write her this thoughtful letter.

Your Grace:

Please accept this letter with Love . . . K-Mart; San Fernando. We have talked with two of your boys at different times. Both had a very negative outlook toward the people they meet.

Do not believe this is in any way as it should be.

These boys happen to represent God. This comes from within. Their outlook must have mercy. We realize this; therefore handpick these little pieces of heaven to place in the middle of these people. Or else it will defeat your purpose.

Love Is. Let it be as it is; with Love or not at all.

My prayers be with you . . . and I beg yours with me.

Yours in God, Blessed Be,
Lynne Ludwig

My dear Lynne Ludwig,

Please accept my blessings. I beg to acknowledge receipt of your letter from California, and I have noted the contents carefully, although due to extensively traveling and preaching in a tour in India I have not had the opportunity to reply to you at length until now. Your complaint is that you have met two of my young disciples in California and they appeared to you to have "a very negative outlook toward the people they meet." Of course, I do not know the case and what the circumstances are, but kindly forgive my beloved disciples for any unkindness or indiscretion on their part. After all, to give up one's life completely for serving the Lord is not an easy thing, and *māyā*, or the illusory, material energy, tries especially hard to again entrap those who have left her service to become devotees. Therefore, in order to withstand the attack of *māyā* and remain strong under all conditions of temptation, young or inexperienced devotees in the neophyte stage of devotional service will sometimes adopt an attitude against those things or persons which may possibly be harmful or threatening to their tender devotional creepers. They may even overindulge in such feelings just to protect themselves, and thus they will appear to some nondevotees, who are perhaps themselves still very much enamored by the material energy of *māyā*, to be negative or pessimistic.

But the actual fact is that this material world is a miserable, negative place, full of danger at every step; it is *duḥkhālayam aśāśvatam*, a temporary abode of death, birth, disease, and old age, a home of suffering and pain only. To come to the platform of understanding these things as they are is not very common, and therefore persons who attain to it are described as "great souls."

mām upetya punar janma duḥkhālayam aśāśvatam
nāpnuvanti mahātmānaḥ saṁsiddhiṁ paramāṁ gatāḥ

This means that those who have understood that the material worlds are places of misery and temporality (*duḥkhālayam aśāśvatam*) never return here again, and because they are *mahātmānaḥ*, the great souls, Kṛṣṇa keeps them with Him because they have qualified themselves to escape this nasty place by becoming His pure devotees. This verse is spoken by Kṛṣṇa, or God Himself, in the *Bhagavad-gītā* [8.15]. Who can be a more final authority? The point is that to make advancement in spiritual life, one must view everything material with a pessimistic eye unless it is utilized to serve and please Kṛṣṇa. We are not very much hopeful for any lasting pleasure or satisfaction for our deepest cravings within this realm of gross matter.

You refer to the word "love" several times in your letter, but the actual fact is that there *is* no love in this material world. That is false propaganda. What they call love here is lust only, or desire for personal sense gratification:

kāma eṣa krodha eṣa rajo-guṇa-samudbhavaḥ
mahāśano mahā-pāpmā viddhy enam iha vairiṇam

Kṛṣṇa tells Arjuna, His disciple, that "It is lust only . . . which is the all-devouring, sinful enemy of this world." [*Bhagavad-gītā* 3.37] In the Vedic language there is no word for materialistic "love," as we call it in the present day. The word *kāma* describes lust or material desire, not love, but the word that we find in the *Vedas* for actual love is *prema*, meaning one's love of God only. Outside of loving God there is no possibility of loving. Rather, there is lusty desire only. Within this atmosphere of matter, the entire range of human activities—and not only every activity of human beings but all living entities—is based upon, given impetus by, and thus polluted by sex desire, the attraction between male and female. For that sex life, the whole universe is spinning around—and suffering! That is the harsh truth. So-called love here means that "you gratify my senses, I'll gratify your senses," and as soon as that gratification stops, immediately there is divorce, separation, quarrel, and hatred. So many things are going on under this false conception of love. Actual love means love of God, Kṛṣṇa.

Everyone wants to repose his loving tendency in some object which is in his opinion worthy. But the question is one of ignorance only, because people have a poor fund of knowledge about where to find that supreme lovable object who is *actually* worthy to accept and reciprocate their love. People simply do not know. There is no proper information. As soon as you have some attachment for anything material, it will kick you upon the face, deteriorate, and disappoint you. It's bound to dissatisfy and frustrate you. That's a fact. But these young boys in your country, and all over the world, are accepting, "Yes, that is a fact," and they are getting the right information from Kṛṣṇa:

bahūnāṁ janmanām ante jñānavān māṁ prapadyate
vāsudevaḥ sarvam iti sa mahātmā sudurlabhaḥ

"After many births and deaths, he who is actually wise surrenders unto Me, knowing Me to be the cause of all causes and all that is. Such a great soul is very rare." [*Bhagavad-gītā* 7.19] Again Kṛṣṇa uses that word *mahātmā*, great soul. Therefore our devotees that you have met are not ordinary boys and girls. No. They are to be considered actually wise, great souls because they have experienced in many births the miserable disease of material life and have become disgusted. Therefore they are seeking higher knowledge—they are seeking something better—and when they find Kṛṣṇa and surrender unto Him, they become *mahātmās,* who are actually situated in knowledge. This material world is just like a prison house; it is a punishing place meant to bring us to that point of becoming disgusted, surrendering at last to Kṛṣṇa, and going back to our original nature of eternal life in bliss and complete knowledge. Therefore it is to the credit of these devotees that they have done what is *su-durlabhaḥ,* very rare among all men in human society.

By surrendering to Kṛṣṇa one will find the final object in which to invest his love: God. Love of God is present in everyone, just like fire in an unlit match, but it is covered over. But if one somehow or other develops his dormant love of God, and Kṛṣṇa becomes his supreme adorable object, supreme friend, supreme master, or supreme lover, than he shall never again become disappointed or unhappy. Rather, because his loving propensity is rightfully placed:

mac-cittā mad-gata-prāṇā bodhayantaḥ parasparam
kathayantaś ca māṁ nityaṁ tuṣyanti ca ramanti ca
[*Bhagavad-gītā* 10.9]

The devotee whose life is surrendered to Kṛṣṇa is always enjoying "great satisfaction and bliss," and he is constantly enlightened, always positive, not negative, as you say. The advanced devotee is the friend of everyone. The *yoga-yukto viśuddhātmā,* purified soul engaged in loving devotional service to Kṛṣṇa, is *sarva-bhūtātma-bhūtātmā,* dear to everyone, and everyone is dear to him. In another place Kṛṣṇa claims that *yo mad-bhaktaḥ sa me priyaḥ,* His devotee, who is very dear to Him, *adveṣṭā sarva-bhūtānāṁ maitraḥ karuṇa eva ca,* is not envious but is a kind friend to all living entities. The devotee is supposed to be, furthermore, equal to everyone (*paṇḍitāḥ sama-darśinaḥ*). He never discriminates, saying, "This one is good, this one is bad." No.

These are descriptions of the more advanced stages of Kṛṣṇa consciousness that devotees get by development of mature knowledge. At present many of our students are young boys. They are learning gradually, and the process is so effective, certain, and authorized that if they stick to it they will come to the right point, as you say, of loving. But that love is not material, so it should not be judged on the false, sentimental platform of ordinary, mundane dealings. That is our point. Therefore to say they are not loving may be true from the materialists' point of view. They have given up affection for family, friends, wife, country, race, and so on, which is all based upon the bodily concept of life, or flickering sense gratification. They have become a little detached from *māyā's* love, or lust, and they want Kṛṣṇa's love, or endless, fully rewarding love, but they have not yet developed to that point, that's all. We cannot expect that all of a sudden your countrymen, who are addicted to so many bad habits, will give up eating flesh, taking intoxicants, having illicit sex life, and so many other nasty things, and overnight become great, self-realized souls. That is not possible. That is utopian. But just being initiated as Kṛṣṇa's devotee puts one in the topmost category of human society. *Sa buddhimān manuṣyeṣu sa yuktaḥ kṛtsna-karma-kṛt:* "He is intelligent in human society. He is in the transcendental position, although engaged in all sorts of activities." And although such a devotee may not yet have advanced to the highest level of spiritual understanding, still he is to be considered the most exalted personality, regardless of any temporary frailties.

api cet su-durācāro bhajate mām ananya-bhāk
sādhur eva sa mantavyaḥ samyag vyavasito hi saḥ

"Even if a devotee commits the most abominable actions, he is to be considered saintly because he is properly situated." [*Bhagavad-gītā* 9.30] As you will say, "To err is human." Therefore in the neophyte stage we may always expect some discrepancies. Kindly see the thing in this light and forgive their small mistakes. The big thing is that they have given everything, even their lives, to Kṛṣṇa—and that is never a mistake.

Your ever well-wisher,
A.C. Bhaktivedanta Swami

AN AWARENESS OF WHAT IS BEST AND MOST BEAUTIFUL

In Rome, during May of 1974, Śrīla Prabhupāda meets with Desmond James Bernard O'Grady, a noted Irish poet: "My request to you is this. You are a poet. Just describe God. You are expert in describing, and therefore I ask you to kindly describe God in your occupation. Then your life will be successful."

Mr. O'Grady: Your edition of the *Bhagavad-gītā* is very nice.
Śrīla Prabhupāda: It is the fifth edition in two years.
Mr. O'Grady: In which country has the Hare Kṛṣṇa movement been the most successful?
Śrīla Prabhupāda: Everywhere. In Africa, America, Canada, Japan, China. But actually it has been most successful in America. Many Americans have taken to Kṛṣṇa consciousness.
Mr. O'Grady: What about here in Rome? Have you had problems with the police?
Śrīla Prabhupāda: We have problems everywhere. The police sometimes harass us, but usually they become tired and eventually don't do anything. [*Laughter.*]
Mr. O'Grady: The system give up? That's marvelous. I feel very tired of the system myself. Something is wrong with the present state of affairs. Maybe you can give me some advice on how to beat the system.
Śrīla Prabhupāda: You Irish people! You are never tired of fighting.
Mr. O'Grady: No. [*Laughter.*] It's inside us.
Śrīla Prabhupāda: Actually, the fighting has been going on constantly.
Mr. O'Grady: Well, what do you suggest we do about it? I mean, is it morally correct for me to be sitting here—
Śrīla Prabhupāda: As long as we remain illusioned by the bodily conception of life, thinking we are these bodies, one man thinking

"I am Irish," another thinking "I am Italian," ". . . American," ". . . Indian," and so on—as long as this goes on, the fighting will go on. You cannot stop fighting between dogs and cats. Why do they fight? The dog simply thinks, "I am a big dog." And the cat thinks, "I am a big cat." In the same way, if we think, "I am an Irishman" or "I am an Englishman," then we are no better than the cats and dogs. As long as people remain in a bodily conception of life, there will be fighting.

Mr. O'Grady: What was Mahatma Gandhi fighting in the House of Commons?

Śrīla Prabhupāda: That was another dog-ism. There is no difference. A dog thinks, "I am a dog," because he has the body of a dog. If I am thinking that I am Indian because this body was born on Indian soil, then how am I different from the dog? The bodily conception of life is simply animalism. When we understand that we are not these bodies but are spirit souls, there will be peace. There cannot be any peace otherwise. *Sa eva go-kharaḥ.* The Vedic literatures state that a person in the bodily concept of life is exactly like a cow or an ass. People have to transcend this inferior conception of the self. How is that done?

māṁ ca yo 'vyabhicāreṇa bhakti-yogena sevate
sa guṇān samatītyaitān brahma-bhūyāya kalpate

"One who engages in the spiritual activities of unalloyed devotional service at once transcends the modes of material nature and is elevated to the spiritual platform." [*Bhagavad-gītā* 14.26]

In our society, there are many Mexicans, Canadians, Indians, Jews, and Muslims, but they no longer consider themselves Muslims, Christians, Jews, or whatever. They are all servants of Kṛṣṇa. That is Brahman realization.

Mr. O'Grady: That's giving it a name also.

Śrīla Prabhupāda: Yes, a name must be there. But although, for example, your name is different from that of another Irishman, you nonetheless all feel that you are Irish. One's name may be different, but that doesn't matter. The quality should be one. That is required. When we acquire Kṛṣṇa's quality, then, despite different names, there will be peace. That is called *so 'ham.* The names of different people in a nation may be different, but all the people feel the same nationality. Varieties may exist, but if the quality is the same, that is oneness, *brahma-bhūta.*

> *brahma-bhūtaḥ prasannātmā na śocati na kāṅkṣati*
> *samaḥ sarveṣu bhūteṣu mad-bhaktiṁ labhate parām*

"One who is thus transcendentally situated at once realizes the Supreme Brahman and becomes fully joyful. He never laments or desires to have anything. He is equally disposed toward every living entity. In that state he attains pure devotional service unto Me." [*Bhagavad-gītā* 18.54] This world is miserable for the materially infected person, but for the devotee, the entire world is as good as Vaikuṇṭha. For the impersonalist, achieving the Brahman stage, becoming one with the Absolute, is the last word.

Mr. O'Grady: Is the Absolute external or internal?

Śrīla Prabhupāda: There is no external or internal. The Absolute is without duality.

Mr. O'Grady: OK, but on an individual level—

Śrīla Prabhupāda: We are not absolute. When we are situated on the absolute platform, we are absolute. However, now we are in the relative world. The Absolute Truth is here also, but our senses are not sufficiently elevated to understand that Absolute Truth. As long as we are under the control of time, there is no question of becoming absolute.

Mr. O'Grady: So "absolute" means life beyond time?

Śrīla Prabhupāda: That is stated in the *Bhagavad-gītā* [4.9]:

> *janma karma ca me divyam evaṁ yo vetti tattvataḥ*
> *tyaktvā dehaṁ punar janma naiti mām eti so 'rjuna*

"One who knows the transcendental nature of My appearance and activities does not, upon leaving the body, take his birth again in this material world, but attains My eternal abode, O Arjuna."

That is absolute—going back home, back to Godhead. As long as one is in the material world and identifies with this body, he transmigrates from one body to another. That is not absolute. This is clearly stated here. When one goes back to the spiritual world, he attains the absolute position.

Mr. O'Grady: All right, but this is my question: Is it sufficient for us to sit here—you sitting there and we as friends sitting with you engaging in the gentle art of conversation, while across the ocean—

Śrīla Prabhupāda: The point you have missed is that although you are sitting in one place and I am sitting in a different place, this difference does not affect our actual existence. We are both human beings. The conceptions of "Irishman," " Englishman," "Protestant," "Catholic," and so on are but different dresses. One has to become free from these designations. When one is thus free, he becomes purified.

sarvopādhi-vinirmuktaṁ tat-paratvena nirmalam
hṛṣīkeṇa hṛṣīkeśa- sevanaṁ bhaktir ucyate
[*Bhakti-rasāmṛta-sindhu* 1.1.12]

When you have purified your senses and engaged those purified senses in the service of the master of the senses, Kṛṣṇa, you have perfected your life. That is nonduality, and that is absolute.

Mr. O'Grady: But the system insists that you think yourself American or Indian or African or whatever.

Śrīla Prabhupāda: Yes. Materialistic society means duality.

Mr. O'Grady: But that is unavoidable. How can you avoid material existence?

Śrīla Prabhupāda: That is possible in Kṛṣṇa consciousness. The lotus lives in the water but never touches the water.

Mr. O'Grady: I don't think you can explain situations in one area with metaphors from another. How can you argue political problems in terms of vague spiritual concepts? Their nature is completely different.

Śrīla Prabhupāda: Sometimes a variety of examples helps us to understand or appreciate the problem better. In the vase there is a variety of flowers, and that variety helps us better appreciate the idea of flowers. From any point of view, Kṛṣṇa can resolve all problems. Why just the problems of Irishmen or Englishmen? All problems. That is called unity in diversity. Our students come from different backgrounds, but because they are all in Kṛṣṇa consciousness, they are unified.

Mr. O'Grady: Very good. Yes, I accept that. I would like to know, though, that when you say "Kṛṣṇa consciousness," is there any difference between that and Christ consciousness?

Śrīla Prabhupāda: No, there is no difference. Christ came to preach the message of God. If you actually become Christ conscious, you become Kṛṣṇa conscious.
Mr. O'Grady: And does becoming Kṛṣṇa conscious or God conscious mean becoming self-conscious? That is, conscious of who we really are?
Śrīla Prabhupāda: Yes, God consciousness includes self-consciousness, but self-consciousness is not necessarily God consciousness.
Mr. O'Grady: But it may be?
Śrīla Prabhupāda: No.
Mr. O'Grady: One may achieve consciousness of the God that is within.
Śrīla Prabhupāda: That means he is God conscious. You are now in the sunlight, and consciousness of the sun includes your ability to see yourself. In the darkness you cannot see yourself. At night you can't even see your own hands or legs, but if you come before the sun, you see the sun and yourself also. Without sunlight, without God consciousness, self-consciousness is incomplete. However, God consciousness makes self-consciousness very clear.
Mr. O'Grady: We meet a lot of young people in our teaching profession, and we don't try to teach them any kind of didactic salvation. We do try to direct them toward an awareness of what is best and what is most beautiful and what is most spiritually nourishing in the world about them—that is, insofar as the system allows us. Very frequently the students are not neutral enough to be in a spiritual condition; they are more in an emotional one. What we are faced with often is the basic question of "Who am I?" or "What is it all about?"
Śrīla Prabhupāda: Yes.
Mr. O'Grady: Or they ask, "Why am I here?"
Śrīla Prabhupāda: Yes, very good.
Mr. O'Grady: We are asked, "Why should I be here? Who are you, teacher, and what gives you the right to tell us what to think or what to be or what not to be? Why should I read Shakespeare? Why should I listen to Mozart? I prefer Bob Dylan." These kinds of questions seem to emanate from a very disillusioned state of mind, and insecurity, and uncertainty, and a lack of credibility in the total structure of things as they are. Frequently we have to answer these questions in a cataclysmic sort of way. Rather than presenting direct

answers, we must answer indirectly, taking account of the conditioning that prompted students to ask these questions in the first place. Do you think that we should try to reach them more directly?
Śrīla Prabhupāda: You are talking about the problem of—
Mr. O'Grady: Modern education.
Śrīla Prabhupāda: Yes. So many questions are there, but they are not answered by modern education. "Why have I come here? What is the purpose?" These questions should be answered perfectly. Therefore the *Vedas* enjoin: *tad-vijñānārthaṁ sa gurum evābhigacchet.* To find answers to all these questions, one must approach a bona fide spiritual master.
Mr. O'Grady: What if you have none? What if we are told that Mr. Nixon is the bona fide spiritual master? What do we do?
Śrīla Prabhupāda: No, no. [*Laughter.*] There is a standard for bona fide spiritual masters. You have only heard one line of the verse. Who is the spiritual master? That is the next line: *śrotriyaṁ brahma-niṣṭham.* The word *śrotriyam* refers to one who has heard from another bona fide source. A spiritual master is he who has taken the message from another qualified spiritual master. This is just like a medical man who has taken the knowledge of medical science from another medical man. Similarly, the bona fide spiritual master must come in a line of successive spiritual masters. The original spiritual master is God.
Mr. O'Grady: Yes. Granted.
Śrīla Prabhupāda: One who has heard from God explains the same message to his disciples. If the disciple doesn't change the message, he is a bona fide spiritual master. That is our process. We take lessons by hearing from Kṛṣṇa, God, and from Him understand who is perfect. Or we hear from His representative, who does not contradict Kṛṣṇa and who has realized His message. It is not that we speak one thing and do all nonsense. One who does so is not a spiritual master.
Mr. O'Grady: Now there's my poor old father, living in western Ireland. A simple old man, seventy-eight now, your generation. He has gotten to the point at his age where he says, "They tell me, the priests, they tell me ultimately that it's God who knows. But I want to know who told God." Then he comes to me and says, "You went to school, and you read books. Tell me, who told God?" So I have no answer. That is the difference between seventy-eight and thirty-nine years.

Śrīla Prabhupāda: No, it is not a difference of age. The difference is knowledge. In the *Brahma-sūtra* the question is raised: Who is God? First of all there is this question.
Mr. O'Grady: Who taught God?
Śrīla Prabhupāda: No. First of all there is the question who *is* God. Then we shall ask who taught God. The *Vedānta-sūtra* says, *athāto brahma jijñāsā:* now we should inquire who is God. Unless you know who God is, how can you raise the question of who instructed God? If you don't know God, the question does not arise who instructed God. Is this not so?
Mr. O'Grady: Yes.
Śrīla Prabhupāda: Who God is, is explained in the *Brahma-sūtra. Janmādy asya yataḥ:* God is He from whom everything emanates. That is God—the Supreme Being from whom everything emanates. Now, what is the nature of that Supreme Being? Is He a dead stone or a living entity? That is also explained. *Janmādy asya yato 'nvayād itarataś cārtheṣv abhijñaḥ svarāṭ* [*Śrīmad-Bhāgavatam* 1.1.1]: the Supreme Being is fully cognizant of everything, directly and indirectly. Unless He is fully cognizant of everything, He cannot be God. Then the question that you raised comes, Who taught God? And that is also answered. *Svarāṭ:* He is fully independent. He does not need to take lessons from anyone. That is God. If one needs to take lessons from others, he is not God. Kṛṣṇa spoke the *Bhagavad-gītā,* and He did not have to learn it from anyone. I had to learn it from my spiritual master, but Kṛṣṇa did not have to learn it from anyone. One who does not need to take lessons from others is God.
Mr. O'Grady: Where does human love come in?
Śrīla Prabhupāda: Everything is coming from God. Being part and parcel of God, we manifest partial love because the original love is there in Him. Nothing can exist if it is not in God; therefore love is there in God.
Mr. O'Grady: And manifestations of love are manifestations of God?
Śrīla Prabhupāda: Unless the loving propensity is there in God, how can we manifest it? A son born of a particular father has the symptoms of the father. Because the loving propensity is in God, we have that same propensity.
Mr. O'Grady: Maybe love is generated in you by the need.
Śrīla Prabhupāda: No, there is no question of "maybe." We are

defining God in absolute terms. *Janmādy asya yataḥ:* God is He from whom everything has emanated. The fighting propensity is also there in God, but His fighting and His loving are absolute. In the material world we experience that fighting is just the opposite of loving, but in God the fighting propensity and the loving propensity are one and the same. That is the meaning of "absolute." We learn from the Vedic scriptures that when the so-called enemies of God are killed by God, they attain liberation.

Mr. O'Grady: Is it possible to arrive at this understanding of God alone?

Śrīla Prabhupāda: No. Therefore we have cited this verse: *tad-vijñānārthaṁ sa gurum evābhigacchet*. The word *abhigacchet* means "must." It is not possible alone. In Sanskrit grammar this is called the *vidhiliṅ* form of a verb, and this form is used when there is no choice. The word *abhigacchet* means that one must approach a guru. That is the Vedic version. Therefore in the *Bhagavad-gītā* you will find that Arjuna was talking to Kṛṣṇa, but when he saw that things were not being resolved, he surrendered himself to Kṛṣṇa and accepted Him as his guru.

kārpaṇya-doṣopahata-svabhāvaḥ
pṛcchāmi tvāṁ dharma-sammūḍha-cetāḥ
yac chreyaḥ syān niścitaṁ brūhi tan me
śiṣyas te 'haṁ śādhi māṁ tvāṁ prapannam

"Now I am confused about my duty and have lost all composure because of miserly weakness. In this condition I am asking You to tell me for certain what is best for me. Now I am Your disciple, and a soul surrendered unto You. Please instruct me." [*Bhagavad-gītā* 2.7] So here we can see that Arjuna is confused about his duty.

Mr. O'Grady: Is this duty to the self, to others, or to the state?

Śrīla Prabhupāda: A soldier's duty is to fight with the enemy. Arjuna was a soldier, and Kṛṣṇa advised him, "The opposite party is your enemy, and you are a soldier. Why are you trying to be nonviolent? This is not good." Then Arjuna said, "Actually, I am confused. In this confusion I cannot make the right decision. I therefore accept You as my spiritual master. Please give me the proper lesson." In a chaotic condition, in a confused state of life, one should approach another, who is in full knowledge of the matter. You go to a lawyer to solve legal problems, and you go to a physician to solve medical problems. Everyone in the material world is confused about spiritual identity. It is therefore our duty to approach a bona fide spiritual master, who can give us real knowledge.

Mr. O'Grady: I am very confused.

Śrīla Prabhupāda: So you must approach a spiritual master.

Mr. O'Grady: And he makes a decision on how to help me stop this confusion?

Śrīla Prabhupāda: Yes, the spiritual master is one who solves all confusion. If the spiritual master cannot save his disciple from confusion, he is not a spiritual master. That is the test.

saṁsāra-dāvānala-līḍha-loka-
trāṇāya kāruṇya-ghanāghanatvam
prāptasya kalyāṇa-guṇārṇavasya
vande guroḥ śrī-caraṇāravindam

This whole confused world is just like a blazing forest fire. In a forest fire all the animals are confused. They do not know where to go to save their lives. In the blazing fire of the material world, everyone is confused. How can that blazing forest fire be extinguished? It is not possible to utilize your man-made fire brigade, nor is it possible to simply pour buckets of water. The solution comes when rain from the clouds falls on the forest fire. Only then can the fire be extinguished. That ability is not in your hands, but is in the mercy of God. So, human society is in a confused state, and it cannot find a solution. The spiritual master is one who has received the mercy of God, and he can deliver the solution to the confused man. One who has received the mercy of God can become a spiritual master and deliver that mercy to others.

Mr. O'Grady: The problem is to find this spiritual master.

Śrīla Prabhupāda: That is not the problem. The problem is whether you are sincere. You have problems, but God is within your heart. *Īśvaraḥ sarva-bhūtānām.* God is not far away. If you are sincere, God sends you a spiritual master. Therefore God is also called *caitya-guru,* the spiritual master within the heart. God helps from within and from without. Everything is thus described in the *Bhagavad-gītā.* This material body is like a machine, but within the heart is the soul, and with the soul is the Supersoul, Kṛṣṇa, who gives directions. The Lord says, "You wanted to do this; now here is the chance. Go and do it." If you are sincere, you say, "Now, God, I want You." Then He will give you directions. "Yes, now you come and get Me like this." This is His kindness. However, if we want something else, that is all right. We can have it. God is very kind. When I want something, He is in my heart directing me and telling me how to have it. So why should He not give directions on how to have a spiritual master? First of all we must again be eager to revive our God consciousness. Then God will give us a spiritual master.

Mr. O'Grady: Thank you very much.

Śrīla Prabhupāda: Thank you very much. My request to you is this. You are a poet. Just describe God. You are expert in describing, and therefore I ask you to kindly describe God in your occupation. Then your life will be successful. And if one hears you, his life will also be successful. That is the injunction:

idaṁ hi puṁsas tapasaḥ śrutasya vā
sviṣṭasya sūktasya ca buddhi-dattayoḥ
avicyuto 'rthaḥ kavibhir nirūpito
yad uttamaśloka-guṇānuvarṇanam
[*Śrīmad-Bhāgavatam* 1.5.22]

There are many leaders in society who are poets, scientists, religionists, philosophers, politicians, and so on. Those who are so expert are given this injunction: Your duty is to perfect your occupation by describing the glories of the Supreme Being.

Mr. O'Grady: My experience is that, for some extraordinary reason, one is chosen to do a particular thing.

Śrīla Prabhupāda: That reason is given here. *Avicyutaḥ.* The infallible choice is this: "Let them describe the glories of the Lord."

Mr. O'Grady: But you were saying that the spiritual master is chosen. The spiritual master, the poet, the priest, is chosen by God. This person is chosen to write poems or paint pictures or make music.

Śrīla Prabhupāda: So when you compose music, compose music about God. That is your perfection.

Mr. O'Grady: When one works for God in his line, then his line becomes his perfection?

Śrīla Prabhupāda: Yes.

Mr. O'Grady: Thank you very much.

VIII. REACHING LIFE'S PERFECTION

"THE HUMAN FORM OF LIFE IS MEANT FOR GOD REALIZATION"

Śrīla Prabhupāda gives an address at London's Conway Hall, in 1969: "If one thinks like that—'I am no one else's servant; my business is to serve God'—then he is liberated. His heart is immediately cleansed, and he is liberated. And after one has reached that, then all one's cares and anxieties in this world are over, because one knows, 'I am a servant of God. God will give me protection. Why should I worry about anything?'"

Today's subject matter is our relationship with God. That is self-realization. The *saṅkīrtana* movement is the easiest process for self-realization because it cleanses the heart. Our misunderstanding of our identity is due to the dust covering the mirror of the mind. In a mirror that is covered with dust one cannot see himself. But if it is very clear, then one can see himself. So meditation is a process for cleansing the heart. Meditation means to try to understand one's relationship with the Supreme.

With everything with which we come in contact there is a relationship. Because I am now sitting on this cushion, the relationship is that I shall sit and the cushion will hold me. You have relationships. You are Englishmen or Indians, so there is a relationship with your society, with your family, with your friends. So what is our relationship with God?

If you ask everyone, very few people will be able to explain their relationship with God. They say, "What is God? God is dead. I don't believe in God, what to speak of a relationship." Because these dirty things are covering their hearts, they cannot see. We have a relationship with everything—why do we not try to understand our relationship with God? Is that very intelligent? No. That is ignorance. All the creatures in this material world are covered by the three modes of material nature. Therefore they cannot see God. They cannot understand God, nor do they try to understand Him. But

God is there. In England in the morning there is mist, so you cannot see the sun behind the fog. But does this mean that there is no sun? You cannot see it because your eyes are covered. But if you send a telegram to another part of the world, they will say, "Yes, the sun is here. We can see it. It is very dazzling, full of light." So when you deny the existence of God or you cannot ascertain your relationship with God, that means that you are lacking in knowledge. It is not that there is no God. We are lacking. The sun is not covered. The sun cannot be covered. The fog or the cloud or the mist does not have the power to cover the sun. How big the sun is! It is so many times bigger than this earth. And the clouds can cover at most ten or twenty or a hundred miles. So how can the clouds cover the sun? No. The clouds cannot cover the sun. They cover your eyes. When an enemy comes and a rabbit cannot defend himself, the rabbit closes his eyes and thinks, "My enemy is now gone." Similarly, we are covered by the external energy of God and are thinking, "God is dead."

The Lord has three kinds of energies. In the *Viṣṇu Purāṇa* there are descriptions of the energy of the Supreme Lord. And in the *Vedas* also, in the *Upaniṣads*, there are descriptions of the energies of the Supreme Lord. *Parāsya śaktir vividhaiva śrūyate* [*Śvetāśvatara Upaniṣad* 6.8]. *Śakti* means "energy." The Lord has multienergies. The *Vedas* say, "God has nothing to do." We have to work because we have no other means to exist—we have to eat, we wish to enjoy this, that—but why should God work? God does not have to work. Then how can we say that God created this universe? Is that not work? No. Then how did it happen? His multifarious energies are so strong that they are acting naturally and are full of knowledge. We can see how a flower blooms and grows and systematically displays multicolors: one side a little spot, another side a little spot, white on one side, more white on the other side. The butterfly also exhibits such artistic symmetry. So this is all being painted, but in such a perfect way and so swiftly that we cannot see how. We cannot understand how it is being done, but it is being done by the energy of the Lord.

It is due to a lack of knowledge that people say that God is dead, that there is no God, and that we have no relationship with God. These thoughts have been compared to the thoughts of a man haunted by a ghost. Just as a haunted man speaks all nonsense, when we become covered by the illusory energy of God we say that God is dead. But this is not a fact. Therefore, we need this chanting process to cleanse our heart. Take to this simple process of chanting the Hare Kṛṣṇa mantra. In that way, in your family life, in your club, in your home, on the road—everywhere—chant Hare Kṛṣṇa, and this darkness covering your heart, covering your real position, will be removed. Then you'll understand your real constitutional position.

Lord Caitanya Mahāprabhu recommended: *ceto-darpaṇa-mārjanam. Mārjanam* means "cleansing," and *darpaṇa* means "mirror." The heart is a mirror. It is like a camera. Just as a camera takes all kinds of pictures of days and nights, so also our heart takes pictures and keeps them in an unconscious state. Psychologists know this. The heart takes so many pictures, and therefore it becomes covered. We do not know when it has begun, but it is a fact that because there is material contact, our real identity is covered. Therefore *ceto-darpaṇa-mārjanam:* one has to cleanse his heart. There are different processes to cleanse the heart—the *jñāna* process, the yoga process, the meditation process, pious activities. Karma also cleanses the heart. If one acts very piously, his heart will gradually be cleansed. But although these processes are recommended for cleansing the heart, in this age they are all difficult. To follow the path of philosophical knowledge one must become a very learned scholar, one must read so many books, one must go to learned professors and scholars and speculate. One must search out a person who has seen the light. So these are all philosophical processes. Meditation is also a recommended process. One should question, "What am I?" Just consider: Am I this body? No. Am I this finger? No, this is *my* finger. If you contemplate your leg, you will see, "Oh, this is *my* leg." Similarly, you will find everything to be "mine." And where is that "I"? Everything is mine, but where is that "I"? When one is searching for that "I," that is meditation. Real meditation means concentrating all the senses in that way. But that meditation process is very difficult. One must control the senses. The senses are dragging one outward, and one has to bring them inward for introspection. Therefore there are eight processes in the yoga system. The first is controlling the senses by regulative principles. Then sitting postures—that will help to concentrate the mind. If one sits leaning over, that will not help; if one sits up straight, that will help. Then controlling the breathing, then meditation, then *samādhi*. But today these are very, very difficult processes. No one can immediately perform them. The so-called yoga processes are fragmental—only the sitting postures and a few breathing exercises are practiced. But that cannot bring one to the perfectional stage. The actual yoga process, although a recommended Vedic process, is very difficult in this age. Similarly one can try to get knowledge by the speculative philosophical process: "This is Brahman, this is not Brahman, so what is Brahman? What is spirit soul?" Such empiric philosophical discussion is also recommended, but it is useless in this age.

Therefore Śrī Caitanya Mahāprabhu—not only Caitanya Mahāprabhu but also the Vedic literature—says:

harer nāma harer nāma harer nāmaiva kevalam
kalau nāsty eva nāsty eva nāsty eva gatir anyathā

Kalau means "in this age." *Nāsty eva, nāsty eva, nāsty eva*—three times *nāsty eva*. *Eva* means "certainly," and *nāsti* means "not." "Certainly not, certainly not, certainly not." What is that "certainly not"? One cannot realize oneself by karma. That is the first "certainly not." One cannot realize oneself by *jñāna*. That is the second "certainly not." One cannot realize oneself by yoga. Certainly not. *Kalau*. *Kalau* means "in this age." *Kalau nāsty eva nāsty eva nāsty eva gatir anyathā*. In this age one certainly cannot achieve success by any of these three methods. Then what is the recommended process? *Harer nāma harer nāma harer nāmaiva kevalam*. Simply chant the Hare Kṛṣṇa mantra. *Kevalam* means "only." Simply chant Hare Kṛṣṇa. It is the easiest and most sublime process. This is recommended, practical, and authorized. So take it. Accept it in any condition of life. Chant. There is no expenditure, there is no loss. We are not chanting a secret. No. It is open. And by chanting you will cleanse your heart.

In this material world no one wants misery, but it comes. Unexpectedly, like a forest fire that starts without anyone's striking a match, it comes. No one wants a war, but war is fought. No one wants famine, but famine comes. No one wants pestilence, but it comes. No one wants fighting, but there is fighting. No one wants misunderstanding, but it comes. Why? This is like a blazing fire in the forest. And it cannot be extinguished by fire engines. This blazing fire of problems cannot be extinguished by our so-called advancement of knowledge. No. That is not possible. Just as one cannot extinguish a forest fire by sending a fire engine or by bringing some water, the problems of our life cannot be solved by material processes.

There are many examples. Prahlāda Mahārāja says, "My dear Lord, the father and mother are not actually the protectors of the children." The father and mother take care of their children; that is their duty. But they are not the ultimate protectors. When nature's law calls the child, the father and mother cannot protect him. Therefore although generally it is considered a fact that the father and mother are the protectors of the child, actually it is not a fact. If someone is sailing the ocean and he thinks he has a very nice boat, will that protect him? No. Still he may drown. A nice airplane is flying in the sky, everyone is safe, but all of a sudden it crashes. Nothing material can protect us. Suppose someone is diseased. He may engage a good physician who gives good medicine, but that will not guarantee that he will live. Then what is the ultimate guarantee? Prahlāda Mahārāja says, "My dear Lord, if You neglect someone, nothing can protect him."

This is our practical experience. We can invent so many methods to solve the problems presented by the laws of material nature, but they are not sufficient. They will never solve all the problems, nor will they give actual relief. This is the fact. Therefore Kṛṣṇa says in the *Bhagavad-gītā*, "*Māyā,* this external energy, is very, very strong. No one can surpass it. It is almost impossible." Then how can one get free from this material nature? Kṛṣṇa says, "Simply by surrendering unto Me one can get relief from the onslaught of material nature." That is a fact. So we have to cleanse the heart to learn what is our relationship with God.

In the *Kaṭha Upaniṣad* it is stated, *nityo nityānāṁ cetanaś cetanānām.* The Supreme Absolute Personality of Godhead, or the Absolute Truth, is eternal. God is eternal, and we are also eternal. But the *Vedas* indicate that He is the supreme living creature. He is not dead. If He is not living, how is this world working? In the *Bhagavad-gītā* Kṛṣṇa says, "Under My supervision things are going on." In the Bible also it is said, "God created." That is a fact. Not that at one time there was a chunk and then this happened and then that. No. The *Vedas* tell us the actual facts, but we have to open our eyes to see. *Ceto-darpaṇa-mārjanam*. That is the process of cleansing our hearts. When we cleanse our hearts, then we will be able to understand what Kṛṣṇa and the *Vedas* say. We need to be purified. If a man is suffering from jaundice and you give him a piece of sugar candy, he will say that it is very bitter. But is sugar candy bitter? No, it is very sweet. And the medicine for jaundice is that sugar. Modern science prescribes this, and it is prescribed in the Vedic literature also. So if we take a great quantity of this sugar candy, then we will be relieved from jaundice. And when there is relief, then one says, "Oh, this is very sweet." So the modern jaundice of a godless civilization can be cured by this chanting of Hare Kṛṣṇa. In the beginning it may appear bitter, but when one advances, then he will see how pleasing it is.

As soon as one understands his identity, his relationship with God, then immediately he becomes happy. We are so full of miseries because we have identified ourselves with the material world. Therefore we are unhappy. Anxieties and fearfulness are due to our misidentifying with the material world. The other day I was explaining that one who identifies with this bag of bones and skin is like an animal. So by chanting Hare Kṛṣṇa this misunderstanding will be cleansed. Cleansing of the heart means that one will understand that he does not belong to this material world. *Ahaṁ brahmāsmi:* I am spirit soul. As long as one identifies oneself with England, with India, or with America, this is ignorance. Today you are an Englishman because you were born in England, but in your next life you may not take your birth in England; it may be in China or Russia or some other country. Or you may not get this human form of body. Today you are a nationalist, you are a very great follower of your country, but tomorrow if you stay in your country you may be a cow being taken to the slaughterhouse.

So we have to thoroughly know our identity. Caitanya Mahāprabhu says that the actual identity of every living creature is that he is the eternal servant of God. If one thinks like that—"I am no one else's servant; my business is to serve God"—then he is liberated. His heart is immediately cleansed, and he is liberated. And after one has reached that, then all one's cares and anxieties in this world are over because one knows, "I am a servant of God. God will give me protection. Why should I worry about anything?" It is just like a child. A child knows that his mother and father will take care of him. He is free. If he should go to touch fire, his mother will take care of him: "Oh, my dear child, don't touch." The mother is always looking after him. So why don't you put your trust in God? Actually, you are under the protection of God.

People go to church and say, "God, give us our daily bread." Actually, if He did not give it to us, we would not be able to live. That is a fact. The *Vedas* also say that the one Supreme Personality supplies all the necessities of every other living creature. God is supplying food for everyone. We human beings have our economic problem, but what economic problem is there in societies other than human society? The bird society has no economic problem. The beasts have no economic problem. There are 8,400,000 species of life, and out of that, human society is very, very small. So they have created problems—what to eat, where to sleep, how to mate, how to defend. These are problems for us, but the majority of creatures—the aquatics, the fish, the plants, the insects, the birds, the beasts, and the many millions upon millions of other living creatures—do not have such problems. They are also living creatures. Don't think that they are different from us. It is not true that we human beings are the only living creatures and that all others are dead. No. And who is providing their food and shelter? It is God. The plants and animals are not going to the office. They are not going to the university to get technological education to earn money. So how are they eating? God is supplying. The elephant eats hundreds of pounds of food. Who is supplying? Are you making arrangements for the elephant? There are millions of elephants. Who is supplying?

So the process of acknowledging that God is supplying is better than thinking, "God is dead. Why should we go to church and pray to God for bread?" In the *Bhagavad-gītā* it is said, "Four kinds of people come to Kṛṣṇa: the distressed, those who are in need of money, the wise, and the inquisitive." One who is inquisitive, one who is wise, one who is distressed, and one who is in need of money—these four classes of men approach God. "My dear God, I am very hungry. Give me my daily bread." That's nice. Those who approach God in this way are recommended as *sukṛtinaḥ. Sukṛti* means "pious." They are pious. Although they are asking for money, for food, they are considered pious because they are approaching God. And others are just the opposite. They are *duṣ-*

kṛtinaḥ, impious. *Kṛti* means "very meritorious," but the word *duṣkṛti* indicates that their energy is being misused to create havoc. Just like the man who invented atomic weapons. He has a brain, but it has been misused. He has created something that is dreadful. Create something that will insure that man will no longer have to die. What is the use of creating something so that millions of people will immediately die? They will die today or tomorrow or after a hundred years. So what have the scientists done? Created something so that man will *not* die immediately, so that there will be no more disease, so that there will be no more old age. Then you will have done something. But the *duṣkṛtinas* never go to God. They never try to understand God. Therefore their energy is misdirected.

The gross materialists who ignore their relationship with God are described in the *Bhagavad-gītā* as *mūḍhas. Mūḍha* means "ass," "donkey." Those who are working very, very hard to earn money are compared to the donkey. They will eat the same four *capātīs* [whole-wheat–bread patties] daily, but they are unnecessarily working to earn thousands of dollars. And others are described as *narādhama. Narādhama* means "the lowest of mankind." The human form of life is meant for God realization. It is the right of man to try to realize God. One who understands Brahman, God, is a *brāhmaṇa,* not others. So that is the duty of this human form of life. In every human society there is some system that is called "religion" and by which one may try to understand God. It doesn't matter whether it is the Christian religion, the Muhammadan religion, or the Hindu religion. It doesn't matter. The system is to understand God and our relationship with Him. That's all. This is the duty of the human beings, and if this duty is ignored in human society, then it is animal society. Animals have no power to understand God and their relationship with God. Their only interests are eating, sleeping, mating, and defending. If we are only concerned with these things, then what are we? We are animals. Therefore the *Bhagavad-gītā* says that those who ignore this opportunity are the "lowest of mankind." They got this human form of life after evolving through 8,400,000 births and yet did not utilize it for God realization but simply for the animal propensities. Therefore they are *narādhama,* the lowest of mankind. And there are other persons who are very proud of their knowledge. But what is that knowledge? "There is no God. I am God." Their actual knowledge has been taken away by *māyā*. If they are God, then how have they become dog? There are so many arguments against them, but they simply defy God. Atheism. Because they have taken to the process of atheism, their actual knowledge is stolen away. Actual knowledge means to know what is God and what is our relationship with God. If one does not know this, then it is to be understood that his knowledge has been taken away by *māyā*.

So in this way, if we try to understand our relationship with God, there are ways and means. There are books, and there is knowledge, so why not take advantage of them? Everyone should take advantage of this knowledge. Try to understand that in the *Bhagavad-gītā* and other Vedic literatures, everywhere, it is said that God is great and that although we are qualitatively one with God, we are minute. The ocean and the minute particle of water have the same quality, but the quantity of salt in the drop of water and the quantity of salt in the ocean are different. They are qualitatively one but quantitatively different. Similarly, God is all-powerful, and we have some power. God creates everything, and we can create a small machine to fly, just like the small machines with which children play. But God can create millions of planets flying in the air. That is the qualification of God. You cannot create any planets. Even if you can create a planet, what is the benefit of that? There are millions of planets created by God. But you also have the creative power. God has power, and you have power. But His is so great that yours cannot compare to it. If you say, "I am God," that is foolishness. You can claim that you are God, but what acts have you performed so extraordinary that you can claim that you are God? This is ignorance. The knowledge of one who thinks himself God has been taken away by the spell of *māyā*. So our relationship is that God is great and we are minute. In the *Bhagavad-gītā* Kṛṣṇa clearly says, "All living entities are My parts and parcels. Qualitatively they are one with Me, but quantitatively they are different." So we are simultaneously one with and different from God. That is our relationship. We are one because we have the same qualities as God. But if we study ourselves minutely, we will find that although we have some great qualities, God has them all in greater quantities.

We cannot have anything that is not in God. That is not possible. Therefore in the *Vedānta-sūtra* it is said that everything that we have is also found in God. It is emanating from God. So our relationship is that because we are small, because we are minute, we are the eternal servitors of God. In this material world also, in ordinary behavior, we see that a man goes to serve another man because the other man is greater than he and can pay him a nice salary. So naturally the conclusion is that if we are small, our duty is to serve God. We have no other business. We are all different parts and parcels of the original entity.

A screw that is connected with a machine is valuable because it is working with the whole machine. And if the screw is taken away from the machine, or if it is faulty, it is worthless. My finger is worth millions of dollars as long as it is attached to this body and is serving the body. And if it is cut off from this body, then what is it worth? Nothing. Similarly, our relationship is that we are very small particles of God; therefore our duty is to dovetail our energies with Him and cooperate with Him. That is our relationship. Otherwise we are worthless. We are cut off. When the finger becomes useless the doctor says, "Oh, amputate this finger. Otherwise the body will be poisoned." Similarly, when we become godless we are cut off from our relationship with God and suffer in this material world. If we try to join again with the Supreme Lord, then our relationship is revived.

THE HIGHEST LOVE

"Spiritual life means to be in association with the Supreme Lord and to exist in bliss and knowledge eternally. Such eternal association means to play with Kṛṣṇa, to dance with and love Kṛṣṇa. Or Kṛṣṇa can become your child—whatever you like. . . . Unless one can love Kṛṣṇa, unless one finishes with love for cats, dogs, country, nation, and society and instead concentrates his love on Kṛṣṇa, there is no question of happiness."

If one protects the tender creeper of devotional service nicely, then gradually it will produce the fruit of unalloyed love for God. Unalloyed love for God means love that is not tinged by desire for material benefit, for mere philosophical understanding, nor for fruitive results. Unalloyed love is to know, "God is great, I am His part and parcel, and therefore He is my supreme lovable object." This consciousness is the highest perfection of human life and the ultimate aim of all methods of self-realization. If one reaches this point—God is my only beloved, Kṛṣṇa is the only lovable object—then one's life is perfect. And when one tastes that transcendental relationship with Kṛṣṇa, then one feels real happiness. The devotional creeper will then be so strongly protected that just by catching hold of it, one will be able to reach the supreme destination. If one climbs steadily up a tree, one eventually comes to the very top. Similarly, if one can achieve love of Godhead by catching that devotional creeper, there is no doubt that one will reach the transcendental abode of Kṛṣṇa and will associate with Him personally, just as we are associating here, face to face.

God is not fictional or imaginary. He is as real as we are. (Actually, we are under illusion; we are living as if this body were our factual self, although this body is not at all reality, but only a temporary manifestation.) We dare to presume that there is no God or that He has no form. This mental speculation is due to a poor fund of knowledge. Lord Kṛṣṇa and His abode exist, and one can go there, reach Him, and associate with Him. That is a fact. Spiritual life means to be in association with the Supreme Lord and to exist in bliss and knowledge eternally. Such eternal association means to play with Kṛṣṇa, to dance with and love Kṛṣṇa. Or Kṛṣṇa can become your child—whatever you like.

There are five primary relationships with Kṛṣṇa: as a passive devotee, as a servant, as a friend, as a parent, and as a lover. The cows in Kṛṣṇa's abode are also liberated souls. They are called *surabhi* cows. There are many popular pictures showing how Kṛṣṇa loves the cows, how He embraces and kisses them. That passive relationship with Kṛṣṇa is called *śānta*. Their perfect happiness is achieved when Kṛṣṇa comes and simply touches them.

Other devotees are inclined to actually give service. They think, "Kṛṣṇa wants to sit down. I will arrange a place for Him. Kṛṣṇa wants to eat. I will get Him some nice food." And they actually make these arrangements. Other devotees play with Kṛṣṇa as friends on equal terms. They do not know that Kṛṣṇa is God; to them, Kṛṣṇa is their lovable friend, and they cannot forget Him for a moment. All day and all night, they think of Kṛṣṇa. At night, when they are sleeping they think, "Oh, in the morning I shall go and play with Kṛṣṇa." And in the morning they go to Kṛṣṇa's house and stand by while Kṛṣṇa is decorated by His mother before going out to play with His friends in the fields. There is no other activity in Kṛṣṇaloka [Kṛṣṇa's abode]. There is no industry, no rushing to the office, or any such nonsense. There is sufficient milk and butter, and everyone eats plentifully. Kṛṣṇa is very fond of His friends, and sometimes He enjoys stealing butter for them. One can actually live this way, and that is the perfection of existence. We should hanker for that perfectional stage of life. Kṛṣṇa consciousness is the process to attain it.

But as long as one has even a slight attachment for this material world, one has to remain here. Kṛṣṇa is very strict. He does not allow anyone to enter into His association who has any tinge of the material conception of life. *Bhakti* must be free from material contamination. Do not think, "I am a very learned scholar. I shall find out what is the Absolute Truth by mental speculation." That is nonsense; one can go on and on speculating and will never find the source of all sources. It is said in the *Brahma-saṁhitā*, "One can go on speculating about the Absolute Truth for millions and millions of years, and still it will not be revealed." One can rot in this material world as he is and can go on speculating, but that is not the right process. Here is the process—*bhakti-yoga*.

Lord Caitanya says that to render devotional service to Kṛṣṇa is the highest perfectional stage of life, and compared to this, other things for which people are hankering in this material world are like bubbles in the ocean. Generally, people are after rewards, and therefore they become religious. They say, "I am a Hindu," "I am a Christian," "I am a Jew," "I am Muhammadan," "I am this, I am that, and therefore I cannot change my religion. I cannot accept Kṛṣṇa." This is called religiosity, *dharma*. With such a materialistic, sectarian idea of religion, they will rot in this material world, stuck to rituals and faith. They are under the impression that if they follow their religious principles, they will get material prosperity. Of course, if one sticks to any kind of religious faith, he will get facilities for material life.

Why do people want this material prosperity? For sense gratification. They are thinking, "I shall have a very nice wife. I shall have very good children. I shall have a very good post. I shall become president. I shall become prime minister." This is sense gratification. And when one is frustrated and has seen that to be rich or to attain the presidency cannot give him happiness, after squeezing out all the taste of sex life, when he is completely frustrated, then perhaps he takes to LSD and tries to become one with the void. But this nonsense cannot give happiness. Here is happiness: one must approach Kṛṣṇa. Otherwise, it will end in LSD confusion and roaming in impersonal void concepts. People are frustrated. They must be frustrated if they do not have genuine spiritual life, because a person is spiritual by nature.

How can anyone be happy without Kṛṣṇa? Suppose one is thrown into the ocean. How can he be happy there? That is not for us. One may be a very good swimmer, but how long will he be able to swim? He eventually becomes tired and drowns. Similarly, we are spiritual by nature. How can we be happy in this material world? It is not possible. But men are trying to remain here, making so many temporary adjustments for survival. This patchwork is not happiness. If one really wants happiness, here is the process: one must attain love of Godhead. Unless one can love Kṛṣṇa, unless one finishes with love for cats, dogs, country, nation, and society and instead concentrates his love on Kṛṣṇa, there is no question of happiness. Rūpa Gosvāmī has given a very nice example in this regard: there are many drugs that saturate one with ideas or hallucinations. But Rūpa Gosvāmī says that unless one tastes that final drug of love of Godhead, *kṛṣṇa-prema,* he will have to be captivated by meditation, impersonal monism, and so many other distractions.

Caitanya Mahāprabhu describes that to attain unalloyed love of Kṛṣṇa one has to execute devotional service, or Kṛṣṇa consciousness. One has to engage oneself exclusively in serving Kṛṣṇa. The highest perfectional stage of unalloyed devotion is to be free from all material desires, all mental speculation, and all fruitive activities. The basic principle of unalloyed devotion is that one cannot maintain any desire other than to become fully Kṛṣṇa conscious. Even if one knows that all other forms of God are also Kṛṣṇa, one should not worship any other form, but should concentrate on the Kṛṣṇa form. Kṛṣṇa has many forms, but one only has to worship Kṛṣṇa in His form with the flute, as in the Rādhā-Kṛṣṇa Deity. Simply concentrate on that form, and all mental speculation and fruitive activities will fall away. One has to cultivate Kṛṣṇa consciousness favorably, and that means to execute service by which Kṛṣṇa becomes satisfied. Kṛṣṇa consciousness is not attained by manufacturing one's own way. I may think that I am doing something in Kṛṣṇa consciousness, but who has sanctioned it? For instance, in the *Bhagavad-gītā,* Arjuna hesitated to fight, for certain moral reasons, but he was viewing the situation from the platform of fruitive activities, on which one has to enjoy or suffer the results. He was considering that if he killed his family members, he would then be subjected to many reactions. This conclusion, however, was not sanctioned by Kṛṣṇa. The law of action and reaction in the material world is called karma, but devotional service transcends karma.

Unalloyed love must be free of all tinges of fruitive activities (karma) and all tinges of mental speculation and material desire. That unalloyed devotional service should be favorably fixed on Kṛṣṇa. "Favorably" means in accordance with what He desires. Kṛṣṇa desired that the Battle of Kurukṣetra take place; it was all arranged by Him. Arjuna was told, "You are thinking in your own way, but even if you do not fight, rest assured that because it has been arranged by Me, none of these warriors who are assembled here are going back to their homes. They will be killed here. It has already been arranged." God's desire is such that one cannot change it. Kṛṣṇa has two qualities: He can protect, and He can also kill. If He wants to kill someone, there is no power in the world that can protect him, and if He protects someone, there is no power in the world that can kill him. Kṛṣṇa's desire is supreme. Therefore, we have to dovetail our desires with Kṛṣṇa's. Whatever Kṛṣṇa desires, no one can make null and void because He is the Supreme Lord. Therefore, our duty is to dovetail our acts with Kṛṣṇa's desire, not to manufacture an action and then declare: "I am doing this action in Kṛṣṇa consciousness." We have to be very careful to ascertain whether Kṛṣṇa actually wants it. Such authorized knowledge is instructed by the representative of Kṛṣṇa. In our prayers of praise to the spiritual master, we are singing daily, "If the spiritual master is satisfied, then God will be satisfied. And if one dissatisfies his spiritual master, then there is no way for him to please God."

Therefore, as far as possible, one has to execute the order of one's spiritual master. That will enable one to progress. That is the essence of the favorable execution of Kṛṣṇa consciousness. In my old age, I have come to America, and I am trying to teach Kṛṣṇa consciousness, because my spiritual master gave me an order that I must do it. It is my duty. I do not know whether I shall be a success or failure. It doesn't matter; my duty is completed if I can present before you whatever I have heard from my spiritual master. This is called the favorable execution of Kṛṣṇa consciousness. Those who are actually serious should take the order of Kṛṣṇa through the representative of Kṛṣṇa as their entire life and soul. One who sticks to this principle is sure to progress. Caitanya Mahāprabhu spoke in that way, and my spiritual master used to say, "The spiritual master is the transparent medium." For example, I can see the letters of this book very nicely through these transparent eyeglasses, without which I cannot see because my eyes are defective. Similarly, our senses are all defective. We cannot see God with these eyes, we cannot hear Hare Kṛṣṇa with these ears, we cannot do anything without the medium of the spiritual master. Just as a defective eye cannot see without the medium of spectacles, so one cannot approach the Supreme Lord without the transparent medium of the spiritual master. "Transparent" means that the medium must be free of contamination. If it is transparent, one can see through it.

In unalloyed love of Godhead we have to engage our senses—*sarvendriya,* all the senses. This means that sex is also to be engaged in Kṛṣṇa consciousness. The conception of God as a father or mother does not allow the engagement of one's sex in the service of the Lord because there is no sexual relationship with the father and mother. But in the conception of God as a lover, there is sexual engagement also. Therefore, Caitanya Mahāprabhu gave the most perfect information of our engagement with the Supreme Lord. In other religious conceptions of life, God is at the utmost taken as the father or mother. Many worshipers in India take the goddess Kālī to be the representation of God. Of course, that is not sanctioned, but the belief is there, and also in the Christian religion the conception of God is as a father. But Caitanya Mahāprabhu informs us that one can even have sexual engagement with the Lord. This information is Caitanya Mahāprabhu's unique contribution. In this material world, sexual engagement is considered to be the highest engagement, the greatest pleasure, although it exists only in a perverted form. No one, however, has conceived that there can be sexual engagement in the spiritual world. There is not a single instance of such theology anywhere in the entire world. This information is given for the first time by Caitanya Mahāprabhu: one can have the Supreme Personality of Godhead as one's husband, as one's lover. This is possible in the worship of Rādhā and Kṛṣṇa, but no one, especially the impersonalists, can understand Rādhā-Kṛṣṇa. The impersonalists have no idea; they cannot even conceive that God has form. But Caitanya Mahāprabhu says that not only does God have form, but He has sex life also. This is the highest contribution of Caitanya Mahāprabhu.

One can serve the Supreme Lord in various relationships, but in the material world those relationships exist only as perverted reflections. What is our engagement in relationship to this material world? What are our ideas of society, friendship, and love? They are all based on the material conception of life. In our society, someone is engaged as a father or mother to a son, and others are engaged as husband and wife, lover and beloved. There are other *rasas* (relationships) also, such as to be engaged with another as an enemy. There are twelve different relationships, out of which five are predominant. The other seven are indirect relationships, such as, for example, to be someone's enemy. There is usually a relationship between enemies, even between a murderer and the one he murders. As far as our relationship with Kṛṣṇa is concerned, however, even if one establishes a relationship as His enemy, then his life is successful. Therefore, when one engages his senses with Kṛṣṇa, a relationship can be established in one of twelve different varieties, of which five varieties are direct and seven are indirect.

When Kṛṣṇa appeared in the arena of Kaṁsa, there were many big wrestlers prepared to kill Him. In fact, He was invited there to be killed. His enemy Kaṁsa thought, "Soon the boys will come. We have tried for sixteen years to kill Them, but that boy Kṛṣṇa could not be killed. But now I have invited Him as a guest, and when He arrives He will fight with these wrestlers, and they will kill Him." The demoniac or atheistic people are always thinking of Kṛṣṇa, or God, in terms of killing Him. Therefore they present their theories that God is dead. They think that if God becomes dead, then they will be free to act however they please. But as far as their actual activities are concerned, God may be dead or alive, but God's agent, the material energy, is so strong that no one can freely do any wrong. As soon as anyone does something wrong, there is immediate punishment. It does not require the presence of God. God may be dead or alive, but the material energy is sufficient to punish anyone who violates the material laws, even to the slightest degree. God has set these conditions, but foolish people do not understand.

Lord Caitanya, however, speaks of favorably engaging all the senses in the service of Kṛṣṇa in pure devotional life. One should favorably engage one's senses and should do whatever Kṛṣṇa wants. Yet even if one engages one's senses against the will of Kṛṣṇa but still thinks of Kṛṣṇa, that is also advantageous. The demon Pūtanā, for example, thought of killing Kṛṣṇa. Just as the occupation of godly persons is to serve God, so the demons and atheists are always prepared to kill God. Pūtanā thought, "I shall kill Kṛṣṇa. He is only a child." This is another mistake of the demoniac. They think Kṛṣṇa, or God, to be an ordinary child or man. So in this way Pūtanā was thinking: "Let me smear my breast with poison, and when the child goes to suck my milk, He will die." As we study this, we see that she approached Kṛṣṇa as His enemy, and yet He accepted her as a friend because He is so merciful. He did not take the demoniac portion of her mentality, but He accepted her. Every living entity is conditioned, but Kṛṣṇa is not. A doctor or psychiatrist treats madmen, but he does not become mad. Sometimes a patient may become angry with him or call him ill names, but the doctor is sober and simply treats him. Similarly, if someone regards Kṛṣṇa as his enemy, Kṛṣṇa does not become his enemy.

Pūtanā came to poison Kṛṣṇa, but He took it otherwise. He thought, "I have sucked her breast milk. Therefore she has become My mother." Kṛṣṇa treated her as His mother, and therefore she became liberated to the same position as Kṛṣṇa's real mother, Yaśodā. The conclusion is that the highest perfection is to establish a favorable relationship with Kṛṣṇa, but even if one engages himself unfavorably, Kṛṣṇa is so merciful that He at least gives one salvation. All the enemies killed by Kṛṣṇa were immediately liberated.

Two classes of men may merge into the impersonal *brahmajyoti:* those who are intentionally aspiring to merge into the impersonal *brahmajyoti* may enter, and those who are enemies of Kṛṣṇa and are killed by Him may also do so. Therefore, the devotee concludes, Why should I accept a condition that is offered even to God's enemies?

Caitanya Mahāprabhu recommends pure devotional service. There should be no desire to fulfill one's own material desires, there should be no attempt to understand Kṛṣṇa by experimental philosophy, and there should be no fruitive activities to derive material benefits from Kṛṣṇa. The only desire should be to serve Him favorably, as He desires. If Kṛṣṇa wants something, then we should do it. Suppose I were to ask a disciple, "My dear student, please give me a glass of water." It is then his duty to give me a glass of water. If he thinks, "Prabhupāda wants a glass of water, but why not give him something better? Why not a glass of hot milk?" that is not service. In his consideration, hot milk is very palatable and is better than water, yet because I have asked for water, he has to give me water, not milk. That is favorable service. One has to understand what Kṛṣṇa wants. When there is that intimate relationship, then one can serve Kṛṣṇa most favorably. And as long as there is not that intimate relationship, one must take information of what Kṛṣṇa wants through the transparent medium of the spiritual master.

A Vaiṣṇava never thinks that he has a direct relationship with Kṛṣṇa. Lord Caitanya says, "I am the servant of the servant of the servant of the servant—a hundred times the servant of the servant—of Kṛṣṇa." We have to agree to become the servant of the servant of the servant. This is the process of disciplic succession, and if one wants real, transcendental love of God, then he has to adopt this process. Because people do not accept this process, they do not develop real love of God. They speak of God, but actually they do not love God; because there is no cultivation of pure devotional service, they love dog.

We may say, "love of God," but unless we adopt this principle, then we will have to love dog, not God. That is the mistake. Caitanya Mahāprabhu says that if one really wants love of God, then one has to follow the process of pure devotional service. It is not that Caitanya Mahāprabhu is speaking out of His own mental concoction; His statements are confirmed in Vedic scriptures such as the *Nārada-pañcarātra* and the *Śrīmad-Bhāgavatam*. These two books, and the *Bhagavad-gītā,* are very authentic scriptures meant for devotees. Caitanya Mahāprabhu quotes from a verse in the *Nārada-pañcarātra: hṛṣīkeṇa hṛṣīkeśa-sevanaṁ bhaktir ucyate.* This is the definition of pure devotional service. *Hṛṣīkeṇa hṛṣīkeśa-sevanam. Hṛṣīkeṇa* means "by one's senses." We have to engage our senses; it is not that we engage only our minds. If someone says, "I am always thinking of Kṛṣṇa," that is not pure devotional service. Meditation is thinking, but no one thinks of Kṛṣṇa; they think of void or something impersonal. If someone is thinking of Kṛṣṇa or Nārāyaṇa or Viṣṇu, as prescribed in the Vedic scriptures, that is real yoga; yoga meditation means to focus one's mind upon the Supersoul. The Supersoul is the representation of Kṛṣṇa in the form of four-handed Nārāyaṇa. Even Patañjali, an authority on the yoga system, prescribes meditation on Viṣṇu. But just as people are manufacturing bogus religious processes, the so-called yogīs of today have manufactured their own way of thinking of something void.

But the *Nārada-pañcarātra* says, *hṛṣīkeṇa hṛṣīkeśa-sevanam:* one must engage not only one's mind but one's senses. Engage the senses in the service of the master of the senses. These three Sanskrit words are very significant. *Hṛṣīkeśa* means "the Lord of the senses." So *bhakti-yoga* means to serve with the senses the Lord of the senses. The Lord of the senses is Kṛṣṇa. We should always remember that we have our senses because we wanted to enjoy this material world, and therefore the Lord has given us a particular set of senses for our enjoyment. The hog has a particular type of body and senses because he wanted to enjoy eating stool. Similarly, a man has a particular type of body and senses because he wanted to enjoy something else. We have a particular set of conditioned senses with which to enjoy this material world, and this is what we have to purify. Our senses are original, but now they are covered by material desires. We have to cure ourselves and become free from such desires. When one's senses are no longer inclined toward material sense gratification, one's status is called pure devotion.

From this verse of the *Nārada-pañcarātra,* we can understand that the spirit soul has original senses. However small a body it may have entered, the spirit soul is not impersonal; it has senses. Perhaps one may find a bug on one's book. It is so small, smaller than a pinpoint, but still it moves; it has all the senses. The small bacteria also move, and they have their senses. Originally, all living entities have senses. It is not that the senses have developed under certain material conditions. The atheistic theory is that under material conditions we have developed senses, that in the spiritual condition there are no senses, and that we are impersonal. By logic and reason, however, that cannot be so. A minute particle of spiritual force, even if it is smaller in size than an atom, has its senses. These senses, being covered by material elements, manifest themselves in a perverted way. We have to purify the senses, and when the senses are purified, we can engage them for the pleasure of the master of the senses. Kṛṣṇa is the master and proprietor of the senses. Therefore, because we are part and parcel of the Supreme Lord, our senses are borrowed from Him; they are on rental. The best thing is to use the senses for His sense satisfaction, and not for our own. This is the process of pure Kṛṣṇa consciousness.

From the *Śrīmad-Bhāgavatam,* Lord Caitanya gives an example of pure devotion: it is said in the *Bhāgavatam* that Kṛṣṇa is situated in everyone's heart. Therefore, just as rivers flow and their natural tendency is to reach the sea, so as soon as one hears the glories of the Lord, his soul is at once attracted toward the Supreme Lord. This is the beginning of pure devotional service. As soon as there is the chanting vibration, Hare Kṛṣṇa, immediately Kṛṣṇa's paraphernalia, Kṛṣṇa's name, Kṛṣṇa's fame, Kṛṣṇa's abode, Kṛṣṇa's associates—everything—all of a sudden become manifested within because He is present. This is the beginning of one's Kṛṣṇa consciousness. To remember by reference to a context means that as soon as one hears a code word, one at once remembers all the information behind that code. Similarly, when our minds are attracted to Kṛṣṇa and everything about Kṛṣṇa simply by hearing a little glorification of His qualities, that is the beginning of pure Kṛṣṇa consciousness. Then there is no more *gati,* or movement of the mind.

It was just that way with the *gopīs:* as soon as they heard the sound of Kṛṣṇa's flute, they gave up everything. Some of them were lying down, some were working in their family affairs, some were taking care of their children, but as soon as they heard Kṛṣṇa's flute, they forgot everything and rushed to Him. Their husbands, their brothers, and their fathers said, "Why are you going and leaving your duty?" But they did not care—they simply left. There is no impediment and no stumbling block in that merge of the mind with Kṛṣṇa. This is the beginning of pure devotion.

Puruṣottama means Kṛṣṇa. The word *puruṣa* means "enjoyer." The conditioned living entities are false enjoyers, imitation enjoyers. Here in this material world, all living entities are acting as *puruṣas.* The more exact meaning of *puruṣa* is "male." The male is considered to be the enjoyer, and the female is considered to be the enjoyed. In the material world, whether one has a male or a female body, everyone has the propensity to enjoy, and therefore everyone is called *puruṣa.* But actually the only *puruṣa* is the Supreme Lord. We living entities are His energy, and He is the supreme enjoyer. We are not *puruṣa.* Energies are employed for enjoyment, and we are energies, instruments of the Supreme Person. Therefore Puruṣottama is the supreme transcendental person, Kṛṣṇa. When our pure devotion for the Supreme Personality of Godhead is employed and there are no impediments or stumbling blocks, that is the symptom of pure Kṛṣṇa consciousness.

There is no ambition or motive in pure Kṛṣṇa consciousness. Every other transcendental function or mode of worship is backed by a motive: someone wants salvation, someone wants material prosperity, someone wants to go to a higher planet, someone wants to go to Kṛṣṇaloka. These ambitions should not be there. A pure devotee has no such ambitions. A pure devotee does not even desire to go to the supreme abode of Kṛṣṇa. Of course, he goes, but he has no desire. He simply wants to engage himself fully in Kṛṣṇa's service.

There are different kinds of salvation. There is *sālokya* liberation, to live on the same planet as the Supreme Lord. The residents of the Vaikuṇṭha planets live on the same planet as the Supreme Personality of Godhead. *Sārṣṭi* liberation means to have almost the same opulence as Nārāyaṇa. The liberated individual soul can appear just like Nārāyaṇa, with four hands, the four emblems, almost the same bodily features, the same opulence, the same ornaments, the same buildings, everything. *Sārūpya* means to have the same form or features. *Sāmīpya* means never to be far away but always to be associated with the Supreme Lord. For example, just as we are sitting together, so one can associate with the Lord. This is called *sāmīpya-mukti,* the liberation of being nearer. Pure devotees, however, do not accept these various forms of liberation. They only want to be engaged in Kṛṣṇa's service. They are not concerned with any kind of liberation. Those who are actually Kṛṣṇa conscious achieve the association of the Supreme Lord, but they do not desire it; their only ambition is to be engaged in the transcendental loving service of the Lord. The highest perfection of devotional service, or Kṛṣṇa consciousness, is exhibited when a devotee refuses to accept any benediction or profit from the Supreme Lord. Prahlāda Mahārāja was offered whatever he liked, he had only to ask for it, but he said, "My Lord, I am Your eternal servant. It is my duty to serve You, so how can I accept any benefit from it? Then I would not be Your servant; I would be a merchant." He replied in that way, and that is the sign of a pure person. Kṛṣṇa is so kind that He fulfills all the desires of a devotee, even if he wants material benedictions. If at the bottom of the devotee's heart there is some desire, He also fulfills that. He is so kind. But the sublime position of *bhakti-yoga,* or devotional service, is that a pure devotee refuses to accept the various kinds of liberation, even if offered by the Supreme Lord.

If one has material desires or motives within himself, and for fulfillment of such desires he engages himself in devotional service, the result will be that he will never get pure love of God. If one is thinking, "I am engaged in Kṛṣṇa consciousness, in Kṛṣṇa's devotional service, because I want such and such an opulence," that desire may be fulfilled, but he will never get such unalloyed love of Kṛṣṇa as the *gopīs* had. If one has a motive, even though he discharges his devotional duty, he still will not be able to reach the stage of pure love of Godhead. In a verse from the *Bhakti-rasāmṛta-sindhu,*

Rūpa Gosvāmī says, "As long as one desires some material benefit [*bhukti*], or even if he wants salvation [*mukti*], then he must take those ghostly representations." As long as that *māyā* exists within one's heart, how can one enjoy the spiritual bliss derived from pure love of Godhead? In other words, if one has material desires, or even a desire for salvation, he cannot attain pure love of Godhead. Pure devotion is devoid of all desires—it is simply to render loving service for its own sake.

There is a nice example in the life of Rūpa Gosvāmī. Rūpa Gosvāmī and his brother Sanātana Gosvāmī were living separately in Vṛndāvana and going on with their *bhajana*, devotional service. Rūpa was living in the forest, and there was no facility for cooking nice food or begging from the village for a *capātī* to eat. Rūpa Gosvāmī was the younger brother, and he thought, "If I could get some foodstuffs, then I could prepare nice dishes and offer them to Kṛṣṇa and invite my elder brother." He had that desire. The next moment, a nice girl about twelve years old came and delivered an abundance of foodstuffs—milk, flour, ghee, etc. That is the Vedic system; sometimes householders present foodstuffs to mendicants and sages in the renounced order of life. Rūpa Gosvāmī was very glad that Kṛṣṇa had sent so many things and that he could now prepare a feast. He prepared a feast and then invited his elder brother.

When Sanātana Gosvāmī came, he was astonished. "How have you secured such things? You have prepared such a nice feast in this forest. How is it possible?"

So Rūpa Gosvāmī explained, "In the morning I desired for it, and by chance Kṛṣṇa sent me all these things. A nice girl came, and she offered it to me." He was describing the girl: "A very nice girl."

Then Sanātana said, "This nice girl is Rādhārāṇī. You have taken service from Rādhārāṇī, the Lord's eternal consort. It is a great blunder." That is their philosophy. They would not accept service from the Lord. They simply wanted to render service. But Kṛṣṇa is so clever that He also wants to serve His devotee. He looks for an opportunity to serve His devotee. This is spiritual competition. A pure devotee does not want anything from Kṛṣṇa; he simply wants to serve Him. And Kṛṣṇa also looks for the opportunity to serve His devotee. Kṛṣṇa is always as anxious to please His devotee as the devotee is to please Him.

This is the transcendental world. On the absolute plane, there is no exploitation. Everyone wants to serve; no one wants to take service. In the transcendental world, everyone wants to give service. You want to give service to me, and I want to give service to you. This is such a nice attitude. This material world means that I want to pickpocket you, and you want to pickpocket me. That's all. This is the material world. We should try to understand it. In the material world, everyone wants to exploit his friend, his father, his mother, everyone. But in the transcendental world, everyone wants to serve. Everyone has Kṛṣṇa as the central point of serving, and all the devotees, either as friends or servants or parents or lovers of Kṛṣṇa, all want to serve Him. And at the same time, Kṛṣṇa also wants to serve them. This is a transcendental relationship; the main function is service, although there is no necessity of service, for everyone is full. There is no hunger, there is no necessity of eating, but still everyone offers nice things to eat. This is the transcendental world. Unless we attain the stage of simply serving Kṛṣṇa or His devotee, we cannot relish the transcendental pleasure of service. If we have any motive, then that sense will never be awakened. Without a motive, without desire for personal sense gratification, service should be rendered to the Supreme Lord and His devotees.

APPROACHING KṚṢṆA WITH LOVE

"This is the formula—we should not try to satisfy our senses separately but should try to satisfy Kṛṣṇa's senses. Then naturally we will become satisfied. A Kṛṣṇa conscious person is always trying to give satisfaction to Kṛṣṇa."

When Kṛṣṇa was on this earth, all the residents of Vṛndāvana loved Him. Indeed, they knew nothing but Kṛṣṇa. They did not know whether Kṛṣṇa is God or not God, nor were they disturbed by such thoughts as "I shall love Kṛṣṇa if He is God." Their attitude was one of pure love, and they thought, "He may or may not be God—it doesn't matter. We love Kṛṣṇa, that's all." This then is the platform of real, unalloyed love. When one thinks, "If Kṛṣṇa is God, I shall love Him," it should be known that this is not the platform of pure love but of conditional love. While on earth, Kṛṣṇa exhibited extraordinary powers, and the *vraja-vāsīs,* the residents of Vṛndāvana, often thought, "Oh, Kṛṣṇa is such a wonderful child. Maybe He is some demigod." They thought in this way because people were generally under the impression that the demigods were all-powerful. Within the material world the demigods are powerful, but people are not aware that Kṛṣṇa is above all of them. The highest of the demigods, Brahmā, gave his opinion of this matter in the verse *īśvaraḥ paramaḥ kṛṣṇaḥ sac-cid-ānanda-vigrahaḥ:* "Kṛṣṇa is the supreme controller, and His body is full of knowledge, bliss, and eternality." Little did the residents of Vṛndāvana know of Kṛṣṇa's power as the ultimate controller and master of all the demigods. What is noteworthy is that their love for Him was not subject to such considerations.

As the residents of Vṛndāvana loved Kṛṣṇa unconditionally, similarly Kṛṣṇa loved them unconditionally. *Vraja-jana-vallabha, giri-vara-dhārī.* When the inhabitants of Vṛndāvana stopped performing sacrifices to Lord Indra, the chief demigod of the heavens, they placed themselves in a very dangerous position. Indra became very angry and sent powerful clouds that rained over Vṛndāvana incessantly for seven days. The whole area began to flood, and the inhabitants became very disturbed. Although He was only seven years old, Kṛṣṇa saved the inhabitants of Vṛndāvana by lifting Govardhana Hill and holding it up as an umbrella to shield the village. Lord Kṛṣṇa thus taught the demigod Indra that his disturbances could be stopped simply by His little finger. Seeing this, Lord Indra bowed down before Kṛṣṇa.

Thus Kṛṣṇa also became known as Gopījana-vallabha, which indicates that His only business is to protect the *gopī-jana*. This Kṛṣṇa consciousness movement aims at teaching people how to become *gopī-janas*, or pure lovers of Kṛṣṇa. When we reach that stage of pure love of God, the Lord will save us from any danger, even if it means His lifting a hill or a mountain. Kṛṣṇa did not have to practice some yoga system in order to lift Govardhana Hill. As God, He is all-powerful, even as a child. He played like a child and dealt with others like a child, but when there was need, He manifested Himself as God Almighty. That is the nature of Kṛṣṇa, or God: He does not have to practice meditation or follow some system of yoga in order to become God. He is not a manufactured type of God, but is God eternally.

Although He is God, He enjoys loving relationships with His devotees, and in order to satisfy His devotees, He often takes roles that appear to be subsidiary. Kṛṣṇa often likes being the child of a devotee, and thus He became the beloved child of Yaśodā, Yaśodā-nandana. Because He is God and everyone worships Him, no one chastises Him. However, Kṛṣṇa enjoys being chastised by His devotee father and mother, and because Kṛṣṇa takes pleasure in being chastised, the devotees also take up the role, saying, "All right, I shall become Your father and chastise You." Similarly, when Kṛṣṇa wants to fight, one of His devotees becomes the demon Hiraṇyakaśipu and fights with Him. In this way, all Kṛṣṇa's activities are carried out in connection with His devotees. If we aspire to become such associates of Kṛṣṇa, we must develop Kṛṣṇa consciousness, awareness of Kṛṣṇa.

Yaśodā-nandana vraja-jana-rañjana. Kṛṣṇa's only business is satisfying the *vraja-janas*, and their only business is satisfying Kṛṣṇa. This is the reciprocation of love. *Yāmuna-tīra-vana-cārī:* Kṛṣṇa, the

Supreme Personality of Godhead, wanders on the banks of the Yamunā to please the *gopīs,* the cowherd boys, the birds, the bees, and the cows and calves. These are not ordinary birds, bees, cows, calves, or men; they have all reached the summit of self-realization and thus, after many, many lives, have attained a position whereby they can play with Kṛṣṇa. This Kṛṣṇa consciousness movement can enable everyone to go to Kṛṣṇaloka and become Kṛṣṇa's associate as a friend, servant, father, or mother. Kṛṣṇa is agreeable to take any of these positions in relation to His devotee. How He does so is all described in our book *Teachings of Lord Caitanya.* To realize our relationship with Kṛṣṇa, we have but to follow in the footsteps of Lord Caitanya and His chief associates, the Six Gosvāmīs—Śrī Rūpa, Sanātana, Śrī Jīva, Gopāla, Raghunātha Dāsa, and Raghunātha Bhaṭṭa. These Gosvāmīs were always engaged in chanting Hare Kṛṣṇa and dancing in ecstasy. They taught that when one is merged in *kṛṣṇa-kīrtana,* or the chanting of the holy names of Kṛṣṇa, he merges into the ocean of love of Kṛṣṇa. As soon as the sound of Kṛṣṇa's name is vibrated, one can immediately merge into the ocean of love. That is the sign of pure devotion. Thus at *kīrtanas* the Six Gosvāmīs would merge immediately into the ocean of love of Godhead.

The Six Gosvāmīs were dear not only to the other devotees of Lord Caitanya Mahāprabhu but to the nondevotees as well. A pure devotee's position is that he has no enemy because he is not envious. A pure devotee is always open to everyone, and he does not discriminate that this person can be allowed to chant Hare Kṛṣṇa and that person should not be allowed. On the material platform, which is a platform of dualism, there are differences between high and low, man and woman, and this or that, but on the spiritual platform there are no such distinctions. The pure devotee, seeing everything with an equal mind, is therefore nonenvious. Because he is nonenvious, he is worshipable. Indeed, it may even be said that a person is worshipable simply if he is nonenvious, for it is only possible to be nonenvious on the spiritual platform. This is also the verdict of the *Bhagavad-gītā* [5.18–19]:

vidyā-vinaya-sampanne brāhmaṇe gavi hastini
śuni caiva śvapāke ca paṇḍitāḥ sama-darśinaḥ

ihaiva tair jitaḥ sargo yeṣāṁ sāmye sthitaṁ manaḥ
nirdoṣaṁ hi samaṁ brahma tasmād brahmaṇi te sthitāḥ

"The humble sages, by virtue of true knowledge, see with equal vision a learned and gentle *brāhmaṇa,* a cow, an elephant, a dog, and a dog-eater. Those whose minds are established in sameness and equanimity have already conquered the conditions of birth and death. They are flawless like Brahman, and thus they are already situated in Brahman."

Such a position can be obtained by one who has acquired the mercy of Lord Caitanya. Upon obtaining His mercy, a person can deliver suffering humanity from material contamination. Because the Six Gosvāmīs were such devotees, we offer our respectful obeisances unto them with the mantra *vande rūpa-sanātanau raghu-yugau śrī-jīva-gopālakau.* The Six Gosvāmīs were expert in scrutinizingly studying all the scriptures with the aim to establish real religion in the world. They left many books to guide us, the most famous of which is Śrī Rūpa Gosvāmī's *Bhakti-rasāmṛta-sindhu* (*The Nectar of Devotion*), which gives the neophyte devotee initial direction. The Gosvāmīs always worked very hard, day and night, and their business was simply writing books, chanting, and dancing. Indeed, they were practically released from the bodily necessities of eating, sleeping, mating, and defending themselves out of fear. There was no question of mating at all, nor was there any question of fearing or defending, for they were totally absorbed in Kṛṣṇa. At most they used to sleep one and a half hours daily, and they ate practically nothing. Whenever they felt hungry, they would simply go to a householder's home and beg one or two pieces of bread.

The mission of such saintly persons is but to make suffering humanity happy by elevating everyone to spiritual consciousness. In the material world, everyone is trying to exploit one another—one nation is trying to exploit another nation, one society is trying to exploit another, one businessman is trying to exploit another, etc. This is called the struggle for existence, and out of it the people who are struggling have invented a law called "Might is right," but we can actually see that even the most powerful must struggle, just as in the current world situation. There is a great struggle going on between Russia, America, and China. Because of such a struggle, everyone is suffering. Indeed, the very struggle for existence means suffering. The pure devotees of Kṛṣṇa, however, are interested not in exploiting others but in helping people become happy, and therefore they are worshiped on all planets. Cāṇakya Paṇḍita even said that a rich man and a learned man cannot be compared, for a rich man may be honored in his own country or on his own planet, but a learned man, a devotee of God, is honored wherever he goes.

Nor for a devotee is there a distinction between heaven and hell, because Kṛṣṇa is with him in both places. Where there is Kṛṣṇa, there is no question of hell; every place is Vaikuṇṭha. Haridāsa Ṭhākura, for instance, did not enter the Jagannātha temple at Purī, for he was born in a Muhammadan family, and the Hindus opposed the Muhammadans' entering the temple. Haridāsa Ṭhākura did not let this disturb him, however. He thought, "Oh, why should I go and disturb them? I shall chant here." Consequently Lord Caitanya, who is Lord Jagannātha Himself, came daily to see Haridāsa. This is the power of a pure devotee: he doesn't have to go to Jagannātha; Jagannātha comes to him. Lord Caitanya Mahāprabhu used to go see Haridāsa Ṭhākura daily when the Lord was going to bathe in the sea. The Lord would enter Haridāsa's cottage and ask, "Haridāsa, what are you doing?" and Haridāsa would reply, "Please come in, my Lord." This then is the actual position of a devotee. Therefore Kṛṣṇa says that worship of His devotee is even more valuable than worship of Himself. The devotee is actually able to deliver Kṛṣṇa, for he knows the science of Kṛṣṇa consciousness, the science of hearing Kṛṣṇa's words, eating *kṛṣṇa-prasādam*, and enjoying Kṛṣṇa. The impersonalists and voidists may preach dry philosophical treatises on *ahaṁ brahmāsmi*—"I am spirit"—but ultimately who will be attracted? What is the difference between someone who thinks, "I am a stone," and someone who thinks, "I am void"? Why should we become stone, wood, or void? Our actual position should be in reciprocating loving affairs with Kṛṣṇa.

The spark of love for Kṛṣṇa is struck by the spiritual master, the pure devotee. As for myself, my spiritual master, His Divine Grace Oṁ Viṣṇupāda Bhaktisiddhānta Sarasvatī Gosvāmī Prabhupāda, ordered me to take up the responsibility of spreading Kṛṣṇa consciousness in the Western world. His Divine Grace had a great desire to preach Lord Caitanya's message in the West, and my success is both his grace and pleasure. When I first met my spiritual master, I was a very young man in India, a nationalist, engaged in a very responsible office. But although I did not want to go, one of my friends, who is still living in Calcutta, forcibly took me to His Divine Grace. I was reluctant to see him because in our home our father used to receive many *sannyāsīs* and I was not very satisfied with their dealings. I thought that Bhaktisiddhānta Sarasvatī Gosvāmī Mahārāja might be a similar man, and if he were, what business would I have in seeing him? But my friend took me forcibly. "Why not see him?" he asked. I finally relented and went with him, and I profited.

On my first visit, His Divine Grace said that it was necessary for educated boys like me to go to foreign countries and preach the gospel of Caitanya Mahāprabhu. I replied that India was a foreign-dominated nation and that no one would hear our messages. Actually, at the time foreigners considered Indians very insignificant because in the face of so many independent nations India was still dependent, being dominated by Britain. At the time there was one Bengali poet who actually lamented that even uncivilized nations were independent, whereas India was dependent on the British. His Divine Grace convinced me that dependence and independence are simply temporary conditions, and he pointed out that because we are concerned with the eternal benefit of humanity, we should take up this challenge of Caitanya Mahāprabhu. This meeting with His Divine Grace, my Guru Mahārāja, took place in 1922, half a century ago.

I was officially initiated in 1933, just three years before the passing of Guru Mahārāja from this mortal world. At the last moment, just a fortnight before his passing away, he wrote me a letter repeating his instructions. He specifically said that I should try to preach this gospel among English-speaking people. After receiving this letter, I sometimes dreamed that Guru Mahārāja was calling me and that I was leaving home and following him. I was dreaming in this way and thinking, "I have to give up my home. My Guru Mahārāja wants me to give up my home and take *sannyāsa*." At the same time I thought, "This is horrible. How can I leave my home? My wife? My children?" This is called *māyā*. Actually I did not want to give up my home life, but Guru Mahārāja made me give it up. Following his orders, I left my home, including a few children, but now Guru Mahārāja has given me many nice children all over the world. Thus by serving Kṛṣṇa no one becomes a loser, and this is an example from my own practical experience.

When I left India alone in 1965, I feared that I would have a great deal of trouble. The Indian government would not allow me to take any money out of the country, so I came with only a few books and forty rupees. I arrived in New York City in such a condition, but it was all by the grace of Guru Mahārāja and Kṛṣṇa. Everything happens by the combined mercy of Kṛṣṇa and the spiritual master. In the *Caitanya-caritāmṛta* it is stated that the mercy of Kṛṣṇa and guru are combined. This is the secret of the success of this Kṛṣṇa consciousness movement. Kṛṣṇa is always within us, and consequently He knows everything about our purposes, and He gives us the opportunity to work as we decide. If we decide to enjoy this material world, Kṛṣṇa gives us the intelligence to become a very shrewd businessman or a popular politician or a cunning man so that we can earn money and enjoy ourselves. According to the standards of material life, many people are becoming great. They begin as very poor men and soon, by good fortune, become millionaires. We Should not think, however, that they are attaining such success by their own puny endeavors. Without intelligence, no one can improve, and that intelligence is given by Kṛṣṇa. In the *Bhagavad-gītā* Kṛṣṇa states that He is seated in everyone's heart as the Supersoul and that by His will a man can remember, and by His will a man can forget. Kṛṣṇa supplies forgetfulness and remembrance according to the living entity's desire. If we want to forget Kṛṣṇa and enjoy the material world, He will give us the necessary intelligence so that we can forget Him for good.

Many people are thinking, "I can enjoy this material world very nicely. Everyone is having such a good time. There is no reason I can't enjoy myself as much as they." This idea is illusion because there is no real enjoyment in the material world. We may rise to a very high position like President Kennedy. We may be very good-looking, very famous, very intelligent, and well educated, very wealthy and very powerful, and we may have a very beautiful wife and children and hold the highest position in the country—but at any moment we are subject to be shot down. This is the nature of the material world: we have to face danger at every step. There is no question of having pleasure without impediments. Even when the pleasures are earned, they are earned after a great deal of struggle and sacrifice, and whatever pleasure may be acquired is temporary, for in the material world there is no pleasure that can give us constant and unending enjoyment. Only Kṛṣṇa can give us that.

Therefore Kṛṣṇa instructs in the *Bhagavad-gītā* that it is the welfare of every living entity to give up this nonsensical material activity and just surrender unto Him. Unfortunately, in this age people are so attracted by the glitter of material nature, to illusion, or *māyā*, that they are not very interested. Kṛṣṇa even declares that if one surrenders unto Him, He will give all protection from all sinful reactions, but still people are so attached that they cannot do it. People always fear that by surrendering to Kṛṣṇa they will lose something, just as I feared losing my family by going to the Western world and preaching. But Kṛṣṇa is so kind that if He takes anything away, He will reward us a thousandfold.

The spiritual master is also kind in that he begs from door to door, country to country, town to town: "My dear ladies and gentlemen, my dear boys and girls, please take to Kṛṣṇa consciousness." In this way he renders very confidential service to Kṛṣṇa. Kṛṣṇa is the Supreme Lord who gives the orders, and the spiritual master executes those orders; therefore the spiritual master is very dear to Kṛṣṇa. Whether Kṛṣṇa sends him to heaven or to hell makes no difference to him. For the spiritual master, a pure devotee, heaven and hell are both the same if there is no Kṛṣṇa consciousness. In hell people are suffering in so many ways, and in heaven they are enjoying their senses in so many ways, but a devotee of the Lord can live any place where there is Kṛṣṇa consciousness, and since he brings this consciousness with him, he is always self-satisfied. If he is sent to hell, he will be satisfied simply chanting Hare Kṛṣṇa. In fact, he does not believe in hell but in Kṛṣṇa. Similarly, if he were put into heaven, where there are so many opportunities for sense gratification, he would also remain aloof, for his senses are satisfied by Kṛṣṇa Himself. Thus for the service of the Lord a devotee is prepared to go anywhere, and for this reason he is very dear to Kṛṣṇa.

Renounced impersonalist philosophers say that this world is false and that the impersonal Brahman is truth. But if they are asked to go out into society where material sense gratification predominates, they will refuse for fear of being affected by those conditions. For a Kṛṣṇa conscious person, however, there is no such difficulty. Because he is controlled and has taken shelter of Kṛṣṇa, he is not afraid of going anywhere.

Consequently, when devotees meet in a place where there is no Kṛṣṇa consciousness, there is no harm, for they take the opportunity to chant Hare Kṛṣṇa and infuse the place with Kṛṣṇa consciousness. This opportunity should always be taken. It is not that one should close himself up in a room and chant alone. The great sage Nārada is a spaceman who travels all over the universe. Although he can dwell in the most elevated planets, he sometimes goes to hell and preaches there. That is the beauty of a servant of God—he is always acting out of love for Kṛṣṇa and His parts and parcels.

The underlying principle of devotional service is unalloyed love for Kṛṣṇa. Regardless of the position of a particular devotee—as friend, servant, parent, or lover of Kṛṣṇa—his service is unconditional, for Kṛṣṇa consciousness is not dependent on any material condition. It is transcendental and has nothing to do with the modes of material nature. A devotee is not afraid to go anywhere, and because of this he sees all material conditions as equal. In the world we may say that this is a good place to be and that is a bad place, but, as pointed out before, the devotee is not subject to these mental concoctions. For him the basic principle of material existence is bad, for material existence means forgetfulness of Kṛṣṇa.

In the neutral stage of devotion one may give more importance to the impersonal effulgence of the Lord and to the Supersoul within the heart, but Kṛṣṇa consciousness actually develops when one thinks, "Kṛṣṇa is my very intimate master of intimate relationships." In the beginning, of course, impersonal realization and realization of the Supersoul are part of Kṛṣṇa consciousness. The partial realization of God in His impersonal aspect or in His aspect as Supersoul enables one to develop veneration for the Lord, but when one has an intimate relationship with Kṛṣṇa as a friend, master, son, or lover, then the veneration disappears.

This platform of personal relationship is certainly higher than the impersonal platform or the platform of Supersoul, or Paramātmā, realization. In the neutral conception, one simply realizes that he and the Absolute Truth are one in quality, or he realizes that he is part and parcel of the Supreme. That is certainly knowledge, for when one develops a personal relationship with Kṛṣṇa as servant, he begins to appreciate the full opulence of the Supreme Lord. One who realizes that God is full in six opulences actually begins rendering service. As soon as one becomes aware of the greatness of Kṛṣṇa and understands Kṛṣṇa's superiority, his service begins. The awareness of God's greatness increases when transcendental service is rendered. A person who serves the Lord in order to satisfy the senses of the Lord becomes satisfied, because Kṛṣṇa is the Supersoul and the individual living entity is His part and parcel. If He is satisfied, then the living entity is satisfied. If the stomach is satisfied, then all the parts of the body are satisfied, for they receive nourishment through the stomach. When one of my Godbrothers began to fan my Guru Mahārāja on a very hot day, Guru Mahārāja asked, "Why are you fanning me all of a sudden?" The boy replied, "Because if you are satisfied, we are all satisfied." This is the formula—we should not try to satisfy our senses separately, but should try to satisfy Kṛṣṇa's senses. Then naturally we will become satisfied.

A Kṛṣṇa conscious person is always trying to give satisfaction to Kṛṣṇa, and this is the beginning of Kṛṣṇa consciousness. Because in the impersonal conception there is no form of God, there is no opportunity to satisfy His senses. However, one who sees Kṛṣṇa as master can render service. In the *Bhagavad-gītā* Kṛṣṇa is referred to as Hṛṣīkeśa, master of the senses. When it is understood that the Absolute Truth is the master of the senses, that our senses are products of His senses, and that they should therefore be utilized for the satisfaction of His senses, Kṛṣṇa consciousness, which is dormant within everyone, begins to awaken. Once Caitanya Mahāprabhu asked, "What is the difference between the neutral position in relation to Kṛṣṇa and the relationship of master and servant?" In both cases one can understand that Kṛṣṇa is great, but in the neutral position there is no inclination for service. Therefore the master-servant relationship between Kṛṣṇa and the living entity is more elevated. Then when one attains friendship with Kṛṣṇa, another transcendental quality is added. There is the conception that God is great and that service must be rendered unto Him, but there is also an extra feeling: "Kṛṣṇa is my friend. Therefore I must treat Him in such a way that He will be happy." With a friend we are not simply content with rendering service but in making him actually happy and satisfied. There is also equality in such a relationship, for Kṛṣṇa and the devotee relate on equal terms. Thus devotees in this position actually forget Kṛṣṇa's superiority. When

Kṛṣṇa's boyfriends used to ride on His shoulders playing games, they did not think that they were greater than Him. There is no question of sense gratification or self-glorification, for the relationship is based on pure love. The devotee's only desire is to give pleasure to Kṛṣṇa, and Kṛṣṇa also takes His friends on His shoulders to derive pleasure from them. Sometimes a person simply accepts the fact that his friend will slap his face—but there is no question of inferiority in such an action. When friendship and mutual pleasure are the basis of the relationship, there is no question of insult or inferiority.

The whole basis of Kṛṣṇa consciousness and a relationship with Kṛṣṇa is the pleasure potency of Kṛṣṇa Himself. Śrīmatī Rādhārāṇī, the damsels of Vraja, and Kṛṣṇa's cowherd boyfriends are all expansions of Kṛṣṇa's pleasure potency. We all have a tendency toward pleasure, because the source from which we emanate is fully potent in pleasure. Impersonalists cannot think in these terms, for they deny the pleasure potency; therefore the impersonalist philosophy is incomplete and inferior. Those who are in Kṛṣṇa consciousness recognize the pleasure potency in Kṛṣṇa and in all His paraphernalia—His friends, servants, father, mother, and consort. All relationships with Kṛṣṇa that aim at satisfying Kṛṣṇa's senses are manifestations of Kṛṣṇa's pleasure potency.

As far as the individual soul is concerned, it is originally a part and parcel of this pleasure potency, of the reservoir of pleasure Himself. However, due to contact with material nature, the soul has forgotten its actual position and has become trapped in the evolutionary process of transmigration from one body to another. Thus one struggles hard for existence. Now we must extricate ourselves from the sufferings of the struggle, from the countless transmigrations that force us to suffer the miseries of birth, old age, disease, and death, and come to the point of our eternal life in Kṛṣṇa consciousness. That eternal life is possible. If one tries his best in this human form of life, in his next life he will get a spiritual body. The spiritual body is already within the gross material body, but it will develop only as soon as one becomes free from the contamination of this material existence. That is the aim of human life and the actual self-interest of all people. Self-interest is actually realizing, "I am part and parcel of God. I have to return to the kingdom of God and join with Him." Just as we have a social life here, God has a social life in the spiritual kingdom, and we can join Him there. It is not that after finishing this body we become void. In the *Bhagavad-gītā* [2.12] Kṛṣṇa told Arjuna, "Never was there a time when I did not exist, nor you, nor all these kings, nor in the future shall any of us cease to be." Our existence is therefore eternal, and the changes of birth and death are simply the changes of the temporary material bodies.

The actual process for achieving eternal life is not at all difficult. This process of Kṛṣṇa consciousness is based on knowledge received from Kṛṣṇa, the most perfect being. Knowledge received from others is defective because the conditioned soul is certain to commit mistakes, certain to be illusioned, certain to cheat, and certain to have imperfect senses. The knowledge received from Kṛṣṇa, however, actually enables us to see Kṛṣṇa. Someone may challenge, "Can you show me God?" and our answer is, "Yes. God can be seen at every moment." Kṛṣṇa says, *raso 'ham apsu kaunteya:* "I am the taste of water." We drink water every day, and the taste of water is there, so if we think of this taste as Kṛṣṇa, we will have begun realizing God every day. In the *Bhagavad-gītā* Kṛṣṇa further says, *prabhāsmi śaśi-sūryayoḥ:* "I am the light of the sun and the moon." Every day we receive sunlight, and in the evening there is moonshine, so if we think of the source of these emanations, we will ultimately become God conscious. There are so many similar instances given in the *Bhagavad-gītā,* for Kṛṣṇa is the beginning, middle, and end of all manifestations. If we want to become God conscious and realize our own essence, it is not very difficult. We only have to understand God in truth—how He appears, how He disappears, and what His functions are—then we can become eligible to enter into the kingdom of God. After quitting this material body, a person who understands God, Kṛṣṇa, does not return again to earth to accept another material body. Where does he go? Kṛṣṇa says, *mām eti:* "He comes to Me." That should be the aim of any intelligent human being.

APPENDIXES

THE AUTHOR

His Divine Grace A. C. Bhaktivedanta Swami Prabhupāda appeared in this world in 1896 in Calcutta, India. He first met his spiritual master, Śrīla Bhaktisiddhānta Sarasvatī Gosvāmī, in Calcutta in 1922. Bhaktisiddhānta Sarasvatī, a prominent religious scholar and the founder of sixty-four Gauḍīya Maṭhas (Vedic institutes), liked this educated young man and convinced him to dedicate his life to teaching Kṛṣṇa consciousness. Śrīla Prabhupāda became his student and, in 1932, his formally initiated disciple.

At their first meeting, in 1922, Bhaktisiddhānta Sarasvatī asked Śrīla Prabhupāda to broadcast Kṛṣṇa consciousness in English. In the years that followed, Śrīla Prabhupāda wrote a commentary on the *Bhagavad-gītā*, assisted the Gauḍīya Maṭha in its work, and, in 1944, started *Back to Godhead*, an English fortnightly magazine. Single-handedly, Śrīla Prabhupāda edited it, typed the manuscripts, checked the galley proofs, and even distributed the individual copies. The magazine is now being continued by his followers.

In 1950 Śrīla Prabhupāda retired from married life, adopting the *vānaprastha* (retired) order to devote more time to his studies and writing. He traveled to the holy city of Vṛndāvana, where he lived in humble circumstances in the historic temple of Rādhā-Dāmodara. There he engaged for several years in deep study and writing. He accepted the renounced order of life (*sannyāsa*) in 1959. At Rādhā-Dāmodara, Śrīla Prabhupāda began work on his life's masterpiece: a multivolume commentated translation of the 18,000-verse *Śrīmad-Bhāgavatam* (*Bhāgavata Purāṇa*). He also wrote *Easy Journey to Other Planets.*

After publishing three volumes of *Śrīmad-Bhāgavatam,* Śrīla Prabhupāda came to the United States, in September 1965, to fulfill the mission of his spiritual master. Subsequently, His Divine Grace wrote more than fifty volumes of authoritative commentated translations and summary studies of the philosophical and religious classics of India.

When he first arrived in New York City, Śrīla Prabhupāda was nearly penniless. Only after a year of great difficulty did he establish the International Society for Krishna Consciousness, in July of 1966. Before he passed away on November 14, 1977, he had guided the Society and seen it grow to a worldwide confederation of more than one hundred *āśramas*, schools, temples, institutes, and farm communities.

In 1972 His Divine Grace introduced the Vedic system of primary and secondary education in the West by founding the *gurukula* school in Dallas, Texas. Since then his disciples have established similar schools throughout the United States and the rest of the world.

Śrīla Prabhupāda also inspired the construction of several large international cultural centers in India. The center at Śrīdhāma Māyāpur is the site for a planned spiritual city, an ambitious project for which construction will extend over many years to come. In Vṛndāvana are the magnificent Kṛṣṇa-Balarāma Temple and International Guesthouse, *gurukula* school, and Śrīla Prabhupāda Memorial and Museum. There are also major cultural and educational centers in Mumbai, New Delhi, Baroda, Tirupati, Siliguri, Ahmedabad, and Ujjain. Other centers are planned in many important locations on the Indian subcontinent.

Śrīla Prabhupāda's most significant contribution, however, is his books. Highly respected by scholars for their authority, depth, and clarity, they are used as textbooks in numerous college courses. His writings have been translated into over fifty languages. The Bhaktivedanta Book Trust, established in 1972 to publish the works of His Divine Grace, has thus become the world's largest publisher of books in the field of Indian religion and philosophy.

In just twelve years, in spite of his advanced age, Śrīla Prabhupāda circled the globe fourteen times on lecture tours that took him to six continents. In spite of such a vigorous schedule, Śrīla Prabhupāda continued to write prolifically. His writings constitute a veritable library of Vedic philosophy, religion, literature, and culture.

GLOSSARY

Words in SMALL CAPITALS are defined elsewhere in the glossary.

A

adhibhautika — miseries caused by conflict with other living entities.

adhidaivika — miseries caused by the forces of nature.

adhyātmika — miseries caused by one's own mind and body.

Advaita Ācārya — an incarnation of the Lord who appeared as a principal associate of another incarnation, Lord CAITANYA MAHĀPRABHU.

Age of Kali — *See:* KALI-YUGA.

Akrūra — an uncle of Lord KṚṢṆA.

Ānandagiri — a prominent follower of ŚAṄKARĀCĀRYA.

apavarga — *See:* MUKTI.

Arjuna — one of the five PĀṆḌAVA brothers; Lord KṚṢṆA became his chariot driver during the battle of KURUKṢETRA and spoke the BHAGAVAD-GĪTĀ to him.

āśrama(s) — (1) the four Vedic developmental divisions of the human life cycle that are meant to elevate one to spiritual perfection; these begin with *brahmacarya* (celibacy and study), proceed to *gṛhastha* (married life) and *vānaprastha* (retirement), and culminate in *sannyāsa* (complete renunciation of family life and material obligations). *See also:* VARṆĀŚRAMA-DHARMA. (2) A residence where spiritual life is practiced.

aṣṭāṅga-yoga — the eight-step process of meditation, beginning with sitting postures and breath control, and culminating with realization of the Lord's form in the heart.

Aśvatthāmā — the nefarious son of the great military teacher Droṇa, who murdered the children of the PĀṆḌAVA brothers.

ātmā — *See:* JĪVA.

avatāra — literally "one who descends"; the appearance on earth of the Supreme Lord or His representative.

B

Bādarāyaṇa — *See:* VYĀSADEVA.

Baladeva — *See:* JAGANNĀTHA, BALADEVA, and SUBHADRĀ.

Bhagavad-gītā — the paramount scripture of the Vedic tradition, embodying the teachings of Lord KṚṢṆA to His devotee ARJUNA, and expounding devotion to the Supreme Lord as both the principal means and the ultimate end of spiritual perfection.

Bhagavān — the Supreme Lord, who is the ultimate possessor of all opulence.

Bhāgavatam, Bhāgavata Purāṇa — *See:* ŚRĪMAD-BHĀGAVATAM.

bhakta — a devotee of the Supreme Lord.

bhakti (bhakti-yoga) — the practice of devotional service to the Supreme Lord.

Bhakti-rasāmṛta-sindhu — RŪPA GOSVĀMĪ's definitive explanation of devotional service to the Supreme Lord, beginning with the most elementary practices and ending with the ultimate perfection of a personal relationship with the Lord.

Bhaktisiddhānta Sarasvatī — (1874–1936) the "grandfather" of the International Society for Krishna Consciousness; the spiritual master of His Divine Grace A. C. Bhaktivedanta Swami Prabhupāda.

Bhaktivedānta — a title meaning "one who has realized that devotional service to the Supreme Lord is the end of all knowledge."

Bhaktivinoda Ṭhākura — (1838–1915) the "great-grandfather" of the International Society for Krishna Consciousness; the father of Śrīla BHAKTISIDDHĀNTA SARASVATĪ.

Bhārata — a name of ARJUNA meaning "descendant of Bharata."

Bharata Mahārāja — a great devotee of the Lord who because of neglect of spiritual duties took birth as a deer; in his following birth, as a human, he attained perfection.

Bhārata-varṣa — the traditional and scriptural name for India.

Bhīṣma — the most powerful and oldest warrior in the Battle of KURUKṢETRA; he is recognized as one of the chief authorities on devotional service to the Lord.

Brahmā — the first created living being in the universe; he creates the multiplicity of life forms, planets, and living conditions under the supervision of the Supreme Lord.

brahmacārī, brahmacarya — *See:* ĀŚRAMAS.

brahmajyoti — the bodily effulgence of the Supreme Lord.

Brahman — the impersonal, all-pervasive aspect of the Supreme Lord.

brāhmaṇa — *See:* VARṆAS.

Brahma-saṁhitā — a nutshell description of the glories of the Lord, including prayers to the Lord by BRAHMĀ.

Bṛhan-nāradīya Purāṇa — *See:* PURĀṆAS.

Buddha — a disguised incarnation of the Supreme Lord who preached atheism in order to divert the people of that time from misusing the ritualistic sacrifices of the VEDAS as a license for animal slaughter.

C

Caitanya-caritāmṛta — Kṛṣṇadāsa Kavirāja Gosvāmī's presentation of the life and philosophy of Lord CAITANYA MAHĀPRABHU.

Caitanya Mahāprabhu — the incarnation of the Supreme Lord disguised as His own devotee, who descended to teach love of God through the process of congregational chanting of the holy names of the Lord.

caitya-guru — the Supreme Lord, who acts as spiritual guide from within the heart.

Cāṇūra — a powerful wrestler and a servant of the demonic KAṀSA; Lord KṚṢṆA as a young boy killed him.

Cārvāka — an atheistic philosopher whose motto was "Beg, borrow, or steal, but somehow or other enjoy life."

Chāndogya Upaniṣad — *See:* UPANIṢADS.

crore — ten million

D

Daridra-nārāyaṇa — "poor Nārāyaṇa"; refers to the misconception that since the Supreme Lord is in everyone's heart, anyone can be accepted as God and thus service to the poor is the same as direct service to God.

Devakī — the wife of VASUDEVA and mother of Lord KṚṢṆA.
Devī — *See:* DURGĀ.
dharma — the eternal function of the living entity.
Dhṛtarāṣṭra — the father who collaborated with his sons to cheat the PĀṆḌAVA brothers of their kingdom and fight against them in the Battle of KURUKṢETRA.
Droṇa — the military teacher of the PĀṆḌAVA brothers who was obliged to fight against them in the Battle of KURUKṢETRA.
Durgā — the personified material energy of the Lord, and the wife of the demigod ŚIVA.
Duryodhana — the son of DHṚTARĀṢṬRA who led the fight against the PĀṆḌAVA brothers in the Battle of KURUKṢETRA.

G

Gadādhara Paṇḍita — a principal associate of Lord CAITANYA MAHĀPRABHU.
Gaṇeśa — the demigod in charge of material wealth.
Ganges (Gaṅgā) — India's most sacred river.
Garga Muni — the family priest of the Yadu dynasty, the dynasty in which Lord KṚṢṆA chose to incarnate.
Gauḍīya Maṭha (Gauḍīya Mission) — the KṚṢṆA conscious association of temples and preaching institutions established by Śrīla Bhaktisiddhānta Sarasvatī in the early part of the twentieth century.
Gaurāṅga — *See:* CAITANYA MAHĀPRABHU.
Goloka — the supreme planet in the spiritual world, VAIKUṆṬHA.
Gopāla Bhaṭṭa Gosvāmī — one of the six Vaiṣṇava spiritual masters who directly followed Lord CAITANYA MAHĀPRABHU and systematically presented His teachings.
gopīs — the cowherd girlfriends of Lord KṚṢṆA in VṚNDĀVANA, who are His most surrendered and confidential devotees.
gosvāmī — *See:* SWAMI.
Govinda — a name of the Supreme Personality of Godhead meaning "one who gives pleasure to the land, the cows, and the senses."
gṛhastha — *See:* ĀŚRAMAS.
guru — a spiritual master who is perfectly God realized and who speaks and acts only in accordance with the scriptures.

gurukula — a school of Vedic learning; children begin at the age of five and live as celibate students through young adulthood, guided by a spiritual master.

H

Hare (Harā) — *See:* RĀDHĀ.

Hari — a name of the Supreme Personality of Godhead meaning "He who removes all obstacles to spiritual progress."

Haridāsa Ṭhākura — a great devotee of Lord CAITANYA MAHĀPRABHU famous for chanting three hundred thousand names of God every day.

hari-kīrtana — *See:* KĪRTANA.

Hari-vaṁśa — a supplement to the MAHĀBHĀRATA.

I

Indra — the king of the heavenly planets and chief administrative demigod.

Īśopaniṣad — *See:* UPANIṢADS.

J

Jagad-guru — spiritual master of the universe.

Jagannātha, Baladeva, and Subhadrā — the Deity of Lord KṚṢṆA as Jagannātha ("Lord of the Universe"), together with His brother Baladeva and sister, Subhadrā.

Jagannātha Purī (Jagannātha-dhāma) — a city on the coast of Orissa, a province in eastern India; the holy city of the temple and Deity of Lord JAGANNĀTHA.

Jayadratha — a chief enemy of the PĀṆḌAVAS in the battle of KURUKṢETRA.

jīva — the individual living entity, who is an eternal minute part of the Supreme Lord.

Jīva Gosvāmī — one of the six Vaiṣṇava spiritual masters who directly followed Lord CAITANYA MAHĀPRABHU and systematically presented His teachings.

jñānī — one who tries to reach the Supreme Absolute by cultivation of empirical, speculative knowledge.

K

Kālī — *See:* DURGĀ.

Kali-yuga — the current Vedic historical age (fourth and last in a cycle of four progressively degenerating ages) characterized by a progressive decline in spiritual knowledge and, consequently, the degeneration of human civilization.

kalpa-taru — literally "desire tree." It grows in the spiritual world and can immediately yield any fruit desired.

kāma — material desire; lust.

Kaṁsa — a demonic king who, after instigating many fruitless attempts to kill KṚṢṆA, was himself killed by KṚṢṆA.

karma — activity in the material world, which always entangles one in some reaction, whether good or bad.

karma-kāṇḍa — rituals recommended in the VEDAS for those interested in material benefits.

karmī — a person who is trying to enjoy the results of his material activities.

Karṇa — a stepbrother of the PĀṆḌAVAS who fought against them in the Battle of KURUKṢETRA.

Kaṭha Upaniṣad — *See:* UPANIṢADS.

Keśava Kāśmīrī — a famous scholar defeated in a poetry competition by Lord CAITANYA MAHĀPRABHU.

kīrtana — singing or speaking in glorification of the Supreme Lord. *See also:* SAṄKĪRTANA.

Kṛpa — a great warrior who fought against the PĀṆḌAVA brothers in the Battle of KURUKṢETRA.

Kṛṣṇa — the Supreme Personality of Godhead, appearing in His original, two-armed form, which is the origin of all of the Lord's other forms and incarnations.

Kṛṣṇaloka — *See:* GOLOKA.

kṛṣṇa-prasāda — *See:* PRASĀDA.

kṛṣṇa-prema — *See:* PREMA.

kṣatriya — *See:* VARṆAS.

Kuntī — the mother of the PĀṆḌAVAS and aunt of Lord KṚṢṆA.

Kurukṣetra— an ancient pilgrimage site near New Delhi where the Battle of KURUKṢETRA was fought and the BHAGAVAD-GĪTĀ spoken. *See also:* DHṚTARĀṢṬRA and PĀṆḌAVAS.

L

Lakṣmī — the goddess of fortune and the eternal consort of the Supreme Personality of Godhead NĀRĀYAṆA.

M

Madhvācārya — a thirteenth-century Vaiṣṇava spiritual master who preached the theistic philosophy of "pure dualism," which maintains that the Lord and the living entities are always distinct from one another.

Mahābhārata — VYĀSADEVA's epic history of ancient India, within which he included the BHAGAVAD-GĪTĀ.

mahājanas — the chief authorities on the process of devotional service to the Lord.

mahā-mantra — the great chanting for deliverance: Hare Kṛṣṇa, Hare Kṛṣṇa, Kṛṣṇa Kṛṣṇa, Hare Hare/ Hare Rāma, Hare Rāma, Rāma Rāma, Hare Hare.

Mahārāja — a title. *See specific names.*

mahātmā — a "great soul"; devotee of God.

Māṇḍūkya Upaniṣad — *See:* UPANIṢADS.

mantra — a syllable, word, or verse with special spiritual potency chanted or meditated upon to invoke spiritual understanding and realization.

Manu-saṁhitā — the ancient Vedic law book for human society.

Martya-loka — "the world of death"; planet earth.

Marut (Vāyu) — the demigod in charge of the wind.

māyā — the material energy; the illusory energy of the Lord that deludes the living entities into forgetfulness of their real, spiritual nature.

Māyāvāda — the monistic philosophy that there is no difference between God and the living entities. *See also:* ŚAṄKARĀCĀRYA.

mleccha — one who does not follow Vedic culture.

mṛdaṅga — a clay drum used in musical glorification of the Lord.

mukti — liberation from the cycle of repeated birth and death.

Muṇḍaka Upaniṣad — *See:* UPANIṢADS.

N

Nanda Mahārāja — the king of VRAJA and the foster father of Lord KṚṢṆA.

Nārada-pañcarātra — Nārada Muni's book containing instructions for practicing devotional service to the Lord.

Nārāyaṇa — a name of the Supreme Personality of Godhead meaning "one who is the source and the goal of all living beings."

Navadvīpa — a city in the Nadia province of West Bengal; the birthplace of Lord CAITANYA MAHĀPRABHU.

The Nectar of Devotion — a summary study by His Divine Grace A. C. Bhaktivedanta Swami Prabhupāda of the book BHAKTI-RASĀMṚTA-SINDHU, by RŪPA GOSVĀMĪ.

New Vrindavan — the first farm community, located in West Virginia, of the International Society for Krishna Consciousness.

Nimāi Paṇḍita — the name of Lord CAITANYA MAHĀPRABHU during His pastimes as a young scholar.

Nityānanda Prabhu — an incarnation of the Lord who appeared as the chief associate of another incarnation, Lord CAITANYA MAHĀPRABHU.

O

oṁkāra — the sacred sound *oṁ,* which is the beginning of many Vedic mantras, and which represents the Supreme Lord.

P

Padma Purāṇa — *See:* PURĀṆAS.

Pāṇḍavas — YUDHIṢṬHIRA, Bhīma, Arjuna, Nakula, and Sahadeva: the five warrior-brothers who were intimate friends of Lord KṚṢṆA and who fought to regain their kingdom from the sons of DHṚTARĀṢṬRA in the Battle of KURUKṢETRA.

Para-brahman — the Supreme Personality of Godhead, who is superior to His impersonal aspect of BRAHMAN.

Paramātmā — the form of the Supreme Lord that dwells in the heart of and accompanies every living entity as the living entity transmigrates from body to body in the material world.

Parāśara Muni — the father of VYĀSADEVA and original narrator of several of the PURĀṆAS.

Parīkṣit Mahārāja — a great Vedic king and devotee of the Lord who heard ŚRĪMAD-BHĀGAVATAM from ŚUKADEVA GOSVĀMĪ and thus attained perfection.

Patañjali — the author of the original yoga system.

Prahlāda Mahārāja — a devotee of the Lord who was persecuted by his demonic father but protected and saved by the Lord.

Prakāśānanda Sarasvatī — an impersonalist SANNYĀSĪ who, after being defeated in scriptural argument by Lord CAITANYA MAHĀPRABHU, became a disciple along with his forty thousand followers.

prakṛti — the predominated energies of the Supreme.

praṇava — *See:* OṀKĀRA.

prasāda — food that is sanctified by first being offered to the Lord for His enjoyment.

Prayāga — a pilgrimage site near Allahabad where two holy rivers, the GANGES and the Yamunā, flow together.

prema — love of God that is free from any selfish motive.

Purāṇas — the eighteen texts expounding the teachings of the VEDAS through historical and allegorical narrations.

puruṣa — The Supreme Lord as the supreme predominator of PRAKṚTI.

Pūtanā — a demoniac witch who wanted to kill Lord KṚṢṆA during His childhood, but who was killed by the Lord.

Purī — *See:* JAGANNĀTHA PURĪ.

R

Rādhā (Rādhārāṇī) — Lord KṚṢṆA's most intimate eternal consort, who is the personification of His spiritual pleasure potency.

Raghunātha Bhaṭṭa Gosvāmī and Raghunātha Dāsa Gosvāmī — two of the six Vaiṣṇava spiritual masters who directly followed Śrī CAITANYA MAHĀPRABHU and systematically presented His teachings.

rajas — the material mode of passion, characterized by materialistic endeavor and the desire for sense gratification.

Rāma — a name of the Supreme Personality of Godhead meaning "the source of all pleasure."

Rāmacandra — an incarnation of the Lord who demonstrated the behavior of a perfect king.

Rāmānanda Rāya — a confidential associate of Lord CAITANYA MAHĀPRABHU.

Rāmānujācārya — an eleventh-century Vaiṣṇava spiritual master who began the theistic attack against ŚAṄKARĀCĀRYA's philosophy of monism.

rasa — the specific "taste" of a specific personal relationship with the Supreme Lord.

Ratha-yātrā — the annual festival of Lord JAGANNĀTHA, in which the Deity is carried on huge carts in a parade.

Ṛg Veda — one of the four original VEDAS, containing hymns to various demigods.

Rudra — *See:* ŚIVA.

Rūpa Gosvāmī — the chief of the six Vaiṣṇava spiritual masters who directly followed Lord CAITANYA MAHĀPRABHU and systematically presented His teachings.

S

śabda-brahma — the VEDAS , which are considered purely spiritual sound vibration.

sac-cid-ānanda — perfect spiritual existence, which is eternal (*sat*), fully knowledgeable (*cit*), and completely happy (*ānanda*).

Śalya — an uncle of the PĀṆḌAVA brothers who fought against them in the battle of KURUKṢETRA.

samādhi — fixed meditation on the personal form of the Lord.

Sāma Veda — one of the four original VEDAS, containing sacrificial prayers and their melodic and metrical settings.

Sanātana Gosvāmī — one of the six Vaiṣṇava spiritual masters who directly followed Śrī CAITANYA MAHĀPRABHU and systemically presented His teachings.

Śaṅkarācārya — the famous and influential ninth-century teacher of monism, a philosophy that maintains that there is no distinction between God and the living entity.

Sāṅkhya — the branch of philosophy that deals with analysis of material elements.

saṅkīrtana — congregational chanting of the holy names of God.
sannyāsa — See: ĀŚRAMAS.
Śārīraka-bhāṣya — the famous commentary on the VEDĀNTA-SŪTRA by ŚAṄKARĀCĀRYA, in which he presents his philosophy of monism.
Sārvabhauma Bhaṭṭācārya — a great scholar who was philosophically defeated by Lord CAITANYA MAHĀPRABHU and who then surrendered to the Lord as a disciple.
śāstras — authoritative scriptures. *See also:* VEDIC LITERATURE.
Satya-yuga — a Vedic historical age (first and best in a cycle of four progressively degenerating ages) characterized by a spiritually advanced human civilization. *See also:* KALI-YUGA.
Śikṣāṣṭaka — eight instructive prayers written by Lord CAITANYA MAHĀPRABHU.
Sindhu — the river forming the western boundary of India.
Śiva — the demigod who supervises the material quality of ignorance and the final destruction of the material cosmos.
śloka — a Sanskrit verse.
smṛti — literature supplementary to the four VEDAS, such as the PURĀṆAS, BHAGAVAD-GĪTĀ, and MAHĀBHĀRATA.
śraddhā — the faith necessary to hear submissively from a proper authority.
Śrī, Śrīla, Śrīmatī, Śrīpāda — titles. *See: specific names following title.*
Śrī-kṣetra — *See:* JAGANNĀTHA PURĪ.
Śrīmad-Bhāgavatam (Bhāgavata Purāṇa) — Vyāsadeva's "spotless PURĀṆA," which deals exclusively with pure devotional service to the Supreme Lord.
Śrīnivāsa Ācārya — a great Vaiṣṇava spiritual master and a direct follower of RŪPA, SANĀTANA, and JĪVA GOSVĀMĪS.
Śrīvāsa Ṭhākura — one of the principal associates of Lord CAITANYA MAHĀPRABHU.
śruti — the original four VEDAS.
Subhadrā — *See:* JAGANNĀTHA, BALADEVA, and SUBHADRĀ.
śūdra — *See:* VARṆAS.
Śukadeva Gosvāmī — the sage who spoke ŚRĪMAD-BHĀGAVATAM to King PARĪKṢIT just prior to the king's death.
Śvetāśvatara Upaniṣad — *See:* UPANIṢADS.

swami — one who has by spiritual strength become the master of his senses.

T

tamas — the material mode of ignorance, characterized by ignorance, lethargy, and madness.

tapasya — austerity; material inconvenience accepted in the pursuit of spiritual realization.

Teachings of Lord Caitanya — a summary study by His Divine Grace A. C. Bhaktivedanta Swami Prabhupāda of the book CAITANYA-CARITĀMṚTA.

Ṭhākura Bhaktivinoda — *See:* BHAKTIVINODA ṬHĀKURA.

U

Upaniṣads — the philosophical division of the VEDAS, meant for bringing the student closer to understanding the personal nature of the Absolute Truth.

V

Vaikuṇṭha — the eternal, spiritual world beyond the material cosmos.

Vaiṣṇava — a devotee of KṚṢṆA, or of any other form of the Supreme Personality of Godhead.

vaiśya — *See:* VARṆAS.

Vālmīki Muni — the author of the original *Rāmāyaṇa,* the epic of Lord RĀMACANDRA'S pastimes.

vānaprastha — *See:* ĀŚRAMAS.

varṇas — the four social-occupational divisions of Vedic society: *brāhmaṇas* (priests, teachers, and intellectuals), *kṣatriyas* (military and public administrators), *vaiśyas* (farmers and business people), and *śūdras* (laborers and craftsmen). *See also:* VARṆĀŚRAMA-DHARMA.

varṇa-saṅkara — lit. "of mixed caste"; children conceived irreligiously and without consideration of Vedic social and religious principles.

varṇāśrama-dharma — the ancient Vedic system of arranging society into four socio-occupational divisions (VARṆAS) and four spiritual divisions (ĀŚRAMAS) to promote social, economic, and political well-being and the spiritual advancement of all members of society.

Vāyu — the demigod in charge of air.

Vasudeva — the father of Lord KṚṢṆA.

Vāsudeva — a name of the Supreme Personality of Godhead as the Supreme Lord of all spiritual and material worlds.

Vedānta-sūtra (Vedānta) — VYĀSADEVA's summary of the theistic philosophy of the Vedic literature, written in the form of concise codes.

Vedas — the four scriptures, *Ṛg, Yajur,* SĀMA, and *Atharva,* and in a broader sense, including the UPANIṢADS and *Vedānta-sūtra.*

Vedic literature — the four VEDAS, the UPANIṢADS, VEDĀNTA-SŪTRA, PURĀṆAS, MAHĀBHĀRATA, other histories and supplements, and also more recent works written in pursuance of the Vedic conclusion.

Vikarṇa — a warrior who fought against the PĀṆḌAVAS in the battle of KURUKṢETRA.

Viṣṇu — a name of the Supreme Personality of Godhead as the creator and maintainer of the material universes.

Viṣṇu Purāṇa — *See:* PURĀṆAS.

Viśvanātha Cakravartī Ṭhākura — a Vaiṣṇava spiritual master and commentator on ŚRĪMAD-BHĀGAVATAM in the disciplic succession from Lord CAITANYA MAHĀPRABHU.

Viveka-cūḍāmaṇi — the best-known work of ŚAṄKARĀCĀRYA, in which he presents his philosophy of monism.

Vraja (Vrajabhūmi) — *See:* VṚNDĀVANA.

Vṛndāvana — Lord KṚṢṆA's most intimate and personal abode, where He engages in loving pastimes with His devotees.

Vyāsadeva — the original compiler of the VEDAS and PURĀṆAS, and author of the VEDĀNTA-SŪTRA and MAHĀBHĀRATA.

Vyāsa-pūjā — the appearance day of the spiritual master, on which he is honored as the representative of VYĀSADEVA and the direct representative of the Supreme Lord.

Y

Yamarāja — the demigod who is in charge of punishing the sinful after death, and who is also recognized as one of the chief authorities on devotional service to Lord KṚṢṆA.

Yaśodā — the foster-mother of Lord KṚṢṆA and the wife of NANDA MAHĀRĀJA.

yavana — a barbarian.

yoga — various processes of spiritual realization, all ultimately meant for attaining the Supreme.

yogī — one who is striving in one of the YOGA processes.

Yudhiṣṭhira — the eldest of the PĀṆḌAVA brothers; Lord KṚṢṆA established him as king after the Battle of KURUKṢETRA.

GUIDE TO SANSKRIT PRONUNCIATION

The system of transliteration used in this book conforms to a system that scholars have accepted to indicate the pronunciation of each sound in the Sanskrit language.

The short vowel **a** is pronounced like the **u** in b**u**t, long **ā** like the **a** in f**a**r. Short **i** is pronounced as in p**i**n, long **ī** as in p**i**que, short **u** as in p**u**ll, and long **ū** as in r**u**le. The vowel **ṛ** is pronounced like the **ri** in **ri**m, **e** like the **ey** in th**ey**, **o** like the **o** in g**o**, **ai** like the **ai** in **ai**sle, and **au** like the **ow** in h**ow**. The *anusvāra* (**ṁ**) is pronounced like the **n** in the French word *bo***n**, and *visarga* (**ḥ**) is pronounced as a final **h** sound. At the end of a couplet, **aḥ** is pronounced **aha**, and **iḥ** is pronounced **ihi**.

The guttural consonants—**k, kh, g, gh,** and **ṅ**—are pronounced from the throat in much the same manner as in English. **K** is pronounced as in **k**ite, **kh** as in Ec**kh**art, **g** as in **g**ive, **gh** as in di**g h**ard, and **ṅ** as in si**ng.**

The palatal consonants—**c, ch, j, jh,** and **ñ**—are pronounced with the tongue touching the firm ridge behind the teeth. **C** is pronounced as in **ch**air, **ch** as in staun**ch-h**eart, **j** as in **j**oy, **jh** as in he**dgeh**og, and **ñ** as in ca**ny**on.

The cerebral consonants—**ṭ, ṭh, ḍ, ḍh,** and **ṇ**—are pronounced with the tip of the tongue turned up and drawn back against the dome of the palate. **Ṭ** is pronounced as in **t**ub, **ṭh** as in ligh**t-h**eart, **ḍ** as in **d**ove, **ḍh** as in re**d-h**ot, and **ṇ** as in **n**ut. The dental consonants—**t, th, d, dh,** and **n**—are pronounced in the same manner as the cerebrals, but with the forepart of the tongue against the teeth.

The labial consonants—**p, ph, b, bh,** and **m**—are pronounced with the lips. **P** is pronounced as in **p**ine, **ph** as in u**ph**ill, **b** as in **b**ird, **bh** as in ru**b-h**ard, and **m** as in **m**other.

The semivowels—**y, r, l,** and **v**—are pronounced as in **y**es, **r**un, **l**ight, and **v**ine respectively. The sibilants—**ś, ṣ,** and **s**—are pronounced, respectively, as in the German word s*prechen* and the English words **sh**ine and **s**un. The letter **h** is pronounced as in **h**ome.

AN INTRODUCTION TO ISKCON AND THE DEVOTIONAL WAY OF LIFE

The International Society for Krishna Consciousness (ISKCON), popularly known as the Hare Kṛṣṇa movement, is a worldwide association of devotees of Kṛṣṇa, the Supreme Personality of Godhead. The same God is known by many names in the various scriptures of the world. In the Bible He is known as Jehovah ("the almighty one"), in the Koran as Allah ("the great one"), and in the *Bhagavad-gītā* as Kṛṣṇa, a Sanskrit name meaning "the all-attractive one."

The movement's main purpose is to promote the well-being of human society by teaching the science of God consciousness (Kṛṣṇa consciousness) according to the timeless Vedic scriptures of India. The most important of these have been translated and provided with learned commentary by ISKCON's founder and spiritual guide, His Divine Grace A. C. Bhaktivedanta Swami Prabhupāda, known to his followers as Śrīla Prabhupāda.

Five Thousand Years of Spiritual Wisdom

Scholars worldwide have acclaimed Śrīla Prabhupāda's translations of Vedic literature. Garry Gelade, a professor at Oxford University's Department of Philosophy, wrote of them: "These texts are to be treasured. No one of whatever faith or philosophical persuasion who reads these books with an open mind can fail to be moved and impressed." And Dr. Larry Shinn, Dean of the College of Arts and Sciences at Bucknell University, wrote, "Prabhupāda's personal piety gave him real authority. He exhibited complete command of the scriptures, an unusual depth of realization, and an outstanding personal example, because he actually lived what he taught."

The best known of the Vedic texts, the *Bhagavad-gītā* ("Song of

God"), is the philosophical basis for the Hare Kṛṣṇa movement. Dating back five thousand years, it is sacred to nearly a billion people today. This exalted work has been praised by scholars and leaders the world over. Mahatma Gandhi said, "When doubts haunt me, when disappointments stare me in the face and I see not one ray of hope, I turn to the *Bhagavad-gītā* and find a verse to comfort me." Ralph Waldo Emerson wrote, "It was the first of books; it was as if an empire spoke to us, nothing small or unworthy, but large, serene, consistent, the voice of an old intelligence which in another age and climate had pondered and thus disposed of the same questions which exercise us." And Henry David Thoreau praised the *Gītā* in this way: "In the morning I bathe my intellect in the stupendous and cos-mogonal philosophy of the *Bhagavad-gītā*."

As Dr. Shinn pointed out, Śrīla Prabhupāda's *Bhagavad-gītā* (titled *Bhagavad-gītā As It Is*) possesses unique authority not only because of his erudition but because he lived what he taught. Thus unlike the many other English translations of the *Gītā* that preceded his, which is replete with extensive commentary, Śrīla Prabhupāda's has sparked a spiritual revolution throughout the world.

Lord Kṛṣṇa teaches in the *Bhagavad-gītā* that we are not these temporary material bodies but are spirit souls, or conscious entities, and that we can find genuine peace and happiness only in spiritual devotion to God. The *Gītā* and other world scriptures recommend that people joyfully chant the holy name of God.

A Sixteenth-Century Incarnation of Kṛṣṇa

Kṛṣṇa incarnated again in the sixteenth century as Śrī Caitanya Mahāprabhu and popularized the chanting of God's names all over India. He constantly sang these names of God, as prescribed in the Vedic literature: Hare Kṛṣṇa, Hare Kṛṣṇa, Kṛṣṇa Kṛṣṇa, Hare Hare/ Hare Rāma, Hare Rāma, Rāma Rāma, Hare Hare. The Hare Kṛṣṇa mantra is a transcendental sound vibration. It purifies the mind and awakens the dormant love of God in the hearts of all living beings. Lord Caitanya requested His followers to spread this chanting to every town and village of the world.

Anyone can take part in chanting Hare Kṛṣṇa and learn the science of spiritual devotion by studying *Bhagavad-gītā As It Is*. This easy and practical process of self-realization will awaken our natural state of peace and happiness.

The Hare Kṛṣṇa Way of Life

The devotees seen dancing and chanting in the streets, dressed in traditional Indian robes, are for the most part full-time students of the Hare Kṛṣṇa movement. The vast majority of followers, however, live and work in the general community, practicing Kṛṣṇa consciousness in their homes and attending temples on a regular basis.

There are about 15,000 full-time devotees throughout the world and 500,000 congregational members outside of India. The movement is presently comprised of 350 temples, 40 rural communities, 26 schools, and 75 restaurants in 85 countries. The basic principle of the Hare Kṛṣṇa way of life is "simple living and high thinking." Devotees of Kṛṣṇa are encouraged to use their time, energy, talents, and resources in devotional service to God, and not to hanker for selfish ambitions or pleasures, which result in frustration and anxiety.

To cultivate their inherent spiritual qualities of compassion, truthfulness, cleanliness, and austerity, devotees follow four regulative principles, which also help them control the insatiable urges of the mind and senses. These principles are:

1. No eating of meat, fish, or eggs.
2. No gambling.
3. No sex other than for procreation within marriage.
4. No intoxicants, including all recreational drugs, alcohol, tobacco, tea, and coffee.

According to the *Bhagavad-gītā* and other Vedic literature, indulgence in the above activities disrupts our physical, mental, and spiritual well-being and increases anxiety and conflict in society

A Philosophy for Everyone

The philosophy of the Hare Kṛṣṇa movement (a monotheistic tradition) is summarized in the following eight points:

1. By sincerely cultivating the authentic spiritual science presented in the *Bhagavad-gītā* and other Vedic scriptures, we can be-

come free from anxiety and achieve a state of pure, unending, blissful consciousness.

2. Each of us is not the material body but an eternal spirit soul, part and parcel of God (Kṛṣṇa). As such, we are all the eternal servants of Kṛṣṇa and are interrelated through Him, our common father.

3. Kṛṣṇa is the eternal, all-knowing, omnipresent, all-powerful, and all-attractive Personality of Godhead. He is the seed-giving father of all living beings and the sustaining energy of the universe. He is the source of all incarnations of God, including Lord Buddha and Lord Jesus Christ.

4. The *Vedas* are the oldest scriptures in the world. The essence of the *Vedas* is found in the *Bhagavad-gītā,* a literal record of Kṛṣṇa's words spoken five thousands years ago in India. The goal of Vedic knowledge—and of all religions—is to achieve love of God.

5. We can perfectly understand the knowledge of self-realization through the instructions of a genuine spiritual master—one who is free from selfish motives, who teaches the science of God explained in the *Bhagavad-gītā,* and whose mind is firmly fixed in meditation on Kṛṣṇa.

6. All that we eat should first be offered to Lord Kṛṣṇa with a prayer. In this way Kṛṣṇa accepts the offering and blesses it for our purification.

7. Rather than living in a self-centered way, we should act for the pleasure of Lord Kṛṣṇa. This is known as *bhakti-yoga,* the science of devotional service.

8. The most effective means for achieving God consciousness in this Age of Kali, or quarrel, is to chant the holy names of the Lord: Hare Kṛṣṇa, Hare Kṛṣṇa, Kṛṣṇa Kṛṣṇa, Hare Hare/ Hare Rāma, Hare Rāma, Rāma Rāma, Hare Hare.

Kṛṣṇa Consciousness at Home

by Mahātmā Dāsa

In *The Science of Self-Realization* Śrīla Prabhupāda makes it clear how important it is for everyone to practice Kṛṣṇa consciousness, devotional service to Lord Kṛṣṇa. Of course, living in the association of Kṛṣṇa's devotees in a temple or ashram makes it easier to practice devotional service. But if you're determined, you can follow at home the teachings of Kṛṣṇa consciousness and thus convert your home into a temple.

Spiritual life, like material life, means practical activity. The difference is that whereas we perform material activities for the benefit of ourselves or those we consider ours, we perform spiritual activities for the benefit of Lord Kṛṣṇa, under the guidance of the scriptures and the spiritual master. The key is to accept the guidance of the scripture and the guru. Kṛṣṇa declares in the *Bhagavad-gītā* that a person can achieve neither happiness nor the supreme destination of life—going back to Godhead, back to Lord Kṛṣṇa—if he or she does not follow the injunctions of the scriptures. And *how* to follow the scriptural rules by engaging in practical service to the Lord—that is explained by a bona fide spiritual master. Without following the instructions of a spiritual master who is in an authorized chain of disciplic succession coming from Kṛṣṇa Himself, we cannot make spiritual progress. The practices outlined here are the timeless practices of *bhakti-yoga* as given by the foremost spiritual master and exponent of Kṛṣṇa consciousness in our time, His Divine Grace A. C. Bhaktivedanta Swami Prabhupāda, founder-*ācārya* of the International Society for Krishna Consciousness (ISKCON).

The purpose of spiritual knowledge is to bring us closer to God, or Kṛṣṇa. Kṛṣṇa says in the *Bhagavad-gītā* (18.55), *bhaktyā māṁ abhijānāti:* "I can be known only by devotional service." Knowledge guides us in proper action. Spiritual knowledge directs us to satisfy the desires of Kṛṣṇa through practical engagements in His loving service. Without practical application, theoretical knowledge is of little value.

Spiritual knowledge is meant to direct us in all aspects of life. We should endeavor, therefore, to organize our lives in such a way as to follow Kṛṣṇa's teachings as far as possible. We should try to do our best, to do more than is simply convenient. Then it will be possible for us to rise to the transcendental plane of Kṛṣṇa consciousness, even while living far from a temple.

Chanting the Hare Kṛṣṇa Mantra

The first principle in devotional service is to chant the Hare Kṛṣṇa *mahā-mantra* (*mahā* means "great"; *mantra* means "sound that liberates the mind from ignorance"):

Hare Kṛṣṇa, Hare Kṛṣṇa, Kṛṣṇa Kṛṣṇa, Hare Hare
Hare Rāma, Hare Rāma, Rāma Rāma, Hare Hare

You should chant these holy names of the Lord as much as possible—anywhere and at any time—but it is also very helpful to set a specific time of the day to regularly chant. Early morning hours are ideal.

The chanting can be done in two ways: singing the mantra, called *kīrtana* (usually done in a group), and saying the mantra to oneself, called *japa* (which literally means "to speak softly"). Concentrate on hearing the sound of the holy names. As you chant, pronounce the names clearly and distinctly, addressing Kṛṣṇa in a prayerful mood. When your mind wanders, bring it back to the sound of the Lord's names. Chanting is a prayer to Kṛṣṇa that means "O energy of the Lord [Hare], O all-attractive Lord [Kṛṣṇa], O Supreme Enjoyer [Rāma], please engage me in Your service." The more attentively and sincerely you chant these names of God, the more spiritual progress you will make. Since God is all-powerful and all-merciful, He has kindly made it very easy for us to chant His names, and He has also invested all His powers in them. Therefore the names of God and God Himself are identical. This means that when we chant the holy names of Kṛṣṇa and Rāma we are directly associating with God and being purified. Therefore we should always try to chant with devotion and reverence. The Vedic literature states that Lord Kṛṣṇa is personally dancing on your tongue when you chant His holy name.

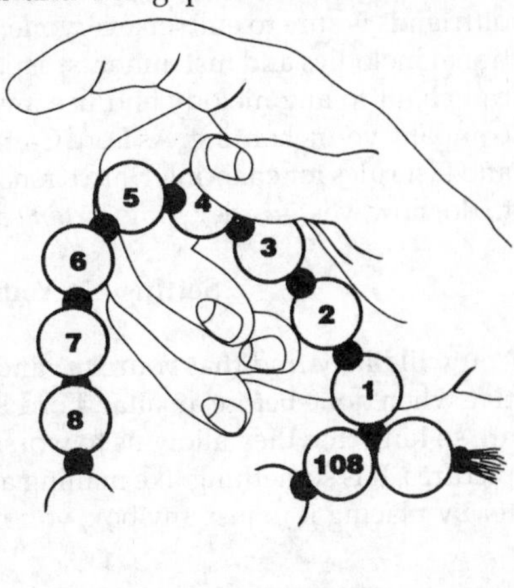

When you chant alone, it is best to chant on *japa* beads (provided in the Mantra Meditation Kit, which is available in the advertisement section at the end of this book). This not only helps you fix your attention on the holy name, but it also helps you count the number of times you chant the mantra daily. Each strand of *japa* beads contains 108 small beads and one large bead, the head bead. Begin on a bead next to the head bead and gently roll it between the thumb and middle finger of your right hand as you chant the full Hare Kṛṣṇa mantra. Then move to the next bead and repeat the process. In this way, chant on each of the 108 beads until you reach the head bead again. This is one round of *japa*. Then, without chanting on the head bead, reverse the beads and start your second round on the last bead you chanted on.

Initiated devotees vow before the spiritual master to chant at least sixteen rounds of the Hare Kṛṣṇa mantra daily. But even if you can chant only one round a day, the principle is that once you commit yourself to chanting that round, you should try to complete it every day without fail. When you feel you can chant more, then increase the minimum number of rounds you chant each day—but don't fall below that number. You can chant more than your fixed number, but you should maintain a set minimum each day. (Please note that the beads are sacred and therefore should never touch the ground or be put in an unclean place. To keep your beads clean, it's best to carry them in a special bead bag, such as the one that comes as part of the Mantra Meditation Kit.)

Aside from chanting *japa,* you can also sing the Lord's holy names in *kīrtana*. While you can perform *kīrtana* individually, it is generally performed with others. A melodious *kīrtana* with family or friends is sure to enliven everyone. ISKCON devotees use traditional melodies and instruments, especially in the temple, but you can chant to any melody and use any musical instruments to accompany your chanting. As Lord Caitanya said, "There are no hard and fast rules for chanting Hare Kṛṣṇa." One thing you might want to do, however, is order some *kīrtana* and *japa* recordings (see ads).

Setting Up Your Altar

You will likely find that your *japa* and *kīrtana* are especially effective when done before an altar. Lord Kṛṣṇa and His pure devotees are so kind that they allow us to worship them even through their pictures. It is something like mailing a letter: You cannot mail a letter by placing it in just any box; you must use the mailbox autho-

rized by the government. Similarly, we cannot imagine a picture of God and worship that, but we can worship the authorized picture of God, and Kṛṣṇa accepts our worship through that picture.

Setting up an altar at home means receiving the Lord and His pure devotees as your most honored guests. Where should you set up the altar? Well, how would you seat a guest? An ideal place would be clean, well lit, and free from drafts and household disturbances. Your guest, of course, would need a comfortable chair, but for the picture of Kṛṣṇa's form a wall shelf, a mantelpiece, a corner table, or the top shelf of a bookcase will do. You wouldn't seat a guest in your home and then ignore him; you'd provide a place for yourself to sit, too, where you could comfortably face him and enjoy his company. So don't make your altar inaccessible.

What do you need for an altar? Here are the essentials:

1. A picture of Śrīla Prabhupāda.
2. A picture of Lord Caitanya and His associates.
3. A picture of Śrī Śrī Rādhā-Kṛṣṇa.

In addition, you may want an altar cloth, water cups (one for each picture), candles with holders, a special plate for offering food, a small bell, incense, an incense holder, and fresh flowers, which you may offer in vases or simply place before each picture. If you're interested in more elaborate Deity worship, ask any of the ISKCON devotees or get in touch with the BBT (see the toll-free number and website address at the end of this book).

The first person we worship on the altar is the spiritual master.

The spiritual master is not God. Only God is God. But because the spiritual master is His dearmost servant, God has empowered him, and therefore he deserves the same respect as that given to God. He links the disciple with God and teaches him the process of *bhakti-yoga.* He is God's ambassador to the material world. When a president sends an ambassador to a foreign country, the ambassador receives the same respect as that accorded the president, and the ambassador's words are as authoritative as the president's. Similarly, we should respect the spiritual master as we would God, and revere his words as we would His.

There are two main kinds of gurus: the instructing guru and the initiating guru. Everyone who takes up the process of *bhakti-yoga* as a result of coming in contact with ISKCON owes an immense debt of gratitude to Śrīla Prabhupāda. Before Śrīla Prabhupāda left India in 1965 to spread Kṛṣṇa consciousness abroad, almost no one outside India knew anything about the practice of pure devotional service to Lord Kṛṣṇa. Therefore, everyone who has learned of the process through his books, his *Back to Godhead* magazine, his recordings, or contact with his followers should offer respect to Śrīla Prabhupāda. As the founder and spiritual guide of the International Society for Krishna Consciousness, he is the instructing guru of us all.

As you progress in *bhakti-yoga,* you may eventually want to accept initiation. Before he left this world in 1977, Śrīla Prabhupāda encouraged his qualified disciples to carry on his work by initiating disciples of their own in accordance with his instructions. At present there are many spiritual masters in ISKCON. To learn how you can get spiritual guidance from them, ask a devotee at your nearby temple, or write to one of the ISKCON centers listed at the end of this book.

The second picture on your altar should be one of the *pañca-tattva,* Lord Caitanya and His four leading associates. Lord Caitanya is the incarnation of God for this age. He is Kṛṣṇa Himself, descended in the form of His own devotee to teach us how to surrender to Him, specifically by chanting His holy names and performing other activities of *bhakti-yoga.* Lord Caitanya is the most merciful incarnation, for He makes it easy for anyone to attain love of God through the chanting of the Hare Kṛṣṇa mantra.

And of course your altar should have a picture of the Supreme

Personality of Godhead, Lord Śrī Kṛṣṇa, with His eternal consort, Śrīmatī Rādhārāṇī. Śrīmatī Rādhārāṇī is Kṛṣṇa's spiritual potency. She is devotional service personified, and devotees always take shelter of Her to learn how to serve Kṛṣṇa.

You can arrange the pictures in a triangle, with the picture of Śrīla Prabhupāda on the left, the picture of Lord Caitanya and His associates on the right, and the picture of Rādhā and Kṛṣṇa, which, if possible, should be slightly larger than the others, on a small raised platform behind and in the center. Or you can hang the picture of Rādhā and Kṛṣṇa on the wall above.

Carefully clean the altar each morning. Cleanliness is essential in Deity worship. Remember, you wouldn't neglect to clean the room of an important guest, and when you establish an altar you invite Kṛṣṇa and His pure devotees to reside as the most exalted guests in your home. If you have water cups, rinse them out and fill them with fresh water daily. Then place them conveniently close to the pictures. You should remove flowers in vases as soon as they're slightly wilted, or daily if you've offered them at the base of the pictures. You should offer fresh incense at least once a day, and, if possible, light candles and place them near the pictures when you're chanting before the altar.

Please try the things we've suggested so far. It's very simple, really: If you try to love God, you'll gradually realize how much He loves you. That's the essence of *bhakti-yoga*.

Prasādam: How to Eat Spiritually

By His immense transcendental energies, Kṛṣṇa can actually convert matter into spirit. If we place an iron rod in a fire, before long the rod becomes red hot and acts just like fire. In the same way, food prepared for and offered to Kṛṣṇa with love and devotion becomes completely spiritualized. Such food is called *kṛṣṇa-prasādam,* which means "the mercy of Lord Kṛṣṇa."

Eating *prasādam* is a fundamental practice of *bhakti-yoga*. In other forms of yoga one must artificially repress the senses, but the *bhakti-yogī* can engage his or her senses in a variety of pleasing spiritual activities, such as tasting delicious food offered to Lord Kṛṣṇa. In this way the senses gradually become spiritualized and bring the devotee more and more transcendental pleasure by being engaged in devotional service. Such spiritual pleasure far surpasses any material experience.

Lord Caitanya said of *prasādam,* "Everyone has tasted these foods before. However, now that they have been prepared for Kṛṣṇa and offered to Him with devotion, these foods have acquired extraordinary tastes and uncommon fragrances. Just taste them and see the difference in the ex-perience! Apart from the taste, even the fragrance pleases the mind and makes one forget any other fragrance. Therefore, it should be understood that the spiritual nectar of Kṛṣṇa's lips must have touched these ordinary foods and imparted to them all their transcendental qualities."

Eating only food offered to Kṛṣṇa is the perfection of vegetarianism. In itself, being a vegetarian is not enough; after all, even pigeons and monkeys are vegetarians. But when we go beyond vegetarianism to a diet of *prasādam,* our eating becomes helpful in achieving the goal of human life—reawakening the soul's original relationship with God. In the *Bhagavad-gītā* Lord Kṛṣṇa says that unless one eats only food that has been offered to him in sacrifice, one will suffer the reactions of karma.

How to Prepare and Offer Prasādam

As you walk down the supermarket aisles selecting the foods you will offer to Kṛṣṇa, you need to know what is offerable and what is not. In the *Bhagavad-gītā,* Lord Kṛṣṇa states, "If one offers Me with love and devotion a leaf, a Íower, a fruit, or water, I will accept it." From this verse it is understood that we can offer Kṛṣṇa foods prepared from milk products, vegetables, fruits, nuts, and grains. (See the ads for some of the many Hare Kṛṣṇa cookbooks.) Meat, fish, and eggs are not offerable. And a few vegetarian items are also forbidden—garlic and onions, for example, which are in the mode of darkness. (Hing, or asafetida, is a tasty substitute for them in cooking and is available at most Indian groceries and ISKCON temple stores.) Nor can you offer to Kṛṣṇa coffee or tea that contain caffeine. If you like these beverages, purchase caffeine-free coffee and herbal teas.

While shopping, be aware that you may find meat, fish, and egg products mixed with other foods; so be sure to read labels carefully. For instance, some brands of yogurt and sour cream contain gelatin, a substance made from the horns, hooves, and bones of slaughtered animals. Also, make sure the cheese you buy contains no animal rennet, an enzyme from the stomach tissues of slaughtered calves. Most hard cheese sold in America contains this rennet, so be careful about any cheese you can't verify as being free of animal rennet.

Also avoid foods cooked by nondevotees. According to the subtle laws of nature, the cook acts upon the food not only physically but mentally as well. Food thus becomes an agent for subtle influences on your consciousness. The principle is the same as that at work with a painting: a painting is not simply a collection of strokes on a canvas but an expression of the artist's state of mind, which affects the viewer. So if you eat food cooked by nondevotees—employees working in a factory, for example—then you're sure to absorb a dose of materialism and karma. So as far as possible use only fresh, natural ingredients.

In preparing food, cleanliness is the most important principle. Nothing impure should be offered to God; so keep your kitchen very clean. Always wash your hands thoroughly before entering the kitchen. While preparing food, do not taste it, for you are cooking the meal not for yourself but for the pleasure of Kṛṣṇa. Arrange portions of the food on dinnerware kept especially for this purpose; no one but the Lord should eat from these dishes. The easiest way to offer food is simply to pray, "My dear Lord Kṛṣṇa, please accept this food," and to chant each of the following prayers three times while ringing a bell (see the Sanskrit Pronunciation Guide on page 338):

1. Prayer to Śrīla Prabhupāda:

nama oṁ viṣṇu-pādāya kṛṣṇa-preṣṭhāya bhū-tale
śrīmate bhaktivedānta-svāminn iti nāmine

namas te sārasvate deve gaura-vāṇī-pracāriṇe
nirviśeṣa-śūnyavādi-pāścātya-deśa-tāriṇe

"I offer my respectful obeisances unto His Divine Grace A. C. Bhaktivedanta Swami Prabhupāda, who is very dear to Lord Kṛṣṇa on this earth, having taken shelter at His lotus feet. Our respectful obeisances are unto you, O spiritual master, servant of

Bhaktisiddhānta Sarasvatī Gosvāmī. You are kindly preaching the message of Lord Caitanyadeva and delivering the Western countries, which are filled with impersonalism and voidism."

2. Prayer to Lord Caitanya:

namo mahā-vadānyāya kṛṣṇa-prema-pradāya te
kṛṣṇāya kṛṣṇa-caitanya-nāmne gaura-tviṣe namaḥ

"O most munificent incarnation! You are Kṛṣṇa Himself appearing as Śrī Kṛṣṇa Caitanya Mahāprabhu. You have assumed the golden color of Śrīmatī Rādhārāṇī, and You are widely distributing pure love of Kṛṣṇa. We offer our respectful obeisances unto You."

3. Prayer to Lord Kṛṣṇa:

namo brahmaṇya-devāya go-brāhmaṇa-hitāya ca
jagad-dhitāya kṛṣṇāya govindāya namo namaḥ

"I offer my respectful obeisances unto Lord Kṛṣṇa, who is the worshipable Deity for all *brāhmaṇas,* the well-wisher of the cows and the *brāhmaṇas,* and the benefactor of the whole world. I offer my repeated obeisances to the Personality of Godhead, known as Kṛṣṇa and Govinda."

Remember that the real purpose of preparing and offering food to the Lord is to show your devotion and gratitude to Him. Kṛṣṇa accepts your devotion, not the physical offering itself. God is complete in Himself—He doesn't need anything—but out of His immense kindness He allows us to offer food to Him so that we can develop our love for Him.

After offering the food to the Lord, wait at least five minutes for Him to partake of the preparations. Then you should transfer the food from the special dinnerware and wash the dishes and utensils you used for the offering. Now you and any guests may eat the *prasādam.* While you eat, try to appreciate the spiritual value of the food. Remember that because Kṛṣṇa has accepted it, it is nondifferent from Him, and therefore by eating it you will become purified.

Everything you offer on your altar becomes *prasādam,* the mercy of the Lord. Flowers, incense, the water, the food—everything you offer for the Lord's pleasure becomes spiritualized. The Lord enters into the offerings, and thus the remnants are nondifferent from Him. So you should not only deeply respect the things you've offered, but you should distribute them to others as well. Distribution of *prasādam* is an essential part of Deity worship.

Everyday Life: The Four Regulative Principles

Anyone serious about progressing in Kṛṣṇa consciousness must try to avoid the following four sinful activities:

1. Eating meat, fish, or eggs. These foods are saturated with the modes of passion and ignorance and therefore cannot be offered to the Lord. A person who eats these foods participates in a conspiracy of violence against helpless animals and thus stops his spiritual progress dead in its tracks.
2. Gambling. Gambling invariably puts one into anxiety and fuels greed, envy, and anger.
3. The use of intoxicants. Drugs, alcohol, and tobacco, as well as any drinks or foods containing caffeine, cloud the mind, overstimulate the senses, and make it impossible to understand or follow the principles of *bhakti-yoga*.
4. Illicit sex. This is sex outside of marriage or sex in marriage for any purpose other than procreation. Sex for pleasure compels one to identify with the body and takes one far from Kṛṣṇa consciousness. The scriptures teach that sex is the most powerful force binding us to the material world. Anyone serious about advancing in Kṛṣṇa consciousness should minimize sex or eliminate it entirely.

Engagement in Practical Devotional Service

Everyone must do some kind of work, but if you work only for yourself you must accept the karmic reactions of that work. As Lord Kṛṣṇa says in the *Bhagavad-gītā* (3.9), "Work done as a sacrifice for Viṣṇu [Kṛṣṇa] has to be performed. Otherwise work binds one to the material world."

You needn't change your occupation, except if you're now engaged in a sinful job such as working as a butcher or bartender. If you're a writer, write for Kṛṣṇa; if you're an artist, create for Kṛṣṇa; if you're a secretary, type for Kṛṣṇa. You may also directly help the temple in your spare time, and you should sacrifice some of the fruits of your work by contributing a portion of your earnings to help maintain the temple and propagate Kṛṣṇa consciousness. Some devotees living outside the temple buy Hare Kṛṣṇa literature and distribute it to their friends and associates, or they engage in a variety of services at the temple. There is also a wide network of devotees who gather in each other's homes for chanting, worship, and study. Write to your local temple or the Society's secretary to learn of any such programs near you.

The International Society for Krishna Consciousness

CENTERS AROUND THE WORLD

Founder-*Ācārya:* His Divine Grace A. C. Bhaktivedanta Swami Prabhupāda

CANADA

Brampton-Mississauga, Ontario — 6 George St. South, 2nd floor, L6Y 1P3/ Tel. (416) 648-3312/ iskconbrampton@gmail.com

Calgary, Alberta — 313 Fourth St. N.E., T2E 3S3/ Tel. (403) 265-3302/ vamanstones@shaw.ca

Edmonton, Alberta — 9353 35th Ave. NW, T6E 5R5/ Tel. (780) 439-9999/ edmonton@harekrishnatemple.com

Montreal, Quebec — 1626 Pie IX Boulevard, H1V 2C5/ Tel. & fax: (514) 521-1301/ iskconmontreal@gmail.com

◆ **Ottawa, Ontario** — 212 Somerset St. E., K1N 6V4/ Tel. (613) 565-6544/ radha_damodara@yahoo.com

Regina, Saskatchewan — 1279 Retallack St., S4T 2H8/ Tel. (306) 525-0002 Or -6461/ jagadishadas@yahoo.com

Scarborough, Ontario — 3500 McNicoll Avenue, Unit #3, M1V 4C7/ Tel. (416) 300 7101/ iskconscarborough@hotmail.com

◆ **Toronto, Ontario** — 243 Avenue Rd., M5R 2J6/ Tel. (416) 922-5415/ toronto@iskcon.net

◆ **Vancouver, B.C.** — 5462 S.E. Marine Dr., Burnaby V5J 3G8/ Tel. (604) 433-9728/ akrura@krishna.com/ Govinda's Bookstore & Cafe: (604) 433-7100 or (888) 433-8722

RURAL COMMUNITY

Ashcroft, B.C. — Saranagati Dhama, Venables Valley (mail: P.O. Box 99, V0K 1A0)/ info@saranagati.ca

U.S.A.

Atlanta, Georgia — 1287 South Ponce de Leon Ave., N.E., 30306/ Tel. & fax: (404) 377-8680/ admin@atlantaharekrishnas.com

Austin, Texas — 10700 Jonwood Way, 78753/ Tel. (512) 835-2121/ sda@backtohome.com

Baltimore, Maryland — 200 Bloomsbury Ave., Catonsville, 21228/ Tel. (410) 744-1624/ contact@iskconbaltimore.org

Berkeley, California — 2334 Stuart Street, 94705/ Tel. (510) 540-9215/ info@iskconberkeley.net

Boise, Idaho — 1615 Martha St., 83706/ Tel. (208) 344-4274/ boise_temple@yahoo.com

Boston, Massachusetts — 72 Commonwealth Ave., 02116/ Tel. (617) 247-8611/ info@iskconboston.org

◆ **Chicago, Illinois** — 1716 W. Lunt Ave., 60626/ Tel. (773) 973-0900/ chicagoiskcon@yahoo.com

Columbus, Ohio — 379 W. Eighth Ave., 43201/ Tel. (614) 421-1661/ premvilasdas.rns@gmail.com

◆ **Dallas, Texas** — 5430 Gurley Ave., 75223/ Tel. (214) 827-6330/ info@radhakalachandji.com

◆ **Denver, Colorado** — 1400 Cherry St., 80220/ Tel. (303) 333-5461/ info@krishnadenver.com

Detroit, Michigan — 383 Lenox Ave., 48215/ Tel. (313) 824-6000/ gaurangi108@hotmail.com

Gainesville, Florida — 214 N.W. 14th St., 32603/ Tel. (352) 336-4183/ kalakantha.acbsp@pamho.net

Hartford, Connecticut — 1683 Main St., E. Hartford, 06108/ Tel. & fax: (860) 289-7252/ pyari108@gmail.com

Hillsboro, Oregon — 612 N 1st Ave. 97124 / Tel.: (503) 567-7363/ info@iskconportland.com

◆ **Honolulu, Hawaii** — 51 Coelho Way, 96817/ Tel. (808) 595-4913/ hawaii.iskcon@gmail.com

Houston, Texas — 1320 W. 34th St., 77018/ Tel. (713) 686-4482/ management@iskconhouston.org

Kansas City, Missouri — Rupanuga Vedic College, 5201 Paseo Blvd., 64110/ Tel. (816) 924-5640/ rvc@rvc.edu

Laguna Beach, California — 285 Legion St., 92651/ Tel. (949) 494-7029/ info@lagunatemple.com

Las Vegas, Nevada — Govinda's Center of Vedic India, 7181 Dean Martin Dr., 89118/ Tel. (702) 434-8332/ info@govindascenter.com

◆ **Los Angeles, California** — 3764 Watseka Ave., 90034/ Tel. (310) 836-2676/ membership@harekrishnala.com

◆ **Miami, Florida** — 3220 Virginia St., 33133 (mail: 3109 Grand Ave., #491, Coconut Grove, FL 33133)/ Tel. (305) 442-7218/ devotionalservice@iskcon-miami.org

Mountain View, California — 1965 Latham St., 94040/ Tel. (650) 336 7993 / isvtemple108@gmail.com

New Orleans, Louisiana — 2936 Esplanade Ave., 70119/ Tel. (504) 304-0032 (office) or (504) 638-1944 (temple)/ gopal211@aol.com
New York, New York — 305 Schermerhorn St., Brooklyn, 11217/ Tel. (718) 855-6714/ ramabhadra@aol.com
Orlando, Florida — 2651 Rouse Rd., 32817/ Tel. (407) 257-3865/ info@iskconorlando.com
Philadelphia, Pennsylvania — 41 West Allens Lane, 19119/Tel. (215) 247-4600/ info@iskconphiladelphia.com
Philadelphia, Pennsylvania — 1408 South St., 19146/ Tel. (215) 985-9303/ govindasvegetarian@gmail.com
Phoenix, Arizona — 100 S. Weber Dr., Chandler, 85226/ Tel. (480) 705-4900/ premadhatridd@gmail.com
◆ **St. Louis, Missouri** — 3926 Lindell Blvd., 63108/ Tel. (314) 535-8085 or 255-2207/ root@iskconstlouis.org
Salt Lake City, Utah — 965 E. 3370 South, 84106/ Tel. (801) 487-4005/ utahkrishnas@gmail.com
San Antonio, Texas — 6538 Thunderbird Dr., 78240 / Tel. (210) 420-1182/ ashram5monks@gmail.com
San Diego, California — 1030 Grand Ave., Pacific Beach, 92109/ Tel. (858) 483-2500/ krishna.sandiego@gmail.com
Seattle, Washington — 1420 228th Ave. S.E., Sammamish, 98075/ Tel. (425) 246-8436/ info@vedicculturalcenter.org
◆ **Spanish Fork, Utah** — Krishna Temple Project & KHQN Radio, 8628 S. State Road, 84660/ Tel. (801) 798-3559/ utahkrishnas@gmail.com
Tallahassee, Florida — 4601 Crawfordville Rd., 32305/ Tel. 850-727-5785/ tallahassee.iskcon@gmail.com
Towaco, New Jersey — 100 Jacksonville Rd. (mail: P.O. Box 109), 07082/ Tel. & fax: (973) 299-0970/ madhupati.jas@pamho.net
◆**Tucson, Arizona** — 711 E. Blacklidge Dr., 85719/ Tel. (520) 792-0630/ sandaminidd@cs.com
Washington, D.C. — 10310 Oaklyn Dr., Potomac, Maryland 20854/ Tel. (301) 299-2100/ info@iskconofdc.org

RURAL COMMUNITIES

Alachua, Florida (New Raman Reti) — 17306 N.W. 112th Blvd., 32615 (mail: P.O. Box 819, 32616)/ Tel. (386) 462-2017/ alachuatemple@gmail.com
Carriere, Mississippi (New Talavan) — 31492 Anner Road, 39426/ Tel. (601) 749-9460 or 799-1354/ talavan@hughes.net
Gurabo, Puerto Rico (New Govardhana Hill) — Carr. 181, Km. 16.3, Bo. Santa Rita, Gurabo (mail: HC-01, Box 8440, Gurabo, PR 00778)/ Tel. & fax: (787) 767-3530 or 737-1722/ manoratha@gmail.com
Hillsborough, North Carolina (New Goloka) — 1032 Dimmocks Mill Rd., 27278/ Tel. (919) 732-6492/ bkgoswami@earthlink.net
◆ **Moundsville, West Virginia (New Vrindaban)** — 3759 McCrearys Ridge Rd., 26041/ Tel. (304) 843-1600 (Guesthouse extension: 111)/ mail@newvrindaban.com
Mulberry, Tennessee (Murari-sevaka) — 532 Murari Lane, 37359 Tel. (931) 759-6888/ murari_sevaka@yahoo.com
Port Royal, Pennsylvania (Gita Nagari) — 534 Gita Nagari Rd., 17082/ Tel. (717) 527-4101/ dhruva.bts@pamho.net
Sandy Ridge, North Carolina (Prabhupada Village) — 1283 Prabhupada Rd., 27046/ Tel. (336) 593-2322/ prabhupadavillage@gmail.com

ADDITIONAL RESTAURANTS

Hato Rey, Puerto Rico — Tamal Krishna's Veggie Garden, 131 Eleanor Roosevelt, 00918/ Tel. (787) 754-6959/ tkveggiegarden@aol.com

UNITED KINGDOM AND IRELAND

Belfast, Northern Ireland — Brooklands, 140 Upper Dunmurray Lane, BT17 OHE/ Tel. +44 (028) 9062 0530/ hk.temple108@gmail.com
Birmingham, England — 84 Stanmore Rd., Edgbaston B16 9TB/ Tel. +44 (121) 420 4999/ iskconbirmingham@gmail.com
Cardiff, Wales — The Soul Centre, 116 Cowbridge Rd., Canton/ Tel. +44 (29) 2039 0391/ the.soul.centre@pamho.net
Coventry, England — Kingfield Rd., Coventry (mail: 19 Gloucester St., Coventry CV1 3BZ)/ Tel. +44 (24) 7655 2822 or 5420/ haridas.kds@pamho.net
Dublin, Ireland — 83 Middle Abbey St., Dublin 1/ Tel. +353 (1) 661 5095/ dublin@krishna.ie; Govinda's: info@govindas.ie
Leicester, England — 31 Granby Street, LE1 6EP/ Tel. +44 (0) 7597 786 676/ pradyumna.jas@pamho.net
Lesmahagow, Scotland — Karuna Bhavan, Bankhouse Rd., Lesmahagow, Lanarkshire, ML11 0ES/ Tel. +44 (1555) 894790/ karunabhavan@aol.com
◆ **London, England (city)** — 10 Soho St., W1D

3DL/ Tel. +44 (20) 7437-3662; residential /pujaris, 7439-3606; shop, 7287-0269; Govinda's Restaurant, 7437-4928/ london@pamho.net

◆ **London, England (country)** — Bhaktivedanta Manor, Dharam Marg, Hilfield Lane, Watford, Herts, WD25 8EZ/ Tel. +44 (1923) 851000/ info@krishnatemple.com; (for accommodations:) bmguesthouse@krishna.com

London, England (south) — 42 Enmore Road, South Norwood, SE25 5NG/ Tel. +44 7988857530/ krishnaprema89@hotmail.com

London, England (Kings Cross) — 102 Caledonian Rd., Kings Cross, Islington, N1 9DN/ Tel. +44 (20) 7168 5732/ foodforalluk@aol.com

Manchester, England — 20 Mayfield Rd., Whalley Range, M16 8FT/ Tel. +44 (161) 226-4416/ contact@iskconmanchester.com

Newcastle-upon-Tyne, England — 304 Westgate Rd., NE4 6AR/ Tel. +44 (191) 272 1911

◆ **Swansea, Wales** — Govinda's, 8 Craddock St., SA1 3EN/ Tel. +44 (1792) 468469/ info@iskconwales.org.uk; restaurant: info@govindas.org.uk

RURAL COMMUNITIES

London, England — (contact Bhaktivedanta Manor)

Upper Lough Erne, Northern Ireland — Govindadwipa Dhama, Inisrath Island, Derrylin, Co. Fermanagh, BT92 9GN/ Tel. +44 (28) 6772 1512/ govindadwipa@pamho.net

ADDITIONAL RESTAURANTS

Dublin, Ireland — Govinda's, 4 Aungier St., Dublin 2/ Tel. +353 (1) 475 0309/ info@govindas.ie

Nottingham, England — Govinda's Nottingham, 7–9 Thurland Street, NG1 3DR/ Tel. +44 115 985 9639/ govindasnottingham@gmail.com

AUSTRALASIA

AUSTRALIA

Adelaide — 25 Le Hunte St. (mail: P.O. Box 114, Kilburn, SA 5084)/ Tel. & fax: +61 (8) 8359-5120/ iskconsa@tpg.com.au

Brisbane — 32 Jennifer St., Seventten Mile Rocks, QLD 4073 (mail: PO Box 525, Sherwood, QLD 4075)/ Tel. +61 (7) 3376 2388/ info@iskcon.org.au

Canberra — 44 Limestone Ave., Ainslie, ACT 2602 (mail: P.O. Box 1411, Canberra, ACT 2601)/ Tel. & fax: +61 (2) 6262-6208/ iskcon@harekrishnacanberra.com

Melbourne — 197 Danks St. (mail: P.O. Box 125), Albert Park , VIC 3206/ Tel. +61 (3) 9699-5122/ melbourne@pamho.net

Newcastle — 28 Bull St., Mayfield, NSW 2304/ Tel. +61 (2) 4967-7000/ iskcon_newcastle@yahoo.com.au

Perth — 155–159 Canning Rd., Kalamunda (mail: P.O. Box 201 Kalamunda 6076)/ Tel. +61 (8) 6293-1519/ perth@pamho.net

Sydney — 180 Falcon St., North Sydney, NSW 2060 (mail: P.O. Box 459, Cammeray, NSW 2062)/ Tel. +61 (2) 9959-4558/ admin@iskcon.com.au

Sydney — Govinda's Yoga and Meditation Centre, 112 Darlinghurst Rd., Darlinghurst NSW 2010 (mail: P.O. Box 174, Kings Cross 1340)/ Tel. +61 (2) 9380-5162/ sita@govindas.com.au

RURAL COMMUNITIES

Bambra, VIC (New Nandagram) — 50 Seaches Outlet, off 1265 Winchelsea Deans Marsh Rd., Bambra VIC 3241/ Tel. +61 (3) 5288-7383

Cessnock, NSW (New Gokula) — Lewis Lane (off Mount View Rd., Millfield, near Cessnock) (mail: P.O. Box 399, Cessnock, NSW 2325)/ Tel. +61 (2) 4998-1800/

Murwillumbah, NSW (New Govardhana) — Tyalgum Rd., Eungella (mail: P.O. Box 687), NSW 2484/ Tel. +61 (2) 6672-6579/ ajita@in.com.au

RESTAURANTS

Brisbane — Govinda's, 99 Elizabeth St., 1st floor, QLD 4000/ Tel. +61 (7) 3210-0255/ brisbane@pamho.net

Brisbane — Krishna's Cafe, 1st Floor, 82 Vulture St., West End, QLD 4000/ Tel. +61 (7) 0417-3027/ brisbane@pamho.net

Burleigh Heads — Govindas, 20 James St., Burleigh Heads, QLD 4220/ Tel. +61 (7) 5607-0782/ ajita@in.com.au

Maroochydore — Govinda's Vegetarian Cafe, 2/7 First Avenue, QLD 4558/ Tel. +61 (7) 5451-0299

Melbourne — Crossways Food for Life, 1st Floor, 123 Swanston St., VIC 3000/ Tel. +61 (3) 9650-2939

Melbourne — Gopal's, 139 Swanston St., VIC 3000/ Tel. +61 (3) 9650-1578

Newcastle — Govinda's Vegetarian Cafe, 110 King Street, NSW 2300/ Tel. +61 (02) 4929-6900/ info@govindascafe.com.au

Perth — Govinda's Restaurant, 194 William St., Northbridge, W.A. 6003/ Tel. +61 (8) 9227-1648/ perth@pamho.net

Perth — Hare Krishna Food for Life, NSW 2300/ Tel. +61 (02) 4929-6900/ info@govindascafe.com.au

NEW ZEALAND AND FIJI

Christchurch, NZ — 83 Bealey Ave. (mail: P.O. Box 25-190)/ Tel. +64 (3) 366-5174/ iskconchch@clear.net.nz
Hamilton, NZ — 188 Maui St., RD 8, Te Rapa/ Tel. +64 (7) 850-5108/ rmaster@wave.co.nz
Labasa, Fiji — Delailabasa (mail: P.O. Box 133)/ Tel. +679 812912
Lautoka, Fiji — 5 Tavewa Ave. (mail: P.O. Box 125)/ Tel. +679 6664112/ regprakash@excite.com
Nausori, Fiji — Hare Krishna Cultural Centre, 2nd Floor, Shop & Save Building, 11 Gulam Nadi St., Nausori Town (mail: P.O. Box 2183, Govt. Bldgs., Suva)/ Tel. +679 9969748 or 3475097/ vdas@frca.org.fj
Rakiraki, Fiji — Rewasa (mail: P.O. Box 204)/ Tel. +679 694243
Sigatoka, Fiji — Sri Sri Radha Damodar Temple, Off Mission St., Sigatoka Town/ Tel. +679 9373703/ drgsmarna@connect.com.fj
Suva, Fiji — 166 Brewster St. (mail: P.O. Box 4299, Samabula)/ Tel. +679 3318441/ iskconsuva@connect.com.fj
Wellington, NZ — 105 Newlands Rd., Newlands/ Tel. +64 (4) 478-4108/ info@iskconwellington.org.nz
Wellington, NZ — Gaura Yoga Centre, 1st Floor, 175 Vivian St. (mail: P.O. Box 6271, Marion Square)/ Tel. +64 (4) 801-5500/ yoga@gaurayoga.co.nz

RURAL COMMUNITY

Auckland, NZ (New Varshan) — Hwy. 28, Riverhead, next to Huapai Golf Course (mail: R.D. 2, Kumeu)/ Tel. +64 (9) 412-8075/

RESTAURANT

Wellington, NZ — Higher Taste Hare Krishna Restaurant, Old Bank Arcade, Ground Flr., Corner Customhouse, Quay & Hunter St., Wellington/ Tel. +64 (4) 472-2233

INDIA (partial list)

Ahmedabad, Gujarat — Satellite Rd., Gandhinagar Highway Crossing, 380 054/ Tel. (79) 686-1945, -1645, or -2350/ iskcon.ahmedabad@pamho.net (Guesthouse: guesthouse.ahmedabad@pamho.net)
Allahabad, UP — Hare Krishna Dham, 161 Kashi Raj Nagar, Baluaghat 211 003/ Tel. (532) 2416718/ iskcon.allahabad@pamho.net
Amritsar, Punjab — Chowk Moni Bazar, Laxmansar, 143 001/ Tel. (183) 2540177
Amravati, Maharashtra — Saraswati Colony, Rathi Nagar 444 603/ Tel. (721) 2666849 or 9421805105/ iskconamravati@ymail.com
Aravade, Maharashtra — Hare Krishna Gram, Tal. Tagaon, Dist. Sangli/ Tel. (2346) 255-766
Bangalore, Karnataka — ISKCON Sri Jagannath Mandir, No.5 Sripuram, 1st cross, Sheshadripuram, 560 020/ Tel. 9901060738 or 9886709603/ varada.krsna.jps@pamho.net
Baroda, Gujarat — Hare Krishna Land, Gotri Rd., 390 021/ Tel. (265) 2310630 or 2331012/ iskcon.baroda@pamho.net
◆ **Bhubaneswar, Odisha** — N.H. No. 5, IRC Village, 751 015/ Tel. (674) 2553517, 2553475, or 2554283/ gm.iskconbbsr.ggs@pamho.net
Chandigarh, Punjab — Hare Krishna Dham, Sector 36-B, 160 036/ Tel. (172) 2601590 or 2603232/ iskcon.chandigarh@pamho.net
Chennai (Madras), TN — Hare Krishna Land, off ECR, Akkarai, Sholinganallur, Chennai 600 119/ Tel. (44) 24530921 or 24530923/ iskconchennai@gmail.com
◆ **Coimbatore, TN** — Jagannath Mandir, Hare Krishna Land, Aerodrome P.O., Opp. CIT, 641 014/ Tel. (422) 2626509 or 2626508/ info@iskcon-coimbatore.org
Dwarka, Gujarat — Bharatiya Bhavan, Devi Bhavan Rd., 361 335/ Tel. (2892) 34606
Guwahati, Assam — Ulubari Chariali, South Sarania, 781 007/ Tel. (361) 2525963/ iskcon.guwahati@pamho.net
Haridwar, Uttaranchal — Srila Prabhupada Ashram, G. House, Nai Basti, Mahadev Nagar, Bhimgoda, 249 401/ Tel. (1334) 260818
Hyderabad, AP — Hare Krishna Land, Nampally Station Rd., 500 001/ Tel. 8106130279 or (40) 24744969/ iskcon.hyderabad@pamho.net; Guesthouse: guesthouse.iskconhyd@pamho.net
Imphal, Manipur — Hare Krishna Land, Airport Rd., 795 001/ Tel. (385) 2455693/ manimandir@sancharnet.in
Indore, MP — ISKCON, Nipania, Indore/ Tel. 9300474043/ mahaman.acbsp@pamho.net
Jaipur, Rajasthan — ISKCON Road, Opp. Vijay Path, Mansarovar, Jaipur 302 020 (mail: ISKCON, 84/230, Sant Namdev Marg, Opp. K.V. No. 5, Mansarovar, Jaipur 302 020)/ Tel. (414) 2782765 or 2781860/ jaipur@pamho.net
Jammu, J&K — Srila Prabhupada Ashram, c/o Shankar Charitable Trust, Shakti Nagar, Near AG Office/ Tel. (191) 2582306

Kolkata (Calcutta), WB — 3C Albert Rd. (behind Minto Park, opp. Birla High School), 700 017/ Tel. (33) 3028-9258 or -9280/ iskcon.calcutta@pamho.net
◆ **Kurukshetra, Haryana** — ISKCON, Main Bazaar, 136 118/ Tel. (1744) 234806 or 235529
Lucknow, UP — 1 Ashok Nagar, Guru Govind Singh Marg, 226 018/ Tel. (522) 2635000, 2630026; or 9415235050/ iskcon.lucknow@pamho.net
◆ **Mayapur, WB** — ISKCON, Shree Mayapur Chandrodaya Mandir, Mayapur Dham, Dist. Nadia, 741313/ Tel. (3472) 245620, 245240 or 245355/ mayapur.chandrodaya@pamho.net
◆ **Mumbai (Bombay), Maharashtra** — Hare Krishna Land, Juhu 400 049/ Tel. (22) 26206860/ info@iskconmumbai.com; guesthouse.mumbai@pamho.net
◆ **Mumbai, Maharashtra** — 7 K. M. Munshi Marg, Chowpatty 400 007/ Tel. (22) 23665500/ info@radhagopinath.com
Mumbai, Maharashtra — Shristhi Complex, Mira Rd. (E), opposite Royal College, Dist. Thane, 401 107/ Tel. (22) 28454667 or 28454672/ jagjivan.gkg@pamho.net
Mysore, Karnataka — #31, 18th Cross, Jayanagar, 570 014/ Tel. (821) 2500582 or 6567333/ mysore.iskcon@gmail.com
Nellore, AP — ISKCON City, Hare Krishna Rd., 524 004/ Tel. (861) 2314577 or (92155) 36589/ sukadevaswami@gmail.com
◆ **New Delhi, UP** — Hare Krishna Hill, Sant Nagar Main Road, East of Kailash, 110 065/ Tel. (11) 2623-5133, 4, 5, 6, 7/ delhi@pamho.net; (Guesthouse) guest.house.new.delhi@pamho.net
◆ **New Delhi, UP** — 41/77, Punjabi Bagh (West), 110 026/ Tel. (11) 25222851 or 25227478 Noida, UP — A-5, Sector 33, opp. NTPC office, Noida 201 301/ Tel. (120) 2506211/ iskcon.punjabi.bagh@pamho.net
Patna, Bihar — Sri Sri Banke Bihariji Mandir, Golok Dham, Budha Marg, Patna-1/ Tel. (612) 2220794, 2687637, or 2685081; or 09431021881/ krishna.kripa.jps@pamho.net
Pune, Maharashtra — 4 Tarapoor Rd., Camp, 411 001/ Tel. (20) 41033222 or 41033223/ nvcc@iskconpune.in
Puri, Odisha — Bhakti Kuti, Swargadwar, 752 001/ Tel. (6752) 231440
Secunderabad, AP — 27 St. John's Rd., 500 026/ Tel. (40) 780-5232
Silchar, Assam — Ambikapatti, Silchar, Dist. Cachar, 788 004/ Tel. (3842) 34615
Srirangam, TN — 103 Amma Mandapam Rd., Srirangam, Trichy 620 006/ Tel. (431) 2433945/ iskcon_srirangam@yahoo.co.in
Surat, Gujarat — Ashram Rd., Jahangirpura, 395 005/ Tel. (261) 276-5891 or 276-5516/ surat@pamho.net
◆ **Thiruvananthapuram (Trivandrum), Kerala** — Hospital Rd., Thycaud, 695 014/ Tel. (471) 2328197/ jsdasa@yahoo.co.in
◆ **Tirupati, AP** — K.T. Rd., Vinayaka Nagar, 517 507/ Tel. (877) 2231760 or 2230009/ revati.raman.jps@pamho.net; Guestouse: guesthouse.tirupati@pamho.net
Udhampur, J&K — Srila Prabhupada Ashram, Srila Prabhupada Marg, Srila Prabhupada Nagar 182 101/ Tel. (1992) 270298/ info@iskconudhampur.com
Ujjain, MP — 35–37 Hare Krishna Land, Bharatpuri, 456 010/ Tel. (734) 2535000 or 2531000, or 9300969016/ iskcon.ujjain@pamho.net
Varanasi, UP — ISKCON, B 27/80 Durgakund Rd., Near Durgakund Police Station, Varanasi 221 010/ Tel. (542) 246422 or 222617
◆ **Vrindavan, UP** — Krishna-Balaram Mandir, Bhaktivedanta Swami Marg, Raman Reti, Mathura Dist., 281 124/ Tel. & Fax: (565) 2540728/ iskcon.vrindavan@pamho.net; (Guesthouse:) Tel. (565) 2540022; ramamani@sancharnet.in

ADDITIONAL RESTAURANT
Kolkata, WB — Govinda's, ISKCON House, 22 Gurusaday Rd., 700 019/ Tel. (33) 24866922, 24866009

EUROPE (partial list)
Amsterdam — Van Hilligaertstraat 17, 1072 JX/ Tel. +31 (20) 675-1404 or -1694/ amsterdam@pamho.net
Bergamo, Italy — Villaggio Hare Krishna (da Medolago strada per Terno d'Isola), 24040 Chignolo d'Isola (BG)/ Tel. +39 (035) 4940705/ villagio.hare.krsna@hare.krsna.it
Budapest — III. Lehel Street 15–17 (Csillaghedy), 1039 Budapest/ Tel. +36 (1) 391-0435 or 397-5219/ budapest@pamho.net
Copenhagen — Skjulhøj Alle 44, 2720 Vanløse, Copenhagen/ Tel. +45 4828 6446/ iskcon.denmark@pamho.net
Grödinge, Sweden — Radha-Krishna Temple, Korsnäs Gård, 14792 Grödinge, Tel. +46 (8) 53025062/ bmd@pamho.net

Helsinki, Finland — Malmi Manor, Latokartanontie 11, 00700/ Tel. +358 9 6949879/ info@krishna.fi

◆ **Lisbon** — Rua Dona Estefãnia, 91 R/C 1000 Lisboa/ Tel. & fax: +351(1) 314-0314 or 352-0038

Madrid — Espíritu Santo 19, 28004 Madrid/ Tel. +34 91 521-3096

Paris — 230 Avenue de la Division Leclerc, 95200 Sarcelles Village/ Tel. +33 682590079/ paris@pamho.net

◆ **Radhadesh, Belgium** — Chateau de Petite Somme, 6940 Septon-Durbuy/ Tel. +32 (86) 322926 (restaurant: 321421)/ radhadesh@pamho.net

◆ **Rome** — Govinda Centro Hare Krsna, via Santa Maria del Pianto, 16, 00186/ Tel. +39 (06) 68891540/ govinda.roma@harekrsna.it

◆ **Stockholm** — Fridhemsgatan 22, 11240/ Tel. +46 (8) 654-9002/ Restaurant: Tel. & fax: +46 (8) 654-9004/ lokanatha@hotmail.com

Zürich — Mohini, Weinbergstr, 15, 8011/ Tel. +41 (44) 252-5211/ info@mohini.ch

RURAL COMMUNITIES

France (La Nouvelle Mayapura) — Domaine d'Oublaisse, 36360, Lucay le Mâle/ Tel. +33 (2) 5440-2395/ oublaise@free.fr

Germany (Simhachalam) — Zielberg 20, 94118 Jandelsbrunn/ Tel. +49 (8583) 316/ info@simhachalam.de

Hungary (New Vraja-dhama) — Krisna-völgy, 8699 Somogyvamos, Fö u, 38/ Tel. & fax: +36 (85) 540-002 or 340-185/ info@krisnavolgy.hu

Italy (Villa Vrindavan) — Via Scopeti 108, 50026 San Casciano in Val di Pesa (FL)/ Tel. +39 (55) 820054/ isvaripriya@libero.it

Spain (New Vraja Mandala) — (Santa Clara) Brihuega, Guadalajara/ Tel. +34 949 280436

ADDITIONAL RESTAURANTS

Barcelona — Restaurante Govinda, Plaza de la Villa de Madrid 4–5, 08002/ Tel. +34 (93) 318-7729

Copenhagen — Govinda's, Nørre Farimagsgade 82, DK-1364 Kbh K/ Tel. +45 3333 7444

Milan — Govinda's, Via Valpetrosa 5, 20123/ Tel. +39 (2) 862417

Oslo — Krishna's Cuisine, Kirkeveien 59B, 0364/ Tel. +47 (2) 260-6250

COMMONWEALTH OF INDEPENDENT STATES (partial list)

Kiev — 16, Zoryany pereulok. 04078/ Tel. +380 (44) 4338312, or 4347028, or 4345533

Moscow — Leningradsky Prospect, Vladenie 39 (mail: Begovaya str., 13, OPS 284, a/ya 17, 125284 Moscow)/ Tel. +7 (495) 7394377/ temple@veda.ru

ASIA (partial list)

Bangkok, Thailand — Soi3, Tanon Itsarapap, Toonburi/ Tel. +66 (2) 9445346 or (81) 4455401 or (89) 7810623/ swami.bvv.narasimha@pamho.net

Dhaka, Bangladesh — 79 Swamibag, Dhaka-11/ Tel. +880 (2) 7122747 or 7122448/ info@iskconbd.org

Hong Kong — 6/F Oceanview Court, 27 Chatham Road South (mail: P.O. Box 98919)/ Tel. +852 (2) 739-6818/ iskconhk@iskconhk.org

Jakarta, Indonesia — Yayasan Radha-Govinda, P.O. Box 2694, Jakarta Pusat 10001/ Tel. +62 (21) 489-9646/ matsyads@bogor.wasantara.net.id

Kathmandu, Nepal — Budhanilkantha (mail: GPO Box 3520)/ Tel. +977 (1) 4373790 or 4373786/ iskconkathmandu@gmail.com

Kuala Lumpur, Malaysia — Lot 9901, Jalan Awan Jawa, Taman Yarl, 58200 Kuala Lumpur/ Tel. +60 (3) 7980-7355/ president@iskconkl.com

Manila, Philippines — Radha-Madhava Center, #9105 Banuyo St., San Antonio village, Makati City/ Tel. +63 (2) 8963357/ iskconmanila@yahoo.com

Myitkyina, Myanmar — ISKCON Sri Jagannath Temple, Bogyoke Street, Shansu Taung, Myitkyina, Kachin State/ mahanadi@mptmail.net.mm

Tai Pei City, Taiwan — Zhong Xiao East Rd. Section 2, Lane 39, Alley 2, No. 3, 2F/ Tel. +886 (2) 2395-6010 or 2395-6715/ bhavna@ms22.hinet.net

Tokyo, Japan — 2-23-4 Funabori, Edogawa-ku, Tokyo 134-0091/ Tel. +81 (3) 3877-3000/ iskcon.new.gaya.japan@gmail.com

LATIN AMERICA (partial list)

Buenos Aires, Argentina — Ciudad de la Paz 394, Colegiales CP 1427/ Tel. +54 4554-0113 or 3532-9996/ Iskconargentina@gmail.com/ Restaurante Naturaleza Divina/ Tel. 3532-9996/ nat.div@gmail.com

Caracas, Venezuela — Av. Los Proceres (con Calle Marquez del Toro), San Bernardino/ Tel. +58 (212) 550-1818

Guayaquil, Ecuador — 6 de Marzo 226 and V. M. Rendon/ Tel. +593 (4) 308412 or 309420

◆ **Lima, Peru** — Schell 634 Miraflores/ Tel. +51 (14) 444-2871

Mexico City, Mexico — Tiburcio Montiel 45, Colonia San Miguel, Chapultepec D.F., 11850/ Tel. and

fax: +52 (55) 5272-5944/ iskcon@krishnamexico.com
Rio de Janeiro, Brazil — Estrada da Barra da Tijuca, 1990, Itanhangá, Rio de Janeiro, RJ/ Tel. +55 (21) 3563-1627/ contato@harekrishnarj.com.br
San Salvador, El Salvador — 8a Avenida Norte, Casa No. 2–4, Santa Tecla, La Libertad/ Tel. +503 2288-2900/ mail@harekrishnaelsalvador.com
São Paulo, Brazil — Rua Tomas Goncalves 70, Butanta, 05590-030/ Tel. +55 (11) 8496-3158/ comunicacao@harekrishnasp.com.br
West Coast Demerara, Guyana — Sri Gaura Nitai Ashirvad Mandir, Lot "B," Nauville Flanders (Crane Old Road), West Coast Demerara/ Tel. +592 254 0494

AFRICA (partial list)

Accra, Ghana — Samsam Rd., Off Accra-Nsawam Hwy., Medie, Accra North (mail: P.O. Box 11686)/ Tel. & fax +233 (21) 229988/ srivas_bts@yahoo.co.in
Cape Town, South Africa — 17 St. Andrews Rd., Rondebosch 7700/ Tel. +27 (21) 6861179
◆ **Durban, South Africa** — 50 Bhaktivedanta Swami Circle, Unit 5 (mail: P.O. Box 56003), Chatsworth, 4030/ Tel. +27 (31) 403-3328/ iskcon.durban@pamho.net
Johannesburg, South Africa — 7971 Capricorn Ave. (entrance on Nirvana Drive East), Ext. 9, Lenasia (mail: P.O. Box 926, Lenasia 1820)/ Tel. +27 (11) 854-1975 or 7969/ iskconjh@iafrica.com
Lagos, Nigeria — No. 23 Egbeyemi St., Off Coker Rd., Illupeju, Lagos (mail: P. O. Box 8793, Marina)/ Tel. +234 8069245577 or 7066011800
Mombasa, Kenya — Hare Krishna House, Sauti Ya Kenya and Kisumu Rds. (mail: P.O. Box 82224, Mombasa)/ Tel. +254 (11) 312248
Nairobi, Kenya — Hare Krishna Close, Off West Nagara Rd., Nairobi 0100 (mail: P.O. Box 28946)/ Tel. +254 (20) 3744365/ iskcon_nairobi@yahoo.com
◆ **Phoenix, Mauritius** — Hare Krishna Land, Srila Prabhupada St., Pont Fer/ Tel. +230 6965804/ iskcon.phoenix@intnet.mu
Port Harcourt, Nigeria — Umuebule 11, 2nd tarred road, Etche (mail: P.O. Box 4429, Trans Amadi)/ Tel. +234 8033215096
Pretoria, South Africa — 1189 Church St., Hatfield, 0083 (mail: P.O. Box 14077, Hatfield, 0028)/ Tel. & fax: +27 (12) 342-6216/ iskconpt@global.co.za

RURAL COMMUNITY

Mauritius (ISKCON Vedic Farm) — Hare Krishna Rd., Vrindaban/ Tel. +230 418-3185 or 418-3955

To save space, we've skipped the calling codes for North America (1) and India (91).

◆ Temples with restaurants or dining

Far from a Center?
Call us at 1-800-927-4152
Or contact us on the Internet

http://www.krishna.com
E-mail: bbt.usa@krishna.com

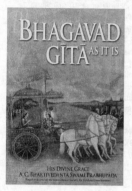

The Nectar of Devotion

Read the classic on which the practices of the Hare Kṛṣṇa movement are based. (Offer valid in US only.)

Take advantage of this special offer and purchase *The Nectar of Devotion: The Complete Science of Bhakti-Yoga,* for only **$9.75**. This is a saving of **25% off** the regular price. To receive this discount you must mention the following code when you place your order: NOD_SSR-S.

ORDER TOLL FREE 1-800-927-4152

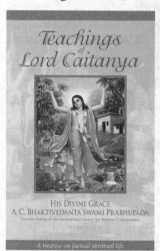

BEYOND BIRTH AND DEATH

What's the self? Can it exist apart from the physical body? If so, what happens to the self at the time of death? What about reincarnation? Liberation? In *Beyond Birth and Death* Śrīla Prabhupāda answers these intriguing questions and more.

Softbound, 96 pages...US$1.00 #BBD

THE HIGHER TASTE

A Guide to Gourmet Vegetarian Cooking and a Karma-Free Diet

Illustrated profusely with black-and-white drawings and eight full-color plates, this popular volume contains over 60 tried and tested international recipes, together with the why's and how's of the Krishna conscious vegetarian lifestyle.

Softbound, 176 pages...US$1.50 #HT

LIFE COMES FROM LIFE

In this historic series of talks with his disciples, Śrīla Prabhupāda uncovers the hidden and blatantly unfounded assumptions that underlie currently fashionable doctrines concerning the origins and purpose of life.

Softbound, 96 pages...US$1.50 #LCFL

CIVILIZATION AND TRANSCENDENCE

In this book Śrīla Prabhupāda calls the bluff of modern materialistic culture: "They have created a society that is simply a dog's race. The dog is running on four legs, and thay are running on four wheels. That's all. And they think the four-wheel race is advancement of civilization." The learned, astute person will use this life to gain what he has missed in countless prior lives—namely, realization of self and realization of God.

The Bhaktivedanta
Book Trust
CATALOG